Political Economy, Growth, and Business Cycles

Political Economy, Growth, and Business Cycles

edited by
Alex Cukierman, Zvi Hercowitz,
and Leonardo Leiderman

The MIT Press
Cambridge, Massachusetts
London, England

This book was set in Palatino by Asco Trade Typesetting Ltd., Hong Kong, and was printed and bound in the United States of America.

Library of Congress Cataloging-in-Publication Data

Political economy, growth, and business cycles / edited by Alex Cukierman,
    Zvi Hercowitz, Leonardo Leiderman.
        p.   cm.
    Includes bibliographical references and index.
    ISBN 0-262-03194-9
    1. Economic development. 2. Economic policy. 3. Business cycles.
I. Cukierman, Alex. II. Hercowitz, Zvi. III. Leiderman, Leonardo, 1951–   .
HD75.P64   1992
338.9—dc20   92-25514
                                                                        CIP

Contents

Introduction

The last decade witnessed important new developments in the areas of growth and the business cycle, as well as in the seemingly unrelated areas that explore the interactions between politics and economics. The new growth theory stresses the effects of externalities and knowledge spillovers on long-term growth. Recent business cycle literature investigates the features of modern economies that can generate business cycles within general equilibrium dynamic frameworks. These two areas of research focus on the endogenous generation of long-term growth and short-term fluctuations in frameworks that generally abstract from distributional considerations. The new political economy literature views economic policy as the outcome of a process in which distributional considerations and political competition play a key role. This literature emphasizes the ensuing endogenous political process as an important determinant of economic policy.

These two branches of research have evolved, however, along separate tracks. A major theme of this volume is that these areas are fundamentally related. Economic policy affects both the process of growth and the cyclical behavior of the economy. Given the central role of governments in modern economies, a full understanding of these processes requires comprehension of the forces that shape economic policy.

The recent analysis of economic policy formation has evolved along two different paths. One, of which Barro (1979) is an early representative, views policymakers as social planners who devise policy so as to maximize social welfare or minimize distortions. The other views the choice of policy as the outcome of a distributional struggle among individuals. This struggle is resolved through the political system by majority rule or by some other mechanism of public choice. An early example of this approach is in Meltzer and Richard (1981).

This volume brings together a collection of essays dealing with economic growth and the business cycle and their interaction with economic policy and institutions. Covering a wide range of approaches to those topics, some essays focus on the interaction between growth and the choice of policy within frameworks in which policy reacts to economic and distributional considerations through a majority rule process. Other essays take the policy as given and focus on the empirical estimation of the speed of convergence of rates of growth across states and regions and the importance of externalities and knowledge spillovers for the rate of growth.

The essays dealing with the business cycle fall into two broad categories. One, which takes its roots from the new political economy tradition, focuses on the effect of elections and of various paths of price decontrols on the business cycle. The other explores the implications of optimal policies in a representative agent framework for the cyclical behavior of the economy.

The unifying theme of the book is growth and business cycles. Some of the essays deal with these topics from a purely economic point of view that takes policy as given. Other essays integrate economic behavior with a political economy choice of policy. The essays are therefore organized around a two-way classification: one concerns the subject—growth or business cycles, the other concerns the scope of behaviors considered within each subject and include either a combination of economic and political behavior or just economic behavior. The following matrix illustrates the two-ways classification:

	Growth	*Business Cycle*
Political and Economic Behavior	Persson-Tabellini Alesina-Rodrik Londregan-Poole	Alesina-Cohen-Roubini van Wijnbergen
Only Economic Behavior	Helpman Caballero-Lyons Barro-Sala-i-Martin Parente-Prescott	Chari-Christiano-Kehoe Greenwood-Hercowitz Christiano-Eichenbaum

The book is divided accordingly into the following parts, which correspond to the four cells in the matrix:

I Growth within politico-economic frameworks

II Growth within purely economic frameworks

III Business cycles within politico-economic frameworks

IV Business cycles within purely economic frameworks

Additionally, the book includes the following part:

V Labor market regulations and industry equilibrium

This part contains the chapter by Hopenhayn-Rogerson. Although their essay does not quite fit into the mold above, the main question it poses is motivated by activities that usually arise from politico-economic interactions.

Part I features three papers that deal with various aspects of the interaction between politics and growth. Persson and Tabellini survey the burgeoning literature at the intersection of endogenous growth and endogenous policy making. They emphasize that policy cannot be viewed as an exogenous process. The endogenous growth literature shows that differences in policy can play a major role in explaining differences in growth. Persson and Tabellini argue that in order to understand differences in growth rates, it is necessary to understand why policies differ across countries. More specifically, they consider two mechanisms that link the distributions of income and land ownership to different tax policies and through them to growth. The first mechanism operates only in democratic societies. The more unequal the distribution of income, the higher is the tax on the return to investment that is chosen by the decisive median voter. The higher the tax rate, the lower the level of investment and the lower, therefore, the growth rate. Thus, inequality is harmful for growth in democracies. The second mechanism operates in all types of regimes. It is based on the notion that when the benefits of a policy are highly concentrated, although its costs are diffused, the small group of individuals that benefits is likely to be organized more effectively and to be more successful in lobbying and bargaining activities than the rest of the population. Using this notion Persson and Tabellini derive the implication that sectoral taxes on the capital intensive sector are higher and the rate of growth lower, the higher is the concentration of land ownership.

The Alesina-Rodrik essay also considers the interrelationship between distribution and growth, but it focuses on the functional distribution of income between labor and capital rather than on the general distribution of income and the concentration of land ownership. Output in their model is produced by means of an aggregate production function that uses three factors of production: capital, labor, and the flow of government spending on productive infrastructure. Government spending is financed by a tax on capital, which creates a production externality. Each capitalist disregards the fact that by saving more he or she increases the tax base and the input of productive infrastructure. Using a model in which each individual receives income only from labor or only from capital, Alesina and Rodrik derive the tax rate on capital that maximizes the rate of growth of the economy. Then they show that when workers have some power, the tax on capital is set above its growth maximizing level. Some of the tax may be used in this case for purely distributive transfers to workers. They also consider a more general version of the model in which each individual gets income from both labor and capital but in which the capital/labor ratio differs across individuals. As a consequence each individual weighs the benefits of taxation for infrastructure against the burden of capital taxation differently. Alesina and Rodrik show within the extended framework that the more unequal the distribution of wealth, the higher the tax rate on capital that arises under majority rule and the lower, therefore, the rate of growth of the economy.

A major implication of both the Alesina-Rodrik and the Persson-Tabellini chapters is that, in democratic societies, higher levels of inequality should be associated with lower rates of growth. Both papers present independent empirical evidence in favor of this implication, with the most convincing evidence being a significant relation between inequality and growth in democracies but not in other countries.

Londregan and Poole describe extensive cross-country evidence on the simultaneous relationship between growth and military coups. This is done by presenting a reduced-form, bivariate model of coups and growth and by using a maximum likelihood simultaneous estimation. The major conclusion of the chapter is that there exists a "poverty trap" and a "coup trap." Low levels of income and low growth rates increase the probability of a coup, and countries with more past coups are more likely to experience another coup. In addition, coups do not seem to affect subsequent economic growth, but the presence of a nonconstitutional leader does. In particular a nonconstitutional rule reduces the annual growth rate by as much as half a percentage point per year.

Part II includes four chapters that deal with purely economic aspects of growth. Helpman surveys recent developments in the theory of endogenous growth, focusing on a family of models that highlight the following elements. First, innovations respond to economic incentives and are, therefore, endogenous to the economic system. By investing more resources in research and development, entrepreneurs can increase the stock of knowledge, but they engage in such activity only when it is profitable at the individual level. Second, new knowledge (like blueprints, scientific principles, and more efficient methods for producing a product) has a positive externality. Hence, the private rate of return to inventive activity is below the social return to such activity. Two main vehicles are used to investigate the effect of those factors on aggregate growth. One is a model of expanding product variety and the other is a quality ladders model. In the first case innovation takes the form of an expanding product variety, and in the second case innovation takes the form of a stochastic improvement in the quality of the same good. In both cases there exists a spillover of knowledge from current to future innovations during the process of growth. Old brands are never totally discontinued in the first case, whereas lower quality brands are eventually fully replaced by higher quality brands in the second case. The survey uses those models to discuss welfare, the effect of policy, and to characterize some of the factors that are conducive to a higher rate of innovation. In particular it finds that a larger initial resource base, a lower rate of time preference in consumption, a higher degree of monopoly power, and a higher intertemporal elasticity of substitution are all conducive to a higher rate of innovation.

The chapter by Caballero and Lyons is an extensive survey of recent empirical attempts to determine the degree of internal returns to scale and external economies in manufacturing, and to sort out the external effects into demand-driven externalities and productive externalities that operate through intermediate goods linkages. The chapter surveys evidence suggesting that there are large and very significant, activity-related, cross-industry, external economies in the manufacturing sectors of both Europe and the United States. New four-digit-level, input-output evidence surveyed in the chapter suggests that demand-driven transaction externalities are significant for explaining the short-run behavior of total factor productivity. Over longer horizons, however, linkage between an industry and its suppliers becomes the dominant factor. The chapter concludes by adding production externalities to the list of potential explanations for short-run increasing returns along with labor hoarding and internal increasing returns.

An important economic question is whether differences in income between poor and rich areas tend to narrow or to widen over time. The evidence in the Barro and Sala-i-Martin chapter suggests that in the United States and Europe they tend to narrow. The chapter presents extensive evidence on long-run patterns of convergence of per capita output and per capita income across states in the United States since 1880 and across 73 regions of 7 European countries since 1950. The overall evidence weighs heavily in favor of slow but clear convergence. Poor states and regions tend to grow faster in terms of per capita income and product than rich ones. However, the gap between the typical poor and rich state or region diminishes at a slow rate of roughly two percent per year. Interestingly, this rate is of the same order of magnitude in the United States and in Europe. The chapter interprets the results in terms of the standard neoclassical growth model and analyzes the interplay between net migration and economic growth.

Parente and Prescott link the disparities in rates of growth to the disparity in the institutional arrangements of different countries. The chapter stresses that the adoption of new technology requires investments not only in tangible but also in intangible capital, such as the training of personnel in the use of new technology. Some institutions are more conducive to the adoption of new technology than others. Parente and Prescott model the effect of institutional arrangements as a tax on the returns to tangible and intangible capital in the business sector. They embed this feature in a general equilibrum dynamic model and use data from the United States and Japan to calibrate the model. The main lesson is that differences in the implicit tax on tangible capital (imposed by different institutional arrangements) can produce dramatic differences in steady state levels of output.

Part III, which deals with politico-economic interactions within the context of the business cycle, includes two chapters. Alesina, Cohen, and Roubini reviews and extend prior empirical work on the political business cycle for all the OECD countries that have been democracies during the period 1960 to 1987. The chapter presents an extensive battery of cross-countries as well as within countries tests of various aspects of the political business cycle. The chapter finds very little pre-electoral effects on real economic variables like GNP growth and unemployment. But there is evidence of a political cycle in policy instruments. In particular, monetary policy is expansionary in election years, and there are indications of soft fiscal policy prior to elections. In addition, inflation exhibits a postelectoral jump. The chapter concludes that these results support the rational approach to modeling voters' beliefs (Cukierman and Meltzer 1986; Rogoff and Sibert 1988) but do not support the myopic approach to the modeling of those beliefs (Nordhaus 1975).

Van Wijnbergen presents a politico-economic analysis of the cyclical behavior of sales for alternative methods of decontrolling prices. The analysis is motivated by the recent move toward price flexibility in centrally planned economies like Poland and the former USSR. Van Wijnbergen is interested in finding out whether—in view of the interaction between shortages and political vulnerability—gradual or cold turkey methods for decontrolling prices are preferable. To answer this question the chapter considers a simple dynamic framework in which producers of a storable good can store it. Storage takes place if producers expect the price of the good to be sufficiently higher in the future. Voters are unsure about the magnitude of the supply response to changes in the price of the good and learn from the size of sales during the first phase of decontrols about its likely magnitude. If the government decides to raise controlled prices gradually, producers expect prices to be even higher in the second phase of decontrol and store a large fraction of output for future sale. As a consequence, the currently observed supply response is smaller than under a cold turkey method of decontrol, and a larger fraction of voters becomes convinced that the response of output to price changes is negligible or even nonexistent. When a sufficiently large fraction of voters becomes convinced that this is the case, the government abandons the decontrol program altogether. This event is more likely under gradualism than under the cold turkey method, and the latter is therefore more likely to succeed in transforming a typical centrally planned economy into a market economy.

Part IV includes three essays. The first explores the potential of dynamically optimal taxation over the cycle as a positive theory of taxation. The second focuses on home production and the cyclical behavior of household capital, and the third takes a new empirical look at the liquidity effect of money on interest rates and economic activity.

Chari, Christiano, and Kehoe characterize the properties of dynamically optimal taxation (including seigniorage) over the business cycle. This is done in a complete markets-general, equilibrium-dynamic framework using the cash-credit goods construct of Lucas and Stokey (1983). The optimal fiscal and monetary policies are obtained by maximizing the welfare of a representative agent, subject to the constraint that the resulting outcomes constitute a competitive equilibrium—this under the assumption that the social planner is able to precommit policy. The main findings are the following. First, tax rates on labor are roughly constant over the business cycle. Second, capital income taxes are close to zero on average. Third, the Friedman rule is optimal (nominal interest rates should be zero), and money should be countercyclical with respect to technology shocks and procyclical with respect to government spending shocks. Some of these results are based on parameter values that are considered as plausible for the U.S. economy. Although it abstracts from issues like heterogeneity and nominal rigidities, the chapter provides a useful benchmark for the characterization of optimal dynamic taxation in a stochastic economy.

The second essay, by Greenwood and Hercowitz, is motivated by two observations. One is that the stock of household capital (residences and consumer durables) in the United States is higher than the stock of business capital. The other observation is that household investment is strongly procyclical, leading the cycle. In terms of this volume, which stresses economic policy issues, it is interesting to point out the asymmetric tax treatment of producer and household capital stressed in this essay: income from the first is taxed, but services from the second are not. This asymmetry is found to be responsible for the relatively large size of household capital. The main issue in the chapter is the interaction between household capital and household time (leisure) and its implications for the cyclical behavior of labor supply and household demand for capital. Given the leading role of household investment, this interaction seems relevent for understanding the origin of macroeconomic fluctuations.

A common feature of traditional macroeconomic thinking is that monetary policy operates through liquidity effects. That is, a monetary expansion is envisioned to be accompanied by a drop in nominal and real interest rates, which in turn cause an expansion in output. The chapter by Christiano and Eichenbaum documents new evidence on the relation between money growth, interest rates, and aggregate real output for the United States. Hence, this study helps to determine the extent to which a liquidity effect is found in the U.S. data. Christiano and Eichenbaum use various measures of money and different identifying assumptions to measure monetary policy shocks. At variance with existing ambiguous results, based on the monetary base and on Ml, they find robust evidence about the effects of monetary policy on interest rates when nonborrowed reserves are used as the monetary aggregate. In this case, unanticipated monetary expansions drive down short-term interest rates for substantial periods of time and generate increases in real GNP. Thus, liquidity effects appear to be an important mechanism for the transmission of (properly measured) changes in monetary policy into aggregate business cycles.

The book concludes in part V with the chapter by Hopenhayn and Rogerson, which develops a framework designed to assess the quantitative impact of various labor market regulations. These regulations normally result from the political process that redistributes resources among different groups in the economy. The case of legislated severance payments, analyzed in the chapter, can be viewed as an attempt by labor to extract resources from capital through the political process. The present work extends an earlier model of a multifirm industry equilibrium with entries and exits. In the model, the aggregate properties of the industry are constant over time, but individual firms are continually changing either by expanding, contracting, and/or starting up or closing down. The framework can be used to analyze the effects of many labor market policies such as policies that make it costly for firms to dismiss workers, policies that create incentives for firms to hire workers, and policies that subsidize start-ups of new firms. The essay characterizes the stationary equilibrium, calibrates the model, and uses it to determine the effect of imposing firing costs on firms. This policy change is shown to result in less job destruction and in firms becoming more cautious about job creation. Furthermore, total employment is decreasing in firing costs, and there is a fairly strong trade-off between the average duration of a job and the total number of jobs. Higher severance payments also increase the average firm size.

Taxation plays an important role in many of the chapters, but its treatment in various parts of the book differs in a fundamental way. Some of the chapters in part I (such as those by Persson-Tabellini and Alesina-Rodrik) view the determination of taxes as the outcome of a political equilibrium in which differences in endowments or in abilities across individuals play a central role. On the other hand, the chapter by Chari, Christiano, and Kehoe in part IV represents the approach of optimal taxation. There is obviously a tension between those two approaches, particularly if they are to be viewed as positive theories of taxation. Although still in its infancy, the political economy approach seems more realistic as a positive theory of taxation. Essays in this volume illustrate the tension between a tight economic theory of optimal taxation derived from a representative individual framework and the insights about a positive theory derived from a political equilibrium framework. This tension is an exciting open issue that is beyond the scope of this book. It should and most likely will be the object of future research.

The essays in this book were presented at The Pinhas Sapir Center Conference on "The Political Economy of Business Cycles and Growth," Tel Aviv University, Israel, June 2 and 3, 1991. The authors are grateful to Terry Vaughn and Sandra Minkkinen at The MIT Press for their valuable editorial and production guidance.

References

Barro, Robert J. 1979. On the determination of the public debt. *Journal of Political Economy* 87:940–971.

Cukierman, Alex, and Meltzer, Allan H. 1986. A positive theory of discretionary policy, the cost of democratic government and the benefits of a constitution. *Economic Inquiry* 24:367–388. Reprinted in Meltzer, Allan H., Alex Cukierman, and Scott F. Richard, 1991. *Political Economy*. Oxford: Oxford University Press.

Lucas, Robert E., and Stokey, Nancy L. 1983. Optimal monetary and fiscal policy in an economy without capital. *Journal of Monetary Economics* 12:55–93.

Meltzer, Allan H., and Richard, Scott F. 1981. A rational theory of the size of government. *Journal of Political Economy* 89:914–927. Reprinted in Meltzer, Allan H., Alex Cukierman, and Scott F. Richard, 1991. *Political Economy*. Oxford: Oxford University Press.

Nordhaus, William. 1975. The political business cycle. *The Review of Economic Studies* 42:169–190.

Rogoff, Kenneth, and Sibert, Anne. 1988. Equilibrium political business cycles, *The Review of Economic Studies* 55:1–16.

I   Growth within Politico-Economic Frameworks

1

Growth, Distribution, and Politics

Torsten Persson and
Guido Tabellini

A glaring fact of economic development is the difference in the growth rate across countries. Table 1.1 displays the average growth rate of real GDP per capita between 1960 and 1985—as well as other statistical indicators of growth—in about eighty developing countries, grouped by continent. Asian countries have, on average, grown twice as fast as Latin American countries and three times as fast as African countries, and the differences within each continent are much larger. Explaining this fact is still one of the most challenging questions in economics. In this paper we review some recent attempts at an answer that have focused on the interaction of economics and politics.

Consider the stylized aggregate production function: $Y = AF(K, N)$, where Y is GDP, A is a measure of technology, K is "capital," and N is population. Any theory of economic growth must then ultimately explain the variables appearing on the right hand side of the following equation:

$$g^y = g^A = RI - \alpha g^N. \tag{1}$$

In equation (1) g^y is the rate of growth of per capita GDP, g^A and g^N are the rates of exogenous technical progress and of population growth, R is the marginal product of capital, I is the investment rate (expressed as a percentage of GDP), and α is the income share of capital.

The early growth accounting literature ascribed a large share of growth to g^A. But the recent literature on endogenous growth has basically widened the definition of capital to include not only physical capital but also other cumulative factors such as human capital and productive knowledge. Under this view, I includes all such productive accumulation, while residual exogenous technical progress, g^A, becomes a negligible number. Suppose further that the population growth rate is primarily determined by non-economic factors, and the capital share of income (broadly defined) is fairly constant across countries.[1] We are then left with only two reasons for why

Table 1.1
Average growth rates

	Number of Countries	Growth 1960–1985	GDP 1960	S.E. Growth	Range Growth
Asia	23	3.08	1,434	2.28	−0.39, 7.44
Latin America	19	1.55	1,835	1.54	−1.61, 4.79
Africa	41	0.96	585	0.94	−2.83, 5.40

Source: Summers and Heston (1988). The country groupings are based on the IMF classification. GDP 1960 is average per capita income in 1960.

countries grow at different rates: either their investment rates differ or their marginal products differ. We now want to argue that economic policy, and in particular bad economic policy, plays a central role in explaining both differences.

Consider first the marginal product of capital, broadly defined. It is difficult to argue that in the slow-growth African and Latin American countries the *potential* marginal product is lower than in the rest of the world. These are the countries where cumulative factors are scarce. Any reasonable economic model would then suggest that investment would be very productive—if anything, more productive than elsewhere. So if marginal products are low, it must be because *realized* marginal products are low. This could happen for a variety of reasons, but most of them have to do with policy. First, investment could go to the wrong sector or firm or be the wrong kind of investment. Second, there may be indivisibilities that prevent investment on a sufficiently large scale. Third, high marginal product investment may be something like infrastructure, with a considerable public-goods component. And so on. But in all these cases, economic policy could either correct the distortions or else it is directly responsible for them. It seems plausible that a "benevolent dictator" in a poor African country would not face a lower physical marginal product of capital than elsewhere in the world. So if slow growth is due to a low marginal product, we must ask why economic policy preserves a gap between the potential and the realized marginal product of capital in some countries but not in others.

Consider next the investment rate. One reason why countries may invest little is that they cannot afford to save. Rebelo (1992) and Atkeson and Ogaki (1990) have recently shown how plausible forms of preferences lead to low savings rates at low levels of income. Taken literally, this argument says that poor countries *prefer* to grow slowly. More generally, it says that there may be a role for policy in attracting foreign direct investment.[2] A second reason why the investment rate differs across countries is more directly related to policy. The marginal product of capital, R in equation (1), need not coincide with the rate of return that can be privately appropriated by investors. Any externality or any explicit or implicit tax on investment income would create a wedge between them. Two countries with the same marginal product will have different investment rates if investors face different appropriable returns. Therefore, policies that define the property rights of investors become a major determinant of growth.

The new research program on endogenous growth, in fact, stresses how economic policy can play a major role in explaining growth. Indeed, one reason why this research program is generating so much excitement is that it is making progress on analyzing the growth consequences of alternative economic policies with the powerful tools of modern economic theory.[3] However, the research on endogenous growth typically views cross-country differences in economic policy as exogenous to the analysis. Policy plays the role of a free parameter in a theoretical model or is an exogenous variable in cross-country regressions, as for instance in Fischer (1991) or in Easterly (1991). In a sense, the early development literature—with its emphasis on planning and government intervention—had a similar mechanistic view of policy: an exogenous set of instruments that could freely be set to achieve desired results.

But this view of policy is hard to swallow. Economic policy is not a random variable that varies freely across countries. Rather, policy is the result of deliberate and purposeful choices by individuals and groups, who have specific incentives and constraints, just like private economic agents. If we maintain that it is policy differences that explain growth differences, what we ultimately have to explain is why these deliberate and purposeful choices differ systematically across countries. To us, the most promising avenue toward such an explanation is to be found in the study of political incentives and political institutions. This is indeed the view of many modern development economists. For instance Kreuger (1990), in a recent paper on the state of development economics, sketches an ambitious research agenda entailing theoretical and empirical work on "the interaction between political and economic forces" and "the functioning of alternative institutions."

We very much agree with the agenda, and we believe that the right way to make progress is to borrow the insights from modern development economics and the tools from neoclassical economics. Operationally, this means that the theory of endogenous growth must be married with the theory of endogenous policy.[4] The next section describes a recent body of research—the first offspring of this marriage.

1.1   Property Rights and Economic Growth

This recent literature starts from the argument that the enforcement of property rights determines the incentive to invest in cumulative factors. To explain differences in growth rates, it attempts to explain why property rights are enforced differently across countries.

Benhabib and Rustichini (1991) address the question in a model without an explicit institutional structure or political mechanism. In their model, two groups of agents consume and invest. Property rights are not well defined, so at any point in time the two groups may also try to redistribute consumption toward themselves from the resources available in the economy. The paper shows how the quest for redistribution may impose binding incentive constraints on the two groups, which manifest themselves in low accumulation and growth. It also shows how the incentives to redistribute may reduce growth at low, as well as high, levels of income. An advantage of this framework is its generality. Because the analysis is highly abstract, the results do not depend on the specific assumptions about the policy instruments or the political environment. But the generality is not without costs. In particular, it becomes difficult to obtain precise testable implications.

Other papers on the topic are more explicit about the political mechanism and the policy formation process. A first group of papers studies conflict over the *size* distribution of income in a democratic society. The model of redistribution borrows from Meltzer and Richard (1981), where rational voters choose a linear income tax and the revenue is distributed lump sum. The outcome depends primarily on the degree of inequality among voters: with more inequality more voters favor redistribution, and the equilibrium tax rate is higher. Persson and Tabellini (1991a) embed such a political mechanism in an overlapping-generations model, where redistribution is harmful for growth, and obtain the testable prediction that more inquality brings about slower growth. Perotti (1990) obtains a similar result in a model that focuses on educational investment, with the qualification that in a poor society, where educational investment is indivisible, more inequality may lead to higher growth. Similarly, Saint-Paul and Verdier (1991) show that more inequality may lead to higher growth if it leads to more redistribution in the form of public education.[5]

A second group of papers focuses instead on conflict over the *functional* distribution of income. In Alesina and Rodrik (1991) and Bertola (1991) there are two kinds of factors: "capital," which is cumulative, and "labor," which is fixed. Different individuals own these factors in different proportions. The government taxes factor income directly, and a tax on the cumulative factor is bad for growth. Under democratic government, the equilibrium policy depends on how factor ownership is distributed among the voters. If wealthy voters have relatively more capital, these models again predict that income inequality is bad for growth because it leads to more capital taxation.

However, the same observable input typically contains a combination of both fixed and cumulative factors, and there is no way to tax them separately. For example, income from labor reflects a combination of human capital and a fixed input. And income from land reflects a combination of improvements to the quality and fertility of the soil and a fixed input. It is only to the extent that different observable variables contain different combinations of income from fixed and cumulative factors that economic policy can redistribute across factors. Persson and Tabellini (1991b) analyze a model of sectoral policy, where different sectors rely on different factors in different proportions. The government observes only the output produced in different sectors. A policy that redistributes away from the capital intensive sector is bad for growth. But conflict over the functional distribution of income still drives the results, since individuals differ in their factor ownership. The model predicts that growth is slower if the owners of the fixed factor have a strong influence over sectoral policy. A good example would be a country where land owners have the balance of power and manage to induce a policy that favors agriculture at the expense of manufacturing.

The next section illustrates some of these ideas in a common analytical framework.

1.2   A Simple Model

In this section we formulate a simple model that illustrates some of the results derived in the previously mentioned literature. The model branches out into two special cases, each one of which illustrates a different aspect of the interaction between growth and income distribution.

In the basic model all individuals live for two periods and have the following identical preferences:

$$U(c^i) + d^i + f^i. \tag{2}$$

A variable with an i superscript is specific to the ith consumer and a variable without such a superscript denotes an average. In equation (2) c denotes first-period consumption, while d and f denote second-period consumption of two goods, which are produced in different sectors. In period 1 there is no production, but individuals derive income from given initial endowments. In Period 2 good d is produced only with a cumulative factor, k, which we call capital, according to the linear technology: $d = k^d$. Good f is produced with capital and a fixed input l, which we call land, according to the concave constant-returns technology: $f = F(k^f, l)$. Since the two goods are perfect substitutes in consumption, their relative consumption price is fixed at unity. Consumers may differ in two dimensions. They may have different first-period income, and they may own different amounts of land. For simplicity, we assume that land cannot be traded, so land holdings only enter the consumer budget constraint in the second period. Finally, there is one-period-ahead commitment: policy is chosen in the first period but takes effect in the second period.

Income Taxes

Consider first a tax on all second-period income, used to finance a lump-sum transfer payment. Here sectoral differences are only of secondary importance, so we assume that all individuals own the same amount of land. Let e^i denote the first-period income of the ith individual, and let θ denote the income tax. Then the consumer budget constraints are

$$e^i \geqslant k^{id} + k^{if} + c^i \tag{3a}$$

$$(1 - \theta)(k^{id} + k^{if} + F_l l) + g \geqslant d^i + f^i, \tag{3b}$$

where k^{ix} is individual i's holdings of capital in sector x, and where F_l is the partial of $F(k^f, l)$ with respect to l. We have also used the fact that equilibrium returns to capital in the two sectors are equalized: $(1 - \theta) = (1 - \theta)F_k(k^f, l)$. The government budget constraint is $g = \theta(k + F_l l)$, where $k = k^d + k^f$ is average capital.

Solving the consumer problem we find that individuals accumulate capital in direct proportion to their first-period income:

$$k^i \equiv k^{id} + k^{if} = e^i - U_c^{-1}(1 - \theta) \equiv e^i - C(\theta). \tag{4}$$

Using equations (3), (4), and the government budget constraint to substitute into the ith consumer's utility function, we can then write the consumer's indirect utility, v^i, as a function of Policy θ.

$$v^i = v(\theta) + (1 - \theta)(e^i - e). \tag{5}$$

In equation (5), $v(\theta) \equiv U(C(\theta)) + e - C(\theta) + F_l l$ is the indirect utility of an individual with average first-period income e.[6] Since the tax distorts the savings decision and is purely redistributive, this average individual has nothing to gain from the tax. Hence, $v(\theta)$ is strictly decreasing in θ. Clearly then, individuals richer than the average are harmed by the tax, while individuals poorer than the average may gain from it since the tax redistributes in their favor.

Suppose now that tax policy is chosen democratically, under majority rule. It is easy to show that the voters' preferences are single peaked under a mild restriction on the form of $U(c)$. Then, the equilibrium tax is that preferred by the median voter, the voter with first period income given by e^m. From equations (4) and (5), the voter's optimum value of θ must satisfy the first-order condition

$$(E - e^m) - \theta C_\theta(\theta) = 0. \tag{6}$$

The lower is median income relative to average income, the more the median gains from redistributing, and the higher is the equilibrium tax. Since a higher tax discourages investment—that is, $C_\theta(\theta)$ is positive—we obtain the testable prediction that investment is lower in more unequal democracies.

Persson and Tabellini (1991a) use a similar framework embedded in an overlapping generations model, which permits endogenous growth because of an intertemporal (and intergenerational) externality. In such a model, predictions for investment translate into predictions for growth: the equilibrium growth rate thus becomes a decreasing function of income inequality.

Sectoral Taxes

We now slightly modify the model to allow for a sector-specific tax. Let the tax, τ, be a tax on the capital intensive sector, d. Again, the tax is chosen in period 1, enacted in period 2, and the proceeds are distributed lump sum to all individuals. Since aggregate income no longer plays a central role, let us assume that all individuals have the same first-period income, e. Given the preferences in equation (2), every consumer will then save the same amount, k. The second-period budget constraint can now be written as

$$(1 - \tau)k^d + F_k k^f + F_l l^i + g \geqslant d^i + j^i. \tag{7}$$

Consumers allocate capital optimally across time and across sectors, such that

$$F_k(k^f, l) = (1 - \tau) = U_c(e - k). \tag{8}$$

Because $F_{kk}(\cdot)$ and $U_{cc}(\cdot)$ are both negative, these conditions make k a decreasing function of τ and k^f an increasing function of τ. Hence, k^d becomes a decreasing function of τ. Since $F_{lk} > 0$, the returns to land are increasing in the tax rate: $Q(\tau) = F_l(k^f, l)$, with $Q_\tau > 0$. Intuitively, a tax on the capital intensive sector drives down the marginal return to capital, reducing aggregate investment. And since capital flows to the land-using sector, the return on land rises.

Imposing the government budget constraint, $g = \tau k^d$, we can again write the indirect utility of the ith individual as a function of the policy and of his relative endowment. But here it is the relative endowment of land, not relative first-period income, that matters

$$v^i = v(\tau) + Q(\tau)(l^i - l). \tag{9}$$

The indirect utility of the average landowner $v(\tau)$ is decreasing in τ for two reasons, both revealed by equation (8): the tax distorts both the savings and the capital allocation decisions . Since $Q_\tau > 0$, we now obtain the result that individuals with less than average land are harmed by the tax, while individuals with more than average land may benefit from it, the more so the larger is their relative land endowment.

It is not very plausible to view a sector-specific policy as chosen under majority rule, even in a democracy. Unlike a general policy like a broad income tax, the benefits of a sectoral policy are highly concentrated among a possibly small subset of individuals, while its costs are broadly distributed among the population at large. It is more plausible to follow the tradition in the trade policy literature and view equilibrium policy as the outcome of lobbying or bargaining between different organized groups in society.[7] With this view, we should expect the individuals who have the most to gain from the policy to have the strongest incentives to organize themselves and take costly political action. These individuals will thus acquire the most power over the policy process.

In the context of our model, it is evident from equation (9) that the individuals with the most "intense" policy preferences are those with a large concentration of land. We thus predict that τ is higher and aggregate investment lower the more concentrated is the ownership of land. Persson and Tabellini (1991b) embed a similar framework in a dynamic model with altruistic overlapping generations and obtain the prediction that land concentration is harmful for growth.[8]

Discussion

To summarize, we have described a stylized model where equilibrium policy depends on conflicting interests over the distribution of income. The *size* distribution of income matters for the choice of a general income tax. The *functional* distribution of income—and particularly the distribution of the fixed factor—matters for the choice of a sectoral tax.

However, the way income distribution shapes policy depends critically on political institutions, because it is political institutions that aggregate conflicting interests into public policy. We argued that in a democracy a general income tax is likely to reflect the preferences of the majority of the population. For this reason, we expect the tax to be higher in more unequal democracies. But this prediction does not apply to nondemocracies, where there may not be any mapping at all from the income distribution of the population at large to the redistributive policy preferred by the decisive individual or group. We also argued that a sectoral tax is more likely to reflect the intensity of preferences of those who gain, rather than the number of gainers and losers in the population. So we expect policies that redistribute in favor of the sectors where factor ownership is more concentrated and organized. Moreover, since the political pressure is likely to operate through other forms of political participation than voting, there are strong reasons to believe that organized lobbies and pressure groups should be able to shape sectoral policies both in democracies and in dictatorial regimes.

We would also like to add that the tax policies in our simple model need not be taken literally. Taxation can be either explicit or implicit, and many other policies are similar, in that they affect the incentives for productive accumulation and entail a redistributive component. Most important among general policies—that is, policies that affect different sectors symmetrically—are probably some aspects of the regulatory system: patent legislation and enforcement of intellectual and general property rights. Most important among sectoral policies—that is, policies that affect different sectors asymmetrically—are probably trade, industrial, and regional policies, and sectoral regulation. Other policies of this type can be analyzed in a similar way and with similar conclusions.

The discussion in this section leaves us with a number of testable hypotheses regarding the effect of income distribution on economic growth. First, growth should be higher in more equal democracies, but it should not be related to the size distribution of income in nondemocratic countries.

Second, growth should be lower in countries where land ownership is highly concentrated, irrespective of the form of government. The next section asks if the available evidence is consistent with these hypotheses.

1.3   Some Evidence

As in our other work (Persson and Tabellini (1991a and b)), we estimate regressions of growth on income distribution and on other explanatory variables. Income distribution is measured at the start of the period over which we measure growth, so as to avoid reverse causation. Our sample includes both developing and industrial countries. The list of countries and the available data are shown in table 1.2. The dependent variable is the average growth rate of per capita real GDP between 1960 and 1985, drawn from the Summers and Heston (1988) data set.

The sample size is constrained by the availability of data on income distribution and land ownership. Paukert (1973) provides data on the pretax income distribution of households around 1960 in about fifty countries. Our measure of income *equality* is the fraction of income received by the third quintile of the distribution: MIDDLE. The third quintile includes median income, so MIDDLE measures the distance between median and mean income. We expect MIDDLE to have a positive effect on growth. Taylor and Hudson (1972) and Taylor and Jodice (1983) provide data on the concentration of land ownership in about seventy countries. Our measure of land concentration is the Gini coefficient for the distribution of land ownership: GINILA. We expect this variable to have a negative effect on growth. Combining these two sources, we are left with a sample of about forty countries for which we have both measures of distribution.[9]

The other variables in the regressions are the same as in Persson and Tabellini (1991a and b) and control for other features of the economy that contribute to explain growth differentials. They are: the percentage of the relevant age group enrolled in primary school, PSCHOOL, as a measure of human capital;[10] the initial level of real GDP per capita in 1960, GDP, as a measure of initial development; and the percentage of the labor force in the agricultural sector, AGRIL, as a measure of the structure of production as well as an additional measure of the relative political strength of the agricultural sector. All these variables are sampled at the start of the period.[11]

The results of the OLS estimation are shown in table 1.3. In column 1 we report the basic regression, where all the variables have been included. The fit of the regression is very good for a cross section, all the estimated

Table 1.2
List of variables

Country	Growth	GDP	PSCHOOL	AGRIL	MIDDLE	GINILA
United States	2.12	7380	118	7	17.6	71.0
United Kingdom	2.22	4970	92	4	16.6	72.3
Austria	3.31	3908	105	24	.	70.7
Denmark	2.74	5490	103	18	18.8	45.8
France	3.19	4473	144	22	14.0	52.5
Germany	2.88	5217	133	14	13.7	66.8
Italy	3.32	3233	111	31	14.6	73.2
Netherlands	2.65	4690	105	11	16.0	57.9
Norway	3.70	5001	100	20	18.5	67.6
Sweden	2.62	5149	96	14	17.4	50.6
Switzerland	1.77	6834	118	11	.	49.4
Canada	2.79	6069	107	13	.	55.8
Japan	5.76	2239	103	33	15.8	47.0
Finland	3.27	4073	97	36	15.4	35.1
Greece	4.43	1474	102	56	13.3	48.8
Ireland	2.86	2545	110	36	.	59.4
Australia	2.14	5182	103	11	17.8	88.2
New Zealand	1.45	5571	108	15	.	73.4
South Africa	1.57	2627	89	32	10.2	70.0
Argentina	0.48	3091	98	20	13.2	86.7
Bolivia	0.84	882	64	61	12.0	.
Brazil	4.79	991	95	52	10.2	84.5
Chile	0.69	2932	109	30	12.0	.
Colombia	2.64	1344	77	51	9.0	86.4
Costa Rica	1.86	1663	96	51	11.2	78.2
Ecuador	2.95	1143	83	57	16.1	86.4
El Salvador	0.48	1062	80	62	8.8	82.7
Guatemala	0.95	1268	45	67	.	86.0
Honduras	0.79	748	67	70	.	75.7
Mexico	2.45	2157	80	55	11.1	69.4
Nicaragua	0.90	1588	66	62	.	80.1
Panama	3.37	1255	96	51	13.8	73.5
Paraguay	2.80	991	98	56	.	.
Peru	0.82	1721	83	53	8.3	93.3
Venezuela	−1.61	5308	100	35	16.0	90.9
Jamaica	0.63	1472	92	39	10.8	77.0
Trinidad, Tobago	1.36	4904	88	22	14.6	69.1
Iran	3.03	1839	41	54	.	62.5
Iraq	0.43	2527	65	53	8.0	88.2
Israel	3.17	2838	98	14	18.6	.
Jordan	2.52	1124	77	44	.	.
Egypt	3.49	496	66	58	.	.
Bangladesh	1.51	444	47	87	.	.
Sri Lanka	1.83	974	95	56	13.8	.
Hong Kong	6.62	1737	87	8	.	.
India	1.37	533	61	74	16.0	64.0
Korea	5.95	690	94	66	18.0	38.7

Table 1.2 (continued)

Country	Growth	GDP	PSCHOOL	AGRIL	MIDDLE	GINILA
Malaysia	4.52	1103	96	63	15.7	47.3
Nepal	0.38	478	10	95	.	.
Pakistan	2.90	558	30	61	15.5	51.8
Philippines	1.77	874	95	61	12.0	53.4
Singapore	7.45	1528	111	8	.	.
Thailand	4.06	688	83	84	.	46.0
Burundi	−0.71	412	18	90	.	.
Cameroon	3.08	507	65	87	.	44.5
Central Africa	−0.44	485	32	94	.	37.2
Chad	−2.83	515	17	95	15.4	37.7
Congo, Peop	3.46	563	78	52	.	28.9
Benin	−0.46	595	27	55	.	.
Ethiopia	0.34	285	7	88	.	.
Ghana	−1.70	534	38	64	.	.
Cote d'Ivoire	0.85	743	46	89	12.0	42.2
Kenya	0.96	470	47	86	.	69.2
Madagascar	−1.13	659	52	93	11.3	.
Mauritania	1.14	414	8	91	.	.
Morocco	3.25	542	47	62	7.7	.
Niger	1.65	284	5	95	15.6	.
Nigeria	0.20	552	36	71	9.0	.
Zimbabwe	1.73	615	96	69	.	.
Rwanda	1.34	244	49	95	.	.
Senegal	−0.01	756	27	84	10.0	.
Sierra Leone	1.82	281	23	78	9.1	45.8
Somalia	−1.31	483	9	88	.	.
Sudan	−0.84	667	25	86	14.3	.
Tanzania	2.14	208	25	89	11.0	.
Togo	0.66	415	44	80	.	.
Tunisia	3.51	852	66	56	10.0	.
Uganda	0.30	322	49	89	.	.
Zambia	−0.95	740	42	79	11.1	75.7
Papua, New Guinea	1.24	1008	32	89	.	.

Note: Total number of countries: 80.

coefficients have the expected sign, and many of them are significantly different from zero. In particular, the coefficients on the two distributional measures have the right sign; GINILA is clearly significant, MIDDLE is not, strictly speaking, but still has a marginal significance level (p-value) of 0.145. Checking the residuals reveals that there is one outlier: Chad, with an average growth rate of −2.8 percent. Column 2 displays the same regression, once we drop Chad from the sample. The fit of the regression improves and all variables are now statistically significant. In the remaining regressions, we leave this outlier in the sample, even though the results continue to improve if we exclude it.

Table 1.3
Growth, investment, and distribution

Dependent variable	Growth				
	1	2	3	4	5
# OBS	36	35	36	48	50
CONSTANT	5.093	4.575	7.315	4.189	5.600
	(1.673)	(1.698)	(1.985)	(1.691)	(2.546)
GDP	−0.11E-2	−0.91E-3	−0.12E-2	−0.99E-3	−0.79E-3
	(−4.112)	(−3.885)	(−4.199)	(−4.102)	(−3.902)
PSCHOOL	0.038	0.029	0.034	0.024	0.029
	(3.187)	(2.727)	(2.081)	(1.862)	(2.494)
AGRIL	−0.061	−0.045	−0.063	−0.040	−0.048
	(−2.572)	(−2.109)	(−2.690)	(−1.895)	(−2.526)
MIDDLE	0.135	0.171	−0.067	−0.042	
	(1.466)	(2.076)	(−0.475)	(−0.343)	
GINILA	−0.039	−0.042	−0.028		−0.028
	(−2.595)	(−3.191)	(−1.076)		(−1.794)
MIDDLEDM			0.352	0.406	
			(1.814)	(2.484)	
GINILADM			−0.009		−0.027
			(−0.269)		(−1.193)
DEMOCRACY			−3.631	−4.750	2.014
			(−0.848)	(−2.298)	(1.204)
$\bar{R}^2$	0.540	0.556	0.563	0.427	0.481
SEE	1.258	1.111	1.225	1.376	1.232

Note: Method of estimation: OLS.

As we argued at the end of the previous section, the theory has more detailed predictions for the link between growth and income distribution in countries governed by different political systems. Specifically, we expect growth to be positively related to income equality in democracies but not in dictatorships. And we expect concentration of land ownership to have a negative effect on growth irrespective of the political regime. To test this more specific prediction, we add to the regressions a dummy variable, DEMOCRACY, taking a value of 1 for democratic countries and 0 otherwise. This variable is entered in the regressions by itself (to control for an independent effect of the political system on growth), and interactively with the two distributional variables: a DM suffix at the end of a variable indicates that it is interacted with DEMOCRACY. We expect to find MIDDLE to have a significant impact on growth only when interacted with DEMOCRACY, and we expect the opposite result for GINILA. The results, shown in column 3, are weakly supportive of the theory. The estimated coefficients are of the sign predicted by the theory, and MIDDLE has a much stronger effect on growth when interacted with DEMOCRACY, while the opposite is true for GINILA, also as predicted by the theory. But the coefficients on the distributional variables are not statistically significant (even though MIDDLEDM has a t-statistic of 1.814, p-value 0.083).

The problem is probably that there are too few observations. Most of the countries in the sample with both distributional variables are democracies (we only have data for ten nondemocratic countries), so there is not enough variability in the political regime. To gain observations, we then run two separate regressions—one where only income equality is included and the other where only land concentration is included. Again, the income distribution variable is interacted with DEMOCRACY. The results, shown in columns 4 and 5, are now exactly as predicted by the theory. Equality of income is the right sign and significant only when interacted with DEMOCRACY, and land concentration has the same negative effect on growth in democracies and nondemocracies.[12]

As a further check on the robustness of our results, in table 1.4 we report the results of some sensitivity analysis. The first two columns add a second measure of human capital, the percentage of individuals enrolled in secondary school (SSCHOOL), to columns 4 and 5 of table 1.3. The new variable is almost significant and of the right sign in one of the two regressions, but the results of table 1.3 are otherwise confirmed. In particular, MIDDLEDM and GINILA are both significant and of the predicted sign. We also tried adding to the regression the percentage of the population living in urban areas, but it was generally insignificant and it did not change the other estimated coefficients.

The estimated residuals reveal a systematic pattern. They tend to be larger for the poor countries in the sample. As a possible correction for this heteroskedasticity, we reestimated the model by weighting observations with GDP. The results are shown in columns 3 and 4 of table 1.4. Again, they remain very similar to those of table 1.3. We obtained similar results for other specifications, not reported in the table.

Next, we ask if our results are robust to the possibility of measurement error and apply the techniques of Klepper and Leamer (1984). Following their approach, we estimate column 1 of table 1.3 minimizing in the direction of all the independent variables potentially measured with error. Klepper and Leamer (1984) show that if all the estimated coefficients thus obtained retain their signs from table 1.3, then the results are robust to measurement error. Furthermore, the two maximum likelihood coefficients lie in a known and bounded interval. In our case, the variables most likely

Table 1.4
Some sensitivity analysis

Dependent variable	Growth				Investment
	1	2	3	4	5
# OBS	46	49	48	50	31
CONSTANT	2.780	5.394	2.550	6.926	4.886
	(1.129)	(2.533)	(1.009)	(3.058)	(0.318)
GDP	−0.99E-3	−0.73E-3	−0.88E-3	−0.719E-3	−0.12E-2
	(−4.325)	(−3.808)	(−4.577)	(−4.386)	(−0.973)
PSCHOOL	0.024	0.024	0.032	0.0159	0.123
	(2.025)	(2.156)	(2.671)	(1.494)	(2.306)
SSCHOOL	0.033	0.016			
	(1.789)	(1.148)			
AGRIL	−0.023	−0.034	−0.278	−0.049	−0.078
	(−1.095)	(−1.825)	(−1.532)	(−2.969)	(−0.661)
MIDDLE	0.039		−0.066		0.747
	(−0.310)		(−0.418)		(1.743)
GINILA		−0.034		−0.037	0.038
		(−2.301)		(−1.750)	(0.505)
MIDDLEDM	0.325		0.396		
	(1.960)		(2.065)		
GINILADM		−0.016		−0.013	
		(−0.762)		(−0.525)	
DEMOCRACY	−4.174	1.111	−4.074	1.500	
	(−2.065)	(0.683)	(−1.697)	(0.785)	
$\bar{R}^2$	0.443	0.475	0.399	0.480	0.365
SEE	1.339	1.136	57.096	51.520	5.544

Note: Method of estimation: Columns 1, 2, 5: OLS. Columns 3, 4: weighted least squares, with GDP as weight.

to be measured with error are GDP, AGRIL, and the two measures of distribution, MIDDLE and GINILA. Hence we ran four "reverse regressions," in each of which we replaced the dependent variable by one of the incorrectly measured regressors. The estimated coefficients retain their sign only in three out of the four regressions. In particular, if we assume that one of the two distributional variables (it does not matter which one) is measured correctly, then we can compute consistent bounds for the coefficients of the remaining three variables. But if both MIDDLE and GINILA are measured with error, then we can argue that the results are robust (in the sense of retaining their sign) only if we are willing to assign specific priors to the percent size of measurement error in the regressors relative to the true R^2. We conclude that our results are somewhat sensitive to the

possibility of measurement error in the variables MIDDLE or GINILA, but not in the remaining variables.

As a further check on our measures of income distribution, we replaced the variable MIDDLE with other measures of income inequality, such as the percentage of income received by the top 5 percent of the population or the Gini coefficient obtained from the distribution of pretax income (the source is always Paukert (1973)). The results, not reported in the table, were essentially unchanged.

From these results taken together, we conclude that they are supportive of the theory: a more unequal size distribution of income is bad for growth in democracies, while more land concentration is bad for growth every-where. These effects of distribution on growth are also quantitatively significant: a one-standard-deviation change in MIDDLE and in GINILA both affect average annual growth by at least half a percentage point (according to the point estimates in table 1.2).

Finally, the theory also has predictions for investment in cumulative factors. As explained in the previous section, distributional variables are important for growth because they affect the investment rate of different countries. In the last column of table 1.4 we change the dependent variable, replacing the average growth rate with the average physical investment rate between 1960 and 1985 (the source is still Summers and Heston (1988)).[13] The results are now less supportive of the theory. The size distribution of income enters with the correct sign and is almost significant. But land ownership is not significantly different from zero and has the wrong sign. In a sense this is not too surprising, since the measure of investment does not correspond with the implications of the theory. First, our measure of investment is the sum of public and private investment, while the theory only refers to private investment. Second, accumulation of human capital and of productive knowledge is not included in the measure of investment, while it should be according to the theory.

1.4   Conclusions

The main predictions of the simple theory outlined in the paper seem to be largely supported by the data. Income inequality and land concentration are bad for growth. In principle, these facts are consistent with other, non-political reasons for why income distribution and the distribution of land ownership influence growth.[14] Our theory, however, also predicts that the distributional variables interact in a specific way with the form of govern-ment. This additional prediction is also consistent with the data and thus

discriminates in favor of a political explanation of why distribution matters for growth.

The theory has predictions about the link between income distribution and policy and about the link between policy and growth. Future empirical research should try to identify both these links, rather than estimating reduced forms, as we have done in this chapter. We think this is going to be pretty hard work though. As we argued in section 1.2, "taxes" in the model can be interpreted in a variety of ways. These various general and sectoral policies are going to be hard to measure in a satisfactory way across countries.

The literature surveyed here has studied the link between income distribution at a point in time and policies affecting growth. But the evidence collected by development economists and economic historians suggests that the relationship between growth and income goes both ways: the literature on the Kuznets curve argues that income distribution is systematically related to the income level.[15] Future theoretical research should try to study the joint dynamics of growth, income distribution, and policy formation. A natural, but difficult, way to do this would be to extend earlier work on human capital and income distribution to incorporate endogenous policy formation.[16] Another challenging task involves building a bridge to the literature, surveyed by Aghion and Bolton (1991), on growth and income distribution under incomplete capital markets.

Notes

Much of the work on this paper was done when we were visiting the Research Department of the International Monetary Fund. We gratefully acknowledge financial support from the Fund, from the Swedish Social Science Research Council, from the Mattei Foundation, and from the NSF, grant S.E.S-8909263. We thank Giuseppe Bertola, John Londregan, Ariel Rubinstein, and the editors of this volume for helpful comments, and we thank Kerstin Blomqvist for secretarial assistance.

1. However, there is a literature that studies optimizing fertility choice and thus makes population growth the object of economic analysis (see, for instance, the recent paper by Barro and Becker (1990)).

2. The contribution of foreign direct investment to GDP growth may be particularly important if there are indivisibilities or other nonconvexities that keep the marginal product of capital low when capital is scarce. The relationship between foreign direct investment, domestic policy, and growth has been recently studied by Cohen and Michel (1991).

3. See for instance Barro and Sala-i-Martin (1992) and Rebelo (1991).

4. The theory of endogenous economic policy has developed in two somewhat different traditions. One development—surveyed by Persson and Tabellini (1990)—is oriented toward macroeconomic policy and public finance. The other development—surveyed by Hillman (1989) and Magee, Brock, and Young (1989)—is oriented toward trade policy.

5. Glomm and Ravikumar (1991) study an overlapping-generations model with heterogenous agents where income taxes finance public education. They obtain the conclusion that more inequality produces less growth. But their assumptions are such that all agents prefer the same tax rate, so there is no distributional conflict in their model.

6. F_l, the return to land in the expression for v, is pinned down by the requirement that $F_k(k^f, l) = 1$ and thus does not depend on the tax.

7. See Hillman (1989) and Magee, Brock, and Young (1989).

8. A tax on the capital intensive sector here is bad for growth for two reasons. First, there is the disincentive to save, which was also present in the other model. Second, capital is driven out of the capital intensive sector, which is typically the sector driving growth. This sectoral distortion further reduces the growth rate (on this point see also Easterly (1991)).

9. For six countries, GINILA is observed in the early 1970s, but for all other countries it is observed in the early 1960s.

10. This is a flow measure of human capital. A stock measure, such as the literacy rate, would be more closely tied to the model, but it is measured with much bigger error than school enrollment.

11. The source for GDP is Summers and Heston (1988). The source for AGRIL and PSCHOOL is the World Development Report, 1988.

12. The correlation coefficient between MIDDLE and GINILA is -0.28. This is not very high, but under the null hypothesis that both variables should be included in the regression, excluding one of them may bias the estimates.

13. We leave the other independent variables in the equation. PSCHOOL may not seem to belong there, but it does—according to some versions of endogenous growth theory—since human capital may increase the return to physical investment (see Romer (1990)).

14. For example, Murphy, Shleifer, and Vishny (1989), building on earlier work in development economics, have suggested another, purely economic, reason why more equality may be good for growth: you may need a sufficiently large middle class to generate demand for manufacturing products that is sufficient for a growth takeoff.

15. Regarding the evidence on the Kuznets curve, see Williamson (1989) and Lindert and Williamson (1985) for an overview of the historical evidence, and Fields (1980) for an overview of the postwar evidence across developing countries.

16. The papers mentioned in section 1.1, by Perotti (1990), Saint-Paul and Verdier (1991), and Glomm and Ravikumar (1991), all take some steps in this direction but

are forced to make simplifying assumptions that rule out an interesting part of the problem.

References

Aghion, P. and P. Bolton. 1991. Distribution and Growth in Models with Imperfect Capital Markets. Forthcoming in *European Economic Review*.

Alesina, A. and D. Rodrik. 1991. Redistributive Politics and Economic Growth Manuscript.

Atkeson, A. and M. Ogaki. 1990. Engel's Law and Savings. Manuscript.

Barro, R. and G. Becker. 1990. Fertility Choice in .a Model of Economic Growth *Econometrica* 57:481–501.

Barro, R. and X. Sala-i-Martin. 1992. Public Finance in Models of Economic Growth. *Review of Economic Studies*. Forthcoming.

Benhabib, J. and A. Rustichini. 1991. Social Conflict, Growth and Income Distribution. Manuscript.

Bertola, G. 1991. Market Structure and Income Distribution in Endogenous Growth Models. Manuscript.

Cohen, D. and P. Michel. 1991. Property Rights on Foreign Capital and Long-Run Growth. Manuscript.

Easterly, W. 1991. Distortions and Growth in Developing Countries. Manuscript.

Fields, G. 1980. *Poverty, Inequality and Development*. Cambridge: Cambridge University Press.

Fischer, S. 1991. Growth, Macroeconomics and Development. *NBER Macroeconomics Annual* 1991:329–363.

Glomm, G. and B. Ravikumar. 1991. Public vs Private Investment in Human Capital: Endogenous Growth and Income Inequality. Manuscript.

Hillman, A. 1989. *The Political Economy of Protection*. London: Harwood Academic Publishers.

Klepper, S. and E. Leamer. 1984. Consistent Sets of Estimates for Regressions with Errors in all Variables. *Econometrica* 52:163–183.

Krueger, A. 1990. Government Failures in Development. *Journal of Economic Perspectives* 4:9–23.

Lindert, P. and J. Williamson. 1985. Growth, Equality and History. *Explorations in Economic History* 22:341–377.

Magee, S., W. Brock, and L. Young. 1989. *Black Hole Tariffs and Endogenous Policy Theory*. Cambridge: Cambridge University Press.

Meltzer, A. and S. Richard. 1981. A Rational Theory of the Size of Government. *Journal of Political Economy* 52:914–927.

Murphy, K., A. Shleifer, and R. Vishny. 1989. Income Distribution, Market Size and Industrialization. *Quarterly Journal of Economics* 104:537—64.

Paukert, F. 1973. Income Distribution at Different Levels of Development-A Survey of the Evidence. *International Labor Review* 108:97—125.

Perotti, R. 1990. Political Equilibrium, Income Distribution and Growth. Manuscript.

Persson, T. and G. Tabellini. 1990. *Macroeconomic Policy, Credibility and Politics.* London: Harwood Academic Publishers.

Persson, T. and G. Tabellini. 1991a. Is Inequality Harmful for Growth? Theory and Evidence. Manuscript.

Persson, T. and G. Tabellini. 1991b. Factor Ownership, Distribution and Growth. In preparation.

Rebelo, S. 1991. Long-Run Policy Analysis and Long-Run Growth. *Journal of Political Economy* 99:500—21.

Rebelo, S. 1992. Growth in Open Economies. *Carnegie-Rochester Conference Series.* Forthcoming.

Romer, P. 1990. Human Capital and Growth: Theory and Evidence. *Carnegie-Rochester Conference Series* 32:251—83.

Saint-Paul G. and T. Verdier. 1991. Education, Growth and Democracy. Manuscript.

Summers, R. and A. Heston. 1988. A New Set of International Comparisons of Real Product and Price Levels: Estimates for 130 Countries. *The Renew of Income and Wealth* 34:1—25.

Taylor, C. and M. Hudson. 1972. *World Handbook of Political and Social Indicators.* 2nd ed. New Haven: Yale University Press.

Taylor, C. and D. Jodice. 1983. *World Handbook of Political and Social Indicators.* 3rd ed. New Haven: Yale University Press.

Williamson, J. 1989. Inequality and Modern Economic Growth: What Does History Tell Us? Discussion Paper 1448. Cambridge, MA: Harvard University.

World Bank. 1988. *World Development Report.* Washington: The World Bank.

2

Distribution, Political Conflict, and Economic Growth: A Simple Theory and Some Empirical Evidence

Alberto Alesina and Dani Rodrik

The relationship between politics and economic growth is one of the most fundamental issues in political economy. Our objective in this chapter is to address this issue by developing a simple theoretical model and looking at some empirical evidence in support of the model. Our basic argument is as follows. In democracies, where voter preferences presumably influence government policies, more concentrated wealth distributions are conducive to lower rates of economic growth. The reason is that when large segments of the population are economically disenfranchised, they are more likely to be willing to "tax" growth-enhancing resources such as physical and human capital. In authoritarian regimes, the relationship between distribution and growth is ambiguous, as the economically disenfranchised will generally have little voice.

An essay on politics and growth must address at least three questions. First, what is the source of political conflict that we should focus on? The basic cleavage we choose to emphasize here is that between "labor" and "capital." This is one of the central cleavages in any modern society. The quotation marks emphasize that we interpret these class distinctions broadly and metaphorically. In particular, by capital we should understand all productive resources that can be accumulated by investing time and resources. Hence, human capital and technology are included under this definition together with physical capital. Labor, by contrast, stands for raw labor. The basic political conflict of this paper will be the conflict of interest among individuals whose incomes derive in different proportions from resources that can be accumulated and resources that cannot.

Second, how do we view the role of government? We find it helpful and realistic to think of government as providing two distinct functions. The first is a directly redistributive one: to transfer resources from less favored groups to more-favored groups. The second is a directly productive one and consists of the provision of basic infrastructure and other critical services such as law and order. These services allow private production to proceed smoothly; we will model them as government expenditure that increases the productivity of the private sector. We will show, however, that these productive expenditures can also play a redistributive role, even though they may not be targeted on specific groups. As a result, different groups disagree on the desired provision of these public goods.

Finally, there is the question of how to model growth. We are interested in showing (and testing) a relationship between distribution and growth. Thus, we have chosen a model in which growth is endogenous. Our production function is linearly homogeneous in capital and (productive) government services taken together. Despite the fixed labor endowment, then, our economy can grow without limit as long as government services can expand at the same rate as private capital.

The present chapter draws heavily on our previous work on this subject, in Alesina and Rodrik (1991). Here, we present a stripped-down version of our previous model. We sacrifice some generality in order to gain simplicity. Furthermore, we leave aside various dynamic aspects and time consistency issues that were explored in the previous paper. On the other hand, we discuss more explicitly some of the policy implications of the approach and present additional empirical evidence.

Some related papers deserve mention at the outset. In independent work, Bertola (1991) presents a model that is very close in spirit to ours, also focusing on the distinction between accumulated and nonaccumulated factors of production. He notes, as we do, the conflict of interest, when it comes to growth, that exists among individuals with differing sources of income. Pazarbasioglu (1991) analyzes the conflict between labor and capital and models nonvoting mechanisms through which the conflict gets played out. In particular, she focuses on labor unrest, which is conducive to increased transfers to workers but discourages private investment.

Galor and Zeira (1989), Perotti (1990), and Persson and Tabellini (1991) focus on models where income distribution affects the equilibrium level of investment in human capital and hence growth. Galor and Zeira develop the argument that, in the presence of credit constraints, a very skewed distribution of income will prevent poor individuals from investing in education. Persson and Tabellini focus on the incentive of the poor to limit the private appropriability, through the political system, of the return to investment in skills or technology. Perotti's paper combines the imperfect-credit market approach with a political motive. Persson and Tabellini also present empirical evidence on the relationship between income distribution and growth, with results similar to ours.[1] Finally, Benhabib and Rustichini

(1991) develop a more general, game-theoretic model in which individuals can appropriate society's resources to their own benefit (at the cost of future retaliation by others) and analyze the relationship between the level of wealth, income distribution, and growth.

The plan for the chapter is as follows. The next section lays out the basic machinery of the growth model and discusses how the policy preferences of two archetypal individuals, a pure worker and a pure capitalist, are determined. In section 2.2, we extend the framework to a continuum of individuals, distinguished by their relative factor endowments. Section 2.3 discusses the endogenous determination of growth when policy is determined by majority voting. Section 2.4 presents some empirical evidence consistent with the implications of the theory. We conclude the paper in section 2.5.

2.1 The Basic Framework

In order to make our points as clearly as possible, we use a simple endogenous growth model that allows for distributive conflict between labor and capital. The production side of the economy is represented by a Cobb-Douglas production function, adapted from Barro (1990) and Barro and Sala-i-Martin (1990) with slight modification.

$$y = Ak^{\alpha}g^{1-\alpha}l^{1-\alpha}, \qquad 0 < \alpha < 1, \tag{1}$$

A is a technological parameter, k and l are the aggregate stocks of capital and labor respectively, and g is the aggregate level of government spending on productive services. We make use of a continuous time model; the time dependence of each variable is not explicitly shown for economy of notation. The government has a single source of tax revenue, a tax on the capital stock (capital is to be interpreted in the broad sense indicated in the introduction). Tax revenues are used to finance spending on productive services (g) as well as lump-sum transfers to labor. We assume that the government balances its budget at every instant. We also rule out expropriation of capital, in order to avoid dealing with time-inconsistency problems in capital taxation, which are not our focus. If we denote the share of tax revenue that goes to workers as λ, the government's budget constraint requires

$$g = (1 - \lambda)\tau k, \tag{2}$$

where τ is the tax on capital. Transfers are possible only from capitalists to workers, and not vice versa, so $\lambda \geq 0$.[2]

We assume perfect competition in factor markets so that wages and rental rates on capital are determined by the usual marginal productivity conditions. Taking the appropriate partial derivatives of equation (1) and substituting from equation (2), we have

$$r = \partial y / \partial k = \alpha A[(1 - \lambda)\tau]^{1-\alpha} \equiv r(\overset{+}{\tau}, \overset{-}{\lambda}) \tag{3}$$

$$w = \partial y / \partial l = (1 - \alpha)A[(1 - \lambda)\tau]^{1-\alpha}k \equiv \omega(\overset{+}{\tau}, \overset{-}{\lambda})k \tag{4}$$

where we have normalized the economy's aggregate labor endowment (l) to unity. Note that the marginal productivity of capital is independent of the capital stock, thanks to the proportional tax on capital that finances government spending. This prevents diminishing returns from setting in. Furthermore, the marginal productivities of labor and capital are both increasing in the tax rate on capital, as higher taxes allow more government spending on productive services for any given λ and k. By the same token, an increase in λ reduces w and r as it diverts government spending away from directly productive channels. After taxes and transfers, labor and capital income are given by

$$y^k = [r(\tau, \lambda) - \tau]k \tag{5}$$

$$y^l = [\omega(\tau, \lambda) + \lambda\tau]k \tag{6}$$

For the national income identity to be satisfied, it is necessary that $y^k + y^l + g = y$, which is indeed the case here.

To see how differences in factor ownership affect policy preferences, it is useful to focus first on an extreme case where the economy has only two types of individuals, pure capitalists and pure workers. As these terms imply, we assume for the moment that workers consume their entire income and that only capitalists save and accumulate. Let us also assume that the utility function of the representative capitalist is given by

$$U^k = \int \log c^k e^{-\rho t} dt, \tag{7}$$

where c^k is the capitalist's consumption level and ρ is the discount rate.

Since only capitalists accumulate, the economy's growth rate is determined by their behavior. The problem solved by the representative capitalist is:

$$\text{Max } U^k = \int \log c^k e^{-\rho t} dt$$

$$\text{s.t.} \quad dk/dt = (r - \tau)k - c^k. \tag{8}$$

The individual capitalist takes r and τ as given. The solution to this problem gives the familiar growth equation:

$$\gamma \equiv \hat{c}^k = \hat{k} = r - \tau - \rho, \tag{9}$$

where a hat over a variable indicates percent changes. Growth is linear in the difference between the after-tax return to capital and the discount rate. This generalizes to any time-separable, isoelastic utility function. In fact, had we written instantaneous utility as $(c^{1-\sigma} - 1)/(1 - \sigma)$, instead of $\log c$, the corresponding growth rate would have become $\gamma = \sigma^{-1}(r - \tau - \rho)$. Therefore, the higher the after-tax return to capital, the higher the economy's growth rate.

In equilibrium, the economy's growth rate is given by

$$\gamma(\tau, \lambda) = r(\tau, \lambda) - \tau - \rho,$$

$$\gamma_\lambda \equiv \partial\gamma/\partial\lambda = \partial r/\partial\lambda < 0; \tag{10}$$

$$\gamma_\tau \equiv \partial\gamma/\partial\tau = \partial r/\partial\tau - 1 \gtreqless 0 \quad \text{as} \quad \tau \lesseqgtr [\alpha(1 - \alpha)A]^{1/\alpha}(1 - \lambda)^{(1-\alpha)/\alpha}$$

where we have substituted from the definition of r in equation (3). Note that direct redistribution (λ) is harmful to growth as it reduces the provision of productive public services. But the tax on capital has an ambiguous effect: for "small" tax rates, the productivity-enhancing effect of public spending dominates, and the after-tax return to capital *increases* in τ. For "large" tax rates, the after-tax return to capital falls as τ is raised further. Therefore, the relationship between the economy's growth rate and the tax on capital (for any given λ) is represented by an inverse-U curve: the growth rate first increases, and then decreases, as τ is progressively raised.

Now suppose that the government in power represents only the interests of the capitalist class. Such a government would choose those policies that simply maximize the welfare of the representative capitalist. Notice first that putting the capitalists' budget constraint $dk/dt = (r - \tau)k - c^k$ together with the expression (9) for growth, we get $c^k - \rho k$. That is, capitalists consume a constant fraction of the capital stock at every instant. The procapitalist government's decision problem can then be written as follows:

$$\text{Max } U^k = \int \log(\rho k)e^{-\rho t}dt$$
$$\tau, \lambda$$

$$\text{s.t.} \quad \hat{k} = \gamma(\tau, \lambda). \tag{11}$$

By inspection, we can see that the solution to this problem is equivalent to maximizing the growth rate. This gives us the procapitalist government's preferred policy choices:

$$\tau^* = [\alpha(1 - \alpha)A]^{1/\alpha} \qquad \lambda^* = 0.$$

These choices are time invariant; thus, the rate of growth is constant. A government that serves the interests of pure capitalists will want to maximize the economy's growth rate.

Let us now turn to the other extreme of a government that seeks to maximize the well-being of pure workers. As mentioned, pure workers do not save—they consume all their income: $c^l = y^l$. Let us also assume that they have the same discount rate as capitalists, ρ.[3] The problem faced by this government is

$$\text{Max } U^l = \int \log[(\omega(\tau, \lambda) + \lambda\tau)k]e^{-\rho t}dt$$
$$\substack{\tau, \lambda}$$

$$\text{s.t.} \quad \hat{k} = \gamma(\tau, \lambda). \tag{12}$$

Unlike in the case of pure capitalists, workers face a trade-off between *level* and *growth* effects in the choice of optimal policies. Consider, for example, the tax rate τ. An increase in τ raises the level of workers' consumption, as it increases both real wages (since $\omega_\tau > 0$) and the lump-sum transfers they receive (whenever $\lambda > 0$). But as long as τ exceeds the growth-maximizing rate, an increase in τ also reduces the economy's growth rate and therefore the rate of increase of real wages. The optimal choice trades off these two effects. Capitalists, by contrast, do not face this trade-off, as the *level* of their consumption is independent of τ and λ and depends only on the discount rate and the inherited capital stock.

The policy choices $(\tau^{**}, \lambda^{**})$ that provide a solution to equation (12) can be characterized as follows:

(i)   if $\rho \geq [(1 - \alpha)A]^{1/\alpha}$, then:

$$\tau^{**} = \rho \qquad \lambda^{**} = 1 - \rho^{-1}[(1 - \alpha)A]^{1/\alpha}$$

(ii)   if $\rho < [(1 - \alpha)A]^{1/\alpha}$, then:

$$\tau^{**}\{1 - \alpha(1 - \alpha)A\tau^{**-\alpha}\} = \rho(1 - \alpha) \qquad \lambda^{**} = 0 \tag{13}$$

This equation identifies two possible outcomes. If the future is discounted sufficiently heavily (13 [i] above), workers would like to have a strictly positive λ. Otherwise (13 [ii]), they will prefer to set λ to zero. In all cases, policies are once again time invariant.

Whether λ is strictly positive or not, it easy to verify that the resulting growth rate will lie *below* the maximum rate that capitalists would have chosen. The intuition for this can be seen most clearly in terms of the level and growth effects mentioned above: Start from the combination of policies that maximizes the economy's growth rate and ask if we can make workers better off by deviating. Now, by direct application of the envelope theorem a small increase in τ or λ will have only second-order effects on growth. However, the same change(s) will have a first-order effect on the workers' consumption level. Therefore, increases in τ (and possibly λ) from their growth-maximizing levels will always present a good bargain for workers. Put differently, maximizing growth is not in the interest of workers.[4]

In summary, this section has established a basic conflict of interest between workers and capitalists as regards public finance decisions and growth. It remains to be seen, however, whether this conflict also exists in a more realistic framework where we allow all individuals to save and accumulate. In the next section we show that it does.

2.2   The Model with a Continuum of Agents

Pure capitalists and pure workers of the sort we analyzed in the previous section exist only in some Marxist minds (and in stylized models). In reality, every individual is a capitalist to some extent, as the desire to save and accumulate is the only prerequisite for entry to the capitalists' club. That does not mean, of course, that all individuals will end up equal in their capital endowment. Depending on the initial distribution of inherited assets and the rates of time preference within the economy, heterogeneity in outcomes is possible. Here we take one of the simplest cases, assuming that individuals are alike in all respects except for their initial holdings of capital. We also limit the choice of policy instruments to τ only and set $\lambda = 0$, for reasons that will soon become clear.[5]

We start by indexing each individual by his relative factor endowment, σ^i, where

$$\sigma^i = l_t^i / [k_t^i k_t], \qquad \sigma^i \in [0, \infty). \tag{14}$$

An individual with a high σ is a capital-poor individual, while one with low σ is capital rich. (Remember that the aggregate labor endowment of the economy is normalized to unity.) We have now used time subscripts to make it clear that in general there is no guarantee that σ^i will remain constant over time. With time-separable, isoelastic preferences, however, σ^i

turns out to be time invariant, and this will simplify the analysis considerably (at some cost to realism, of course).

Each individual earns income from both capital and labor. Therefore

$$y^i = \omega l^i k + [r - \tau]k^i = \omega k^i \sigma^i + [r - \tau]k^i. \tag{15}$$

Note that income depends both on individual ownership of capital and on the aggregate stock of capital. We assume all individuals have the same logarithmic utility function. The consumption-saving decisions of the individual are determined by solving the following problem:

$$\text{Max } U^i = \int \log c^i e^{-\rho t} dt$$

$$\text{s.t.} \quad dk^i/dt = \omega k^i \sigma^i + [r - \tau]k^i - c^i. \tag{16}$$

This yields:

$$\hat{c}^i = \hat{k}^i = r - \tau - \rho, \qquad \text{for all } i. \tag{17}$$

This is a helpful result that states that everyone accumulates at the same rate (provided they have the same discount rates), or, what amounts to the same thing, that savings are a constant fraction of an individual's capital stock. The initial distribution of factor endowments does not affect the common rate of accumulation, $\gamma(\tau)$. A direct consequence is that the σ^i remain constant over time; the distribution of wealth in the economy is time invariant, given the preferences we have assumed. The result that wealth distribution remains constant over time may not be realistic, but it helps us avoid tricky problems that would otherwise arise.[6]

What is individual i's preferred policy and how does it depend on σ^i? The policy problem for a government that wants to maximize i's well-being is given by

$$\text{Max } U^i = \int \log c^i e^{-\rho t} dt$$
$$\phantom{\text{Max}}_{\tau}$$

$$\text{s.t.} \quad c^i = [\omega(\tau)\sigma^i + \rho]k^i$$

$$\hat{k}^i = \gamma(\tau)$$

$$\hat{k} = \gamma(\tau). \tag{18}$$

Note that the consumption level now has two components, one that depends on ρ and another one that depends on wage earnings; the latter component is increasing in σ^i. The exercise yields the following implicit characterization of individual i's preferred tax, τ^i

$$\tau^i\{1 - \alpha(1 - \alpha)A\tau^{i-\alpha}\} = \rho(1 - \alpha)\mu^i(\tau^i), \tag{19}$$

where:

$$\mu^i(\tau^i) = \omega(\tau^i)\sigma^i/[\omega(\tau^i)\sigma^i + \rho]. \tag{20}$$

Note that $\mu^i(\cdot)$ is the share of labor earnings in consumption expenditures of individual i, and it is increasing in σ^i. It is straightforward to verify that (19)–(20) yield a unique τ^i that increases with σ^i. In words, the more capital poor is an individual, the higher his preferred tax on capital.

It can also be checked that (19)–(20) yield our earlier extreme cases when σ^i is set accordingly. For a pure capitalist, with no income from labor, σ^i is zero. In this case, $\mu^i = 0$, and τ^i simplifies to $\tau^i = [\alpha(1 - \alpha)A]^{1/\alpha} = \tau^*$, which is the pure capitalist's optimal policy from the previous section. For a pure worker, σ^i goes to infinity and μ^i becomes one. In this case the solution for τ^i is the same as that given for τ^{**} in (13[ii]).

2.3 Wealth Distribution and Growth under Majority Rule

Suppose now that τ has to be chosen in a democratic setting. What can we say about the tax rate that will result from political competition? We are in fact just a short step away from endogenizing the choice of policy in a regime where majority rule prevails. The median-voter theorem can be readily applied to our problem, as all of its requirements are satisfied: a single issue (i.e., the selection of τ), and single-peaked individual preferences defined over this particular issue.

Of course, the median-voter theorem does great injustice to how real democracies operate. But in this case we think it is a useful way to formalize the idea that distributional conflicts are likely to be resolved in a democracy in a manner that reflects the preferences of a majority. A statement like this one seems pretty unobjectionable to us; the median-voter theorem is simply a way of making it operational.

Under majority voting, then, the political equilibrium will yield a tax rate, τ^m, which is the preferred tax rate of the median voter, identified by his relative factor endowment σ^m. This tax rate is implicitly defined by the analogue of (19)–(20)

$$\tau^m\{1 - \alpha(1 - \alpha)A\tau^{m-\alpha}\} = \rho(1 - \alpha)\{\omega(\tau^m)\sigma^m/[\omega(\tau^m)\sigma^m + \rho]\}. \tag{21}$$

As before, the more capital poor the median voter (i.e., the higher σ^m), the higher the resulting tax rate and the lower the equilibrium growth rate. For growth to be as high as possible, we need the median voter to own as much capital as possible. Note. however, that it is practically impossible for majority voting to yield the economy's maximum growth rate. Maximum growth is attained only if the median voter has no labor endowment whatsoever, which is not a realistic possibility.

The conclusion that maximum growth cannot be achieved in a democracy should not be interpreted in a normative manner. As the discussion so far should have made clear, care should be exercised in attributing welfare significance to growth in a model such as ours with distributive conflict. Moreover, even from the standpoint of the representative individual (with $\sigma^i = 1$), the desired policy is one that yields a tax rate higher than that which maximizes growth. This can be seen from (19)–(20), where $\sigma^i = 1$ implies $\mu^i = \omega/(\omega + \rho) > 0$ and $\tau^i \leqq \tau^*$.

Consider next the relationship between distribution and growth. Our model has a specific prediction here, namely that the more capital poor the median voter, the lower the growth rate of the economy. In a perfectly egalitarian society, we would have $\sigma^m = \sigma^i = 1$ for all i. A possible measure of inequality, therefore, is $(\sigma^m - 1)$; this measure reflects how much below the average share is the median share of capital ownership. For example, assuming labor is uniformly distributed, $\sigma^m = 2$ implies that the median voter owns only half the capital that would have been his due under equal distribution. This establishes the following result: *in a democracy, the more unequal the distribution of wealth, the lower is the growth rate of the economy.* The basic intuition for this result is simple: when a large segment of the electorate is cut off from the expanding assets of the economy, they are more likely to be willing to tax these assets.

2.4   Empirical Evidence

There are three basic empirical implications of the model developed here. First, we should observe that a concentrated distribution of wealth produces lower rates of economic growth in democracies. Second, the hypothesized link between distribution and growth should hold for democracies only; our model makes no direct prediction for regimes in which majority preferences do not translate into policy outcomes. Third, our model has implications for the relationship between democracy and growth, an issue that has received extensive attention (see Roubini 1990 for a survey). The empirical results on the relationship between democracy and growth have been mixed, and our model can explain why. According to our model, growth should be highest in technocratic or right-wing authoritarian regimes. Growth should be lowest in populist and "kleptocratic" dictatorships.[7] Democracies should lie somewhere between these types of dictatorships. Thus, regressions that do not distinguish between different types of authoritarian regimes and simply compare democracies to dictatorships are bound to find ambiguous results.

In order to test directly this third implication of the model, one would need a classification of the type of authoritarian regimes, which is difficult to accomplish and risks turning into a tautological exercise. Thus, in what follows we concentrate on the first two implications of the model.

We note again that our usage of capital and capital taxation in the context of the model above should be taken metaphorically, not literally. We refer by capital to all factors of production that can be accumulated. Physical capital per se is only one determinant of growth. Others are human capital and technological development. Our distinction between capital and labor is meant to capture the conflict between those individuals in society who derive their income primarily from raw labor as against those whose incomes are based on this broad notion of capital. By the same token, we should not think of τ as an actual capital tax alone. The taxation in question is a metaphor for all kinds of actions that workers can undertake to transfer income to themselves and which, at the same time, hurts the profitability of accumulation. A direct capital tax is one such action. Others are industrial action, such as strikes, and labor militancy in general. When τ is interpreted in this broad fashion, the government budget constraint (2) should in turn be thought of as a reduced-form government-response function that translates worker pressure into real wage gains at the expense of capital.

Consequently, a test of our model that focused on the relationship between distribution and capital taxation would miss the broader point. In reality, τ is a whole vector whose elements are difficult to quantify, and which shows different characteristics in different societies. For this reason, we focus here on the relationship between distribution and growth directly. The disadvantage of this approach is that the evidence will be silent on the intermediate links.[8] But to the extent that the relationship turns out to hold for democracies and not for other regimes, we will at least have some confirmation that the underlying causality is driven by political factors.

There are other difficulties in looking at empirical evidence. Our framework predicts a relationship between the distribution of *wealth* and economic growth. Comparable data on wealth distribution exists for only a handful of countries. We are therefore forced to resort to data on *income* distribution. While such data are available for a relatively large number of countries, the data are not without fault; the quality of the data and the methods used in putting them together vary greatly. Moreover, the statistics usually pertain to different years. We take these problems as inserting possibly large random errors in our regressions, so that any positive result would be very encouraging indeed.

We present cross-country regressions with the average growth rate during 1960–1985 taken as the dependent variable. To limit potential problems with reverse causality (from growth to distribution), we have focused on the largest group of countries for which we could get information on income distribution around a year close to 1960—the beginning of the time horizon for growth. This gave us a group of sixty-seven countries, for the vast majority of which we have an observation on income distribution somewhere between 1956 and 1964. The appendix lists the countries and the relevant years. The data on income distribution are taken from Jain (1975) and Lecallion et al. (1984). As additional explanatory variables, we use the initial level of per capita income (in thousands of 1980 dollars), GDP60, and the primary-school enrollment ratio for 1960, PRIM60. As investment is an endogenous variable in our framework. we do not include it as a separate regressor in the regressions. All the data, except for income distribution, are obtained from Barro and Wolf (1989) and Heston and Summers (1988).

We divided our sample of countries into two subgroups, democracies and nondemocracies. To avoid sample-selection problems, we decided on the split before we ran any regressions. Our classification is shown in the appendix. There are some ambiguous cases, such as Greece and Spain. We classified these two countries as democracies, even though authoritarian regimes were in power during some of the period in each case. But our results turned out to be insensitive to changing the classification of countries such as these two that underwent transformation in their political regimes. We display the main results in tables 2.1, 2.2, and 2.3. The first table shows the regressions for the entire sample; the other two show the results for nondemocracies and democracies, respectively. In each table, we show six regressions with different distributional indicators. These indicators are the income shares of each of the five quintiles in the population and the income share of the top five percentile.

We see for the sample as a whole (table 2.1) that increases in the income shares of the poorer quintiles are associated with increases in growth, while increases in the income shares of the richest quintile and of the top five percent are associated with decreases in growth. That is, countries where income is more equally distributed also grow faster (once we control for initial income and primary enrollment ratios). The distributional indicators are also statistically significant in the case of the third and highest quintiles and the top five percentile.

Table 2.1
Growth regressions: All countries, income distribution measured in the 50s/60s, sample = 67 (t-statistics in parentheses)

Eqn.	CONST.	GDP60	PRIM60	Lowest 20%	Second 20%	Third 20%	Fourth 20%	Highest 20%	Highest 5%	R^2
(1)	−0.522 (−0.63)	−0.432 (−2.94)	0.042 (4.67)	0.063 (0.62)						0.26
(2)	−1.426 (−1.52)	−0.500 (−3.35)	0.042 (4.82)		0.147 (1.70)					0.29
(3)	−2.007 (−1.87)	−0.582 (−3.62)	0.043 (4.90)			0.156 (2.03)				0.30
(4)	−1.513 (−1.07)	−0.513 (−3.11)	0.042 (4.73)				0.074 (1.05)			0.27
(5)	2.070 (1.40)	−0.533 (−3.39)	0.043 (4.85)					−0.040 (−2.03)		0.28
(6)	1.273 (1.42)	−0.533 (−3.53)	0.042 (4.82)						−0.047 (−2.03)	0.30

Sources: See text.

Table 2.2
Growth regressions: Nondemocracies, income distribution measured in the 50s/60s, sample = 43 (t-statistics in parentheses)

Eqn.	CONST.	GDP60	PRIM60	Lowest 20%	Second 20%	Third 20%	Fourth 20%	Highest 20%	Highest 10%	R^2
(1)	0.283 (0.25)	−0.844 (−2.52)	0.043 (3.59)	−0.024 (−0.17)						0.26
(2)	−0.539 (−0.41)	−0.814 (−2.50)	0.044 (3.69)		0.072 (0.60)					0.27
(3)	−1.121 (−0.75)	−0.848 (−2.62)	0.044 (3.75)			0.099 (0.94)				0.28
(4)	−0.762 (−0.43)	−0.891 (−2.60)	0.044 (3.69)				0.048 (0.55)			0.27
(5)	1.252 (0.66)	−0.844 (−2.59)	0.044 (3.70)					−0.021 (−0.63)		0.27
(6)	1.129 (1.00)	−0.863 (−2.67)	0.044 (3.78)						−0.035 (−1.12)	0.28

Sources: See text.

Table 2.3
Growth regressions: Democracies, income distribution measured in the 50s/60s, sample = 24 (t-statistics in parentheses)

Eqn.	CONST.	GDP60	PRIM60	Lowest 20%	Second 20%	Third 20%	Fourth 20%	Highest 20%	Highest 10%	R^2
(1)	−1.806 (−0.91)	−0.384 (−2.29)	0.051 (2.56)	0.123 (0.86)						0.29
(2)	−3.169 (−1.53)	−0.487 (−2.88)	0.051 (2.74)		0.228 (1.78)					0.36
(3)	−4.931 (−1.97)	−0.620 (−3.20)	0.057 (3.04)			0.262 (2.06)				0.39
(4)	−5.611 (−1.78)	−0.576 (−2.95)	0.057 (2.95)				0.210 (1.72)			0.36
(5)	2.525 (1.01)	−0.552 (−3.06)	0.055 (2.95)					−0.075 (−1.91)		0.38
(6)	0.517 (0.29)	−0.504 (−3.02)	0.054 (2.94)						−0.075 (−2.04)	0.39

Sources: See text.

Table 2.2 displays the same regressions for the subsample of non-democracies. None of the distributional variables comes out statistically significant in this subsample, suggesting that the above results are driven by the democratic countries in our sample. Indeed the regressions for the democratic countries (table 2.3) confirm this. Even though the sample is limited to twenty-four countries in this case, the sign pattern is consistent with the theory, and the coefficients of the third and highest quintiles and of the top fifth percentile are statistically significant. These results suggest that growth may be particularly sensitive in a democracy to the income shares of the middle class and of the richest quintile. The income share of the poorest individuals may exert little influence. One possible reason is that the middle class is likely to be politically much more active than poorer income groups.

To see how different countries are stacked against each other, we provide two scatterplots. Figures 2.1 and 2.2 display the relationship between the income share of the top 5 percent of the population around 1960 and the subsequent growth rate during 1960–1985 for the two subsamples. The income share of the richest 5 percent of the population is shown on the horizontal axis. The vertical axis shows the calculated growth residual from the relevant regression when the income share is not allowed to change and is fixed at the sample mean. The scatterplot for the nondemocracies (figure 2.1) is essentially a cloud, with no obvious relationship one way or the other. The scatter plot for democracies (figure 2.2), meanwhile, displays the negative relationship between concentration of income and growth. We note from the vertical axis that differences in income distribution can make quite a bit of difference to growth: going from the most equal to the least equal countries, growth rates vary by 4–5 percentage points.

The information revealed on specific countries is also interesting. Take France and Canada for example. France has grown at an annual rate of 3.2 percent during 1960–1985, compared to 2.8 percent in Canada's case. But figure 2.2 suggests that France has done rather poorly compared to what would have been expected for a country with its initial level of income and human capital, and Canada has done rather well: France has a negative residual of around 1 percent, and Canada a positive residual of an equivalent magnitude. Our regressions suggest that this may have been accounted by the fact that the richest 5 percent of the population held 25 percent of national income in France, but only 14 percent in Canada. Similarly, the scatterplot reveals that Japan and Israel have been helped by their egalitarian distribution, while Costa Rica, Jamaica, and Germany have been hurt by inequality.

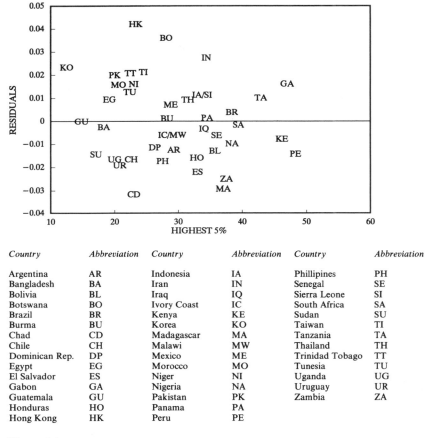

Figure 2.1
Nondemocracies-residuals versus highest 5 percent.

As mentioned, data on income distribution are of dubious quality and comparability. Therefore, we have checked the robustness of our results by also using a more recent data set on income distribution, collected by the World Bank (1990). This gave us a sample of thirty-eight countries, twenty-six of which are democracies, and for which data on income distribution pertain mostly to the early to mid-1980s. Regression results for the full sample and the subsample of democracies are presented in tables 2.4 and 2.5. These confirm our earlier findings. The full sample (table 2.4) shows a very weak relationship between equality and growth. Democracies, on the other hand, yield very strong results in the predicted direction: the distributional variables are now all statistically significant.

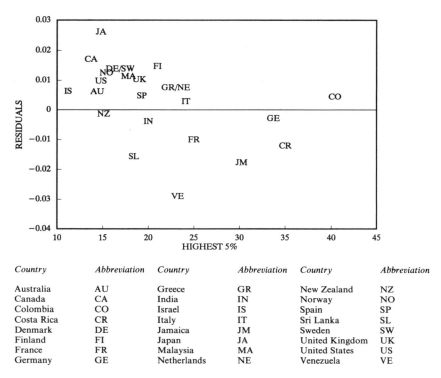

Figure 2.2
Democracies-residuals versus highest 5 percent.

Country	Abbreviation	Country	Abbreviation	Country	Abbreviation
Australia	AU	Greece	GR	New Zealand	NZ
Canada	CA	India	IN	Norway	NO
Colombia	CO	Israel	IS	Spain	SP
Costa Rica	CR	Italy	IT	Sri Lanka	SL
Denmark	DE	Jamaica	JM	Sweden	SW
Finland	FI	Japan	JA	United Kingdom	UK
France	FR	Malaysia	MA	United States	US
Germany	GE	Netherlands	NE	Venezuela	VE

While this second set of results is encouraging, it is also subject to the criticism of reverse causality. Since distribution is now measured during the 1980s, it is possible that causality runs from growth to equality rather than from equality to growth. To correct as best we can for this, we carried out two-stage least squares regressions. We first constructed a compact measure of distribution, denoted by RTL, by taking the ratio of the income shares of the richest quintile in the population to the poorest 40 percent. We then ran first-stage regressions on RTL with GDP60, PRIM60, the secondary enrollment ratio, the agricultural population share, and male life expectancy (all in 1960) used as instruments.[9] The OLS and 2SLS regressions are shown in table 2.6 for the full sample and for democracies.

The OLS results, not surprisingly, confirm those in tables 2.4 and 2.5. The 2SLS results are also consistent with the theory: the coefficient on RTL is larger and has a higher t-statistic (in absolute value) in the subsample of democracies than in the full sample. Therefore, equality is conducive to growth, and this effect operates primarily in democratic regimes.

Table 2.4
Growth regressions: All countries, income distribution measured in the 80s, sample = 38 (t-statistics in parentheses)

Eqn.	CONST.	GDP60	PRIM60	Lowest 20%	Second 20%	Third 20%	Fourth 20%	Highest 20%	Highest 10%	R^2
(1)	−0.373 (−0.23)	−0.417 (−2.17)	0.039 (2.52)	0.117 (0.70)						0.17
(2)	−1.310 (−0.71)	−0.475 (−2.41)	0.037 (2.47)		0.179 (1.16)					0.19
(3)	−2.587 (−1.03)	−0.541 (−2.55)	0.037 (2.45)			0.219 (1.34)				0.20
(4)	−4.657 (−1.05)	−0.568 (−2.45)	0.037 (2.45)				0.250 (1.18)			0.19
(5)	3.134 (1.25)	−0.500 (−2.45)	0.038 (2.50)					−0.055 (−1.19)		0.19
(6)	2.455 (1.25)	−0.514 (−2.48)	0.038 (2.50)						−0.059 (−1.23)	0.19

Sources: See text.
* For this sample of countries we do not have the income share of the richest 5 percent of the population.

Table 2.5
Growth regressions: Democracies only, income distribution measured in the 80s, sample = 26 (t-statistics)

Eqn.	CONST.	GDP60	PRIM60	Lowest 20%	Second 20%	Third 20%	Fourth 20%	Highest 20%	Highest 10%	R^2
(1)	−2.824 (−1.55)	−0.330 (−2.15)	0.043 (2.36)	0.381 (2.18)						0.37
(2)	−5.053 (−2.62)	−0.459 (−3.25)	0.038 (2.29)		0.481 (3.23)					0.49
(3)	−7.858 (−3.66)	−0.622 (−4.41)	0.041 (2.45)			0.517 (4.10)				0.57
(4)	−13.011 (−3.89)	−0.719 (−4.58)	0.049 (3.24)				0.574 (3.95)			0.54
(5)	6.708 (2.78)	−0.584 (−4.18)	0.044 (2.88)					−0.147 (−3.81)		0.54
(6)	4.411 (2.33)	−0.584 (−4.18)	0.044 (2.88)						−0.150 (−3.96)	0.56

Sources: See text.

Table 2.6
Growth regressions on RTL (t-statistics in parentheses)

Sample	OLS		2SLS	
	1	2	1	2
Sample	All	Democracies	All	Democracies
	(n = 38)	(n = 26)	(n = 37)*	(n = 26)
Constant	0.784	2.417	3.237	5.04
	(0.58)	(1.33)	(1.33)	(1.73)
GDP60	−0.434	−0.480	−0.775	−0.576
	(−2.17)	(−3.30)	(−2.64)	(−3.18)
PRIM60	0.038	0.041	0.059	0.037
	(2.45)	(2.48)	(3.03)	(1.91)
RTL	−0.101	−0.863	−1.344	−1.540
	(−0.43)	(−3.08)	(−1.74)	(−2.49)
R^2	0.16	0.47	0.19	0.44

* Botswana, which is included in the OLS regressions, is not included in the 2SLS regressions for lack of data on the variables needed as instruments.

In our model, the linkage between income distribution and growth operates through the effect of inequality on taxation of capital, which lowers investment and growth. As emphasized above, this mechanism regarding the role of investment in physical capital should be taken as illustrative of a more general point. Nonetheless, it is still instructive to examine more directly the relationship between income distribution and physical investment.

Tables 2.7, 2.8, and 2.9 display our results for democracies. The dependent variable is now the average ratio of investment to GDP (over 1960–1985), taken from Heston and Summers (1988).[10] In table 2.7, which is the analogue of table 2.3, we use the income distribution data as measured in the late 1950s and early 1960s. The sign pattern on the coefficients of the various quintiles is identical to that obtained in the growth regressions (see table 2.3). The t-statistics, however, are lower and only borderline (in)significant. In the regression for nondemocracies (not displayed here), the income inequality measures are not significant (and t-statistics lie consistently below one).

Table 2.8, which is the analogue of table 2.4, displays the results with the income distribution data from the 1980s. In these regressions, the distribution variables are strongly significant and with a sign pattern identical to what we had found for growth. To correct for potential reverse causality, we repeat the 2SLS estimation in table 2.9 using the same instruments as in table 2.5. Once again, our results on investment are consistent with those for growth.

Table 2.7
Investment regressions: Democracies, income distribution measured in the 50s/60s, sample = 24* (t-statistics in parentheses)

Eqn.	CONST.	GDP60	PRIM60	Lowest 20%	Second 20%	Third 20%	Fourth 20%	Highest 20%	Highest 5%	R^2
(1)	9.805 (0.97)	0.041 (0.48)	0.136 (1.35)	-0.010 (-0.01)						0.12
(2)	2.513 (0.24)	-0.315 (-0.36)	0.142 (1.47)		0.768 (1.17)					0.18
(3)	-5.329 (-0.41)	-0.880 (-0.88)	0.164 (1.70)			1.011 (1.54)				0.22
(4)	-10.296 (-0.65)	-0.808 (-0.82)	0.168 (1.73)				0.917 (1.49)			0.21
(5)	21.553 (1.66)	-0.526 (-0.56)	0.156 (1.59)					-0.248 (-1.22)		0.18
(6)	15.472 (1.65)	-0.412 (-0.78)	0.154 (1.61)						-0.279 (-1.46)	0.21

*Dependent variable: $\dfrac{I}{GDP60}$ = Total investment in physical capital over GDP; average 1960–85.

Table 2.8
Investment regressions: Democracies only, income distribution measured in the 80s, sample = 25* (t-statistics in parentheses)

Eqn.	CONST.	GDP60	PRIM60	Lowest 20%	Second 20%	Third 20%	Fourth 20%	Highest 20%	Highest 10%	R^2
(1)	1.810 (0.20)	0.520 (0.68)	0.098 (1.07)	1.672 (1.90)						0.27
(2)	−8.53 (−0.87)	−0.064 (−0.09)	0.075 (0.88)		2.178 (2.87)					0.39
(3)	−20.474 (−1.81)	−0.770 (−1.03)	0.091 (1.16)			2.282 (3.34)				0.45
(4)	−42.429 (−2.39)	−1.174 (−1.41)	0.124 (1.55)				2.495 (3.24)			0.43
(5)	43.881 (3.47)	−0.431 (−0.59)	0.091 (1.12)					−0.648 (−3.21)		0.43
(6)	33.305 (3.32)	−0.584 (−0.79)	0.101 (1.26)						−0.649 (−3.23)	0.43

* Dependent variable: $\dfrac{I}{GDP60}$ = see table 2.7.

Table 2.9
Investment regressions on RTL* (t-statistics in parentheses)

	OLS		2SLS	
	1	2	1	2
Sample	All	Democracies	All	Democracies
	($n = 37$)	($n = 25$)	($n = 37$)	($n = 25$)
Constant	3.870	38.728	19.132	25.957
	(0.88)	(2.68)	(1.75)	(2.86)
GDP60	0.074	−0.651	−1.422	−0.184
	(0.11)	(−0.72)	(−1.07)	(−0.25)
PRIM60	0.211	0.066	0.271	0.089
	(4.01)	(0.69)	(3.07)	(1.07)
RTL	−0.951	−7.409	−6.745	−4.085
	(−1.12)	(2.40)	(−1.93)	(−2.91)
R^2	0.53	0.37	0.29	0.39

* Dependent variable: $\dfrac{I}{GDP}$ = see table 2.7.

2.5   Concluding Remarks

Leaving aside our particular model, we think the general idea developed here is one that has substantial appeal. Individuals who have access to the productive assets of an economy are more likely to be restrained in their desire to tax them. This makes an egalitarian distribution good for growth in democracies. It is easier to avoid damaging conflict over redistributive policies when the economy's assets are shared widely.

An argument like this is important in understanding why a large, prosperous middle class is important in laying the foundation for growth in democratic societies. It explains the recurring resort to populist policies, so damaging to growth, in Latin America and other places where wealth distribution has been traditionally skewed. It also explains why distributive conflict has played such a comparatively minor role in the postwar development of three fast-growing Asian countries, Japan, Korea, and Taiwan: in each of these countries, a radical land reform in the aftermath of World War II served to eliminate great disparities in wealth from the outset.

The framework also has implications for the emerging market economies of Eastern Europe. In order to ensure sustainable growth, these countries have to avoid the populist trap that a skewed income distribution can create. Their transition from socialism provides them with a rare opportunity to mold their wealth distribution in an egalitarian manner. In particular, care should be exercised in devising a privatization program that ensures an equitable asset ownership.

Table 2A.1
List of countries

Democracies	Nondemocracies	
Australia (66–67)*	Argentina (61)	Taiwan (59–60) $
Belgium #*	Bangladesh (63–64) $*	Tanzania (64)
Canada (61) $*	Bolivia (68)	Thailand (62) $
Colombia (64)*	Botswana (72) $*	Trinidad and Tobago (57–58)
Costa Rica (69)*	Brazil (60)*	Tunisia (71)
Denmark (63)*	Burma (58)	Uganda (70) $
Finland (62)*	Chad (58)	Uruguay (67) $
France (62)*	Chile (68)	Zambia (59)
Germany (64)*	Dominican Republic (69) $	
Greece (57)	Egypt (64–65) $	
India (56–57)*	El Salvador (65)	
Israel (57)*	Gabon (60)	
Italy (48)*	Ghana #*	
Jamaica (58)*	Guatemala (66) $*	
Japan (57–58)*	Honduras (67–68) $	
Malaysia (63)*	Hong Kong (71) $*	
Netherlands (62)*	Indonesia (71) $*	
New Zealand (66) $*	Iran (59) $	
Norway (63)*	Iraq (56)	
Spain (64–65) $*	Ivory Coast (59)*	
Sri Lanka (63)*	Kenya (69) $	
Sweden (63)*	Korea (66)	
Switzerland #*	Madagascar (60)	
United States (69)*	Malawi (69) $	
United Kingdom (64)*	Mexico (63)	
Venezuela (62)*	Morocco (65)*	
	Niger (60)	
	Nigeria (59)	
	Pakistan (63–64)*	
	Panama (69)	
	Peru (61)*	
	Philippines (61)*	
	Senegal (60)	
	Sierra Leone (68)	
	Singapore #*	
	South Africa (65)	
	Sudan (69)	

Note: The year following each country indicates the date in which income distribution is measured for the regressions in tables 2.4, 2.5 and 2.6.
* = countries included in the regressions of tables 2.7, 2.8 and 2.9.
# = countries *not* included in tables 2.4, 2.5 and 2.6.
$ = data obtained from Jain (1975); for all other countries data are from Lecaillon et al. (1984).

Table 2A.2
Summary statistics for the sample of 67 countries

	Mean	Standard deviation	Minimum	Maximum
GR6085	2.18	1.86	−2.83	6.62
GDP60	2.04	1.86	0.21	7.38
PRIM60	77.61	30.58	5.00	144.00
Lowest 20%	5.18	2.02	1.60	10.00
Second 20%	9.15	2.41	4.20	14.00
Third 20%	13.27	3.03	7.00	18.80
Fourth 20%	19.82	3.39	12.40	26.40
Highest 20%	52.58	8.93	36.00	71.00
Highest 5%	26.47	9.17	11.20	48.30

Notes

We would like to thank Allan Drazen and the conference organizers for useful comments, and Gerald Cohen for excellent research assistance. Alesina gratefully acknowledges financial support from the Sloan Foundation. Rodrik gratefully acknowledges financial support from an NBER Olin Fellowship.

1. Their empirical results cover not only a cross section of countries during the postwar period but also historical experience in a more limited sample of countries.

2. Allowing reverse transfers would be possible, but has little economic content in this framework since we will not allow workers to have a labor-leisure choice. Lump-sum taxation of workers would then enable the government to finance public spending at no distortionary cost.

3. This begs the question of why they would then choose not to save. Since our focus is on extreme cases, we leave this issue aside for the moment. For an analysis of what happens when workers are more impatient than capitalists, see Alesina and Rodrik (1991).

4. In Alesina and Rodrik (1991), we solve the more general problem of a government that cares for both workers and capitalists, and we derive several results concerning the effect on economic growth of the weights attributed by the government to each group's welfare.

5. We could set λ equal to any constant without affecting the results of this section.

6. Most notably, the identity of the median voter would change over time, leading to complicated issues having to do with strategic voting. See Perotti (1991) for an exploration of some of these issues.

7. Our model does not explicitly incorporate the case of "kleptocratic" dictators, who redistribute to themselves rather than to workers. However, following

Grossman and Noh (1990) and using our specification for the growth equation, such a model could be built, with the implication that kleptocratic dictators reduce growth by taxing capital to increase their personal wealth.

8. But see below our results on investment.

9. We are here following Persson and Tabellini (1991).

10. The data are on aggregate investment, not private investment. We have had to use this data as data on private investment are patchy for our sample of countries over the full 1960–1985 period. This introduces some errors from the standpoint of testing our theory. As long as these errors are random, the bias should be in the direction of rejecting the theory.

References

Alesina, Alberto, and Rodrik, Dani. 1991. Distributive politics and economic growth. Working Paper No. 3668. Cambridge, MA: National Bureau of Economic Research.

Barro, Robert. 1990. Government spending in a simple model of economic growth. *Journal of Political Economy* 98:S103–S125.

Barro, Robert, and Sala-i-Martin, Xavier. 1990. Public finance in the theory of economic growth. Manuscript.

Barro, Robert, and Wolf, Holger. 1989. Data appendix for economic growth in a cross-section of countries. Manuscript.

Benhabib, Jess, and Rustichini, Aldo. 1991. Social conflict, growth and income distribution. Manuscript.

Bertola, Giuseppe. 1991. Factor shares, saving propensities, and endogenous growth. Manuscript.

Galor, Oded, and Zeira, Joseph. 1989. Income distribution and macroeconomics. Manuscript.

Grossman, Herschel, and Noh, Suk Jae. 1990. A theory of kleptocracy with probabilistic survival and reputation. *Economics and Politics* 2:157–172.

Heston, Alan, and Summers, Robert. 1988. A new set of international comparisons of real product and price levels: Estimates for 130 countries. *The Review of Income and Wealth* 34:1–25.

Jain, S. 1975. Size distribution of income: A comparison of data. Washington, D.C.: The World Bank. Manuscript.

Lecallion, Jack; Paukert, Felix; Morrison, Christian; and Cemiolis, Dimitri. 1984. Income distribution and economic development: Analytical survey. Geneva: International Labor Office.

Pazarbasioglu, Ceyla. 1991. Private investment in the presence of political uncertainty. Dissertation in progress. Washington, D.C.: Georgetown University.

Perotti, Roberto. 1991. Political equilibrium income distribution and growth. Manuscript.

Persson, Torsten, and Tabellini, Guido. 1991. Is inequality harmful for growth? Theory and evidence. Working Paper No. 91-155. Berkeley, CA: Department of Economics, University of California at Berkeley.

Roubini, Nouriel. 1990. The interactions between macroeconomic performance and political structures and institutions: The political economy of poverty, growth, and development. Manuscript.

World Bank. 1990. *World development report, 1990.* Washington, D.C.

3

The Seizure of Executive Power and Economic Growth: Some Additional Evidence

John Londregan and
Keith Poole

Despite the euphoric wave of democratization that swept the world in 1989, the prevalence of nonconstitutional and coercive rule remains a basic feature of world politics. Although nonconstitutional rulers sometimes gain power legally and then subvert the system that brought them in, as did Hitler, it is more common for them to directly seize the reigns of power by the use or threat of force in a coup d'etat. Because coups are a primary means by which countries become afflicted by coercive rule, a systematic analysis of the determinants and consequences of coups is of more than intrinsic interest.

In earlier work (Londregan and Poole 1990) we assembled a large cross-national data set matching annual data on the incidence of coups and other political events with annual economic time series. In this analysis we review the methods used in that earlier study and compare them with fresh results obtained using a new, and much richer, set of data on leadership change (Bienen and Van De Walle 1990). These results confirm and strengthen our earlier findings. However, using leader-specific data now enables us to learn more about the effects of postcoup rule, which we find inhibits economic growth.

There are substantial discrepancies between the coup counts used in our earlier work, from Jodice and Taylor's (1983) *World Handbook of Political and Social Indicators III* (hereafter referred to as the *World Handbook*), and the numbers we derive from the Bienen and Van De Walle codings. Bienen and Van De Walle employ very conservative criteria when coding for nonconstitutional rule, so that their "nonconstitutional" rulers are a relatively homogeneous group. In contrast, the *World Handbook* coded a number of questionable regime transfers that nevertheless contained elements of legitimacy, such as de Gaulle's 1958 accession to power in France, as "irregular transfers of executive power"; that is, as coups. The Bienen and Van De Walle data have the advantage of reporting leader-specific variables, as well as "event counts" for the country as a whole, enabling us, for example, to observe a leader's constitutional status directly. An additional point in favor of the Bienen and Van De Walle data set is the considerable care taken in its assembly. The Bienen and Van De Walle data set drew on a wider set of sources than the *World Handbook* and was directly coded by the authors, whereas much of the *World Handbook's* coding was delegated to research assistants.[1]

Differences between the two data sets notwithstanding, the substantive results uncovered using the Handbook data are robust to the use of the Bienen and Van De Walle data. Our findings on the fresh data set corroborate the contention (Luttwak 1969 and Finer 1962) that coups are a feature of poverty: they almost never occur in developed countries, but they are commonplace among the poorest nations. We also confirm the finding of a "coup trap": the political culture of a country suffers serious erosion in the wake of a coup d'etat; once the ice is broken more coups follow (Finer 1962). Opposition groups apparently respond to the forceful seizure of executive power with a more ruthless willingness to resort to the same means (Blondel 1980), and the involvement of the military in politics creates a praetorian political climate that fosters further coups (Huntington 1968).

Using the Bienen and Van De Walle leader-specific data, we are now able to address some questions about the nature of the "coup trap." Is it simply the case that nonconstitutional rulers are at a heightened risk of a coup, so that he who lives by the coup dies by the coup, or do the aftereffects of a coup continue to taint a country's politics even after the coup leader has himself lost power? Either of these hypotheses could have led to our earlier findings that a past history of coups affects a country's current probability of a coup. Leader-specific data enable us to directly test whether countries that have suffered past experience with coups are more coup prone even after controlling for the current leader's constitutional status. We find that they are.

Knowing leaders' constitutional status also enables us to separate the economic effects of nonconstitutional rule from the potential economic disruption caused directly by coups. We confirm our earlier result that a country's coup history, as summarized by the number of coups occurring during the most recent six years, and the number of coups occuring in the more distant past, does not affect economic growth. However, nonconstitutional rule *does* slow the pace of economic growth. Our estimates indicate that nonconstitutional rule (as coded by Bienen and Van De Walle) costs about half a percentage point of growth per year. While coups themselves are not damaging to growth, our estimates indicate that postcoup despotism is.

Our analysis also affords an opportunity for a methodological comparison of the robust bootstrap calculation of standard errors in our earlier work with standard errors calculated according to the more conventional delta (δ) method. The bootstrap method is a resampling procedure that provides robust estimates of standard errors (Efron 1979). It involves constructing multiple pseudosamples by drawing observations from the actual sample with replacement. The distribution of parameter estimates among pseudosamples is then used as an estimate of the probability distribution of the actual parameter estimates. In contrast, the delta method uses the analytical asymptotic variance-covariance matrix of the parameter estimates, with estimated parameters used in place of the true, but unknown, parameter values. Although the δ method is less robust to specification errors, it can be calculated directly from the parameter estimates without need for resampling. In the context of the coup data, both methods yield very similar standard error estimates; the main difference is the substantially greater time required to calculate the bootstrap estimates.

The outline of the chapter is as follows: section 3.1 compares the Bienen and Van De Walle data set with the coup data available from the *World Handbook of Political and Social Indicators*. In section 3.2, we estimate a simultaneous equations model of coups and economic growth, analyze the robustness of our results across the two data sets, and check their sensitivity to the use of bootstrapped vs. conventional standard errors. Section 3.3 incorporates leader-specific information into the analysis—extending our results on the effect of political variables on the economy and on the nature of the "coup trap." We conclude in section 3.4.

3.1 The Data

We use Summers and Heston's annual economic data, which cover 130 countries during the interval 1950–1985 (Summers and Heston 1988). To measure income we use real GDP per capita in constant 1980 U.S. dollars. The issues raised by comparing incomes between countries and across time are not trivial (Lucas 1988). However, the data we use were compiled with painstaking sensitivity to differences in consumption patterns, both among sectors of a given country's economy and among different countries.

In our earlier work, we used political data from *The World Handbook of Political and Social Indicators*. The *World Handbook* provides data on political activity at an annual level for 148 countries during the period 1948–1982.

These data include counts of riots, elections, political executions, deaths from domestic political violence, successful irregular transfers of executive power (that is, successful coups), and unsuccessful irregular transfers of executive power (failed coups).

Our analysis draws on newly available leadership data from Bienen and Van De Walle (1990), who catalogue individual characteristics for 2258 modern leaders. These data include some straightforward variables, such as year of entry, age at entry, and number of years in power, and also some qualitative variables that reflect the judgments of the compilers. This second set of variables includes a dichotomous classification of leaders' means of gaining executive power as either nonconstitutional, if they gained power outside the framework of established and regular procedures, or constitutional (Bienen and Van De Walle, pp. 21, 28).

The nonconstitutional rule variable dichotomizes what is in principle a continuous variable. On one end of this continuum we might put Eyadema of Togo, who is said to have murdered the fleeing President Olympio as he tried to reach a foreign embassy during a coup, or Uganda's Idi Amin Dada, who seized power while his predecessor Milton Obote was traveling abroad. At the other extreme we could place the likes of George Bush, who after a long "probationary period" of public service was nominated by a major political party and came to power during a regularly scheduled competitive election.

But many "intermediate" cases have elements of both coercion and constitutionality. Argentina's Frondizi came to power in 1958 with the grudging acquiesence of the junta headed by Aramburu, but after having spent a long career as a civilian politician. Frondizi was hardly a textbook example of a constitutional ruler, yet he clearly had more institutional backing than Eyadema or Amin. An ambiguous case is that of de Gaulle's 1958 rise to power, which was widely popular, and yet took place against a background of military pressure that forced de Gaulle's predecessor, Pfimlin, from office. Moving most, but not all, of the way toward the constitutional end of the spectrum, consider the 1974 electoral defeat of Heath by Wilson, an early election that Heath is generally acknowledged to have called under the pressure of a miners' strike (Blondel 1980). Although the accession of Wilson to the prime ministership took place within the framework of electoral politics, the coercive pressure of the miners' strike did influence the timing of the election so that the succession was not entirely free from extraconstitutional pressure.

The coding of nonconstitutional rule was conservative, accession to power within constitutional frameworks of questionable legitimacy, such as the ascendence of Generals Roberto Viola and subsequently Leopoldo Galtieri of Argentina, who assumed power under the rubric of a constitution imposed by a military junta, are nevertheless coded as constitutional. Because of this conservatism, the nonconstitutional rulers in this sample are a relatively homogeneous sample of illegal entrants, and the constitutional rulers are more eclectic, ranging from rulers who were brought in with the merest trappings of a showcase constitution to leaders of competitive, multiparty parliamentary governments.

The nonconstitutional entry variable thus identifies a relatively homogeneous group of leaders at the coercive end of the constitutional spectrum— the likes of Eyadema and Amin—and leaves all of the others, from Frondizi to Bush, in a residual class labeled "constitutional." Further coding could profitably identify parliamentary regimes, a relatively homogeneous group at the constitutional end of the spectrum.

Other qualitative variables in the Bienen and Van De Walle data set include a characterization of leaders' exits. The coding distinguishes leaders who lost power constitutionally; those who left office nonconstitutionally, either through a politically motivated assassination (John Kennedy is included in this group) or a coup (e.g., Chile's Allende); and leaders who died in office from "nonpolitical" causes (e.g., Franklin Roosevelt). We count as a coup d'etat a case in which a leader lost power by nonconstitutional means, *and* his apparent and immediate successor arrived in power by nonconstitutional means. This is not a variable that Bienen and Van De Walle code for directly, but rather one that we construct from the entry and exit mode codings.

Although the economic data and the data from the *World Handbook* are both available on an annual basis, the leadership data reports the sequence of leaders, including a number who remain in power for less than a year. A further complication is that the Bienen and Van De Walle codings are not a continuous record of the exercise of executive power—interim leaders, and interregnum periods are excluded, as are periods of "shared rule" as in Uruguay between 1951 and 1958, or Yugoslavia after 1978.

There are several years in our sample for which there are multiple rulers, for example, during 1979 Bolivia had a very heterogeneous sequence of five leaders.[2] To integrate leader-specific traits with measures of country-level variables, we must develop some systematic rules for dealing with country/ years with multiple leaders, such as Bolivia in 1979. We adopt the rule of matching each annual observation with the traits of the first leader to hold power during that year. Selecting any subsequent leader could, under some circumstances, lead to no exit being coded for that year, whereas our method guarantees that an exit is always coded for years with multiple leaders. Other alternatives included averaging leader characteristics (raising questions about the interpretation of average values of qualitative variables), and creating multiple records for years with multiple leaders (creating a sample that overrepresents years with leadership turnover). Our choice of assigning the traits of the first leader of the year comes at the cost of allowing some short-term leaders to fall between the cracks: a leader who ruled from January to December of the same year would not be counted.

Because the leadership data do not code for caretaker governments, and because leaders' durations in power are coded as integer values, it is possible that our reconstructed series will erroneously attribute interregnum periods to the preceding leader. A leader who comes to power in 1967 and has a length of time in power of two years may have left office in either 1969 or 1970. If the subsequent leader came to power in 1970, we cannot tell from the leader codings whether that next leader succeeded directly, or after one or more caretakers, with the initial leader leaving in 1969.

Rather than retrace the leader codings to search for caretaker governments, we treat any order of succession that *could* have occurred without an interim caretaker as though it *did*. Thus, a leader who came to power in 1967 and remained in power two years, who is followed by another leader who arrives in 1970, is treated as the head of state at the beginning of 1970 because his term *could* have lasted until his successor's time in power began. If instead his time in power had been one year, then there is clearly an interregnum period between the 1967 leader and the 1970 leader. In this case, we treat the leader as though he held power until 1968.[3] Our analysis of the sample identified several cases that must have involved gaps between leadership spells.[4] Our sample omits these missing years and also drops two intervals of contested multiple leadership.[5]

Although the leadership traits of only the country/year's first leader are included, we count all coups occurring during the year, whether they were staged against the year's first leader or not. This enables us to construct the coup history for these countries as well as to conduct a more careful robustness analysis of our earlier work that was based on annual coup counts.[6]

In our previous work, we matched data from the *World Handbook* with Summers and Heston's economic data. Because of the ambiguity and unreliability of economic data from the centrally planned economies, we omitted these states from the matched data set. This left us with 3,035 observations on 121 countries during the span 1950 through 1982. In recognition of the serial dependence of GDP growth, we then calculated the growth rate and the lagged growth rate, taking first differences in the log of the level of real GDP per capita (measured in 1980 U.S. dollars) leaving us with 2797 observations on 121 countries over the interval 1952 through 1982 (the first two years of the sample being lost in the calculation of current and lagged GDP growth rates). Not all countries contributed the same number of observations to the data set. At one extreme, there is only one post-independence observation for Zimbabwe, whereas other countries, such as the United Kingdom, contributed thirty-one observations, spanning the entire interval from 1952 through 1982.

The matched data set permits us to readily compare the *World Handbook*'s coup counts with those derived from Bienen and Van De Walle's leader codings. The two sets of data are by no means in close accord. The *World Handbook* counts 144 country/years with at least one coup, while the leadership data implies 123 country/years with at least one coup. The reasons for these discrepancies are various. In some cases the *World Handbook* counted transfers of power via what were probably sham constitutions as coups, but the more conservative coding rule of Bienen and Van De Walle did not. Although a case can be made for counting the leaders who gained power by such means as nonconstitutional (imposing a less strict threshold for nonconstitutional rule), it would not be appropriate to count the transfer of power, typically acknowledged as proper by the exiting leader, as nonconstitutional.[7] Such transfers, though unpalatable to proponents of democratic institutions, are not coups. In other cases, it appears that the *World Handbook* and Bienen and Van De Walle disagree about the year in which a coup occurred.[8]

Some discrepancies were more complex and reflect not only the conservatism of the Bienen and Van De Walle codings but also the difference in their emphasis, which is the duration of leadership, rather than coups directly. For example, on October 28, 1963, Col. Soglo seized power from Benin's President Maga. However, he then proceeded to set up an interim government whose cabinet consisted of the country's three leading civilian politicians, including Maga. Soglo announced that the government was provisional. Elections were held in January, 1964, and convincingly won by Sourou-Migan Apithy, who assumed the office of president. Soglo stepped down to resume his duties as army chief of staff. Bienen and Van De Walle code this as nonconstitutional exit by Maga, followed by constitutional entry for Apithy, with Soglo's three-month sojourn in power counted as a period of interim rule (unlike his postcoup rule beginning in 1965). The *World Handbook* codes this as a successful irregular transfer of executive power (i.e., coup). In this case, both sets of codings appear to be right.

The conservative coup-counting rule we have adopted—counting as coups only cases of nonconstitutional exit followed by nonconstitutional entry by the successor—misses several coups, as in the case of the 1963 coup d'etat in Benin; however, it is very resistant to falsely counting a transfer as a coup. A further argument in favor of this approach is the extra care taken by Bienen and Van De Walle in coding entry and exit dates. They coded leadership spells directly from country-level histories using country and regional biographical indexes, news summary sources, and interviews with area experts as supplements. The primary sources for the *World Handbook* were news summaries, such as the *New York Times Index* and *Keesings*, and much of the *World Handbook*'s coding was delegated to research assistants. In no case have we found the Bienen and Van De Walle identification of a transition as nonconstitutional exit followed by non-constitutional entry to be incorrect, but we have identified several factual errors in the *World Handbook*'s coup codings.

3.2 A Parametric Model of Coups and Income Growth

In earlier work (Londregan and Poole 1990) we estimated a simultaneous model of income growth and coups using matched data from the *World Handbook* and Summers and Heston, described in the previous section. In the reduced form of this model, income growth potentially depends on lagged income, lagged income growth (as in Barro 1989), region-specific effects, and the countries' past experience with coups d'etat. Let y_{it} denote the natural log of per capita GDP during year t in country i, while we define Δy_{it} as

$$\Delta y_{it} \equiv y_{it} - y_{it-1},$$

which is approximately the real GDP growth rate during year t in country i. We let c_{it} denote the number of coups d'etat occurring in country i during year t. Finally, our previous work used Summers and Heston's regions—Africa, Asia, Europe and North America, Central America and the Carribean, South America, and Oceania (they also treat the centrally planned econ-omies as a separate class, but we did not incorporate any of these countries into our analysis). We used region-specific indicator variables for country locations of the form r_{ij}, where $r_{ij} = 1$ if country i is located in region j, and 0 otherwise. We subsequently discarded several regions and combined the United States and Canada with the European countries. This left us with Africa, South America, and a region we labeled North America and Europe, although it did not include Mexico.[9]

The income growth model we estimated is of the form:

$$\Delta y_{it} = \pi_{10} + \pi_{11}\left(\sum_{s=1}^{6} c_{it-s}\right) + \pi_{12}\left(\sum_{s=7}^{\infty} c_{it-s}\right) + \pi_{13}y_{it-1}$$

$$+ \pi_{14}\Delta y_{it-1} + \sum_{j=5}^{7} \pi_{1j}r_{ij} + \varepsilon_{it}. \tag{1}$$

The random error term from this reduced-form growth equation, ε_{it}, is potentially correlated with the occurrence of a coup d'etat.

The second element of our model is an equation explaining the occurrence of coups. We let z_{it} denote the latent "propensity for a coup," and let δ_{it} code dichotomously for the occurrences of coups: $\delta_{it} = 1$ if there is at least one coup in country i during year t, and it equals zero otherwise. We assume that coup occurrence and coup propensity are linked by the crossing of a threshold: if $z_{it} < 0$, then $\delta_{it} = 1$, while for $z_{it} \geq 0$, $\delta_{it} = 0$. This is a standard probit model applied to coups, except that we allow shocks to the latent coup equation, η_{it}, to be correlated with shocks to economic growth. In our earlier work, we estimated a model in which the coup propensity depends on only predetermined variables[10]

$$z_{it}^* = \pi_{20} + \pi_{21}\left(\sum_{s=1}^{6} c_{it-s}\right) + \pi_{22}\left(\sum_{s=7}^{\infty} c_{it-s}\right) + \pi_{23}y_{it-1}$$

$$+ \pi_{24}\Delta y_{it-1} + \sum_{j=5}^{7} \pi_{2j}r_{ij} - \eta_{it}. \tag{2}$$

As with other probitlike models, the variance of η_{it} and the coefficients of the coup equation are only identified up to a scale factor. To pin these estimates down, we adopt the arbitrary, but standard, normalizing restriction that the variance of η_{it} in equation (2) equals 1. This leaves us with two parameters of the variance-covariance matrix to estimate: the variance of ε_{it}, which we denote σ^2, and the correlation between η_{it} and ε_{it}, which we denote ρ.

Notice that the coup equation resembles empirical models of economic voting in U.S. presidential elections (see Fair 1978, Erikson 1989). However, these models typically use election year growth as their economic performance variable. It has been claimed that growth during the two quarters immediately preceding the election is a sufficient statistic for economic performance (Fair 1978; see also Rosenstone 1983). While quarterly data permits the use of lagged (and thus, in the context of our model, predetermined) growth information from as few as five weeks before the presidential election, our use of the previous year's growth rate leaves us with information that potentially predates a coup by as much as twenty-three months, and by an average of just under eighteen months.

An alternative specification of the coup equation is to include contemporaneous growth and use lagged growth as an instrument. This results in a model that is just identified, and so we cannot test the restriction. It seems reasonable that, to the extent that growth rates affect the propensity for a coup, current growth would matter more than lagged growth. However, although our exclusion restriction seems sensible, we must interpret our results with the caveat that if both current and lagged growth exert independent influences on the coup propensity (as they do not appear to do for U.S. presidential voting (Fair 1978)), our model will be misspecified.

The specification of the coup equation with current growth is of the form

$$z_{it}^* = \gamma_2 \Delta y_{it} + \alpha_{20} + \alpha_{21}\left(\sum_{s=1}^{6} c_{it-s}\right) + \alpha_{22}\left(\sum_{s=7}^{\infty} c_{it-s}\right)$$

$$+ \alpha_{23} y_{it-1} + \sum_{j=5}^{8} \alpha_{2j} r_{ij} - \eta_{it} \tag{2'}$$

The parameter estimates we obtain from this procedure provide us with a picture of the relative effects of past coups, economic growth, and the level of income as "risk factors" for a coup.

We can rewrite this model more compactly as:

$$y_{it} = \underline{x}_{it}'\underline{\pi}_1 + \varepsilon_{it} \tag{1a}$$

$$z_{it}^* = \underline{x}_{it}'\underline{\pi}_2 - \eta_{it} \tag{2b}$$

where $\underline{x}_{it}$ denotes the column-vector of explanatory variables, which is the same for both equations

$$\underline{x}_{it} = \left(1, \sum_{s=1}^{6} c_{it-s}, \sum_{s=7}^{\infty} c_{it-s}, y_{it-1}, \Delta y_{it-1}, \{r_{ij}\}_{j=5}^{8}\right)'$$

The likelihood function for our model is

$$l(\underline{\pi}_1, \underline{\pi}_2, \rho, \sigma)$$

$$= \sum_{\text{Coups}} \ln(\Phi((\underline{x}_{it}'[\underline{\pi}_2 + (\rho/\sigma)\underline{\pi}_1] - (\rho/\sigma)y_{it}) \cdot (1 - \rho^2)^{-1/2}))$$

$$+ \sum_{\text{Noncoups}} \ln(\Phi((-\underline{x}_{it}'[\underline{\pi}_2 + (\rho/\sigma)\underline{\pi}_1] + (\rho/\sigma)y_{it}) \cdot (1 - \rho^2)^{-1/2}))$$

$$- \left(\frac{1}{2\sigma^2}\right)\sum(y_{it} - \underline{x}_{it}'\underline{\pi}_1)^2 - \frac{N}{2}\ln(2\pi) - n\ln\sigma$$

We first replicate the full information maximum likelihood (FIML) estimates of the reduced-form model of equations (1) and (2) from our earlier work. The estimation algorithm we use exploits the special structure of our model, converges very quickly (in about forty seconds using Gauss386 computer software on an IBM PS70 machine[11]), and may be of practical interest to applied econometricians and data analysts.[12]

In our earlier work we calculated standard errors using Efron's bootstrap technique, a resampling procedure, with 1,024 replications. With a fresh draw of 1,024 resamples the estimated standard errors will change slightly, but the parameter estimates themselves, and the value of the likelihood function, remain exactly as reported in our earlier work. These estimates are reported in column 1 of table 3.1, and the newly calculated bootstrap standard errors are reported in column 2.

We also calculate the variance-covariance matrix of our parameter estimates by the δ method, using the inverse Hessian of the likelihood function. These standard errors are reported in column 3 of table 3.1. For reference, we report the bootstrap estimates of the standard errors reported in our earlier work in column 4. Comparison of the competing estimates of the standard errors reveals that they are nearly identical;[13] the differences between the estimates obtained by the δ-method and the bootstrap estimates are of the same order of magnitude as the differences between the two sets of bootstrap estimates. This suggests that, in the context of this model and these data, there is little reason to expend the extra effort of calculating the bootstrap estimates. Using our computer system, the δ method estimates standard errors along with the other parameters of our model in forty seconds, the bootstrap (with 1,024 replications) requires over ten hours, and even with only 64 replications, almost three-quarters of an hour would be required.

While using 1,024 bootstrap replications is a cumbersome procedure, smaller numbers may suffice for the purpose of preliminary data analysis. A sensible exploratory analysis of a parametric model such as ours on a new data set might include an initial bootstrap estimation with only 32 or 64 replications. The bootstrap standard errors could then be compared with those generated by the method. If no notable discrepancies were detected, then the further application of the bootstrap could be abandoned in lieu of the less time consuming method. Otherwise, further iteration of the bootstrap would be in order given its more reliable convergence to the underlying distribution of the parameter estimates (see, for example, Efron, 1979). A contingent use of the bootstrap only when the δ method yields notably different results than a small scale application of the bootstrap makes

Table 3.1
Joint maximum likelihood estimation of the reduced form (using coup counts from *World Handbook*)

	1	2	3	4
Growth equation				
Constant	0.0758	0.0134	0.0112	0.013
Coups occurring during the previous six years	0.0007	0.0015	0.0014	0.0016
Coups occurring more than six years earlier	−0.0032	0.0015	0.0009	0.0016
Log of the previous year's per capita GDP	−0.0072	0.0018	0.0014	0.002
The previous year's per capita GDP growth rate	0.1596	0.0311	0.0176	0.032
Africa	−0.0174	0.0034	0.0031	0.003
Europe and North America	0.0131	0.0032	0.0032	0.003
South America	−0.0027	0.0039	0.0038	0.004
Coup equation				
Constant	0.8671	0.4529	0.4953	0.427
Coups occurring during the previous six years	0.1835	0.0431	0.0435	0.043
Coups occurring more than six years earlier	0.0408	0.0321	0.0321	0.032
Log of the previous year's per capita GDP	−0.3675	0.0628	0.0698	0.061
The previous year's per capita GDP growth rate	−1.1014	0.7744	0.6812	0.743
Africa	−0.1839	0.1161	0.1143	0.111
Europe and North America	−0.0337	0.1897	0.1751	0.001
South America	0.5392	0.1273	0.1273	0.131
$\hat{\rho}$	−0.1322	0.0437	0.0371	0.045
$\hat{\sigma}$	0.0571			
Log of the likelihood function:	3,533.0828			
Number of observations:	2,797			
Number of bootstrap replications:	1,024			

Column 1: Parameter estimate.
Column 2: Bootstrap standard errors, calculated from a fresh pseudosample.
Column 3: Standard errors calculated by the δ method.
Column 4: Bootstrap standard errors from Londregan and Poole (1990).

particular sense in case of more elaborate likelihood functions with less tractable convergence properties.

As in our earlier work, we proceed to test the direction of feedback between coups and income growth. This amounts to imposing various exclusion restrictions on our model. Can we omit the coup variables from the growth equation? Can we eliminate the growth and income variables from the coup equation? These are essentially tests of Granger Causality.

We first turn to the question of whether we can exclude the past history of coups from the growth equation, that is, do coups "Granger cause" growth? More formally, we test (with respect to equation (1))

$$H_0: \pi_{11} = \pi_{12} = 0.$$

Rather than reestimate the entire model with these coefficients excluded, we conduct an asymptotically equivalent test that calculates the optimal minimum distance (OMD) estimate of the constrained model from the unconstrained coefficient estimates. Let $\hat{\underline{\alpha}}$ denote the constrained coefficient estimates. In the context of the hypothesis that lagged coups do not affect the current rate of growth, $\pi_{11} = \pi_{12} = 0$, the constrained model becomes

$$\Delta y_{it} = \alpha_{10} + \alpha_{13} y_{it-1} + \alpha_{14} \Delta y_{it-1} + \sum_{j=5}^{7} \alpha_{1j} r_{ij} + \varepsilon_{it} \tag{1''}$$

$$z_{it}^* = \alpha_{20} + \alpha_{21}\left(\sum_{s=1}^{6} c_{it-s}\right) + \alpha_{22}\left(\sum_{s=7}^{\infty} c_{it-s}\right) + \alpha_{23} y_{it-1}$$

$$+ \alpha_{24} \Delta y_{it-1} + \sum_{j=5}^{7} \alpha_{2j} r_{ij} - \eta_{it} \tag{2''}$$

We adopt the general notation $\underline{\pi}(\underline{\alpha})$ for the set of reduced form coefficients that correspond to the vector $\underline{\alpha}$ of structural parameters. We estimate $\hat{\underline{\alpha}}$ using the OMD technique (Rothemberg 1973), which chooses $\hat{\underline{\alpha}}$ as the solution to the following minimization:

$$\text{Min}_{\underline{\alpha}} \ (\hat{\underline{\pi}} - \underline{\pi}(\underline{\alpha}))' \Delta_{\pi}^{-1} (\hat{\underline{\pi}} - \underline{\pi}(\underline{\alpha}))$$

where Δ_{π}^{-1} denotes the variance-covariance matrix of $\hat{\underline{\pi}}$. The solution to this minimization is asymptotically equivalent to the maximum likelihood estimate of the constrained parameter vector. The asymptotic variance-covariance matrix of $\hat{\underline{\alpha}}$ is given by

$$V(\hat{\underline{\alpha}}) = \nabla_{\alpha} \underline{\pi}(\underline{\alpha})' \Delta_{\pi}^{-1} \nabla_{\alpha} \underline{\pi}(\underline{\alpha})$$

where we denote the Jacobian of a vector valued function f with respect to its arguments, $\underline{x}$, by $\nabla_x f(\underline{x})$. Under the null hypothesis, the minimized value of the objective function for the OMD,

$$\chi^2(\hat{\underline{\alpha}}) = (\hat{\underline{\pi}} - \underline{\pi}(\hat{\underline{\alpha}}))' \Delta_{\pi}^{-1} (\hat{\underline{\pi}} - \underline{\pi}(\hat{\underline{\alpha}})),$$

is asymptotically distributed according to an χ^2 distribution with k degrees of freedom, where k is the number of linear restrictions imposed by $\underline{\alpha}$ on the vector of reduced-form coefficients, $\hat{\underline{\pi}}$, which in this case is 2.

These estimates are reported in columns 1 and 2 of table 3.2.[14] The value of the criterion function is 4.534, corresponding to a p-value of 0.103, indicating acceptance at the $\alpha = 0.05$ significance level. Both the parameter estimates and the value of the test statistic echo our earlier finding that a country's coup history does not affect the growth rate. However, using the

Table 3.2
Simultaneous estimation (using coup counts from *World Handbook*)

	1	2	3	4
Growth equation				
Constant	0.0672	0.0089	0.0731	0.0078
Coups occurring during the previous six years	*	*	*	*
Coups occurring more than six years earlier	*	*	*	*
Log of the previous year's per capita GDP	−0.0061	0.0012	−0.0071	0.0010
The previous year's per capita GDP growth rate	0.1478	0.0216	0.1623	0.0124
Africa	−0.0172	0.0024	−0.0170	0.0022
Europe and North America	0.0124	0.0022	0.0144	0.0022
South America	−0.0062	0.0025	−0.0043	0.0026
Coup equation				
Constant	0.7597	0.3182	0.8703	0.3503
Coups occurring during the previous six years	0.1907	0.0303	0.1843	0.0307
Coups occurring more than six years earlier	0.0350	0.0227	0.0370	0.0227
Log of the previous year's per capita GDP	−0.3518	0.0441	−0.3676	0.0493
The previous year's per capita GDP growth rate	−1.2057	0.5458	−1.1046	0.4819
Africa	−0.1817	0.0821	−0.1842	0.0808
Europe and North America	−0.0673	0.1336	−0.0352	0.1239
South America	0.5397	0.0900	0.5411	0.0900

Column 1: OMD parameter estimates using the bootstrap covariance matrix.
Column 2: Standard errors based on the bootstrap OMD estimate.
Column 3: OMD parameter estimates via the δ method covariance matrix.
Column 4: Standard errors based on the δ method covariance matrix.

δ method estimate of Δ_π yields very similar parameter estimates, reported in columns 3 and 4 of table 3.2, but a considerably larger value of the test statistic. Using the δ method, we instead obtain a test statistic of 11.653, with a corresponding p-value of 0.003, indicating rejection at all conventional levels. Our answer to whether coups (as coded by the *World Handbook*) inhibit growth depends on the fairly esoteric question of which variance-covariance matrix estimator to use: the bootstrap or the δ-method.

We also test for the impact of the economy on coups. More formally, we test whether the coefficients of lagged income and lagged growth are simultaneously equal to zero in the coup equation. Using the same methodology as employed in the test of the hypothesis that past coups do not affect the economy, we obtain a test statistic of 34.308 using the bootstrap method, and 31.765 via the δ-method. Under the null hypothesis, each test statistic has an χ^2 distribution with two degrees of freedom. Both test statistics indicate rejection of the null at all standard levels of significance.

The notable discrepancies between the coup counts derived from the Bienen and Van De Walle data and the counts reported by the *World Handbook* raise a serious question about the dependence of our results on the *World Handbook* data. To assess the robustness of our conclusions, we reestimate our model using the Bienen and Van De Walle coup counts. We also adopt their regional definitions, rather than the modified Summers and Heston regions we used in the coup paper. Countries within these regions have been argued to be relatively homogeneous with respect to national unity and political culture (Blondel 1980, pp. 29, 30). The primary change here is the creation of the Middle East as a region distinct from Africa and Asia, and the inclusion of South and Central America under the common heading of Latin America.

With these region definitions, the bootstrap coefficient estimates become somewhat problematic: there are only two coups d'etat, as derived from the Bienen and Van De Walle codings, in the region labeled North America-Europe-Australasia.[15] This implies that in the course of resampling, approximately 13 percent of the pseudosamples drawn by the bootstrap procedure will contain *no* coups for this region, leading to nonconvergence of the probit estimates. For these samples, location in North America-Europe-Australasia will be treated by the probit as making coups "impossible," that is, the algorithm will attempt to assign the coefficient of the indicator variable for this region a value of "$-\infty$."

To cope with nonconvergent pseudosamples, the bootstrap algorithm was modified to omit pseudosamples in which North America-Europe-Australasia was "coup-free," and then the standard errors were calibrated for the remaining subset of the 1,024 bootstrap replications. Thus the bootstrap variance-covariance matrix in this setting is conditional on the occurrence of at least one coup in North America-Europe-Australasia. However, as with the *World Handbook* coup codings, the results for this region are very similar to those generated by the δ method.

Using the Bienen and Van De Walle coup codings, we reestimate the model, with the region definitions suggested by Blondel, but otherwise preserving the list of explanatory variables.[16] Column 1 of table 3.3 reports parameter estimates for this model. Standard errors calculated according to the δ method appear in column 2, while the bootstrap standard errors are listed in column 3. The parameter estimates of column 1 are very similar to the estimates based on the *World Handbook* data. The small but statistically significant effect of coups on growth found in the *World Handbook* data is not present in the new estimates. This may in part be due to the differences in region definitions; coups occurring in the distant past may have proxied

Table 3.3
Joint maximum likelihood estimation of the reduced form (using coup counts derived from Bienen and Van de Walle)

	1	2	3
Growth equation			
Constant	0.0794	0.0112	0.0135
Coups occurring during the previous six years	−0.0007	0.0015	0.0016
Coups occurring more than six years earlier	−0.0008	0.0007	0.0009
Log of the previous year's per capita GDP	−0.0074	0.0015	0.0018
The previous year's per capita GDP growth rate	0.1590	0.0176	0.0330
Africa	−0.0232	0.0037	0.0038
Middle East	−0.0031	0.0044	0.0043
Latin America	−0.0063	0.0042	0.0040
North America-Europe-Australasia	0.0112	0.0045	0.0041
Coup equation			
Constant	0.0947	0.5261	0.4630
Coups occurring during the previous six years	0.1720	0.0452	0.0449
Coups occurring more than six years earlier	0.0558	0.0253	0.0256
Log of the previous year's per capita GDP	−0.2853	0.0778	0.0663
The previous year's per capita GDP growth rate	−1.5451	0.7148	0.7792
Africa	−0.0222	0.1520	0.1555
Middle East	0.1817	0.1855	0.1914
Latin America	0.4537	0.1674	0.1667
North America-Europe-Australasia	−0.3998	0.2984	0.2561
$\hat{\rho}$	−0.1209	0.0391	0.0442
$\hat{\sigma}$	0.0571		
Log of the likelihood function:	3,595.0269		
Number of observations:	2,797		
Number of bootstrap replications:	1,024		

Column 1: Parameter estimate.
Column 2: Standard errors calculated by the δ method.
Column 3: Bootstrap standard errors, calculated from a fresh pseudosample.

for subsaharan Africa in the estimates reported in table 3.1, which aggregate the Maghreb with sub-Saharan Africa, despite the very different experiences of these regions with colonialism.

The effect of lagged growth reaches the threshold of statistical significance using the Bienen and Van De Walle data, while the coup-inhibiting effect of location in North America-Europe-Australasia is significantly negative, unlike the similarly defined Europe and North America variable in the earlier estimates. Aside from these small differences, the coefficient estimates obtained using the new data set are remarkably similar to those appearing in table 3.1. Even the estimates of ρ are much the same: −0.121 using the new leadership data, −0.132 using the *World Handbook* data. Because of the slightly smaller event probability in the new sample, estimates based on the new data set need to be slightly larger to correspond to the same impact on the event probability as those in table 3.2.

The sign patterns of the two sets of coefficient estimates, with the exceptions noted above, are the same. It is also noteworthy that the bootstrap standard errors once again closely resemble those obtained by the δ method, with the one exception of the standard error of the lag coefficient in the growth equation, just as we found using the *World Handbook's* coup codings and region definitions.

The strong resemblance between the parameter estimates derived from the two data sets is a reassuring check on the robustness of the model. Why are the results so robust to what is apparently a substantial dose of measurement error? Probably because the "falsely positive" miscodings in the *World Handbook* tend to occur in countries and during years where the coup propensity was very high anyway—for example, the erroneous dating of the New Year's Eve 1965 coup by Bokassa as occurring in 1966, another year during which the Central African Republic and its leader were prone to a coup. In some of the ambiguous cases, such as the installation of Argentina's Frondizi in 1958, there were likewise many conditions favoring a coup. The propensity to code false positives was shaped by the same empirical regularities that are reflected in our coefficient estimates. In any event, the coup counts derived from Bienen and Van De Walle are, in our view, more reliable.

An important source of difference between the two data sets emerges when we repeat our Granger causality tests using this fresh data. The test of the joint restriction that real income growth is unaffected by the past history of coups is accepted at all standard significance levels using *either* the bootstrap *or* the δ method to calculate the variance-covariance matrix of the vector of reduced-form coefficients. Using the bootstrap, the test statistic, which is asymptotically distributed according to an χ^2 distribution with two degrees of freedom, takes on a value of 0.988; using the δ method the corresponding statistic is 1.361. Both methods lead to the same conclusion: we accept the hypothesis that a country's growth rate is unaffected by its past experience with coups.

As discussed earlier, the coup equation bears a strong resemblance to U.S. presidential voting equations that include economic growth among their explanatory variables. However, to avoid simultaneity bias in our coefficient estimates, we must instrument contemporaneous growth on the right-hand side of our coup equation. Fair (1978) avoids simultaneity bias at low cost by exploiting quarterly data on U.S. growth, using quarters 2 and 3 of the U.S. presidential election year. Because U.S. presidential elections are always held in the fifth or sixth week of quarter 4, using lagged income growth leaves almost no slippage between the realization of the lagged (and thus predetermined) growth variable and the presidential election. However, using the preceding year's growth leaves a larger space between lagged growth and the current coup propensity.

An alternative version of our model holds that it is contemporaneous rather than lagged income that affects coups

$$\Delta y_{it} = \alpha_{10} + \alpha_{13} y_{it-1} + \alpha_{14} \Delta y_{it-1} + \sum_{j=5}^{7} \alpha_{1j} r_{ij} + \varepsilon_{it} \tag{1''}$$

$$z_{it}^{*} = \alpha^{*} \Delta y_{it} + \alpha_{20} + \alpha_{21} \left(\sum_{s=1}^{6} c_{it-s} \right) + \alpha_{22} \left(\sum_{s=7}^{\infty} c_{it-s} \right)$$

$$+ \alpha_{23} y_{it-1} + \sum_{j=5}^{7} \alpha_{2j} r_{ij} - \eta_{it} \tag{2''}$$

Exclusion of lagged growth from the coup equation identifies equation (2″), which we can then estimate using the OMD estimator set forth above. Starting with reduced-form coefficients corresponding to equations (1) and (2), we then recover the parameters of the model given by (1″) and (2″) using the OMD method. We simultaneously impose the additional restriction that coups do not affect economic growth. This leaves us with two overidentifying (and hence testable) restrictions of equation (1) and one identifying (and hence not testable) restriction for the coup equation.

The impact coefficient for current growth is informative in its own right—it calibrates the sensitivity of the coup propensity to each percentage point of growth. Estimates of the model using the Bienen and Van De Walle data, with the variance-covariance matrix calculated by the δ method, appear in column 1, table 3.4; asymptotic standard errors appear in column 2. We also present estimates using the same data, but estimate the variance-covariance matrix via the bootstrap in column 3, with associated standard errors in column 4.

Both sets of estimates are very similar. Notably, the effects of current growth on the coup propensity are large and statistically significant, although not precisely estimated. In our earlier work on coups we found that *lagged* growth had a large but statistically insignificant coup inhibiting effect. Our finding does not lend support to Olson's (1963) theory of the "revolution of rising expectations." While rapid growth may destabilize societies in other ways, it makes Bienen and Van De Walle coded coups *less*, rather than more, likely.

Table 3.4
Simultaneous estimation (using coup counts derived from Bienen and Van de Walle)

	1	2	3	4
Growth equation				
Constant	0.0778	0.0079	0.0773	0.0094
Coups occurring during the previous six years	*	*	*	*
Coups occurring more than six years earlier	*	*	*	*
Log of the previous year's per capita GDP	−0.0073	0.0011	−0.0072	0.0013
The previous year's per capita GDP growth rate	0.1593	0.0125	0.1589	0.0229
Africa	−0.0230	0.0026	−0.0230	0.0027
Middle East	−0.0035	0.0031	−0.0029	0.0030
Latin America	−0.0081	0.0027	−0.0093	0.0024
North America-Europe-Australasia	0.0113	0.0032	0.0111	0.0029
Coup equation				
Constant	0.8516	0.4526	0.8685	0.4285
Coups occurring during the previous six years	0.1711	0.0320	0.1671	0.0309
Coups occurring more than six years earlier	0.0550	0.0179	0.0524	0.0180
Log of the previous year's per capita GDP	−0.3564	0.0597	−0.3557	0.0519
This year's per capita GDP growth rate	−9.7037	3.2912	−10.2003	3.6387
The previous year's per capita GDP growth rate	*	*	*	*
Africa	−0.2460	0.1390	−0.2610	0.1433
Middle East	0.1475	0.1351	0.1429	0.1380
Latin America	0.3768	0.1244	0.3698	0.1262
North America-Europe-Australasia	−0.2900	0.2164	−0.3053	0.1807

Column 1: OMD parameter estimates via the δ method covariance matrix.
Column 2: Standard errors based on the δ method covariance matrix.
Column 3: OMD parameter estimates using the bootstrap covariance matrix.
Column 4: Standard errors based on the bootstrap OMD estimate.

Notice that in both tables 3.2 and 3.4 the coefficient estimates are slightly different when the OMD estimator is calculated using the δ-method instead of the bootstrap. This is because the second stage of the estimation procedure is dependent on Δ_π: the variance-covariance matrix of the reduced-form coefficients.

We also retest the hypothesis that lagged income and income growth do not affect a country's probability of a coup. Both the bootstrap and the δ method lead to decisive rejection of this hypothesis using the new data, although the magnitude of the test statistics is somewhat smaller than we obtained using the *World Handbook* data. Under the null hypothesis of no effect, the test statistic is distributed as χ^2 with two degrees of freedom.

Using the bootstrap, the actual value of the test statistic was 23.976; using the δ method it was 18.412, both corresponding to p-values below 0.001: income Granger causes coups.

Our test of the hypothesis that income does not affect *World Handbook* coded coups was sensitive to the method used to estimate the variance-covariance matrix of the parameters. However, using the more reliably measured Bienen and Van De Walle coded coups, there is no ambiguity—Granger causality tests based on either the bootstrap or the method indicate acceptance of the null hypothesis that the past history of coups does not influence income growth. The greater reliability of the Bienen and Van De Walle codings suggests that coups do not affect income growth, the ambiguities of the *World Handbook*-based estimates notwithstanding. While this conclusion seems justified on empirical grounds, it has less theoretical appeal; misgovernment can certainly disrupt the processes of economic growth, and we would expect that a past history of coups leaves a country at increased risk of bad government. It is with this question in mind that we turn to the leader-specific data of the next section.

3.3   The Effect of Leaders' Characteristics

Using leader-specific data, we are now in a position to more directly test our most surprising finding from the earlier research: the claim that the past history of coups has no effect on the current rate of economic growth. We are left to question whether the governments brought to power via coups have an effect on the economy. One possibility, which the country-level coup counts from the *World Handbook* does not permit us to address, is that although nonconstitutional rule impedes economic growth, most coups simply result in the replacement of one despotic ruler by another, with no independent effect on growth.

More generally, nonconstitutional governments are a heterogeneous lot, with a range of effects on economic performance. Some foster economic growth; the replacement of Turkish President Menderes by General Gursel is often spoken of as such a case. Other nonconstitutional governments reverse decades of economic progress, as in the case of the replacement of Iranian Shah Mohammed Pahlavi by Khomeini. In the aftermath of other nonconstitutional transitions, such as the replacement of Egypt's King Farouk by Nagib, or of Benin's Soglo by Alley, economic matters appear to have remained much as they were. The "average" effect on the economy of this eclectic group may be neutral.

The Bienen and Van De Walle data permit us to conduct a more direct test of whether nonconstitutional rulers are, at least on average, different from their constitutional counterparts. Thus we are able to assess the separate influences of the current leader's constitutional status (controlling for the past history of coups) and the extent of a county's recent experience with coups. The nonconstitutional rule variable also permits a more detailed analysis of the coup trap: is the history of past coups simply telling us about the current leader's nonconstitutional status, or does it exert an independent influence on the probability of further coups?

To implement this test we match the annual coup counts and economic data with data on the first leader to hold power during each year, as described in section 3.1. Two variables are of particular interest: nonconstitutional entry and the current leader's time in power.[17] Bienen and Van De Walle used hazard functions to analyze their leader-specific data and discovered "negative duration dependence": the longer a leader remains in power, the lower his probability of being removed during the current year. Further, the pattern of time dependence for nonconstitutional rulers appeared to differ from the others. The nonconstitutional rulers started with a higher risk of losing power, but over time their risk fell below that for the others.

In light of Bienen and Van De Walle's findings on leadership duration, we include our variables for nonconstitutional rule—time in power and an interaction term that allows the effects of time in power to differ for nonconstitutional rulers. Our model also includes all of the explanatory variables in both the growth equation and the coup equation. The coefficients of time in power and time in power for nonconstitutional rulers are insignificant in both equations. When we constrain the time-in-power variable to have the same effect for both constitutional and nonconstitutional rulers, the variable remains insignificant in both equations. Parameter estimates of our model with the nonconstitutional rule variable appear in column 1 of table 3.5. Column 2 reports estimated standard errors (via the δ method).

This is surprising in light of Bienen and Van De Walle's earlier findings. Yet this is not a direct contradiction of their finding of negative duration dependence. Their dependent variable is the time elapsed until a leader loses power—whether by electoral defeat, resignation, assassination, or coup d'etat. In our analysis we focus only on coups. Our finding does suggest that the negative duration dependence found by Bienen and Van De Walle operates through some other type of risk of losing power; we find no

Table 3.5
Incorporating leader-specific data (using coup counts derived from Bienen and Van de Walle)

	1	2	3	4	5	6
Growth equation						
Constant	0.0833	0.0117	0.0836	0.0083	0.0838	0.0118
This year's coup propensity	*	*	*	*	−0.0016	0.0118
Coups occurring during the previous six years	0.0005	0.0017	*	*	*	*
Coups occurring more than six years earlier	−0.0005	0.0008	*	*	*	*
Log of the previous year's per capita GDP	−0.0078	0.0016	−0.0079	0.0011	−0.0083	0.0038
The previous year's per capita GDP growth rate	0.1583	0.0177	0.1583	0.0125	0.1557	0.0255
Nonconstitutional leader	−0.0055	0.0030	−0.0055	0.0019	−0.0050	0.0045
Leader's time in power	3×10^{-5}	0.0001	0.0000	0.0001	0.0000	0.0001
Africa	−0.0235	0.0037	−0.0234	0.0026	−0.0234	0.0038
Middle East	−0.0036	0.0044	−0.0037	0.0031	−0.0033	0.0054
Latin America	−0.0073	0.0042	−0.0079	0.0027	−0.0069	0.0085
North America-Europe-Australasia	0.0106	0.0045	0.0107	0.0032	0.0102	0.0060
Coup equation						
Constant	0.0474	0.5401	0.8709	0.4734	0.8741	0.6714
Coups occurring during the previous six years	0.1280	0.0514	0.1286	0.0363	0.1257	0.0583
Coups occurring more than six years earlier	0.0471	0.0256	0.0466	0.0181	0.0466	0.0250
Log of the previous year's per capita GDP	−0.2835	0.0789	−0.3613	0.0613	−0.3617	0.0873
This year's per capita GDP growth rate	*	*	−9.8505	3.3235	−9.8459	4.4928
The previous year's per capita GDP growth rate	−1.5583	0.7151	*	*	*	*
Nonconstitutional leader	0.1919	0.1030	0.1371	0.076	0.1391	0.1095

Table 3.5 (continued)

	1	2	3	4	5	6
Leader's time in power	−0.0049	0.0078	−0.0047	0.0056	−0.0048	0.0080
Africa	−0.0149	0.1528	−0.2460	0.1410	−0.2459	0.1969
Middle East	0.2238	0.1875	0.1867	0.1367	0.1873	0.1928
Latin America	0.4955	0.1696	0.4176	0.1259	0.4193	0.1771
North America-Europe-Australasia	−0.3543	0.3010	−0.2483	0.2181	−0.2476	0.3087

$\hat{\rho}$: −0.1178   S.D. $(\hat{\rho})$: 0.0392 $\hat{\sigma}$: 0.0570   Log Lik: 3,598.4828   #Obs: 2797

Column 1: Parameter estimate.
Column 2: Standard errors calculated by the δ method.
Columns 3 and 5: OMD parameter estimates using the δ method covariance matrix.
Columns 4 and 6: Standard errors based on the δ method OMD estimate.

evidence that time in power reduces a leader's risk of losing power in a coup (once a country's past history of coups has been controlled for). Of course, the longer a leader who seized power in a coup continues to rule, the more distant the coup that spawned his rule becomes, and, all else held equal, the lower the count of recent coups. This effect will tend to reduce the leader's coup risk.

In contrast to our findings about time in power, our results indicate that nonconstitutional rule exerts a marginally significant influence on the probability of a coup. Rulers who commit the "original sin" of coming to power outside their country's constitutional framework are themselves at heightened risk of a coup d'etat. We further find that nonconstitutional rule, unlike the lagged coup history, does have a statistically significant impact on the rate of economic growth for the average country in our sample: a nonconstitutional ruler reduces the annual growth rate by about half a percentage point, which is the equivalent of around two months growth for the average country in our sample. While coups themselves may not directly harm the economy, nonconstitutional rule apparently does.

These estimates also shed light on the question of whether lagged coups proxy for nonconstitutional rule in our earlier estimates, or whether instead they exert an independent risk on the probability of further coups, as Finer (1962) suggests they will. After correcting for the effect of nonconstitutional rule, a country's recent coup rate continues to exert an independent influence on the probability of a coup. However, the coefficient estimates for lagged coups are somewhat smaller than in the earlier tables—part of the estimated effect was due to the role of past coups as a proxy for nonconstitutional rule.

When we retest the restriction that lagged coups do not affect growth, it now passes easily, with an χ^2 statistic of 0.5304. Repeating our test of the hypothesis that lagged income variables do not matter for coups, we just as easily reject this hypothesis. Our test statistic, which is asymptotically distributed as χ^2 with two degrees of freedom, takes on a value of 17.9003. Both of these tests are based on the covariance matrix calculated using the δ method.

We estimate the model with current growth in the coup equation, again adopting the identifying restriction that lagged growth does not exert an independent influence. Estimates of the restricted version of the model appear in column 3 of table 3.5, with estimated standard errors in column 4. These estimates are calculated via the δ method. These estimates confirm that current growth has a large, statistically significant, but imprecisely estimated effect on the probability of a coup. The economy affects the choice of ruler, even when this choice is not filtered through the electoral process.

Do coups affect growth? For lagged coups, the answer is consistently no. However, we can use lagged coups as instruments for the current coup propensity in the growth equation. When we do so we obtain the estimates reported in column 5 of table 3.5 (with associated standard errors appearing in column 6). The estimates are little changed from their previous values, with an χ^2 statistic with one degree of freedom of 0.5067 implied by the restriction that lagged coups do not affect growth. The estimated coefficient on the current coup propensity reported in column 5 is very nearly zero and does not even approach the threshold of statistical significance. The message of this model is clear: nonconstitutional rule slows the pace of economic growth, but once this effect is controlled for, additional coups do not exert an additional growth-inhibiting influence.

Our model enables us to gauge the effects of various risk factors for a coup and also the effect of coups on the growth process, but how well does it fit the data? For the growth equation, the answer to this question is straightforward but depressing. The R^2 for our preferred growth model is a mere 0.0584. With 2,798 observations, this R^2 is highly statistically significant. However, there is a high degree of residual noise in the system; 96 percent of the variation in growth rates remains unexplained by our model. By aggregating over time, and estimating a model of, say, five- or ten-year growth rates, we could presumably gain additional accuracy.

For example, using average annual growth rates over the period 1960 through 1985, Barro explains over half the variation in his growth data, using a growth model similar to ours, enriched by data on government spending and educational attainments. By accepting a longer time interval,

Barro gained access to a wider set of variables, those collected with less than annual frequency, and also worked with series in which the very high frequency variation had been removed. We believe that, for our purpose of modeling the structural determinants of coups, the increased sample size and added precision of our coup coefficient estimates is worth the sacrifices entailed by working with annual data. Further work with longer time intervals, such as Barro's, that focused on the interplay of growth and coups could profitably complement our work here.

The picture for coups is more ambiguous. Because coups are a rare event, a model that predicts that coups never occur will be right about 95 percent of the time. Predicting which countries will suffer coups this year is like trying to predict which individuals in a population will suffer heart attacks this year. While we can predict that overweight male smokers over the age of forty with high blood cholesterol, high blood pressure, and a family history of heart disease are at higher risk of a heart attack, there are very few of them for whom the risk this year rises above 50 percent. However, if we aggregate an annual heart attack model and seek to predict which individuals will suffer heart attacks over, say, the next twenty years, we will predict much more accurately.

The case for our coup data is very similar. In only one country/year, Bolivia in 1980, does our model's estimate of the coup probability rise above 0.5. In other words, our model only "predicts" one coup, by the stringent standard of only predicting when the event probability goes above 0.5. When we calculate the correlation between actual coups and the probability of a coup estimated by our model, the association remains low. The mean coup rate for our data set is 0.044, which is also the predicted rate. However, the correlation between our model's predicted annual coup probability and the actual occurrence of coups is only 0.1998.

At an annual level, our model does not do a spectacular job of predicting coups. However, if we pose the somewhat less ambitious task of predicting the total number of coups for each country in our sample, the model does a more impressive job. Of course, on theoretical grounds, any probit model can always get the total number of coups for the sample exactly by simply setting all the response coefficients to zero and adjusting the constant to return the mean event probability. However, there is considerable variation among the 121 countries in our sample. The mean number of coups per country in our sample is 0.9916 (our model predicts 0.9974), with a standard deviation of 1.5744. We construct the predicted number of coups for each country by adding up the annual estimates of the coup probability generated by our model for each country. The correlation between these estimates and the actual coup counts is 0.7993. By this standard, our model does well—over time it does a good job of predicting countries' cumulative experience with coups.

3.4 Conclusion

The findings of our earlier work on coups (Londregan and Poole 1990) are largely confirmed when the model is reestimated using coup counts derived from Bienen and Van De Walle (1990) instead of the counts provided by the *World Handbook*. These findings include the existence of a coup trap, leaving countries that have experienced a coup at greater risk of further seizures of executive power, and the finding that coups are a poor country phenomenon—they almost never occur in high income countries. We substantially corroborate the lack of a feedback effect from coups to growth, though in the *World Handbook* data this conclusion is sensitive to the method of calculating the variance-covariance matrix. However, with the exception of testing for the effect of past coups on current growth rates, we find that our results are robust to the method of calculating standard errors, whether the bootstrap or the δ-method. We find reason to prefer the coup counts based on the Bienen and Van De Walle codings because of their greater accuracy and because the more conservative definition of non-constitutional transfers of executive power leads to the classification of a more homogeneous set of events as coups.

We extend our earlier work by adding leader-specific variables. Our results indicate that nonconstitutional leaders are themselves at greater risk of being forced from power nonconstitutionally: he who lives by the coup dies by the coup, or at least tends to lose power that way. However, this is not the entire story behind the coup trap. Even after correcting for nonconstitutional entry by the current leader, countries' past experience with coups continues to exert an independent coup-provoking influence.

Our results indicate that nonconstitutional rule is an important source of feedback *from* the political system *to* the economy. While the past history of coups does not influence the growth rate, nonconstitutional rule does, reducing annual growth by about a half percentage point per year. In addition to the coup trap there seems to be a "poverty trap" in which poor countries are more coup prone and thus more likely to be saddled with nonconstitutional rulers who will slow the rate at which economic growth eventually immunizes them from yet further coups and more nonconstitutional rule. Coups are not simply an inferior good disproportionately "consumed" by poor countries, they are a very high priced Giffen good, imposing nonconstitutional rule on countries that can least afford it.

Notes

Prepared for the Pinhas Sapir Center Conference on *The Political Economy of Business Cycles and Growth*, Tel Aviv, June 2 and 3, 1991. We thank Torsten Perrson, Guido Tabellini, and conference participants for their helpful comments.

1. To the *World Handbook's* credit, an extensive data appendix details the many descrepancies among the coding decisions of various research assistants. In addition, the *World Handbook* codes a wider set of political variables and does not simply focus on leadership, although for our purposes in this paper, this extra breadth of coverage is irrelevant.

2. Pereda Asbun (a 47-year-old with a military background, who nonconstitutionally seized power in 1978), Padilla Arancibia (a 54-year-old military leader, who grasped control in 1979 by nonconstitutional means), Guavara Arce (a 68-year-old civilian, who gained power "constitutionally" in 1979), Natusch Busch (a 53-year-old from a military background, who seized executive power nonconstitutionally in 1979) and Gueiler Tejeda (a 58-year-old civilian, who came to power in 1979 constitutionally).

3. The rationale being that survival for such a leader until 1969 is an uncertain proposition: a leader who acceded to power in 1967, and lasted for more than one year, but less than two, need not have remained in power until the beginning of 1969.

4. These came following Al-Shaabi of the Yemen Democratic Republic, Boumedienne of Algeria, Donitz of Germany, Gizenga of Zaire, D. Anastasio Somoza of Nicaragua, Souvanna Phouma of Laos, Tito of Yugoslavia, and Villarroel of Bolivia. There were also the cases of Karume of Zanzibar, and Minh of South Viet Nam, the last leaders of their respective countries.

5. The first four years of Zairian independence, and the Uruguayan interval of shared rule (1951–1958).

6. We compile two coup history variables, coups occurring during the previous six years (that is, during years $t - 6$ through $t - 1$), and coups occurring earlier (during $t - 7$ or before). While the Summers and Heston economic data begin with 1950 or later, the leadership data for some countries reach back much further (the early 1800s for some of the Latin American leaders). We create annual coup counts back to 1944 or the first year of independence, whichever comes later. This means that for countries for which leadership data is available as early as 1944, the values of the recent coup history variable are not distorted by "presample" coups from 1950 onward.

7. For example, consider the case of the replacement of Thailand's Thanom by Sanya in 1973. The *World Handbook* codes this as a coup, presumably because it continued an epoch of military rule in Thailand that began with a coup led by Pibun in 1947. However, this transfer took place under the rubric of the constitution imposed by the military.

8. For example, the December 31, 1981 coup of Rawlings against Ghana's Limann is erroneously counted as occuring in 1982 by the *World Handbook* but correctly

placed in 1981 by Bienen and Van De Walle. Likewise, Bokassa's December 31, 1965 overthrow of Dacko in the Central African Republic is miscoded by the *World Handbook* as occurring in 1966 (*Facts on File* also erroneously counts this coup as occurring on January 1).

9. For notational convenience, we index these regions conformably with the following coefficient subscripts: $j = 5$ for Africa, $j = 6$ for Europe and North America, and $j = 7$ for South America.

10. In the sense of Engle, Hendry, and Richard (1983).

11. Using a Gateway 2000 machine, convergence is even faster, taking about 32 seconds.

12. This algorithm is described in detail in the appendix to Londregan and Poole 1990.

13. The one exception being the standard error for lagged income in the growth equation. The bootstrap estimate of this standard error is about twice the standard error estimated by the δ method.

14. These estimates are calculated using the method of Broyden, Fletcher, Goldfarb, and Shanno, with a final iteration of the Newton-Raphson method at the optimum employing numerical gradients and Hessians. Consistent with theory, identical parameter estimates and the same value of the criterion function are yielded by Amemiya's method of generalized least squares, (Amemiya 1978), which essentially calculates generalized least squares estimates of α by regressing the reduced-form parameter estimates, π, on a "selection" matrix D that depends on the set of variables excluded from the structural model.

15. This region corresponds closely to Lipset's (1959) set of "European and English-Speaking Stable Democracies."

16. The lagged coup counts used in this model are, of course, different from those based on *World Handbook* data.

17. We also examined the effect of the leader's military background and age, but neither of these was significant once we had accounted for nonconstitutional entry and time in power.

References

T. Amemiya, T. 1978. "The Estimation of a Simultaneous Equation Generalized Probit Model." *Econometrica* 46:1193–1205.

Barro, Robert. 1989. "A Cross Country Study of Growth, Saving, and Government." NBER Working Paper No. 2855 (February 1989).

Bienen, Henry and Nic Van De Walle. 1990. *Of Time and Power: Leadership Duration in the Modern World*. Stanford: Stanford University Press.

Blondel, Jean. 1980. *World Leaders: Heads of Government in the Postwar Period*. Beverly Hills: Sage Publications.

Efron, Bradley. 1979. "Bootstrap Methods: Another Look at the Jack-Knife." *Annals of Statistics* 7:1–26.

Engle, Robert F., David F. Hendry, and Jean-François Richard. 1983. "Exogeneity." *Econometrica* 51:277–304.

Erikson, Robert. 1989. "Economic Conditions and the Presidential Vote." *American Political Science Review* 83:567–576.

Fair, Ray. 1978. "The Effects of Economic Events on Votes for Presidents." *The Review of Economics and Statistics* 60:159–72.

Finer, Samuel E. 1962. *The Man on Horseback.* London: Pall Mall.

Huntington, Samuel P. 1968. *Political Order in Changing Societies.* New Haven: Yale University Press.

Jodice, D. and Charles Lewis Taylor. 1983. *The World Handbook of Political and Social Indicators III.* New Haven: Yale University Press.

Keesings Contemporary Archives, 1963 and 1964 editions. London: Keesings Ltd.

Lipset, Seymour Martin. 1959. "Some Social Requisites of Democracy: Economic Development and Political Legitimacy." *American Political Science Review* 53:69–105.

Londregan, John B. and Keith T. Poole. 1990. "Poverty, the Coup Trap, and the Seizure of Executive Power. " *World Politics* 42:151–183.

Lucas, Robert E. 1988. "On the Mechanics of Economic Development." *Journal of Monetary Economics,* 22:3–42.

Luttwak, Edward. 1969. *Coup d'Etat: A Practical Handbook.* New York: Knopf.

Newey, Whitney K. 1987. "Efficient Estimation of Limited Dependent Variable Models with Endogenous Explanatory Variables." *Journal of Econometrics* 36:231–50.

Olson, Mancur. 1963. "Rapid Growth as a Destabilizing Force, " *Journal of Economic History* 23:529–52.

Rosenstone, Steven J. 1983. *Forecasting Presidential Elections* New Haven: Yale University Press.

Rothemberg, Thomas J. 1973. "Efficient Estimation with a priori Information." *Cowles Foundation Monograph 23.* New Haven: Yale University Press.

Summers, Robert and Alan Heston. 1988. "A New Set of International Comparisons of Real Product and Prices: Estimates for 130 Countries, 1950–1985." *The Review of Income and Wealth* 34:1–25.

Taylor, Charles Lewis and Michael C. Hudson. 1972. The World Handbook of Political and Social Indicators Second Edition, 1948–1982. New Haven: Yale University Press.

II

**Growth within Purely
Economic Frameworks**

4   Endogenous Macroeconomic Growth Theory

Elhanan Helpman

Fortunes of nations change over time. Leading economic powers of the past have become poorly performing economies of the present, and poor economies of the past have become the new leaders. The determinants of the wealth of nations and its evolution over time have mystified economists ever since the beginnings of our discipline. Why do some countries grow faster than others? And how have the underlying forces of growth changed over time? Complete answers to these questions cannot possibly be provided within the narrow limits of a single branch of economics, such as macroeconomics, nor even within the confines of our profession as commonly perceived. Nevertheless, macroeconomic theories of economic growth have much to offer, as exemplified by the seminal contributions of Ramsey (1928), Harrod (1939), Domar (1946), and Solow (1956).

The neoclassical theory of economic growth has been mostly concerned with capital accumulation. When confronted with data, however, its central tenet could explain only a fraction of the variations in growth rates, and the rest was attributed to technical progress (see Solow 1957 and Maddison 1987). On the other hand, attempts to explain technical progress were, unfortunately, not very successful, with Arrow's (1962a) theory of learning-by-doing being an exception. But that theory suffers from the limitation that it assumes that productivity improvements occur serendipitously as a byproduct of capital accumulation, although deliberate efforts to develop new products and technologies have been very prominent indeed. Recall the dramatic developments in consumer electronics, computers, and pharmaceuticals in order to see the important role of deliberate research and development in raising our standards of living. R&D has grown in importance in all industrial nations. In the OECD countries in particular, real expenditure on R&D has grown at 6 percent per annum in the decade ending in 1985 (see OECD 1989). And some of the large Japanese companies now invest more in R&D than in plant and equipment. We have to bear these facts in mind when constructing our theories.

The new wave of research on economic growth was stimulated by Romer (1986) and Lucas (1988). Their work relies on Arrow's mechanism of learning-by-doing, but following Uzawa (1965), they have redirected its application to the accumulation of knowledge and human capital rather than the accumulation of plant and equipment. Moreover, they have changed the focus toward explanations of sustained long-run growth and cross-country variations in growth rates.

Following Arrow (1962a), they have taken the view that aggregate production exhibits increasing returns to scale. But the returns to scale are external to single economic agents and internal to a sector or larger parts of the economy. Consequently competition can prevail. This approach avoids complications of market conduct and structure that arise when economies of scale are internal to firms. Such complications are unavoidable, however, when we wish to deal explicitly with profit-seeking investment in innovation, as we should, given the rising importance of commercial R&D in the industrial world.

The integration of imperfect competition with innovation-based growth was first achieved by Judd (1985). His main interest was in issues of industrial organization, however. For this reason he did not explore the implications of his work for growth. Romer (1990a) combined Judd's approach with learning-by-doing *in innovation* and thereby developed a model that sustains long-run growth at an *endogenous rate*. This was an important achievement, because it opened the door to a new research line with attractive realistic features.

Learning-by-doing in R&D is a natural phenomenon.[1] Current researchers use the stock of knowledge that has been accumulated over long periods of time. They draw upon the laws of physics and mathematics, properties of chemical compounds, the structure of a cell, and other fruits of past labor. And they make use of accumulated knowledge about commercial traits, such as methods of refrigeration or the architecture of personal computers. Many commercial R&D efforts generate not only an appropriable product such as a technology for the manufacturing of a new good, but also a nonappropriable product such as a new way of using components, or a new material that can be used in a variety of applications. The nonappropriable product adds to society's general stock of knowledge, which is freely used by many parties. These spillovers from industrial research drive a wedge between the private and social return on R&D (see Arrow 1962b). Existing estimates indicate that the social rate of return on R&D is more than twice as high as the private rate of return (see Mansfield et al. 1977 and Scherer 1982). It follows that the uncompensated product of R&D is substantial. Naturally, the incentive of entrepreneurs to innovate derives from the return on the compensated product. These features will be taken into account in what follows.

New innovation-based models of economic growth come closer than ever before to Schumpeter's view of the capitalist system, "Was not the observed performance [of technological progress] due to that stream of inventions that revolutionized the technique of production rather than to the businessman's hunt for profits? The answer is in the negative. The carrying into effect of those technological novelties was of the essence of that hunt" (p. 110). His emphasis on the entrepreneur and the link between innovation and profits are clearly manifested in this literature, as is his belief that the marginal productivity of innovations need not decline, because new inventions can be as productive as old.

4.1   Neoclassical Growth

We are all familiar with the neoclassical theory of economic growth; it has been taught almost unrivaled for about three decades. For this reason there is no need for me to dwell upon it in detail. Nevertheless, my discussion of endogenous growth would be grossly incomplete if I neglected to point out its place in the neoclassical theory. I will therefore lay out conditions needed for sustained endogenous growth in neoclassical models and relate them to similar conditions in innovation-based models of growth.

The main point I wish to make in this regard appears already in Solow's (1956) classic paper and can be seen most clearly with the help of his model. Consider a stripped down version of a Solow economy in which the labor force does not grow, capital does not depreciate, and the state of technology does not change over time. Under these conditions accumulation of capital equals saving:

$$\dot{K} = sF(K, L), \tag{1}$$

where K represents the capital stock, L the labor force, s the savings rate, and $F(\cdot)$ the constant returns to scale production function. Evidently, in this economy the capital stock grows without bound. It follows that output also grows without bound and so does income per capita. But what happens to the growth rate of per capita income?

The rate of growth of income per capita equals

$$g_{Y/L} = sF_K(K, L), \tag{2}$$

where $F_K(\cdot)$ denotes the marginal product of capital. Therefore the long-run growth rate approaches zero unless the marginal product of capital remains positive as capital accumulates without bound. The assumption that the marginal product of capital approaches zero (an Inada condition) has been common in the literature. When this condition holds, growth peters out. Observe, however, that this simple Solow economy sustains long-run growth whenever the marginal product of capital is bounded below by a positive constant.

The condition for sustained growth becomes more demanding in the presence of capital depreciation or population growth. If, for example, the population grows at the rate $g_L > 0$, the lower bound on the marginal product of capital that is needed to sustain long-run growth becomes $F_K(K, L) > g_L/s$ (rather than $F_K(K, L) > 0$). Evidently, this lower bound is higher the higher the rate of population growth and the lower the rate of savings. The main point remains the same, however: *the economy grows in the long run if the marginal product of capital does not decline too much as a result of capital accumulation.*[2]

Our last conclusion depends only partially on the postulated form of saving behavior. As an alternative to the fixed saving rate, take, for example, the case of infinitely lived consumers who optimize over their choice of consumption and saving, using a time-separable intertemporal utility function with a constant elasticity of the marginal utility of consumption. The intertemporal utility function is given by

$$U_t = \int_t^\infty e^{-\rho(\tau-t)}u(\tau)d\tau, \tag{3}$$

where $u(\tau)$ describes the flow of utility at time τ, and ρ represents the subjective rate of time preference, and

$$u = \frac{C_Y^{1-v} - 1}{1 - v}, \qquad v > 0, \tag{4}$$

where C_Y stands for the consumption level of the final product Y. The parameter v represents the elasticity of the marginal utility of consumption while its inverse $1/v$ equals the intertemporal elasticity of substitution. A consumer that maximizes (3)–(4) subject to an intertemporal budget constraint allocates consumption according to the rule

$$\frac{\dot{C}_Y}{C_Y} = \frac{1}{v}\left[r - \rho - \frac{\dot{p}_Y}{p_Y}\right], \tag{5}$$

where r stands for the nominal interest rate and p_Y for the nominal price of output. It follows that consumption grows over time at a rate given by the product of the intertemporal elasticity of substitution and the difference between the real interest rate and the subjective discount rate.

Equation (5) shows clearly that this type of an economy sustains long-run growth only if the real interest rate remains above the subjective discount rate in the long run. As is well known, however, in the absence of capital depreciation the real interest rate equals the marginal product of capital. It follows that income per capita grows in the long run if and only if the marginal product of capital remains higher than the subjective rate of time preference. In this case the long-run rate of growth is higher the lower is the subJective rate of time preference and the higher the intertemporal elasticity of substitution.

We have thus seen that a sufficiently high marginal product of capital leads to long-run growth in per capita income for two forms of saving. It may appear, therefore, that savings behavior does not constrain growth in neoclassical economies. This conclusion is unwarranted, however. First, even in the previously discussed cases parameters of the saving function do matter whenever growth does not peter out. And second, there exist economic structures in which aggregate saving is insufficient to sustain long-run capital accumulation even with high marginal products of capital. Jones and Manuelli (1990b) and Boldrin (1990) provide examples of this phenomenon. They show that in a one-sector overlapping generations model, growth peters out in the long run because the young generation does not have enough resources to purchase an ever increasing capital stock. For this reason aggregate saving, which amounts to the savings of the young, cannot support continued growth.

Leaving aside the case of overlapping generations, recall the role that technical progress can play in the neoclassical theory. With labor augmenting technical progress, the production function takes the form

$$Y = F(K, AL), \tag{6}$$

where A represents the state of technology. Technical progress raises A and thereby the marginal product of capital. Higher marginal productivity of capital leads to a higher real interest rate. Now take the case in which the rate of consumption growth is governed by equation (5). In this case capital accumulation depresses the real interest rate and therefore the rate of consumption growth, while technical progress raises the real interest rate thereby increasing the rate of consumption growth. In steady state the rate of capital accumulation equals the rate of technical progress and the real

interest rate remains constant. This describes the case of exogenous technical progress that leads to exogenous long-run growth.

Following Arrow's analysis of learning-by-doing, however, some growth
theorists have linked the state of technology to cumulative investment
experience. With this view the state of technology parameter A becomes a
function of the economy's capital stock $A(K)$ (see Sheshinski 1967). The
effect of capital on productivity is assumed to be external to an individual
investor. For this reason the real interest rate equals the private marginal
product of capital $F_K[K, A(K)L]$. It follows that with this form of endogenous
technical progress an economy can sustain long-run growth as long as the
state of technology is sufficiently responsive to capital accumulation.

This discussion points to the fact that sustainability of long-run growth
depends critically on the extent to which capital accumulation depresses its
marginal productivity as perceived by investors and on whether there exist
offsetting forces that prevent the marginal product of capital from declining
too much. In the model of learning-by-doing, learning provides an offsetting device, but this mechanism will not suffice if the pace of learning is not
fast enough or learning is bounded.

Now that we have identified the mechanisms of long-run growth in the
neoclassical theory, we may turn to the more recent innovation-based
theories of economic growth. I begin with an approach based on horizontal
product differentiation. This approach suffers from several shortcomings,
some related to the specification of product differentiation and others
related to the mechanism of knowledge accumulation. It is important,
however, to bear in mind that these details are not particularly important, as
they can and will be replaced with more appealing ingredients without
affecting the results in any fundamental way. On the other hand, the
approach I will describe first has the advantage of being simple, and it
brings out in a clear way important characteristics of the innovation-based
approach to economic growth.

4.2   Expanding Product Variety

A particularly simple model of innovation-based growth builds on the Dixit
and Stiglitz (1977) formulation of horizontal product differentiation. We
define an index D by means of the following constant elasticity of substitution function:

$$D = \left[\int_0^n x(j)^\alpha dj \right]^{1/\alpha}, \qquad 0 < \alpha < 1, \tag{7}$$

where $x(j)$ represents the quantity of variety j of a high-tech product, n stands for the measure (the number) of available brands, and α is a paiame- ter. The elasticity of substitution between every pair of brands equals $1/(1 - \alpha)$. The postulated restriction on α implies an elasticity of substitu- tion larger than one, which means that varieties substitute well for each other. Equation (7) yields constant elasticity demand functions with mar- ginal revenue $MR(j) = \alpha p(j)$, where $p(j)$ represents the price of brand j (the demand elasticity with respect to the price equals the elasticity of substitution).

Next assume that all brands require the input of one unit of labor per unit output. Then marginal costs equal the wage rate w for all brands, and $MR(j) = MC(j)$ implies that all brands are equally priced at

$$p = \frac{w}{\alpha}. \tag{8}$$

With this pricing rule operating profits are

$$\pi = (1 - \alpha)\frac{pX}{n} \tag{9}$$

per brand, where X represents aggregate output of high-tech products.

These relationships are well known from the static theory of monopolis- tic competition. In a static environment one would add fixed costs of, say, f units of labor per brand in manufacturing and close this model with Chamberlain's free-entry condition for the large group case that requires zero (excess) profits; that is, $\pi = wf$, and a labor market clearing condition, $X + nf = L$, where L represents available labor.[3]

This simple general-equilibrium model of horizontal product differentia- tion has been extended by Judd (1985) to a dynamic framework. His formulation, like most of the new literature on innovation-based growth, interprets the fixed costs as an R&D expense, where R&D leads to the development of new varieties of the differentiated product. Other specifica- tions assign R&D the role of product improvement (vertical product differ- entiation) or cost reduction (see Aghion and Howitt 1990 and Grossman and Helpman 1991a). A central feature of R&D costs is that they have to be paid up front, before operating profits can be appropriated. Conse- quently operating profits accrue at different points in time from R&D costs. This realistic time structure introduces natural dynamics.

In the dynamic version of monopolistic competition we replace Cham- berlain's static free-entry condition with a dynamic free-entry condition that takes the following form (this discussion follows Grossman and Helpman

1991b, chap. 3). Firms are valued according to their expected profit stream. A typical firm owns the technology for manufacturing a single brand of the differentiated product, and it possesses indefinite monopoly power in the supply of its brand. It follows that the value of a firm equals the present value of its profits,

$$v(t) = \int_t^\infty e^{-R(\tau, t)} \pi(\tau) d\tau, \tag{10}$$

where v represents the value of a firm and $R(\tau, t) = \int_t^\tau r(z) dz$ represents the discount rate from time τ to t. This implies the no arbitrage condition

$$\frac{\pi}{v} + \frac{\dot{v}}{v} = r. \tag{11}$$

It states that the rate of return on the ownership of a firm—consisting of the profit rate π/v (the inverse of the price-earning ratio) and the rate of capital gain $\dot{v}/v$—has to equal the nominal interest rate r.

An entrepreneur who contemplates investing resources in the development of a new brand expects a reward of v on R&D effort and therefore engages in product development unless the cost of R&D exceeds this value. Now suppose that the productivity of research labs rises with the stock of available knowledge K_n. This property plays a central role in bringing about endogenous long-run growth, as we will shortly see. In this case the dynamic free-entry condition implies that at each point in time the value of a firm does not exceed product development costs wa/K_n, where a represents a parameter (because otherwise labs will have an unbounded demand for labor), and the flow of newly invented products equals zero, unless product development costs just equal the value of a firm:

$$v \leq \frac{wa}{K_n}, \qquad \text{with equality whenever } \dot{n} > 0. \tag{12}$$

Now labor market clearing requires employment in R&D plus employment in manufacturing to equal the available labor supply:

$$\frac{a}{K_n} \dot{n} + X = L, \tag{13}$$

where the first term on the left-hand side represents employment in R&D and the second term represents employment in manufacturing.

In this economy investment consists of developing new products (as opposed to building new capital equipment in the neoclassical growth model). This investment has to be financed by savings. For this purpose we may borrow the intertemporal structure of preferences (3) from the previous section, where this time

$$u = \frac{C_D^{1-v} - 1}{1 - v}, \qquad v > 0. \tag{14}$$

As before, the parameter v represents the elasticity of the marginal utility of consumption, while C_D represents consumption in terms of the index D. In equilibrium $C_D = D$. It follows from our discussion in the previous section that in this case too infinitely lived households allocate spending over time according to (see (5))

$$\frac{\dot{C}_D}{C_D} = \frac{1}{v} \left[r - \rho - \frac{\dot{p}_D}{p_D} \right], \tag{15}$$

where p_D is the price index of D, given by

$$p_D = \left[\int_0^n p(j)^{-\alpha/(1-\alpha)} dj \right]^{-(1-\alpha)/\alpha}. \tag{16}$$

This completes the description of the growth model, except for the evolution of knowledge capital.

4.3 Implications

As we will see shortly, long-run properties of economies of the type I have described depend in important ways on the evolution of knowledge capital. For this reason I deal first with the case in which knowledge capital is constant and only later on with the more interesting case of a positive feedback from R&D experience to the knowledge stock.

Constant Knowledge Capital

In the case of a constant stock of knowledge capital, *the economy does not grow in the long run.* This result is important for understanding the forces of long-run growth that I will describe later. It is necessary, however, first to spell out what we mean by growth in the present context. What growth rate should we measure? Real gross domestic product is a natural candidate. So is the real consumption index C_D (= D). For current purposes I use the latter (see, however, Grossman and Helpman 1991b, chap. 3, for the relationship between these two growth rates).

The first thing to observe is that the real consumption index can grow in the long run if either variety expands over time or aggregate output of manufacturing rises over time. For a constant stock of knowledge capital, however, the resource constraint (13) implies that the flow of new goods and the output volume are both bounded. Therefore the rate of innovation g, defined as the rate of increase of the number of products (i.e., $g = \dot{n}/n$), converges to zero, and the rate of growth of the real consumption index also converges to zero.[4]

Rising Knowledge Capital

The assumption of a constant stock of knowledge capital is not realistic. An economy that engages in product innovation expands its knowledge base. It is, however, necessary to distinguish between different forms of knowledge. For even in the above described economy with a constant stock of knowledge capital, innovation leads to an expansion of knowledge, in the sense that it increases the number of brands that the economy knows how to produce. Knowledge, as measured by the number of blueprints, rises over time in an innovating economy, and this knowledge expansion raises the productivity of resources in *manufacturing*. There exists, however, another measure of knowledge that we have termed *knowledge capital*. This stock of knowledge affects productivity in the *research lab*. Cumulative experience in R&D raises the productivity of labs by raising the stock of knowledge capital available to researches, as I have explained in the introduction. Unlike some forms of learning-by-doing, however, such as on-the-job training, important parts of knowledge that accumulates in the process of R&D can be used by other agents.

In order to capture these features I now follow Romer (1990a) in assuming that the stock of knowledge capital equals cumulative experience in R&D as measured by the number of brands that have been developed; namely,

$$K_n = n. \tag{17}$$

This specification implies that every developer of a new brand contributes equally to the future stock of knowledge, but more flexible forms can be used without altering the main thrust of the argument (see Grossman and Helpman 1991b, chap. 3) In our case the economy settles down immediately in a steady state that can be characterized by the following two equations:[5]

$$ag + X = L, \tag{18}$$

$$\frac{(1 - \alpha)X}{\alpha a} = \rho + \beta_D g, \qquad \beta_D = \left[1 + \frac{1 - \alpha}{\alpha}(v - 1) \right]. \tag{19}$$

The first equation represents the resource constraint, where g is the rate of innovation, while the second describes the no-arbitrage condition. The left-hand side of (19) represents the inverse of the price-earning ratio while the right-hand side represents the effective cost of capital; namely, the real interest rate minus the rate of capital gain on equity holdings. I assume $\beta_D > 0$.

Our steady-state conditions are depicted in figure 4.1; line LL represents the resource constraint while NN represents the no-arbitrage condition. The latter may be termed the Schumpeter line, because it embodies the notion that innovation is driven by the quest for profit opportunities. LL slopes downward because an increase in the rate of innovation involves more employment in research labs and therefore less employment in manufacturing. On the other hand NN slopes upward. An increase in the rate of innovation raises the effective cost of capital to an entrepreneur, because it leads to a higher real interest rate and a faster depreciation of the value of a firm. Consequently the entrepreneur requires a higher profit rate (a lower

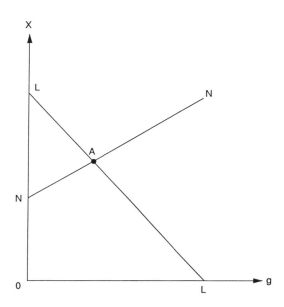

Figure 4.1

price-earning ratio) in order to engage in R&D. To attain a higher profit rate, however, more resources have to be employed in manufacturing. The intersection point A describes a long-run equilibrium.

The figure describes a fundamental trade-off between resource deployment in innovation and manufacturing. Growth is constrained by resource availability on the one hand and by market incentives on the other. One sees from the figure that a country innovates faster when it has: (a) a larger resource base (an expansion of L shifts out the LL line);[6] (b) a lower rate of time preference (a reduction of ρ shifts down the Schumpeter line NN); (c) a higher degree of monopoly power (a reduction of α shifts down the Schumpeter line); and (d) a higher intertemporal elasticity of substitution (a reduction of v shifts down the Schumpeter line). Evidently, the rate of growth is endogenous. These structural determinants of the rate of innovation can also be seen directly from the explicit solution

$$g = \frac{1}{\alpha + (1 - \alpha)v}\left[(1 - \alpha)\frac{L}{a} - \alpha\rho\right].$$
(20)

Note that a positive rate of innovation obtains if and only if $L/a > \alpha\rho/(1 - \alpha)$. This restriction applies whenever the effective size of the country is large enough (as measured by L/a), the degree of monopoly power is large enough (as measured by $1/\alpha$), or the rate of time preference is low enough. Otherwise the country does not innovate.[7]

Welfare

My discussion has concentrated on the determinants of innovation and growth. A natural question that arises is whether the market allocates resources efficiently between innovation and manufacturing. There are four sources of potential market failure.

• First, manufacturers price goods above marginal costs. Relative prices of different brands are not distorted, however, because all suppliers of brands exercise the same degree of monopoly power. In addition, brands of the differentiated product are the only goods supplied. For these reasons the departure from marginal cost pricing does not distort resource allocation (see Lerner 1934).

• Second, an entrepreneur who contemplates the development of a new product does not take into account the contribution of his product to consumer surplus.

• Third, the entrepreneur does not take into account the effect of his R&D effort on profits of competing firms, despite the fact that he depresses the profitability of competing brands. This feature exemplifies Schumpeter's notion of creative destruction.

• Fourth, the benefits to future product developers, who will work with a larger stock of knowledge capital, are not considered in the decision to invest in R&D.

It so happens that in this model underinvestment in product development as a result of the disregard for consumer surplus just equals overinvestment in product development as a result of the disregard for destruction of profits. Thus the allocation of resources *is efficient when product development does not affect the stock of knowledge capital* (see Grossman and Helpman 1991a, chap. 3). *When R&D contributes to the stock of knowledge capital, however, the equilibrium pace of innovation is too slow.*[8]

4.4 Capital Accumulation

Up to this point my description of innovation-based growth has disregarded investment in plant and equipment. I have purposely chosen to present the theory in this way in order to emphasize its novel elements. In practice, however, investment in plant and equipment constitutes a large share of GDP (20 percent or more in many countries), and the share of investment relates positively to the growth rate of GDP (see Barro 1991). For these reasons we need to ensure that the theory can encompass investment in plant and equipment in a suitable way.[9]

The basic story to be formalized later incorporates the type of capital accumulation emphasized in the neoclassical growth model. We have seen that in the neoclassical model technical progress raises the marginal product of capital, thereby raising the profitability of investment in plant and equipment. In this event capital deepening, that ceteris paribus depresses the marginal product of capital, can nevertheless continue indefinitely The same applies here, except that now *technical progress is driven by profit-seeking entrepreneurs.* In other words, the invention of new brands generates the incentive to install more fixed plant and equipment.

In order to demonstrate the role of conventional capital, consider an economy in which the differentiated product is an intermediate input. The economy manufactures a single, final, homogeneous output Y that can be used for either consumption or investment in plant and equipment, just like in the neoclassical model. The production function of Y takes the Cobb-

Douglas form:

$$Y = A_Y D_Y^\eta K^\beta L_Y^{1-\beta-\eta}, \qquad \eta, \beta > 0, 1 > 1 - \beta - \eta > 0, \tag{21}$$

where A_Y is a constant, D_Y denotes a Dixit-Stiglitz index of differentiated products (see (7)), K represents the stock of plant and equipment, and L_Y represents direct labor employment in the production of Y. In this specification the production of final output takes place under constant returns to scale.

In this economy the demand for labor derives from three sources: R&D, manufacturing of differentiated intermediate inputs, and production of the final output. Therefore labor market clearing requires $ag + X + L_Y = L$.

It is shown in Grossman and Helpman (1991a) that in this type of an economy with nondepreciating capital the steady state growth rate of output Y equals

$$g_Y = \frac{\eta}{1 - \beta} \frac{1 - \alpha}{\alpha} g, \tag{22}$$

and the rate of investment equals[10]

$$\frac{\dot{K}}{Y} = \frac{\beta g_Y}{\rho + v g_Y}. \tag{23}$$

Moreover, the equilibrium rate of innovation and the volume of manufacturing of high-tech differentiated products can be described by means of a figure similar to 4.1. An analysis of the figure confirms our earlier findings that a country innovates faster in the long run when its resource base is larger, it is more productive in R&D, it has a lower rate of time preference, its intertemporal elasticity of substitution is larger, or its degree of monopoly power is higher (see Grossman and Helpman 1991b, chap. 5).

Evidently, the rate of investment increases with the rate of output growth while the latter increases with the rate of innovation. Combined with the results concerning the determinants of the rate of innovation, these relationships imply, for example, that countries with low rates of time preference innovate faster, experience faster output growth, and have a higher rate of investment. However, investment is *not* a primary source of growth in these economies. Rather, the primary sources of growth are a variety of factors (such as the rate of time preference and the degree of monopoly power) that affect the incentive for industrial research while the rate of investment adjusts so as to keep the rate of expansion of conventional capital in line with the growth rate of output. In terms of causality, the investment rate and the rate of growth are simultaneously determined by technological progress that affects them in essentially the same direction, whereas the pace of technological progress is endogenously determined by more primitive factors.

4.5 Quality Ladders

In the theory of innovation-based growth that has been described so far, entrepreneurs invest resources in R&D in order to develop new brands of a horizontally differentiated product. Diversity is valuable per se because it raises productivity of manufacturing for a given volume of inputs or household utility for a given volume of consumption. When coupled with productivity gains in R&D as a result of the accumulation of knowledge capital, they lead to sustained long-run growth. The growth rate depends on an economy's resource base, subjective rate of time preference, degree of monopoly power, and parameters of the production function.

This model has several unattractive features, however. First, new goods are no better than old. As a result, every brand competes on equal footing with all existing products. Second, society uses old brands side by side with new ones, without ever dropping a product. Finally, whereas innovation involves risk taking, the model employs a deterministic R&D technology. All of these shortcomings notwithstanding, we have identified a mechanism of economic growth that does not depend on the model's details: (a) profit seeking drives innovation; (b) innovation contributes to the society's stock of knowledge in addition to providing the innovator with an appropriable asset; and (c) an expansion of knowledge capital reduces future innovation costs. This cost reduction mitigates the decline in the profitability of inventive activity that would have taken place in its absence. As a result, the profitability of innovation can be sustained and with it a positive growth rate. The rate of growth depends on structural features and on economic policy.

In this section I describe a model of quality ladders in which innovation improves the quality of a fixed set of goods or reduces their manufacturing costs. New products drive out old products from the market, and R&D is risky. In this model the rate of innovation equals the fraction of goods that are improved per unit time. Despite these marked departures from the model of horizontal product differentiation, I will show that the same mechanism of economic growth also operates in the new model. Moreover, both models have a similar reduced form. For this reason a figure similar to 4.1 can be used to describe its equilibrium. My presentation follows

Grossman and Helpman (1991b, chap. 4), where readers can find the missing details of the arguments.

The economy manufactures a continuum of goods indexed by points on the interval [0, 1]. The utility derived from a good depends on its quality. A consumer enjoys a unit of good j that was improved $m(j)$ times, $j \in [0, 1]$, as much as he would enjoy $\lambda^{m(j)}$ units of the good had it never been improved; $\lambda > 1$. In this sense innovation that leads to product improvement raises the quality of a good. One can verify that all the results that follow also apply when innovation leads to cost reduction, whereby a product j that was improved $m(j)$ times requires $\lambda^{-m(j)}$ times the inputs per unit output that would have been required if the product had not been improved at all. I will use the quality improvement interpretation for convenience. Evidently, in this case the consumer chooses to buy a quality of good j that extracts the lowest price per unit quality; that is, the lowest ratio $p(j, m)/\lambda^m$, where $p(j, m)$ represents the price of good j that was improved m times.

We continue to represent intertemporal preferences by means of (3) and the flow of utility by means of (14), as in the case of horizontal product differentiation. This time, however, the real consumption index C_Q, that replaces C_D, takes on the Cobb-Douglas form

$$C_Q = \exp\left[\int_0^1 \log X(j)dj\right],\tag{24}$$

where $X(j)$ represents the quality equivalent consumption level of good j. If, for example, good j was improved only once, it is available in two qualities: $\lambda^0 = 1$ and $\lambda^1 = \lambda$. Then a consumer who purchases quantity $x(j, 0)$ of the lowest quality and $x(j, 1)$ of the improved brand enjoys the quality equivalent consumption level $X(j) = x(j, 0) + \lambda x(j, 1)$. We have argued, however, that a consumer will choose the quality that provides the lowest quality-adjusted price. In the event $X(j) = \tilde{x}(j)$, where $\tilde{x}(j)$ represents the consumption level of the brand that provides the lowest quality-adjusted price. We denote by $\tilde{p}(j)$ the price of this brand. It follows that the price index of real consumption C_Q equals

$$p_Q = \exp\left\{\int_0^1 \log[\tilde{p}(j)\lambda^{-\tilde{m}(j)}]\right\} dj,\tag{25}$$

where $\tilde{m}(j)$ represents the number of improvements of the brand of good j that provides the lowest quality-adjusted price. This price index can be used to calculate the optimal intertemporal allocation of real consumption, in analogy with (19). Namely,

$$\frac{\dot{C}_Q}{C_Q} = \frac{1}{v}\left[r - \rho - \frac{\dot{p}_Q}{p_Q}\right].\qquad(26)$$

We turn next to manufacturers and innovators.

An innovator who succeeds in improving a good can charge a price λ times higher than the next to the top quality brand and remain competitive in the market. Let the manufacturing of a brand require one unit of labor per unit output independent of quality. Then in the ensuing price competition between the suppliers of existing qualities the manufacturer of the top quality brand captures the entire market by charging a price that is a shade lower than λ times marginal manufacturing costs. Consequently, the top of the line brand provides the lowest quality-adjusted price and

$$p = \lambda w.\qquad(27)$$

The same price, which is marked up above marginal costs by the factor λ, applies to the top quality of all goods $j \in [0, 1]$. It follows that profits derived from owning the technology to manufacture a top quality product equal

$$\pi = \left(1 - \frac{1}{\lambda}\right)pX,\qquad(28)$$

where $X = x$ represents the common output level of the top quality brand of every good j as well as aggregate output (recall that the measure of goods equals one). Lower quality products are neither manufactured nor consumed, and the owners of their technologies derive zero profits. An important thing to note at this stage is the resemblance of the pricing and profit equations (27)–(28) to the equivalent equations (8)–(9) for the case of horizontal product differentiation (with $1/\lambda$ replacing α). A significant difference from the point of view of the theory of the firm, however, is that now a firm does not maintain monopoly power forever but rather loses it and shuts down when a better variety of its goods appears on the market. Old products drop out; they are replaced with new brands.

Entrepreneurs have to target particular goods for improvement and they face a risky R&D technology. By employing $\iota(l, j)a$ workers per unit time in lab l that targets good j the lab attains a flow density of $\iota(l, j)$ per unit time of product improvement (as before, a represents a productivity parameter in R&D). An important feature of our R&D technology is that it is available to everybody, and it can improve the top of the line quality. This means that experience in the improvement of a particular good does not provide a lab with future advantages in the improvement of this good.

Whatever learning has taken place during the innovation process becomes public. This assumption introduces a spillover from private R&D to the society's stock of knowledge capital. And this contribution is not appropriable by the innovator.

It follows from this specification that the firm that owns the technology to manufacture the top quality brand of good j faces the hazard rate $\iota(j)$ of losing the monopoly profit stream, where $\iota(j)$ equals the aggregate across labs of $\iota(l, j)$. This hazard rate is the same for all goods in a symmetric equilibrium, and we denote it simply by ι. The stock market will value a firm according to its *expected* present value of profits, implying a no-arbitrage condition

$$\frac{\pi}{v} + \frac{\dot{v}}{v} = r + \iota. \tag{29}$$

Compared with (11) this condition describes the reality that a firm needs to add a risk premium ι to its cost of capital, reflecting the risk of displacement from the market.

An entrepreneur who contemplates investing in product improvement obtains the prize v if successful. In a time interval of length dt, his probability of success is $\iota(l, j)dt$ if he employs $\iota(l, j)a$ workers per unit time. The difference between his expected reward and costs equals $v\iota(l, j)dt - \iota(l, j)wadt$, and he chooses $\iota(l, j)$ so as to maximize this difference. It follows that in equilibrium the value of a firm cannot exceed wa, and it has to equal wa for innovation to take place (compare with (12)):

$$v \leqslant wa, \qquad \text{with equality whenever } \iota > 0. \tag{30}$$

It remains to identify the resource constraint. Workers are employed in research labs and in manufacturing plants. Employment in research labs equals $a\iota$ while employment in manufacturing plants equals X. Therefore, full employment requires (compare with (18))

$$a\iota + X = L. \tag{31}$$

This completes the description of the model. Our next task is to compare implications of quality ladder-based growth with expanding variety-based growth.

4.6 Quality Ladders vs Expanding Product Variety

We can characterize the steady state of the model with quality ladders by means of two equations, just as we have done for the expanding variety model. One equation consists of the resource constraint that was derived in the previous section, (31), whose analogy with the resource constraint (18) has already been pointed out. The second equation consists of a no-arbitrage condition, in parallel with (19). For the quality ladders model it takes the form[11]

$$\frac{(1 - \lambda^{-1})X}{\lambda^{-1}a} = \rho + \beta_Q \iota, \qquad \beta_Q = [1 + (v - 1)\log \lambda]. \tag{32}$$

This equation is indeed very similar to (19).

We may now use a figure similar to 3.1 to describe the resource constraint (31) and the no arbitrage condition (32) (where ι replaces g on the horizontal axis). From this figure we can derive the dependence of the long-run rate of innovation on an economy's parameters. In particular, we find again that the rate of innovation is larger the larger the economy's resource base, the higher its productivity in the lab, the lower its subjective rate of time preference, and the higher its degree of monopoly power. Observe, however, that the degree of monopoly power in the quality ladders model results from limit pricing rather than from monopoly pricing (the price elasticity of demand equals one). It is measured by λ, which determines the extent to which a manufacturer of the top quality can charge a price above his nearest rival. But the rival's price is driven to their common marginal manufacturing costs. Therefore, λ also describes the markup factor above marginal costs.

From (31) and (32) we can solve the equilibrium rate of innovation

$$\iota = \frac{\lambda}{\lambda + (v - 1)\log \lambda} \left[(1 - \lambda^{-1})\frac{L}{a} - \lambda^{-1}\rho \right]. \tag{33}$$

Comparing this equation with (20)—which describes the rate of innovation for the expanding variety model—we see that the terms in brackets are the same in both, with λ^{-1} playing the role of α. If the intertemporal elasticity of substitution in consumption equals one (i.e., $v = 1$), we obtain the remarkable result that there exist no further differences in these equations (see Grossman and Helpman 1991a). Since both λ and $1/\alpha$ describe degrees of monopoly power, it follows that these equations represent exactly the same economic content. When the elasticity of intertemporal substitution in consumption differs from one, however, they differ slightly but do retain the same economic implications concerning the qualitative effects of various parameters on the rate of innovation.

The above similarity is not accidental. Rather, the same economic mechanism sustains long-run growth in both models. Recall that expanding variety-based growth leads to declining profits per brand that are compensated by declining R&D costs. The latter results from the accumulation of knowledge capital. In the model of quality ladders, innovation adds quality. An innovator who improves a good that was improved m times in the past derives profits $(1 - \lambda^{-1})pX/\lambda^{m+1}$ per unit quality of his product (see (28)). It follows that profits per unit quality decline as more innovation takes place (given a constant price). At the same time innovation costs per unit quality decline at an equal pace, because innovation costs equal wa (see (30)) and the price is proportional to the wage rate. Here, as in the case of expanding product variety, there exists a spillover of knowledge from current to future innovators. An innovator who adds the $(m + 1)$th improvement builds on the knowledge that has been accumulated during the past m improvements. The only difference is that with quality ladders every good has its own stock of knowledge while with horizontal product differentiation the same stock of knowledge serves all brands.

The similarity of the models extends to investment in plant and equipment. Parallel to the analysis of capital accumulation by economies with expanding variety in section 4.4, we can develop an analysis of capital accumulation by quality-ladders-driven economies (see Grossman and Helpman 1991b, chap. 5).

Now consider the relationship between the rate of innovation and the rate of real output growth. With quality ladders the real consumption index C_Q provides a good measure of real output. Quality improvements increase this index over time. In a short time interval of length dt, innovators improve a proportion ιdt of the goods. Since consumed quantities are constant in steady state, this implies a real consumption increase $dC_Q = C_Q \iota (\log \lambda) dt$ in this time interval (see (24) and note 11). Therefore the rate of growth of real consumption equals $\iota \log \lambda$.

With Dixit-Stiglitz-type horizontal product differentiation a market economy always innovates too slowly. With quality ladders, on the other hand, it may innovate too slowly or too quickly (see Grossman and Helpman 1991a). This difference affects policy implications, to which I now turn.

4.7   Policy

Whenever economies feature endogenous long-run growth, we expect the growth rate to depend on economic policies. In these circumstances we need to understand how various measures affect the growth rate. This is the more so for economies with innovation-based growth of the type I have

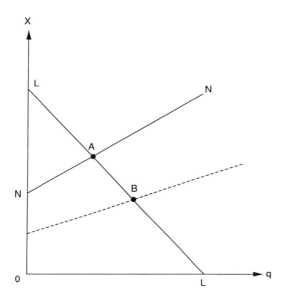

Figure 4.2

described, in which free markets may lead to growth that is either too slow or too fast, and in which growth is only one among several determinants of welfare.

Now let us consider industrial policies in the simple expanding-variety and quality-ladders-based growth models. For this purpose I use a common representation by means of figure 4.2, where q stands for the rate of innovation in both models. The downward sloping line LL represents the economy's resource constraint. The upward sloping line NN describes the no-arbitrage condition. Equilibrium obtains at the intersection point A. The equations behind these lines consist of the steady-state conditions (18)–(19) and (31)–(32):

$$aq + X = L, \tag{34}$$

$$\frac{(1 - \mu)X}{\mu a} = \rho + q\xi, \tag{35}$$

where in the case of expanding product variety q represents the rate of innovation g, $\mu = \alpha$, and $\xi = 1 + (1 - \alpha)(v - 1)/\alpha$, whereas in the case of quality ladders q represents the rate of innovation ι, $\mu = 1/\lambda$ and $\xi = 1 + (v - 1)\log \lambda$. In either case $1/\mu$ represents the markup factor of prices over marginal costs.

First consider a subsidy to R&D. This policy has no effect on the resource constraint. It reduces, however, the cost of innovation and thereby the value of a firm. As a result it reduces the price-earning ratio for a given volume of manufacturing. Therefore the volume of manufacturing has to decline in order to eliminate arbitrage opportunities. In terms of figure 4.2, the provision of an R&D subsidy shifts down NN to the broken line and the equilibrium point to B. It follows that an R&D subsidy raises the rates of innovation and growth. At the same time it contracts the manufacturing sector. The contraction of manufacturing represents the cost of faster innovation.

Is this a good policy? The answer depends on whether the initial rate of innovation was too low or too high. I have argued that expanding product variety leads to an outcome with insufficient innovation. Then a small R&D subsidy that brings about a resource reallocation from manufacturing to labs raises welfare.[12]

Contrary to expanding product variety, quality ladders can lead to either insufficient or excessive innovation. In the former case an R&D subsidy can be useful. In the latter case, however, an R&D subsidy speeds up innovation but hurts welfare. In the event a tax on innovation, which removes the overincentives on creative destruction, raises welfare.

An alternative industrial policy provides direct support to high-tech manufacturing in the form of an output subsidy. This policy does not affect the resource constraint. It also has no effect on the no-arbitrage condition. Therefore it does not change the rate of innovation and growth nor the volume of output (see Grossman and Helpman 1991a).

The ineffectiveness of this policy results from the simple structure of these economies: The existence of a single input and no employment outside the high-tech sector. I now show that if we extend the model to include an additional sector that manufactures traditional goods with constant returns to scale, then an output subsidy to high-tech manufacturing accelerates innovation and increases the output level of high-tech products. The expansion of the high-tech sector comes at the expense of the traditional sector, which contracts.

Suppose that in addition to the high-tech sector the economy manufactures a traditional good Z with a unit of labor per unit output. Perfect competition prevails in the supply of Z. Consumers allocate a fraction σ of their spending to high-tech products and a fraction $1 - \sigma$ to traditional goods. We replace the real consumption index C_D with $C_D^\sigma C_Z^{1-\sigma}$ in the case of horizontal product differentiation and C_Q with $C_Q^\sigma C_Z^{1-\sigma}$ in the case of quality ladders. Under these circumstances the no-arbitrage condition

(35) remains valid, except for the fact that now $\xi = 1 + \sigma(1 - \alpha)(v - 1)/\alpha$ for the expanding variety model and $\xi = 1 + \sigma(v - 1)\log\lambda$ for the model with quality ladders.

Three activities absorb resources: R&D, manufacturing of high-tech goods, and manufacturing of traditional goods. The resource constraint becomes $aq + X + Z = L$, where Z represents output of traditional goods. Consumer preferences imply that relative spending on high-tech goods equals $pX/p_Z Z = \sigma/(1 - \sigma)$ (because in equilibrium $pX = p_J C_J$, $J = D, Q$, and $C_Z = Z$). Commodities are priced according to $p = w/\mu$ and $p_Z = w$. Therefore in equilibrium the output level of traditional goods is proportional to the output level of high-tech goods; $Z = X\mu\sigma/(1 - \sigma)$. It follows that the resource constraint can be represented by

$$aq + \left[1 + \frac{1 + \sigma}{\mu\sigma}\right]X = L. \tag{36}$$

Now (35) and (36) can be used to represent equilibrium of both models with the aid of figure 4.3, which is similar to 4.2 except for the fact that the slopes of lines LL and NN depend on the share of spending on high-tech products. The simpler model represented in figure 4.2 is a special case with $\sigma = 1$.

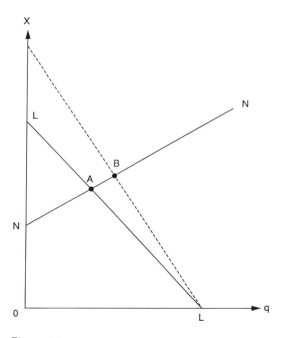

Figure 4.3

In order to see how the equilibrium rate of innovation depends on the composition of consumer spending, consider the case in which the elasticity of intertemporal substitution in consumption does not exceed one; that is, $v \geqslant 1$. In this case an increase in the expenditure share on high-tech products rotates the resource constraint line LL in a clockwise direction around its intersection with the horizontal axis, and the Schumpeter line NN rotates in a clockwise direction around its intersection with the vertical axis. The movement of each line raises the rate of innovation. We therefore conclude that economies with larger spending shares on high-tech products innovate faster.

The existence of a traditional good does not alter the long-run impact of an R&D subsidy. As before, an R&D subsidy does not affect the resource constraint but shifts down the Schumpeter line. Consequently it speeds up innovation and growth and reduces the volume of high-tech products. Since this policy does not affect relative manufacturing volumes X/Z, the traditional sector contracts. It follows that an R&D subsidy induces a resource reallocation from both manufacturing sectors towards research labs.

And what about an output subsidy to high-tech producers? As before, this policy does not affect the no-arbitrage condition. It changes, however, the resource constraint. Recall that $aq + X + Z = L$, $pX/p_z Z = \sigma/(1 - \sigma)$, and $p_z = w$. But with the output subsidy in place, $p = w/\mu(1 + \phi_x)$, where ϕ_x is the subsidy rate. Therefore the subsidy inclusive resource constraint becomes

$$aq + \left[1 \frac{1 - \sigma}{\mu\sigma(1 + \phi_x)}\right]X = L. \tag{37}$$

What this equation shows is that, given the output volume X, an increase in the subsidy reduces the relative price of high-tech products to consumers and thereby demand for traditional products. Consequently it reduces aggregate manufacturing employment. Evidently, an increase in the subsidy rotates clockwise line LL around its intersection point with the horizontal axis, as indicated by the broken line in figure 4.3. The equilibrium point shifts from A to B. We see that this time an output subsidy to high-tech products speeds up innovation and expands manufacturing of high-tech goods. The expansion of the high-tech sector comes at the expense of the traditional sector, which contracts.

Even this result is not robust, however. There exist reasonable economic structures in which a subsidy to high-tech manufacturing will actually reduce the rates of innovation and growth. To see how, suppose that in

addition to labor an economy employs human capital in all three activities
—manufacturing of high-tech goods, manufacturing of traditional goods,
and R&D—with constant input-output ratios. R&D uses the highest ratio
of human capital to labor and traditional manufacturing uses the lowest
ratio. Finally, the supply of human capital is constant. Under these circumstances an expansion of high-tech manufacturing leads to a contraction of
both the manufacturing of traditional goods and R&D, because the factor
intensity of high-tech manufacturing is intermediate between R&D and
traditional manufacturing. In the event an output subsidy to high-tech
products leads to an expansion of high-tech production but to a *slowdown
of innovation and a contraction of the traditional sector* (see Grossman and
Helpman 1991b, chap. 10). Thus, this modeling approach allows us to
investigate whether policies that would appear to promote growth actually
do so.

The two-factor, two-sector model that I outlined can also be used to shed
new light on the relationship between an economy's resource base and its
rate of innovation and growth (see Grossman and Helpman 1991a). Recall
that in the one-factor, one-sector economy the rates of innovation and
growth are higher the larger the economy's resource base. The same applies
to the two-sector, one-factor economy. In the presence of two factors,
however, a larger resource base does not guarantee faster innovation.
Given that the human capital-to-labor ratio is highest in R&D and lowest
in traditional manufacturing, economies with higher stocks of human capital
innovate faster. If in addition the elasticities of substitution in manufacturing exceed one, then economies with more labor also innovate more
quickly. But if instead the elasticities of substitution are low in all three
activities, *economies with more labor innovate more slowly* (see Grossman and
Helpman 1991b, chap. 5).[13] The general point that emerges from this
discussion is that inputs that are used intensively in R&D are conducive to
innovation and growth; inputs that are used intensively in the manufacturing of traditional goods may discourage innovation and growth.

4.8   Further Considerations

My description of the macroeconomic theory of endogenous growth has
been incomplete; it did not cover all existing approaches nor did it deal with
all the issues that have been treated in the literature. Admittedly, my
choices exhibit a large dose of subjectivity. This type of bias is, however,
unavoidable, and I did not intend to survey the literature. I focused my
presentation on one important class of mechanisms that sustain long-run

growth, a small number of models that employ them, and a limited number of issues that demonstrate the usefulness of viewing economic growth in this particular way. In these closing comments I do not wish to take a position on the important issue of which model is best. As a rule I believe in pluralism. We gain much insight by dealing with economic problems from a variety of perspectives. This is the more so for a major problem of the type considered in this paper. For this reason I limit the remaining remarks to a number of issues that were not treated so far, but which I feel deserve special mention.

Real Interest and Growth Rates

The models discussed have the unfortunate implication that, given taste parameters, the real rate of interest increases with the growth rate, although the evidence does not support this relationship (see Barro and Sala-i-Martin 1990). Does this fact destroy the usefulness of these models? I think it does not. The models were designed to study supply-side mechanisms of economic growth that build on the accumulation of physical capital, the accumulation of knowledge capital, and innovation. For this reason they treat consumption in a simple way. Elaborations that allow for different determinants of consumption can break this link without diminishing the role of the supply-side mechanisms in the growth process. One way to proceed would be to replace the time separable preference structure with a nonseparable form of the type studied by Weil (1990) and Epstein and Zin (1989).

An alternative route to the same end would be to use an overlapping generations economy populated by consumers with finite lifetimes. The latter approach has been explored by a number of authors. Using Yaari-Blanchard type consumers and a neoclassical technology that exhibits learning-by-doing in capital accumulation, Alogoskoufis and van der Ploeg (1990) constructed a model in which the rate of long-run growth depends on fiscal variables although the real interest does not. It follows that countries that pursue different fiscal policies may experience different long-run growth rates and nevertheless share the same real interest rate. They show that, other things being equal, countries that maintain a higher public debt-to-output ratio grow slower, because consumers consider government debt to be net wealth and therefore save less in high public debt countries. In the event real interest rates and growth rates are not positively correlated.

Fluctuations

Innovation-based growth can proceed smoothly or in bursts. We have seen two models in which it proceeds smoothly. Of particular interest on this issue is the model of quality ladders. There every good is improved after an irregular interval of time has elapsed. Because there exists a large number of such goods, however, the proportion of goods improved in a given time interval remains constant in the steady state. For this reason the rate of growth of the macroeconomy remains constant as well (out of steady state this rate changes smoothly). Naturally, the smooth pace of progress of the macroeconomy masks substantial turmoil at the industry level.

One may argue that there exist important innovations that are not limited to a particular product, but rather have broad applications, such as general-purpose technologies discussed by Bresnahan and Trajtenberg (1990). In the event a successful innovation leads to a step increase in real output. If such drastic innovations occur infrequently and at irregular intervals of time, the economy exhibits irregular bursts of growth. Then the growth rate exhibits substantial variability even when its mean remains constant.

A model of this nature was analyzed by Aghion and Howitt (1990). In their model output experiences positive shocks at irregular intervals of time and the logarithm of output follows a random walk.

Unemployment

Innovation-based growth entails a constant reallocation of labor. In the presence of horizontal product differentiation, manufacturers of new brands employ labor that has been released by contracting old product lines. In the presence of quality ladders, manufacturers of new products employ labor that has been released by old product lines that shut down, as superior new goods replace lower quality old products. My presentation assumed full employment, implying that these labor shifts take place instantly and without friction. This assumption is obviously extreme, and one expects some frictional unemployment in a reallocation process of this magnitude. This is the more so when labor is heterogeneous and the skill composition of new hires does not necessarily match the skill composition of displaced workers. In short, innovation-driven growth may not be as painless as assumed in our models. In the event one wonders whether growth that generates new jobs on the one hand and destroys jobs on the other raises or reduces the rate of unemployment.

This question has been addressed by Aghion and Howitt (1991). The answer proves to be involved. In particular, the effect of faster innovation and growth on the rate of unemployment depends on the factors that speed up innovation.

International Trade

Economic growth of countries depends on a variety of structural features and government policies. Since my discussion was confined to isolated economies, the structural features and policies that I considered were also confined to isolated economies. Economies are, however, linked with each other by means of international trade, capital flows, imitation of cultural traits, and the transfer of ideas and scientific discoveries. Does this openness affect the growth opportunities of nations? And are the growth processes of open economies interdependent? The answers to both questions are in the affirmative. A recent book-length treatment of innovation and growth in open economies has been provided by Grossman and Helpman (1991b), and I could not possibly deal with this subject in a satisfactory way in the framework of this chapter that has been confined to macroeconomic theory. I therefore provide only brief comments on some open-economy issues that have been investigated.

The integration of a nation into a world-trading system unleashes powerful forces that speed up growth, but it also unleashes forces that are harmful to growth. The former dominate, however, when countries do not differ too much in terms of resource composition, and knowledge flows freely across national borders. The extent to which the accumulation of knowledge capital is country specific or international in scope also plays an important role in the determination of trade patterns and growth differentials across countries. Internationalization of knowledge leads to long-run trade patterns and GDP growth rates that are governed by traditional forces, such as differences in factor composition. In the event initial differences in comparative advantage that result from historical experiences do not affect long-term outcomes. When knowledge accumulation is localized, however, history can extract powerful effects on the evolution of trade patterns and growth rates. Under these circumstances small initial differences in knowledge capital can translate into large long-run differences in sectoral structures, trade patterns, and growth rates.

In open economies trade policies affect innovation and growth. They influence not only the policy-active country but also its trade partners. Other policy measures, such as R&D or output subsidies, spread their influence across national borders and alter the rates of innovation and growth of trade partners.

R&D need not be directed to the invention of new goods or production processes. Less-developed countries invest substantial resources in learning to operate technologies that were originally developed in advanced economies. This process of imitation by the South affects the incentive to innovate in the North, and vice versa. The rate of innovation is jointly determined with the rate of imitation by more fundamental ingredients, and this interdependence can be quite involved.

I have outlined a new approach to economic growth. The emerging theory complements Solow's contribution in explaining technical progress. It provides a richer structure with realistic new attributes, and it is capable of dealing with a variety of new issues. Although there exist a fair number of new empirical studies, some supporting Solow and others supporting the new theory, it is fair to say that at this stage the data do not distinguish sharply enough between the alternatives. This has partly to do with the fact that the neoclassical theory and the new one are complements rather than substitutes, and partly because the existing tests are not powerful enough. We will undoubtedly see much more work on this subject in the coming years.

Notes

This paper was prepared as the Joseph Schumpeter Lecture for the Sixth Annual Congress of the European Economic Association. It is reproduced with permission from the *European Economic Review*, Vol. 36, Spring 1992. My views on the subject of endogenous growth have been profoundly influenced by Gene Grossman, whom I thank for a memorable four years of collaboration and intellectual excitement. Traces of his influence appear on every page of this paper. I also thank the National Science Foundation and the U.S.-Israel Binational Science Foundation for financial support, and Gene Grossman and Torsten Persson for comments on an earlier draft. Part of the work for this paper was done when I was a visiting scholar in the research department of the International Monetary Fund.

1. Empirical studies of productivity have used knowledge capital variables that are based on cumulative R&D expenditure long before their use in the theoretical models; see Griliches 1979.

2. This insight has been exploited in a number of recent studies, such as Rebelo (1991) and Jones and Manuelli (1990a).

3. From these two conditions together with (8) and (9) we calculate the equilibrium number of brands $n = (1 - \alpha)L/f$ and the output level $X = \alpha L$.

4. Since all brands are equally priced, they are used in the same quantities. In the event (7) implies $D = n^{(1-\alpha)/\alpha}X$ and the rate of growth of D equals $((1 - \alpha)/\alpha)g + \dot{X}/X$.

5. The first equation is a direct consequence of the resource constraint (13). The second results from the no-arbitrage condition (11) in the following way. Take the wage rate to be the numeraire; that is, $w(t) = 1$ for all t. Then from the pricing equation (8) $p = 1/\alpha$, a constant, and output per brand equals for all brands (although it may vary over time). It follows from (7) that $\dot{D}/D = (1 - \alpha)g/\alpha$ (because X is constant) and from (16) that $\dot{p}_D/p_D = -(1 - \alpha)g/\alpha$. The consumer's intertemporal allocation rule (15) implies then an interest rate

$$r = \rho + g\frac{1 - \alpha}{\alpha}(v - 1).$$

Assuming positive product innovation (see the discussion that follows in the text), the free-entry condition (12) implies $v = a/n$ and $\dot{v}/v = -g$. Substituting these results together with the profit equation (9) into the no-arbitrage condition (11) yields (19).

6. This result will be qualified later on.

7. When the proposed parameter restriction does not hold, line NN in figure 4.1 lies everywhere above LL in the positive orthand. In this case the intersection point of LL with the vertical axis represents the equilibrium. At this point the present value of profits falls short of R&D costs. In the event entrepreneurs have no incentive to innovate. There also exists a restriction on parameters that prevents innovation from proceeding at a pace that is so rapid as to make the utility level in (3) unbounded. Since D grows at the rate $g(1 - \alpha)/\alpha$, the functional forms in (3) and (14) imply $\rho > g(1 - v)(1 - \alpha)/\alpha$ for that condition to hold. Substituting (20) into this inequality yields a restriction on the economy's parameters. Observe, however, that the inequality is satisfied whenever the intertemporal elasticity of substitution is smaller than one; that is, $v \geqslant 1$.

8. The last point can be seen as follows. It can be shown by means of optimal control or variational methods that the optimal rate of innovation remains constant over time. In this case we can compute consumer welfare from (3) and (14) as

$$U_t = \frac{1}{1 - v}\left[\frac{n(t)^{(1-v)(1-\alpha)/\alpha}X^{1-v}}{\rho - (1 - v)(1 - \alpha)g/\alpha} - \frac{1}{\rho}\right].$$

Maximizing this expression with respect to g and X subject to the resource constraint (18) yields the optimal rate of innovation. The equilibrium rate of innovation (20) is a fraction $(1 - \alpha)v/[\alpha + (1 - \alpha)v]$ of the optimal rate of innovation.

9. My description follows Grossman and Helpman (1991b, chap. 5). For an alternative view see Romer (1990a).

10. These calculations assume that (3)–(4) describe preferences.

11. In steady state ι remains constant and so does the volume of output X (which also equals output per product of the highest quality x because the measure of

goods equals one). Take the wage rate to be the numeraire. Then $p = \lambda$ and $\pi = (1 - \lambda^{-1})\lambda X$ (see (27) and (28)). Suppose also that $\iota > 0$. Then $v = a$ (see (30)) and $\dot{v}/v = 0$. It follows that the no-arbitrage condition (29) can be written as

$$\frac{(1 - \lambda^{-1})X}{\lambda^{-1}a} = r + \iota. \tag{i}$$

It remains to derive the interest rate by means of (24)–(26). In (24) $\log X(j) = \log X + \tilde{m}(j)\log \lambda$, where $\tilde{m}(j)$ represents the number of times good j has been improved (because the top quality product provides the lowest quality adjusted price). Since all goods are equally targeted, the arrival of improvements follows a Poisson process with the arrival probability ι per unit time. In the event

$$\int_0^1 \tilde{m}(j)dj = \iota t \log \lambda$$

in a time interval of length t. Therefore $\dot{C}_Q/C_Q = \iota \log \lambda$. A similar argument establishes that $\dot{p}_Q/p_Q = -\iota \log \lambda$. Substituting these results into (26) we obtain

$$r = \rho + (v - 1)\iota \log \lambda.$$

Finally, substituting this interest rate into the no-arbitrage equation (i) above we obtain (32).

12. The optimal rate of subsidy can be calculated by means of the welfare measure developed in note 8 (see also Grossman and Helpman 1991a). Additional complications arise when the differentiated products are capital goods; see Barro and Sala-i-Martin (1990).

13. Romer (1990b) presents a two-factor, one-sector example in which an expansion of labor, in which manufacturing is relatively intensive, reduces the rate of innovation and growth.

References

Aghion, Philippe and Howitt, Peter. 1990. "A Model of Growth Through Creative Destruction," NBER Working Paper No. 3223.

Aghion, Philippe and Howitt, Peter. 1991. "Growth and Unemployment," Mimeo.

Alogoskoufis, George S. 1990. "On Budgetary Policies and Economic Growth." CEPR Discussion Paper No. 496.

Arrow, Kenneth J. (1962a), "The Economic Implications of Learning by Doing." *Review of Economic Studies* 29: 155–173.

Arrow, Kenneth J. 1962b. "Economic Welfare and the Allocation of Resources for Inventions," in Nelson, Richard R., *The Rate and Direction of Inventive Activity*. Princeton: Princeton University Press for the NBER.

Barro, Robert J. 1991. "Economic Growth in a Cross Section of Countries," *Quarterly Journal of Economics* 106: 407–444.

Barro, Robert J. and Sala-i-Martin, X. 1990. "Public Finance in Models of Economic Growth," NBER Working Paper No. 3362 (forthcoming in the *Review of Economic Studies*).

Boldrin, Michele. 1990. "Dynamic Externalities, Multiple Equilibria and Growth." Santa Fe Institute, Economics Research Program.

Bresnahan, Timothy and Trajtenberg, Manuel. 1990. "General Purpose Technologies and Economic Growth." Mimeo.

Dixit, Avinash and Stiglitz, Joseph E. 1977. "Monopolistic Competition and Optimum Product Diversity." *American Economic Review* 67:297–308.

Domar, Evsey D. 1946. "Capital Expansion, Rate of Growth, and Employment." *Econometrica* 14:137–147.

Epstein, Larry G. and Zin, Stanley E. 1989. "Substitution, Risk Aversion and the Temporal Behavior of Consumption and Asset Returns: A Theoretical Framework." *Econometrica* 57:937–969.

Griliches, Zvi. 1979. "Issues in Assessing the Contribution of Research and Development in Productivity Growth." *Bell Journal of Economics* 10:92–116.

Grossman, Gene M. and Helpman, Elhanan. 1991a. "Quality Ladders in the Theory of Growth." *Review of Economic Studies* 58:43–61.

Grossman, Gene M. and Helpman, Elhanan. 1991b. *Innovation and Growth in the Global Economy*. Cambridge, MA: MIT Press.

Harrod, Roy F. 1939. "An Essay in Dynamic Theory." *Economic Journal* 49:14–33.

Jones, Larry E. and Manuelli, Rodolfo. 1990a. "A Convex Model of Equilibrium Growth." *Journal of Political Economy* 98:1008–1038.

Jones, Larry E. and Manuelli, Rodolfo. 1990b. "Finite Lifetimes and Growth." NBER Working Paper No. 3469.

Judd, Kenneth L. 1985. "On the Performance of Patents." *Econometrica* 53:567–586.

Lerner, Abba P. 1934. "The Concept of Monopoly and the Measure of Monopoly Power." *Review of Economic Studies* 1:157–175.

Lucas, Robert E. Jr. 1988. "On the Mechanics of Economic Development," *Journal of Monetary Economics* 22:3–42.

Maddison, Angus. 1987. "Growth and Slowdown in Advanced Capitalist Economies." *Journal of Economic Literature* 25:649–698.

Mansfield, Edwin, Rapoport, J., Romeo, A., Wagner, S., and Beardsley, G. 1977. "Social and Private Rates of Return from Industrial Innovation." *Quarterly Journal of Economics* 91:221–240.

OECD (1989), *OECD Science and Technology Indicators No. 3: R&D, Production and Diffusion of Technology*. Paris: Organization for Economic Cooperation and Development.

Ramsey, Frank P. 1928. "A Mathematical Theory of Savings." *The Economic Journal* 38:543–559.

Rebelo, Sergio. 1991. "Long Run Policy Analysis and Long Run Growth." *Journal of Political Economy* 99:500–521.

Romer, Paul M. 1986. "Increasing Returns and Long-Run Growth." *Journal of Political Economy* 94:1002–1037.

Romer, Paul M. 1990a. "Endogenous Technological Change." *Journal of Political Economy* 98:S71–S102.

Romer, Paul M. 1990b. "Capital, Labor, and Productivity." *Brookings Papers on Economic Activity* (Microeconomics), pp. 337–367.

Scherer, F. M. 1982. "Interindustry Technology Flows and Productivity Growth." *Review of Economics and Statistics* 64:627–634.

Schumpeter, Joseph. 1942 *Capitalism, Socialism, and Democracy*. New York: Harper.

Sheshinski, Eitan 1967. "Optimal Accumulation with Learning by Doing." in Shell, Karl (ed.), *Essays on the Theory of Optimal Economic Growth*. Cambridge MA: MIT Press.

Solow, Robert M. 1956. "A Contribution to the Theory of Economic Growth." *Quarterly Journal of Economics* 70:65–94.

Solow, Robert M. 1957. "Technical Change and the Aggregate Production Function." *Review of Economics and Statistics* 39:312–320.

Uzawa, Hirofumi. 1965. "Optimal Technical Change in an Aggregative Model of Economic Growth." *International Economic Review* 6:18031.

Weil, Philippe. 1990. "Nonexpected Utility in Macroeconomics." *Quarterly Journal of Economics* 105:29–42.

5   The Case for External Economies

Ricardo J. Caballero and Richard K. Lyons

In this chapter we provide an overview of our previous empirical work on external economies in manufacturing.[1] By looking at these articles in conjunction, we are able to broaden the interpretation and implications of the main results. At the same time, this permits us to address competing interpretations of our findings more comprehensively.

The chapter has three building blocks. The first one reviews our previous results and describes the basic methodology. To the best of our means, we establish six basic facts: (i) there are social *increasing* returns to scale (U.S. and European manufacturing), (ii) there are constant returns to scale at two-digit (U.S. and Europe) and four-digit (U.S.) levels, (iii) results (i) and (ii) are made consistent by the presence of an externality that has most of its impact between the two-digit and the aggregate level, (iv) in the short run, the externality is primarily driven by the relation between industries and their customers, while (v) in the long run, the main transmission channel is the relation between industries and their suppliers, (vi) there is also preliminary evidence on the transmission of externalities across countries' borders.

The second block describes the main alternative explanations of our findings and shows how none of these can account for the full range of results described in the first part of the chapter. If there are short-run internal increasing returns at the firm level, we find that these have disappeared by the four-digit level, thus social increasing returns require spillovers at a fairly aggregate level; to a lesser extent, the same is true in the long run. Labor hoarding competes only with the short-run findings. Moreover, we argue that in its conventional form labor hoarding competes with internal returns not external economies. Finally, technology shocks or real business cycle theories are dealt with by alternative procedures, from the use of demand instruments to the use of time dummies. On top of this, it remains difficult to reconcile real business cycle theories with the fact that it is the customers' activity level as opposed to the suppliers' that matters in the short run; in the end, we conclude that technology shocks and externalities are complements rather than substitutes.

In the final block we establish the links between our work and several different domains, some of which have only recently stressed external effects and their implications (e.g., economic fluctuations) and some of which have recognized an important role for many years (e.g., international trade). We try to determine the specific interpretation and implications of our results in the context of these areas of research.

The remainder of this chapter is divided into four sections: the next three address the issues of the different blocks in order (framework and results, alternative explanations, and literature links), and the last section concludes.

5.1   The General Framework and Results

To motivate our framework, consider as a starting point the general value-added equation previously emphasized by Hall (1990) that relates growth (log change) in value-added output to a cost-weighted input measure and a residual:

$$y = \phi[\alpha_c l + (1 - \alpha_c)k] + w,$$

where y is the rate of growth of manufacturing value added, α_c is the share of labor in total factor costs, l is the growth in labor input, k is the growth in capital input, and w is the rate of technological progress. Letting $x \equiv [\alpha_c l + (1 - \alpha_c)k]$, we can rewrite the previous equation as:

$$y = \phi x + w. \tag{1}$$

The first objective is to estimate ϕ, the coefficient of returns to scale of the aggregate technology. This parameter is crucial for many important issues, ranging from the number of equilibria an economy has to the potential gains from removing barriers to trade. The second objective— where our contribution starts—is to disentangle the components of ϕ. For further discussion, see section 5.3.

If there were no externalities and technologies were similar across firms, then there is nothing to disentangle and ϕ represents the returns-to-scale parameter at the firm level. On the other hand, if externalities at lower levels of aggregation exist, then ϕ "internalizes" them. To see this, let i be a manufacturing two-digit index (variables without the subindex i correspond to aggregate manufacturing). Let us write a value-added function for sector

i similar to equation (1) except for the presence of a canonical externality:

$$y_i = \gamma x_i + \beta y + v_i. \tag{2}$$

It is clear that one can go from equation (2) to equation (1) by summing over all industries i, so:

$$\phi \equiv \frac{\gamma}{1 - \beta} \qquad w = \frac{1}{1 - \beta} v.$$

The externality builds a gap between returns to scale at the two-digit level and aggregate returns to scale. It also magnifies the effect of technology shocks. We postpone the discussion of the second effect until section 5.3. The first effect, on the other hand, is the basis of the next subsection, where we juggle two-digit and aggregate data simultaneously to quantify the externality properly.

Of course, the canonical externality is just a proxy for more complex forms of interactions across different sectors of the economy. Moreover, it is not unlikely that γ already internalizes externalities operative at even lower levels of aggregation. In general, one can write the value-added equation as:

$$y_j = \gamma x_j + \kappa a_j + u_j, \tag{3}$$

where j is an industry at any level of aggregation one may want and a_j is a measure corresponding to the externality (possibly a vector) relevant for that industry.

Though the specification in (3) leaves the connections between internal returns at different aggregation levels unclear, it is well designed for identifying the nature of the externalities involved. This is what we do in section 5.1.2. In particular, we let j be an index of four-digit industries, and the externality index considers different forms of interrelations across sectors based on input-output information.

One would like to distinguish not only between the different channels through which externalities are transmitted but also the frequency at which they are operative. While one can question whether there is much power in the available data to trace the full dynamic path of the different externalities, here we identify the short-run effects by looking at the contemporaneous relations across sectors over the whole time series; to identify the long-run relation, on the other hand, we look at the average relation between sectors (over the entire sample).

To see this, it is convenient to introduce the time subindex in equation (3) and write the model in terms of mean deviations. Using tildes to denote deviations from an industry's mean and the corresponding parameters yields:

$$\tilde{y}_{jt} = \tilde{\gamma}\tilde{x}_{jt} + \tilde{\kappa}\tilde{a}_{jt} + \tilde{u}_{jt}. \tag{4}$$

As noted, we identify this equation with the short run. We use the complement, that is, the industry means, to identify the long-run relationship. Bars denote means:

$$\bar{y}_j = \tilde{\gamma}\bar{x}_j + \tilde{\kappa}\bar{a}_j + \bar{u}_j. \tag{5}$$

The reader may have noticed that a simple regression of equation (4) yields the *within* or *fixed effects* estimator of panel data. A regression of (5), on the other hand, yields the *between* estimator of panel data. In conventional panel data, both are constrained to be the same. By relaxing this constraint we allow for different short- and long-run responses without explicitly modeling the dynamics.[2]

5.1.1   Increasing Social Returns and Macro-Level Externalities

In Caballero and Lyons (1989) we study equations of type (1) and (2) for U.S. manufacturing, expanded to correct for possible structural changes due to the oil shocks. We also notice that at the two-digit level there is too little power in the between dimension of the data, so we only estimate short-run relationships.[3]

We proceed by estimating the aggregate equation (where we avoid the time subindex):

$$\tilde{y} = \tilde{\phi}\tilde{x} + \rho_1 \tilde{p}, \tag{1'}$$

and the system (for all i) of equations:

$$\tilde{y}_i = \tilde{\gamma}\tilde{x}_i + \tilde{\beta}\tilde{y} + \rho_2 \tilde{p}_i, \tag{2'}$$

where p_i is the growth rate of the price of oil relative to sector i's value-added deflator, and ρ_1 and ρ_2 are free parameters.

It is also informative to estimate a system equivalent to (2') but under the assumption that there are no externalities:

$$\tilde{y}_i = \tilde{\theta}\tilde{x}_i + \rho_3 \tilde{p}_i. \tag{6}$$

Simple algebra shows that:

$$\text{plim } \bar{\theta} = \phi(1 - \beta(1 - \psi)) = \gamma[1 + \beta\psi/(1 - \beta)],$$

Table 5.1
Macro-level results

	1	2	3
$\tilde{\phi}$	1.33		
	(0.07)		
$\tilde{\theta}$		1.15	
		(0.06)	
ψ		0.90	
$\tilde{\gamma}$			0.98
			(0.05)
External $\tilde{\beta}$			0.18
			(0.04)
Oil Price ρ	−0.10	−0.11	−0.09
	(0.02)	(0.02)	(0.01)

Column (1): $\tilde{y} = \tilde{\phi}\tilde{x} + \rho\tilde{p}$. Column (2): $\tilde{y}_i = \tilde{\theta}\tilde{x}_i + \rho\tilde{p}_i$. Column (3): $\tilde{y}_i = \tilde{\gamma}\tilde{x}_i + \tilde{\beta}\tilde{y} + \rho\tilde{p}_i$. Standard errors in parentheses.

where ψ is a coefficient between 0 and 1, related to the correlation between x_i and x (see Caballero and Lyons 1989). The importance of this probability limit is that one clear implication of the presence of externalities is:

$$\tilde{\phi} > \tilde{\theta} > \tilde{\gamma}.$$

Table 5.1 summarizes the results, all of them obtained with instrumental variables and three-stage least squares (IV and 3SLS).[4]

Column 1 of table 5.1 presents the results for equation (1') at the level of aggregate manufacturing. The estimate suggests the presence of significant aggregate increasing returns.[5] As mentioned, however, from the estimate of $\tilde{\phi}$ alone it is not clear whether external effects are present.

The oil price coefficient, denoted by ρ here, is significant and negative, as expected. Interestingly, if the oil price is excluded from the regressors $\tilde{\phi}$ rises to 1.52, indicating the considerable effects of the oil shocks on measured total factor productivity.[6]

Column 2 of table 5.1 reports the results under the assumption that no external effects are present (equation (6)). The estimate of $\tilde{\theta}$ is slightly smaller than the aggregate elasticity $\tilde{\phi}$ from column 1. The third row shows that the estimate of ψ is below one; thus, in the limit one would expect the estimate of $\tilde{\theta}$ to be smaller than that of $\tilde{\phi}$ if external economies are present, which is consistent with the results reported in table 5.1.

Column 3 presents the results for equation (2'), which relaxes the assumption that no external effects are present. The externality term, denoted $\tilde{\beta}$ is significant and positive. Its magnitude, about 0.2, implies that when other manufacturing industries expand their output by, say, 10 percent, a given industry's factor productivity is raised by about 2 percent. The estimate of $\bar{\gamma}$ is very close to unity. Moreover, it is also smaller than $\bar{\phi}$ and $\bar{\theta}$ from columns 1 and 2, as suggested by the model in the presence of external economies.

Roughly, the parameter $\bar{\gamma}$ reported here should be interpreted as the *average* short-run response of value added to an increase in inputs when an industry expands in isolation; $\bar{\theta}$ represents the *average* response of value added to an increase in inputs when an industry expands, taking into account the likelihood of other industries expanding simultaneously; finally, $\bar{\phi}$ represents the *average* response of value added to an increase in inputs when all industries expand in lockstep.

Hence, we find that in an *average* sense, constant returns to scale is an accurate description of manufacturing at the two-digit level. In contrast, at the aggregate level an external economy is internalized, which lifts the aggregate returns-to-scale index above one. According to our estimates, if all manufacturing industries simultaneously raise their inputs by 10 percent (given the relative price of oil), aggregate manufacturing value added rises by 13 percent, of which about 3 percent is due to external economies. Hence, when an industry increases its inputs in isolation by 10 percent, its value added rises only by about 10 percent. Of course, isolated versus across-the-board input changes are unrealistic polar extremes.

The above results are robust to estimation in other industrialized countries. In Caballero and Lyons (1990) we apply the same basic methodology to European manufacturing at the NACE two-digit level. The bottom line there is very similar to that in the United States: The external economies coefficients ($\bar{\beta}$'s) for the four countries covered by the study (West Germany, France, the United Kingdom, and Belgium) are all very significant. In the country for which we had the most reliable data, West Germany, our estimate of $\bar{\beta}$ was in the same range (0.26). Additionally, as in the United States, there is very little evidence of internal increasing returns in Europe, though there is strong support for the presence of *increasing social returns*.

5.1.2   Transmission Mechanisms Over the Short and Long-Run

In this section we summarize the basic results in Bartelsman, Caballero, and Lyons (1991). These narrow down the possible transmission channels behind the findings described in the previous section. They also provide insights on externalities operating over the long haul. As noted, there are two basic systems of equations behind our approach:

$$\tilde{y}_{jt} = \tilde{\gamma}\tilde{x}_{jt} + \tilde{\kappa}\tilde{a}_{jt} + \tilde{u}_{jt},\tag{4}$$

$$\bar{y}_i = \bar{v}\bar{x}_j + \bar{\kappa}\bar{a}_{jt} + \bar{u}_{jt}.\tag{5}$$

Since $\tilde{y}_{jt}$ is orthogonal to $\bar{y}_j$ by construction, and the same is true for the regressors and residuals, one can also estimate both sets of parameters in a single regression (system) of the form:

$$y_{jt} = \tilde{\gamma}\tilde{x}_{jt} + \bar{\gamma}\bar{x}_j + \tilde{\kappa}\tilde{a}_{jt} + \bar{\kappa}\bar{a}_j + u_{jt}.\tag{7}$$

This equation, estimated using a panel of four-digit U.S. manufacturing industries, provides the main results.

Broadly speaking, our approach is to consider different variables (or sets of variables) as proxies for the best index of aggregate activity affecting productivity growth at the four-digit level. In Bartelsman, Caballero, and Lyons (1991) we consider many alternatives. We first show that once one corrects for input-output relationships there is no evidence of externalities operative between the two- and four-digit levels. We then use input-output relations to consider the linkages across industries more explicitly. For example, if the externalities are working through the intermediate goods channel, then it would be more appropriate to weight the aggregate activity variable for each industry according to the share of materials *received* from other industries, rather than the simple aggregate. In contrast, if the externality derives from aggregate demand, then weighting the aggregate activity variable according to where output is *going* is more appropriate.

Table 5.2 presents our basic findings from estimation of equation (7) with the constraint $\tilde{\gamma} = \bar{\gamma}$ imposed.[7] Column 1 corresponds to both the within and between results for manufacturing for the case where externalities come only from manufacturing sectors. The second column is similar to the first one but contains one dummy for each year with the purpose of removing the average (across sectors) impact of aggregate shocks. Regardless of whether the dummies are included, both of the short-run (input-weighted and output-weighted) externalities appear significant (rows three and four). Inclusion of the dummies lowers the short-run output-weighted externality, but it remains large and significant.[8]

In contrast to the short-run externalities, over the longer run only the input-weighted aggregate is significant. Hence, these between results suggest that over longer horizons external effects are operating through intermediate goods linkages.

If transactions per se, demand, or both play a major role in boosting industry productivity, there is no reason, besides data availability, to close

Table 5.2
Summary table, mixed within-between estimates

	Manuf. VA		Expanded VA		Expan. Gr. Prod.	
	No T.D.	T.D.	No T.D.	T.D.	No T.D.	T.D.
Const	.013	.021	.010	.018	−.001	.014
	(.002)	(.006)	(.003)	(.006)	(.002)	(.004)
γ	1.009	1.013	1.016	1.016	1.096	1.096
	(.015)	(.015)	(.015)	(.015)	(.007)	(.007)
$\tilde{\kappa}^{IN}$	.139	.156	.026	−.002	.034	.019
	(.040)	(.050)	(.054)	(.066)	(.023)	(.029)
$\tilde{\kappa}^{OW}$	.358	.270	.562	.431	.186	.118
	(.035)	(.037)	(.044)	(.049)	(.022)	(.023)
$\bar{\kappa}^{IN}$	.327	.326	.266	.267	.281	.281
	(.119)	(.117)	(.158)	(.156)	(.101)	(.100)
$\bar{\kappa}^{OW}$	−.134	−.136	−.008	−.008	.070	.070
	(.104)	(.103)	(.116)	(.114)	(.078)	(.077)
$\bar{R}^2$	.38	.40	.39	.40	.76	.76

Notes: Standard errors in parentheses. The superscripts *IW* and *OW* denote input- and output-weighted, respectively. The expanded sector includes activity of the nonmanufacturing sector as providing externalities to the manufacturing sector. The gross production columns use an aggregate activity measure using capital, labor, and materials inputs. No T.D.: without time dummies. T.D.: with time dummies.

the model in manufacturing. In the next two columns of table 5.2 we "expand" the model to include in our weightings the activity levels of nonmanufacturing suppliers and customers in the business sector.

The striking result here is that the row 3 estimates suggest that once the customer weights are fully specified, the input-weighted component of the short-run externality vanishes. Together with row 4, it appears that short-run effects are tied wholly to the activity levels of the sectors an industry supplies, regardless of whether those sectors are principally within manufacturing, such as finished goods, or are principally outside manufacturing, such as construction or transportation. Further, these rows suggest that there is no evidence for the existence of fluctuations-oriented external effects deriving from either specialization of intermediate goods or from inbound transactions. Both of these channels would imply some effect coming from the input-weighted aggregates, yet we find none in the context of our expanded model.

The debate about the virtues and shortcomings of value-added models is an old one.[9] In the last two columns of table 5.2 we reproduce our (expanded) results using gross production instead of value added in order to check whether there is any sensitivity along these lines. These columns demonstrate that the externalities, output-weighted in the short run and input-weighted in the longer run, remain highly significant and positive. It is also apparent, however, that some of the weight moves away from the externality to the own inputs coefficient; we suspect that this is an artifact of the way we construct our expanded gross-production external activity measures (see Bartelsman, Caballero, and Lyons 1991).

5.2 "Competing" Hypotheses and Robustness

5.2.1 "Competing" Hypotheses

In our previous work we have encountered three main alternative hypotheses: internal increasing returns, real business cycle theories, and labor hoarding (together with capacity underutilization). Since the latter, as externalities, is an evasive concept, we devote most of this section to showing why conventional labor hoarding is an imperfect substitute for the externalities we propose.

5.2.1.1 Labor Hoarding

We view the labor-hoarding criticism to externalities as rather clouded. The first question one should ask is which aspects of the facts we document are potentially accountable by conventional labor hoarding. We provide a simple model to define this alternative more properly.

Under the conventional labor-hoarding argument, though l is the growth rate of effective labor, the econometrician observes only l^m, the rate of growth of measured hours. Of course the same applies to capital, so we use x_i and x_i^m to denote effective and measured factor growth, respectively. These two quantities are related at all points in time by:

$$x_{it} = x_{it}^m + f_{it},\tag{8}$$

where f is (tautologically) the growth rate of per-factor effort. Conventional hoarding stories relate factor utilization, or effort, to sector i's activity level, which corresponds to the following specification:

$$f_{it} = \mu(y_{it} - g_i),\tag{9}$$

where μ is a positive constant and g_i is some sector-specific constant such that $b_i \equiv E[y_{it} - g_i]$ is sector i's long-run rate of hoarding growth.

We combine equations (8) and (9) with equation (2), yielding:

$$y_{it} = \gamma x_{it} + \mu\gamma(y_{it} - g_i) + \beta y_t + v'_{it},\tag{10}$$

which we can rewrite as:

$$y_{it} = \frac{\gamma}{1 - \mu\gamma} x_{it} - \frac{\mu\gamma}{1 - \mu\gamma} g_i + \frac{\beta}{1 - \mu\gamma} y_t + v''_{it},\tag{11}$$

where the disturbances absorb the constants.

Removing industry-specific averages from (11), we obtain our short-run equation:

$$\tilde{y}_{it} = \frac{\tilde{\gamma}}{1 - \mu\tilde{\gamma}} \tilde{x}_{it} + \frac{\tilde{\beta}}{1 - \mu\tilde{\gamma}} \tilde{y}_t + v'''_{it}.\tag{12}$$

This equation shows that conventional labor-hoarding stories tend to magnify both the internal and external returns coefficients, but *they are not able to mimic an externality when there is none.*

Clearly then, labor hoarding is a close competitor of "true" increasing returns-to-scale stories. Of course, it is also a competitor of externalities at the most aggregate level, when these become indistinguishable from increasing internal returns. In sum, conventional labor hoarding and externalities are indistinguishable (with our approach) as explanations of *increasing social returns to scale,* but they have very different implications for the less aggregate evidence.

One could argue that the model of labor hoarding we propose is too simple, which we would agree with, and that aggregate variables should enter the effort equation. But this is already an externality, although it could be of the pecuniary type.

As for our long-run findings, taking averages over an equivalent to equation (10) where the externality is of the more general form, a_i, and assuming that the time domain is large, yields our long-run (between) equation:

$$\bar{y}_i = \bar{\gamma}\bar{x}_i + \mu\bar{\gamma}b_i + \bar{\beta}\bar{a}_i + \bar{v}_i.\tag{13}$$

It is obvious from this equation that if effort does not grow or decline (remember that all equations are in rates of growth) systematically within industries, all the b_i's are identically zero, so our findings of long-run externalities cannot be mere proxies for labor hoarding.

Therefore, labor hoarding could account for our long-run results, but this would require that effort varies systematically over long periods of time, and that sectors with fast-growing suppliers of intermediate inputs are the sectors with largest systematic growth in the utilization rate of their factors. We see no a priori reason for any of these conditions to be prevalent.

One could also try to measure effort more directly and include it in the basic equation. This is precisely what Abbott, Griliches, and Hausman

(1989) do. They treat the effects of factor utilization directly in the context of Hall's framework, which is similar to our own. They argue that Hall's finding of increasing returns is an artifact of the correlation between his instruments and factor utilization. Using the number of hours per employee as a proxy for both capital and labor utilization rates, Abbott, Griliches, and Hausman find that internal increasing returns disappear and that the capacity measure plays an important role. To confront the possibility that this argument might undermine our own results, we include their concept of capacity utilization as an explanatory variable in equation (2). Table 5.2 reports the results, where column 1 excludes capacity utilization from the list of intruments and column 2 includes it. In both cases, the coefficient is of the hypothesized sign, though excluding utilization from the list of instruments prevents any statistical significance. On the whole, this suggests that, in addition to the role of oil prices, capacity utilization effects are relevant. Nevertheless, the external economy remains significant and large.

5.2.1.2 *"True" Increasing Returns and Productivity Shocks*

"True" or internal increasing returns compete with the externality interpretation since they both can account for the increasing social returns-to-scale finding; however, the gap between estimates at the aggregate and at less aggregate levels is clearly inconsistent with a purely internal story.

Productivity shocks, on the other hand, are unlikely to have the magnitude required to explain our findings. But even if it were the case that the magnitude is sufficient, we use demand instruments to generate our macroeconomic results; these insruments, if proper, entirely resolve the issue.

As for our more disaggregate findings, we report ordinary least squares (OLS) results so there is the potential for a more serious simultaneity problem. However, our use of time dummies entirely removes the effects of these shocks even if their effect on different sectors is heterogenous. The reason for this is that sectors above the mean will cancel with sectors below the mean; once one imposes that the externality coefficients be the same for all sectors, the result is that the technology shocks cannot generate an artificial externality.

5.2.2 Robustness

5.2.2.1 *Observed Capacity and Labor Hoarding*

The previous section considers the impact of *unmeasured* variations in capacity and labor utilization on our findings. There is also the possibility that our results are affected by the assumption that the dynamic optimiza-

Table 5.3
Capacity utilization

	1	2
γ	1.02	0.99
	(0.07)	(0.05)
External. β	0.32	0.44
	(0.15)	(0.04)
Oil Price ρ	-0.06	-0.05
	(0.03)	(0.01)
Cap. Util.	0.27	0.46
	(0.92)	(0.06)

Standard errors in parentheses. Panel includes a constant per sector. Cap. Util. is the rate of growth of aggregate hours per worker, as in Abbott, Griliches, and Hausman (1989). Column 1 excludes capacity utilization from the list of instruments.

tion problem of a firm can be well approximated by a sequence of (annual) *frictionless* static problems. That is, even if all variations in capacity and labor utilization are precisely measured, misspecification of our model due to neglecting dynamics might generate the results we are interpreting as evidence for external economies (see Morrison 1988).

In Caballero and Lyons (1989) we show that relaxing this assumption to allow for *observed* labor hoarding and excess capacity, interpreted as discrepancies between short- and long-run optimal allocations (not as measurement error), is not likely to yield substantial biases. We provide only an outline of the argument here.

First, we suppose that the factor-demand first-order conditions implied by the static optimization problem are not always satisfied: there is an additional multiplicative factor in both. It is immediately apparent that if the factors vary proportionally then the estimating equation is identical to the one we employ. In other words, observed excess capacity and labor hoarding affect the model only if they do not move proportionally. If excess capacity and labor hoarding do not vary proportionally, then even ratios of the two multiplicative factors as extreme as 0.5 and 2.0 produce biases in the estimate of γ of less than 4 percent under very reasonable assumptions.

5.2.2.2   Classical Measurement Error
Given that we work with industry data, an important issue is whether classical measurement error can be responsible for a spurious external effect; that is, factors of production may be reported with errors or imputed to the wrong industries. In Caballero and Lyons (1989) we show that the sign of the bias of this type of measurement error is ambiguous. Moreover, in order

to explain our findings and conditional on the bias being positive (i.e., resembling a positive externality), the measurement error left after projecting on the set of instruments would have to account for about 60 percent of the covariance between the observable and the instruments.

5.3   Externalities in Economics

Tibor Scitovsky (1954) begins with the statement, "The concept of external economies is one of the most elusive in economic literature." We cannot claim to close the issue here. It is of vital importance, however, that we provide a backdrop for our results so that they can be more properly put in perspective. The first step is to recognize that the existence of externalities in manufacturing is relevant across a broad spectrum of different research domains. Some of those for which externalities are particularly relevant include (i) growth, (ii) macroeconomic fluctuations, (iii) international trade, and (iv) urban economics. Not surprisingly, each area emphasizes particular types of externalities. Here we briefly review the role and types of externalities in each, with the emphasis on providing a few representative examples rather than exhaustive coverage. Then we summarize by providing the implications of our evidence for each of the external effects presented.

5.3.1   Growth

The first appearance of externalities in the literature is due to Marshall (1890). He provides two Primary examples of external effects, both of which are of central importance for the domain of growth. The first is an increase in "trade knowledge," the benefits of which cannot be fully appropriated internally. By using the expression *trade knowledge*, Marshall left the concept open enough to include not only R&D but also knowledge along the lines of process innovation and "best practices" more generally. The second of his two examples is based on growth and specialization of subsidiary trades, implying a kind of division of labor among industries. A quote from Young (1938) provides additional clarification: "It would be wasteful to make a hammer to drive a single nail...How far it pays to go in equipping factories with special appliances for making hammers... depends again upon how many nails are to be driven" (p. 530). This notion that productivity is at least partially a function of the extent of the market is also taken up by Stigler (1951) and others. Perhaps a more precise characterization of these effects would involve a production function that recognizes specialized inputs and the added efficiency derived therefrom. Nevertheless, these effects are observationally equivalent to external economies under standard empirical methodology and have been treated accordingly in the literature (see Romer 1986b).

There is a third type of "externality" that first made its appearance in the context of growth, more specifically in the context of development: the pecuniary externality (see Scitovsky 1951). A *pecuniary externality* is distinguished from a *Marshallian* (or *technological*) externality in that with the technological externality the production technology of one firm is directly affected by activity of others through nonmarket interaction, whereas technology remains unaffected under the pecuniary externality. With pecuniary externalities the operative word is profits rather than technology. A pecuniary externality is said to exist if the profits of a firm depend not only on its own activity but also on the activity of other firms. Hence, this type of effect results purely from market interaction.

Recent theoretical work has proceeded along all three of these lines. The trade-knowledge externality of Marshall is the driving force in the endogenous growth literature spawned by the work of Romer (1986a). In his model the external effects are associated with capital input. This type of externality is also introduced through the labor input as embodied human capital, such as in the model of Lucas (1988). The second of the two Marshallian externalities, that deriving from further industry specialization, is addressed by Romer (1986b). Finally, the pecuniary externality has also received some recent theoretical attention. One such example (Murphy, Shleifer, and Vishny 1989) has imperfectly competitive industries with decreasing cost technologies that are underexploited in the sense that the extent of the market is limited and it does not behoove any industry (firm) to expand in isolation due to relative price effects. Under these conditions, welfare is increased by a coordinated expansion, or big push.

The empirical literature concerning growth externalities is deep, very narrow, and sometimes successful in detecting effects. We refer to it as narrow because it has concentrated on a particular dimension of Marshall's trade knowledge, namely the returns associated with R&D and basic research. The difficulties in doing this kind of empirical work are legion.[10] Here we provide only a few of the more successful examples. Bernstein and Nadiri (1988) develop and estimate a model for five U.S. high-tech industries that allows each industry to be a distinct spillover source, in contrast to previous work that tended to define the R&D spillover as a single aggregate. Their results showed that there were significant differences among industries as both spillover senders and receivers. Bernstein (1989) employs a similar methodology to a wider set of Canadian industries and goes further in determining that for industries that are major sources of spillovers, the social returns to R&D are at least twice the private returns. As a final example, Jaffe (1986) looks at evidence from firms' patents, profits, and market value to come to the conclusion that spillovers from R&D are indeed significant.[11]

5.3.2   Macroeconomic Fluctuations

The Marshallian external effects are likely to be operative only over longer horizons and are therefore not likely to be relevant for fluctuations. There are two such types of external effects that appear in the literature. One was noted as being relevant in the growth context: the pecuniary externality. Only relatively recently has it begun to appear in the context of fluctuations. Also sometimes referred to as an aggregate-demand externality, this effect is clarified within the monopolistically competitive framework of Blanchard and Kiyotaki (1987), among others. The second is the transactions (or thick-market) externality of Diamond (1982). Though also sometimes referred to as an aggregate-demand externality, the transactions externality is distinct since it does indeed imply shifts in measured productivity that are directly linked to aggregate activity. This externality arises in a search framework from the easing of the matching between relevant agents during economic expansions. Hence, this externality focuses more directly on the continuous interface between firms in the course of doing business over the short run. By its nature, it is more relevant for understanding the measured productivity of transactions-oriented labor and capital, both on the incoming and outgoing sides.

One of the central contact points between externalities and the work in macroeconomic fluctuations is the topic of the procyclicality of measured productivity. As mentioned, there have been three predominant explanations for procyclicality: (1) labor hoarding, (2) procyclical productivity shocks, and (3) internal increasing returns. The first of these, labor hoarding, turns on procyclical variations in effective labor and has the longest history of the three. The second, procyclicality of productivity shocks, provides the foundation for existing real business cycle models. In this setting, positive shocks to production possibilities induce higher marginal labor productivity, thereby generating procyclical labor productivity. The third alternative, emphasized recently by Hall (1990), maintains that an important part of the explanation turns on increasing returns to scale at the firm level. These internal increasing returns imply that output increases will entail movement down the average cost curve, generating procyclicality.

Our work, on the other hand, addresses what is perhaps best considered a complementary issue: whether the structural source of procyclical productivity (as opposed to shocks to productivity) stems from properties of the aggregate technology that are within agents' control (internal), or due to properties that are outside their control (external).[12] Stories based upon internal control include increasing returns and traditional labor hoarding. Conceivably, though, part of the explanation for procyclicality may rely on externalities, for example thick-market externalities arising from the easing of the matching between relevant agents during economic expansions (Diamond 1982).

Though the issue of procyclical productivity is an important link between our work and the domain of economic fluctuations, it is by no means the only link. A moment's reflection makes it clear that, in the presence of (positive) external effects, business cycle fluctuations are likely to be more pronounced, since comovements generate important reinforcing cross-effects. This very point is taken up by Baxter and King (1990) in a real business cycle framework. They demonstrate that the character of dynamic responses to shocks is fundamentally tied to whether external effects are present.

5.3.3   International Trade

Though the international trade literature has long considered the impact of external effects on world equilibrium, work in this area has had less to say about what the sources of the effects might be. Authors typically suggest in passing that one of the two Marshallian effects or an effect deriving from a public intermediate input is behind the specification of an equation such as our equation (2).[13] The early role of externalities in trade is evinced by the famous debate between Graham (1923, 1925) and Knight (1924, 1925), not so long after Marshall's initial characterization of the concept. Knight's view was that Graham's analysis of possible losses from trade is valid if economies of scale are external to the firm, but not if they are internal.

Much of the subsequent work on the topic focuses on economies external to the firm but internal to the industry, or industry-specific external effects (see, for example, Ohlin 1933 and Stigler 1951). More directly relevant for our work than the external to the firm/internal to the industry distinction is the theoretical work that considers cross-industry externalities, since our unit of empirical analysis is never finer than four-digit level industry. Examples of work in this area includes Manning and Macmillan (1979), Chang (1981), and Herberg, Kemp, and Tawada (1983).

5.3.4   Urban Economics

At first blush our work might appear quite unrelated to the domain of urban economics in that our work has largely to do with temporal bunching whereas urban economics concerns itself with spatial bunching. However the principal forces pushing toward agglomeration and the formation of cities in the urban economics literature are common among those that have been introduced in the context of the literatures above, namely increasing returns in production (compare pecuniary externality), public goods, and specialized service networks (see Papageorgiou 1979). Of course, there is no one model of agglomeration, and there are a number of forces that appear in the literature that are not listed above; our intention here is only to touch upon a domain that has the concept of externalities at its very core, both positive and negative (e.g., congestion).

In fact, the concept of spatial agglomeration provides the perfect setting in which to consider what is perhaps *the* classic externality example: Meade's (1952) beekeeper and apple grower. It is only due to the physical proximity of the the two that the productivity of honey production is improved as a result of an increase in apple production.

5.3.5   Implications of Our Results

So, what is the relevance of our results for the roles and types of externalities reviewed above? First, it must be recognized that our results, taken literally, imply a shift in the production function, that is, a true technological externality. Hence, regardless of whether one feels pecuniary externalities should be considered externalities at all, our results have nothing to say about their presence.

Second, external effects relevant in the growth context appear to be present, though they do not appear to be operating through the channels emphasized in the current theory—namely, through physical or human capital—but rather through the channel of intermediate inputs. It is of course possible that either of the two Marshallian sources is behind the effects, intermediate inputs simply being the transmission mechanism, but our framework does not admit a ready determination along these lines.

Third, external effects relevant for fluctuations are also present. At the same time we find no evidence of internal increasing returns. And, since our instrumental variables are chosen to be orthogonal to productivity shocks, we are left with labor hoarding and external economies as (potentially complementary) explanations for the remaining procyclicality. Yet, a simple specification of the labor-hoarding view is not sufficient for explaining our measured coefficients. We stress that our message is not that conventional labor hoarding is irrelevant, but rather that the data suggest strongly that it is not the whole story. In addition, our result of increasing social returns with decreasing internal returns suggests the likelihood of multiple equilibria, as demonstrated by a number of authors.[14]

As for implications for international trade, our results support the use of frameworks including a role for externalities. However, it should be recognized that our European intraindustry results (Caballero and Lyons 1991) are suggestive but weak and hence should not be interpreted as lending support for the popular intraindustry specification. On the policy side, a topic receiving considerable attention of late is the potential gains deriving from Europe's 1992 program. The Cecchini Report puts the estimated cost savings from further exploitation of economies of scale in manufacturing production at about 35 percent of the total gains. Our results bear both good and bad news. The bad news is that there appears to be little opportunity, at least in an average sense, for further exploitation of increasing internal returns in European manufacturing (at least for the countries we work with). We do not, however, intend to suggest that certain subindustries will not enjoy significant gains from internal scale economies, particularly those currently shielded by national procurement policies. Yet, these gains do not show up in our more aggregated measures. The good news is that external economies appear to be present. Since there exist social increasing returns, some of the Cecchini Report gains will be recouped.

5.4   Summary and Conclusion

Our framework provides a useful means of both revealing external effects and discriminating between a number of prominent types in an integrated manner. Overall, our results provide evidence along five different fronts: (1) there are social *increasing* returns to scale (U.S. and European manufacturing); (2) there are constant returns to scale at two-digit (U.S. and Europe) and four-digit (U.S.) levels; (3) these two results suggest the presence of an externality that has most of its impact between the two-digit and the aggregate level; (4) in the short run, the externality is primarily driven by the relation between an industry and its customers, while (5) in the long run, the main transmission channel is the relation between an industry and its suppliers.

Expressed compactly, our estimates imply that the elasticity of a four-digit industry's output with respect to own input, holding the input of other industries constant, is about one. This elasticity rises to about 1.3 when industry inputs move in lockstep. Of course, the unconditional elasticity falls somewhere between these two extremes. According to our estimates it, is in the neighborhood of 1.15.

With respect to the fluctuations-oriented externalities, output-weighted aggregates remain significant throughout our within estimation, regardless of whether gross production or value added is used. This is true even in the case in which we remove purely aggregate shocks by including time dummies. In the context of the expanded model, which includes demand categories outside of manufacturing, the output-weighted aggregate becomes the sole indicator of external effects. All this suggests that the external economies are likely to derive from either thick markets or externally driven changes in effort. In addition, the magnitude of the effect is not a function of whether the expanding industries are within a given two-digit sector or are outside. Once the interindustry linkage is fully specified, the measure of closeness in and of itself does not appear to be relevant.

With respect to the growth-oriented externalities, our between estimates indicate that over longer horizons the role of intermediate goods is important in accounting for multifactor productivity growth. This role for intermediates might be coming from either further specialization or the embodiment of knowledge and increased quality derived therefrom. These two mechanisms correspond to the two main external effects referred to originally by Marshall, though the transmission channel of intermediate goods differs from the original conception. These effects do not, however, correspond to the capital-based externalities that drive part of the endogenous growth work. It is not surprising in this light that in looking for capital-related externalities, Benhabib and Jovanovic (1991) could find no evidence, but our procedures appear to have been successful.

Our main contribution to past work of macroeconomic fluctuations is to add externalities to the list of potential explanations of short-run increasing returns, which includes internal increasing returns, technology shocks, and conventional labor hoarding (hoarding that is tied to own-firm activity). The internal/external distinction is important since in many frameworks it has a bearing on the character of dynamic response to shocks. Additional contributions to the areas of fluctuations and trade include the implications of our results for questions such as whether a competitive equilibrium can be supported and whether multiple equilibria are likely. The answer to both of these questions would appear to be yes.

Notes

Columbia University and NBER. We thank Manuel Trajtenberg, Danniel Tsiddon and seminar participants at "The Political Economy of Business Cycles and Growth" organized by the Pinhas Sapir Center for Development for their comments. Ricardo Caballero acknowledges the National Science Foundation for financial support under grant SES-9010443.

1. Caballero and Lyons 1989, 1990, 1991, Bartelsman, Caballero, and Lyons 1991.

2. In a sense, we are exploiting specification error to distinguish short- from long-run effects (see Hausman and Taylor 1981).

3. Strictly speaking, since the between estimators are very imprecise, one could not reject the hypothesis that long- and short-run relationships are the same.

4. The instruments are the rate of growth of real military purchases of goods and services, the log-difference of the relative price of oil in terms of durables, the log-difference of the relative price of oil in terms of nondurables, and a dummy variable for the political party of the president (see Hall 1987). Though not reported here, the externality result is robust to estimation method, in particular to the use of OLS and SUR (although in this case one must proxy externalities by aggregate input growth).

5. The standard errors in this equation are computed using White's (1980) heteroskedasticity-robust procedure.

6. An alternative interpretation maintains that the relative price of oil is picking up discrepancies resulting from the use of double-deflated value added in the context of changing relative materials prices.

7. This constraint is relaxed through most of the estimation in Bartelsman, Caballero, and Lyons (1991); the basic findings are virtually unchanged.

8. The magnitude of the fall in the externality coefficient is a rough indicator of the magnitude of common shocks.

9. See Baily (1986) for a summary of the central issues.

10. See Griliches (1979) for an overview of the difficulties and Mohnen (1991) for a survey of the work; in this area.

11. For more anecdotal evidence of input-output transmission of technological progress see Rosenberg (1982).

12. On the whole our work abstracts from the the role of procyclical productivity shocks; through most of it we use instruments that are taken to be orthogonal to innovations in technology.

13. For a review of work in this area see Helpman (1984).

14. See Diamond (1982), Cooper and John (1988), and Hammour (1989).

References

Abbott III, T., Z. Griliches and J. Hausman. 1989. "Short Run Movements in Productivity: Market Power versus Capacity Utilization." Mimeo.

Baily, Martin N. 1986. Productivity Growth and Materials Use in U.S Manufacturing. *Quarterly Journal of Economics* 00:185–195.

Bartelsman, E., R. Caballero, and R. Lyons. 1991. "Short and Long Run Externalities," NBER Working Paper, September (1991).

Baxter, M. and R. King. 1990. "Productive Externalities and Cyclical Volatility," prepared for the NBER Economic Fluctuations Meeting (1990).

Benhabib, J. and B. Jovanovic. 1991. "Growth Accounting and Externalities." *American Economic Review* 81:82–113.

Bernstein, J. 1989. "The Structure of Canadian Inter-Industry R&D Spillovers, and the Rates of Return to R&D." *The Journal of Industrial Economics* 37:315–328.

Bernstein, J. and M. Nadiri. 1988. "Interindustry R&D Spillovers, Rates of Return, and Production in High-Tech Industries." *American Economic Review Papers and Proceedings* 78:429–434.

Blanchard, O. and N. Kiyotaki. 1987. "Monopolistic Competition and the Effects of Aggregate Demand." *American Economic Review* 77:647–666.

Caballero, R. and R. Lyons. 1989. "The Role of External Economies in U.S. Manufacturing." Columbia University. Mimeo.

Caballero, R. and R. Lyons. 1990. "Internal Versus External Economies in European Industry." *European Economic Review* 34:805–830.

Caballero, R. and R. Lyons. 1991. "External Effects and Europe's Integration," in A. Winters and A. Venables, eds., *European Integration: Trade and Industry* (Cambridge University Press: Cambridge, England).

Cecchini, P. 1988. *The European Challenge: 1992 The Benefits of a Single Market.* (Gower Publishing Company: Brookfield, VT).

Chang, W. W. 1981. "Production Externalities, Variable Returns to Scale, and Theory of Trade." *International Economic Review* 22:511–525.

Cooper, R. and A. John. 1988. "Coordinating Failures in Keynesian Models." *Quarterly Journal of Economics* 103:441–464.

Diamond, P. 1982. "Aggregate Demand Management in Search Equilibrium." *Journal of Political Economy* 90:881–894.

Graham, F. 1923 "Some Aspects of Production Further Considered." *Quarterly Journal of Economics* 37:199–227.

Graham, F. 1925. "Some Fallacies in the Interpretation of Social Costs: A Reply." *Quarterly Journal of Economics* 39:324–330.

Griliches, Z. 1979. "Issues in Assessing the Contribution of Research and Development to Productivity Growth." *Bell Journal of Economics* 10:92–116.

Hall, R. 1987. "Productivity and the Business Cycle." *Carnegie-Rochester Series of Public Policy* 27:421–444.

Hall, R. 1990. "Invariance Properties of Solow's Productivity Residual." in P. Diamond, ed., Growth/Productivity/Employment (MIT Press: Cambridge, MA).

Hammour, M. 1989. "Indeterminacy and Instability in Macro Models with External Effects," Ph.D. diss., MIT.

Hausman, J. A. and W. E. Taylor. 1981. "Panel Data and Unobservable Individual Effects." *Econometrica* 48:1377–1398.

Helpman, E. 1984. "Increasing Returns, Imperfect Markets, and Trade Theory," in R. Jones and P. Kenen, eds., *Handbook of International Economics*, vol. 2. (North Holland: New York).

Herberg, H., M. C. Kemp, and M. Tawada. 1983. "Further Implications of Variable Returns to Scale." *Journal of International Economics* 13:65–84.

Jaffe, A. 1986. "Technological Opportunity and Spillovers of R&D: Evidence From Firms' Patents, Profits, and Market Value." *American Economic Review* 76:984–1001.

Knight, F. 1924. "Some Fallacies in the Interpretation of Social Costs." *Quarterly Journal of Economics* 38:582–606.

Knight, F. 1925. "On Decreasing Costs and Comparative Costs: A Rejoinder." *Quarterly Journal of Economics* 39:331–333.

Manning, R. and J. Macmillan. 1979. "Public Intermediate Goods, Production Possibilities, and International Trade." *Canadian Journal of Economics* 12:243–257.

Marshall, A. 1890. *Principles of Economics*, Macmillan: London.

Meade, J. 1952. "External Economies and Diseconomies in a Competitive Situation." *Economic Journal* 62:54–67.

Morrison, C. 1988. "Quasi-fixed Inputs in U.S. and Japanese Manufacturing: A Generalized Leontief Restricted Cost Function Approach." *Review of Economics and Statistics* 70:275–287.

Murphy, K. M., A. Shleifer, and R. W. Vishny. 1989. "Industrialization and the Big Push." *Journal of Political Economy* 97:1003–26.

Ohlin, B. 1933. *Interregional and International Trade*. (Harvard University Press: Cambridge, MA).

Papageorgiou, G. 1979. "Agglomeration." *Regional Science and Urban Economics* 9:41–59.

Ramey, V. 1991. "Non-convex Costs and the Behavior of Inventories." *Journal of Political Economy* 99:306–334.

Romer, P. 1986a. "Increasing Returns and Long-Run Growth." *Journal of Political Economy* 94:1002–37.

Romer, P. 1986b. "Increasing Returns, Specialization, and External Economies: Growth as Described by Allyn Young." Rochester Center for Economic Research Working Paper No. 64.

Rosenberg, N. 1982. *Inside the Black Box: Technology and Economics*. (Cambridge University Press: New York).

Scitovsky, T. 1954. "Two Concepts of External Economies." *Journal of Political Economy* 54:143–151.

Stigler, G. 1951. "The Division of Labor is Limited by the Extent of the Market." *Journal of Political Economy* 59:185–193.

Young, A. 1938. "Increasing Returns and Economic Progress." *Economic Journal* 38:527–542.

6　Convergence across States and Regions

Robert J. Barro and Xavier Sala-i-Martin

An important economic question is whether poor countries or regions tend to converge toward rich ones. We want to know, for example, whether the poor countries of Africa, South Asia, and Latin America will grow faster than the developed countries, whether the south of Italy will become like its north, whether and how fast the eastern regions of Germany will attain the prosperity of the western regions, and—in a historical context—how the American South became nearly as well off as the North.

Although some economic theories predict convergence, the empirical evidence has been a subject of debate. In this study we add to the evidence by extending our previous analysis of economic growth across the U.S. states.[1] We examine the growth and dispersion of personal income since 1880 and relate the patterns for individual states to the behavior of regions. We then analyze the intelplay between net migration and economic growth. We also study the evolution of gross state product since 1963 and relate the behavior of aggregate product to productivity in eight major sectors. The overall evidence weighs heavily in favor of convergence: both for sectors and for state aggregates, per capita income and product in poor states tend to grow faster than in rich states. The rate of convergence is, however, not rapid; the gap between the typical poor and rich state diminishes at roughly 2 percent a year.

We apply the same framework to patterns of convergence across seventy-three regions of Western Europe since 1950. The process of convergence within the European countries is in many respects similar to that for the United States. In particular, the rate of convergence is again about 2 percent a year.

We conclude by using the findings to forecast the convergence process for the eastern regions of unified Germany. The results are not very encouraging. If the histories of the U.S. states and European regions are useful guides, the convergence process will occur, but only at a slow pace.

6.1   Framework of the Analysis

Our previous study, which we refer to as our 1990 study throughout the rest of this chapter, examined convergence patterns for economic growth across the U.S. states.[2] We based our main analysis on a growth equation that derives, as a log-linear approximation, from the transition path of the neoclassical growth model for closed economies.[3] We follow the same research strategy in this chapter; that is, we begin with the closed-economy framework and then consider how the model would be affected by open-economy elements that are important to U.S. states and European regions.

We showed in our 1990 study that the transitional growth process in the neoclassical model can be approximated as

$$(1/T) \cdot \log(y_{it}/y_{i,t-T}) = x_i^* + \log(\hat{y}_i^*/\hat{y}_{i,t-T}) \cdot (1 - e^{-\beta T})/T + u_{it}, \tag{1}$$

where i indexes the economy, t indexes time, y_{it} is per capita output (equal to income per person as well as income per worker in the standard model), x_i^* is the steady-state per capita growth rate (corresponding to exogenous, labor-augmenting technological progress in the standard model), $\hat{y}_{it}$ is output per effective worker (that is, the number of workers adjusted for the effect of technological progress), $\hat{y}_i^*$ is the steady-state level of output per effective worker, T is the length of the observation interval, the coefficient β is the rate of convergence, and u_{it} is an error term. (The error term is a distributed lag of disturbances between dates $t - T$ and t.) Thus the convergence coefficient, β, indicates the rate at which $\hat{y}_{it}$ approaches $\hat{y}_i^*$.

On the production side, the neoclassical model assumes diminishing returns to capital, exogenous technological progress, full employment, a fixed relation between the labor force and population, and exogenous growth of population. With respect to preferences, the model assumes that the saving rate derives from the choices made by utility-maximizing households over an infinite horizon. (The infinite horizon can represent individuals who are connected to their descendants through a chain of intergenerational transfers.) The steady-state value of output per effective worker, $\hat{y}_i^*$, depends on the parameters of technology and preferences. We can extend the notion of technology to include natural resources, such as geography, fertile land, and the availability of minerals, as well as governmental policies (considered exogenous) that affect property rights, the provision of infrastructure services, tax rates, and so on.

The Rate of Convergence

The convergence coefficient, β, depends on the productivity of capital and the willingness to save. In particular, the source of convergence in the neoclassical growth model is the assumed diminishing returns to capital. If the ratio of capital (and hence output) to effective labor declines relative to the steady-state ratio, then the marginal product of capital rises. Therefore, for a given saving behavior, an economy grows faster the further it is below the steady state, that is, the higher $\hat{y}_i^*/\hat{y}_{i,t-T}$ in equation (1). If we compare different production functions, then β is higher if diminishing returns to capital set in faster. For example, for a Cobb-Douglas production function with capital share α, a smaller α corresponds to a larger β. As the capital share tends to one, so that diminishing returns to capital no longer apply, the rate of-convergence tends to zero. This case corresponds to endogenous growth models with constant returns to a broad concept of capital.[4]

The rate of convergence also depends on saving behavior, although more on the variation in the saving rate over the transition to the steady state than on the level of the saving rate. We have explored these effects in a related paper, one result of which is that a greater willingness to substitute intertemporally tends to raise β.[5]

Although the coefficient β can differ across economies, we neglect these differences in the subsequent discussion. This assumption is probably satisfactory for the U.S. states, which are likely to be similar in terms of the underlying parameters of technology and preferences. The theory also implies that pure differences in the levels of technology—and hence in levels of per capita income that derive from these technological differences—do not affect β. Thus, the convergence coefficients, β, can be similar across economies that appear in other respects to be very different.

We noted in our 1990 study that our empirical estimates of β for the U.S. states—somewhat greater than 2 percent a year—accord with the neoclassical growth model only if diminishing returns to capital set in very slowly. For example, with a Cobb-Douglas production function, the capital-share coefficient, α, has to be in the neighborhood of 0.8. We also argued that this high value for α is reasonable if we take the appropriately broad view of capital to include nonhuman and human components. That is, education and other expenditures on people are important parts of the investment process.

Capital and Labor Mobility

The closed-economy model cannot be applied literally to the U.S. states or
the regions of other countries. If technologies are the same, then convergence in per capita outputs and capital stocks occurs more rapidly in open
economies than in closed economies, whereas convergence in per capita
incomes and assets occurs less rapidly.[6] Models that assume perfect capital
mobility tend to have unrealistic implications, such as the prediction that
the most patient economy, the one with the lowest rate of time preference,
owns everything asymptotically and that less patient economies eventually
have negative assets and negligible consumption per effective worker.[7]
Also, our empirical findings do not exhibit the distinctions in the behavior
of output and income that are predicted by models with perfect capital
markets. We have considered models in which "imperfections" in capital
markets imply that only a fraction of physical capital serves as collateral on
loans.[8] In the context of the U.S. states, such models apply if the residents
or the government of a state cannot borrow nationally to finance all their
expenditures on education and other forms of investment in human capital.
This type of model predicts that product and income eventually behave in
a similar manner and that each exhibits the kind of convergence property
implied by the closed-economy specification of equation (1).

In a model that allows for labor mobility, raw labor tends to migrate
toward richer economies, which have higher wage rates. This movement of
persons lowers the capital-labor ratio in places with initially high ratios;
hence, diminishing returns to capital set in more rapidly and the convergence coefficient, β, is higher for any given parameters of preferences and
technology.[9] In other words, if the other parameters are given, the capital-
share coefficient for a Cobb-Douglas production function would have to be
even higher than 0.8 to be consistent with empirical estimates of β.

The rate of convergence also tends to be higher if we allow for the flow
of technological advances from rich to poor economies.[10] However, differences in levels of technology can alter the implications of capital mobility.
Human and physical capital may move from poor to rich economies and
thereby create a force toward divergence.

Two Concepts of Convergence

We discussed in our 1990 study two concepts of convergence related to
equation (1). The first, called β convergence, relates to poor economies
growing faster than rich ones, and the second, called σ convergence, involves a decline over time in the cross-sectional dispersion of per capita

income or product. The model in this chapter implies a form of *conditional* β convergence in that, for given steady-state values x_i^* and $\hat{y}_i^*$, an economy's per capita growth rate is higher the lower the starting level of per capita output, $y_{i,t-T}$. The convergence is conditional in that $\hat{y}_{i,t-T}$ enters in relation to $\hat{y}_i^*$, which may differ across economies. The coefficient β measures the speed of this conditional convergence. To isolate β empirically we have to hold constant the differences in the steady-state values x_i^* and $\hat{y}_i^*$. Although we included some additional variables as proxies for these differences, we found that the variations in the steady-state values seemed to be minor across the U.S. states. These variations appeared to be more significant across a group of relatively homogeneous countries, such as the OECD members, and were considerably more important across a broad sample of ninety-eight countries.

Even if x_i^* and $\hat{y}_i^*$ are identical across a group of economies, a positive β coefficient need not imply that the cross-sectional dispersion of per capita output, y_{it}, diminishes over time. A positive β tends to reduce the dispersion in $\log(y_{it})$ from equation (1), but new shocks, u_{it}, tend to raise it. Equation (1) implies, for a given distribution of u_{it}, that the cross-sectional standard deviation of $\log(y_{it})$, denoted σ_t, approaches a constant σ. The dispersion, σ_t, falls (or rises) over time if it starts above (or below) σ; hence, β convergence (in the sense of $\beta > 0$) need not imply σ convergence (in the sense of a declining σ_t). If the steady-state value $\hat{y}_i^*$ differs across economies, we could also consider a conditional form of σ convergence. That is, conditional σ convergence applies if the dispersion of the deviations, $\log(\hat{y}_{it}) - \log(\hat{y}_i^*)$, diminishes over time. Because this concept relies heavily on measures of the $\hat{y}_i^*$, we have not attempted to implement this idea.

We can bring out the distinction between β and σ convergence by considering two different kinds of questions. Suppose that we are interested in how fast and to what extent the per capita income of a particular economy is likely to catch up to the average of per capita incomes across economies. Then β convergence is the concept that matters. Suppose, on the other hand, that we want to know how the distribution of per capita income across economies has behaved in the past or is likely to behave in the future. In this case, σ convergence is the relevant concept.[11]

Many disturbances, such as war and shocks to agriculture or oil, affect economies differentially. These disturbances tend to temporarily raise the cross-sectional variance of the error term, u_{it}, and thereby raise σ_t above σ. Subsequently, if the long-run distribution of u_{it}, is unchanged, σ_t tends to fall gradually back to the value σ. Events related to war, agriculture, or oil can also affect groups of economies in a correlated manner; when such an event occurs, the u_{it} are not independent draws over the economies, *i*. In our previous work, we used regional dummies and measures of sectoral composition of output to address this problem. That is, we treated the u_{it} as independent over i once we included these additional variables in the regressions.

The failure to introduce these additional variables can also lead to biased estimates of the coefficient β, contingent on the realization of a particular shock. Consider, for example, an adverse shock to agricultural output in a setting in which agricultural economies start with below-average per capita product. Because of the positive correlation of the shock with $y_{i,t-T}$, we would underestimate β if we did not hold the shock constant.

6.2   Personal Income across U.S. States

Figure 6.1 shows the broad pattern of β convergence for per capita personal income, exclusive of all transfers, for forty-seven U.S. states or territories from 1880 to 1988.[12] The figure shows the strong negative

Annual growth rate, 1880–1988 (percent)

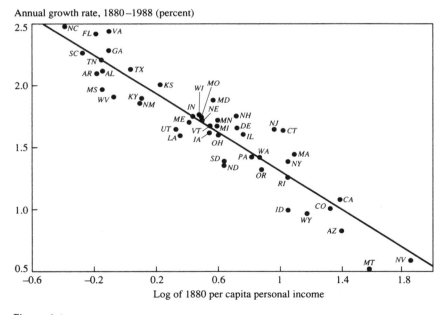

Figure 6.1
Convergence of personal income across U.S. states: 1880 income and income growth from 1880 to 1988. Sources: Bureau of Economic Analysis (1984), Easterlin (1960a, 1960b), and *Survey of Current Business*, various issues. The postal abbreviation for each state is used to plot the figure. Oklahoma, Alaska, and Hawaii are excluded from the analysis.

correlation (-0.93) between the average growth rate from 1880 to 1988 and the log of per capita personal income in 1880. The means and standard deviations for these and other variables are reported in the appendix tables.

As expected the southern states tended to have low per capita income in 1880 and high average growth rates thereafter. Less well known is that the western states had above-average per capita income in 1880 and below-average growth thereafter.

Although regional catch-up is part of the overall convergence story, figures 6.2 and 6.3 show that the pattern between regions (East, South, Midwest, and West) is similar to that within regions. Figure 6.2 shows the four data points that correspond to the regional means. Figure 6.3 shows the pattern when the state growth rates and logs of initial income are measured relative to their respective regional means. The relations between growth rates and starting levels from figures 6.2 and 6.3 are quantitatively similar.

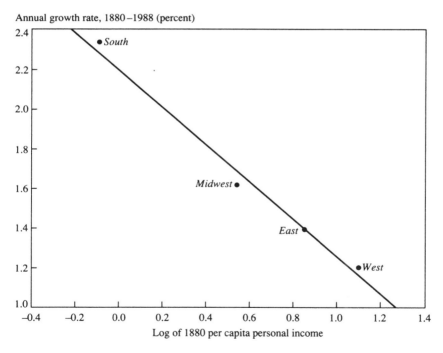

Annual growth rate, 1880–1988 (percent)

Log of 1880 per capita personal income

Figure 6.2
Convergence of personal income across U.S. regions: 1880 income and income growth from 1880 to 1988. Sources: Bureau of Economic Analysis (1984), Easterlin (1960a, 1960b), and *Survey of Current Business*, various issues. The four data points correspond to the regional means.

Relative growth rate, 1880–1988 (percent)[a]

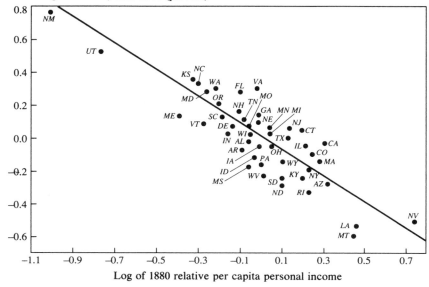

Log of 1880 relative per capita personal income

Figure 6.3
Convergence of personal income, U.S. states relative to regional means: 1880 income and income growth from 1880 to 1988. Sources: Bureau of Economic Analysis (1984), Easterlin (1960a, 1960b), and *Survey of Current Business*, various issues. The postal abbreviation for each state is used to plot the figure. Oklahoma, Alaska, and Hawaii are excluded from the analysis. The figure shows the pattern when the state growth rates and the logs of initial income are measured relative to the respective regional means.
a. Growth is measured by the deviation of the average per capita growth rate of personal income in each state from 1880 to 1988 from the average growth rate for that state's respective region over the same period.

Basic Regression Results

Table 6.1 shows regression estimates of the convergence coefficient, β, for nine subperiods of the U.S. sample from 1880 to 1988. The first column is a form of equation (1) that includes only a constant and the log of each state's initial personal income per capita. Although most of the estimated coefficients are significantly positive, the magnitudes vary a great deal and two of the point estimates are negative. (Recall that we define the coefficient β in equation (1) so that a positive β means that poor economies grow faster than rich ones.) If we constrain the estimate of β to be the same for all subperiods, the resulting joint estimate is $\hat{\beta} = 0.0175$, or in the neigh-

Table 6.1
Regressions for personal income across U.S. states, 1880–1988

Period	Basic equation $\hat{\beta}$	Basic equation $R^2[\hat{\sigma}]$	Equation with regional dummies $\hat{\beta}$	Equation with regional dummies $R^2[\hat{\sigma}]$	Equation with regional dummies and sectoral variables[a] $\hat{\beta}$	Equation with regional dummies and sectoral variables[a] $R^2[\hat{\sigma}]$
1880–1900	0.0101	0.36	0.0224	0.62	0.0268	0.65
	(0.0022)	[0.0068]	(0.0040)	[0.0054]	(0.0048)	[0.0053]
1900–20	0.0218	0.62	0.0209	0.67	0.0269	0.71
	(0.0032)	[0.0065]	(0.0063)	[0.0062]	(0.0075)	[0.0060]
1920–30	−0.0149	0.14	−0.0122	0.43	0.0218	0.64
	(0.0051)	[0.0132]	(0.0074)	[0.0111]	(0.0112)	[0.0089]
1930–40	0.0141	0.35	0.0127	0.36	0.0119	0.46
	(0.0030)	[0.0073]	(0.0051)	[0.0075]	(0.0072)	[0.0071]
1940–50	0.0431	0.72	0.0373	0.86	0.0236	0.89
	(0.0048)	[0.0078]	(0.0053)	[0.0057]	(0.0060)	[0.0053]
1950–60	0.0190	0.42	0.0202	0.49	0.0305	0.66
	(0.0035)	[0.0050]	(0.0052)	[0.0048]	(0.0054)	[0.0041]
1960–70	0.0246	0.51	0.0135	0.68	0.0173	0.72
	(0.0039)	[0.0045]	(0.0043)	[0.0037]	(0.0053)	[0.0036]
1970–80	0.0198	0.21	0.0119	0.36	0.0042	0.46
	(0.0062)	[0.0060]	(0.0069)	[0.0056]	(0.0070)	[0.0052]
1980–88	−0.0060	0.00	−0.0005	0.51	0.0146	0.76
	(0.0130)	[0.0142]	(0.0114)	[0.0103]	(0.0099)	[0.0075]
Nine periods combined[b]						
β restricted	0.0175	...	0.0189	...	0.0224	...
	(0.0013)		(0.0019)		(0.0022)	
Likelihood-ratio statistic[c]	65.6	...	32.1	...	12.4	...
P-value	0.000		0.000		0.134	

Sources: Authors' own calculations using Bureau of Economic Analysis (1984), Easterlin (1960a, 1960b), and *Survey of Current Business*, various issues. All regressions are for the continental states, except for the 1880–1900 period, in which Oklahoma is excluded for all equations and Wyoming is excluded in the last equation. The regressions use nonlinear least squares to estimate equations of the form:

$$(1-T)\log(y_{it}/y_{i,t-T}) = a - [\log(y_{i,t-T})](1 - e^{-\beta T})(1-T) + \text{other variables,}$$

where $y_{i,t-T}$ is the per capita personal income in state i at the beginning of the interval, divided by the overall CPI; $y_{i,t}$ is the real per capita personal income in state i at time t; T is the length of the observation interval; and the other variables are regional dummies and the variables described in note a. Standard errors are in parentheses. The standard errors of the regressions are in brackets.

a. The additional variables in the third column are the share of personal income originating in agriculture at the start of the period, $Agry_{i,t-T}$, and the structural composition variable, S_{it}, described in the text. Data for S_{it} are only available since 1929.

b. The combined regression restricts the value of β to be the same across all nine subperiods. The restricted β are estimated using iterative, weighted, nonlinear least squares.

c. The likelihood ratio test is based on the null hypothesis that the β are the same across all nine subperiods. It follows a chi-squared (χ^2) distribution; the 0.05 χ^2 value with eight degrees of freedom is 15.5.

borhood of 2 percent a year. However, a likelihood-ratio test, shown in the table, strongly rejects the hypothesis that β is stable over the subperiods.[13]

The second equation of table 6.1 introduces regional dummies for each subperiod. These dummies proxy for differences in the steady-state values, x_i^* and $\hat{y}_i^*$, and also absorb fixed regional effects in the error term, u_{it}. Although the fits are improved and the variation in $\hat{\beta}$ over the subperiods is somewhat reduced, the results still reject the hypothesis of β stability over the periods. The restricted point estimate, $\hat{\beta}$, for the nine subperiods, 0.0189, is similar to that reported in the first column. The estimate from the second equation reflects within-region β convergence, whereas that from the first reflects a combination of within- and between-region convergence. Hence, as also suggested by figures 6.1–6.3, the results indicate that the within- and between-region rates of β convergence are similar.

Additional Explanatory Variables

The last equation of table 6.1 adds two additional variables to the regression. The first, denoted $Agry_{i,t-T}$, is the share of personal income originating in agriculture in state i at the start of each subperiod (that is, in year $t - T$). This variable is available for all of the subperiods since 1880. As with the regional dummies, the agriculture variable can hold constant the differences in steady-state values, x_i^* and $\hat{y}_i^*$, as well as the common effects related to agriculture in the error term.

The second variable, denoted S_{it} for structure, relates to the breakdown of state i's personal income into nine standard sectors: agriculture; mining; construction; manufacturing; transportation; wholesale and retail trade; finance, insurance, real estate; services; and government. We first compute the national growth rates of per capita income originating in each sector for each subperiod. Then we weight the national growth rates by the share of each sector in state i's personal income at the start of the subperiod. Hence, the formula for S_{it} is

$$S_{it} = \sum_{j=1}^{9} w_{ij,t-T} \cdot \log(y_{jt}/y_{j,t-T}), \tag{2}$$

where $w_{ij,t-T}$ is the weight of sector j in state i's personal income at time $t - T$, and y_{jt} is the national average of personal income in sector j at time t, expressed as a ratio to national population at time t. Aside from the effect of changing sectoral weights within a state, the variable S_{it} would equal the total growth rate of per capita personal income in state i between years $t - T$ and t if each of the state's sectors grew at the national average rate for that sector. In particular, the variable S_{it} reflects shocks to agriculture, oil, and so on in a way that interacts with state i's concentration in those sectors. We think of S_{it} as a proxy for common effects related to sectoral composition in the error term, u_{it}. Note that S_{it} depends on contemporaneous realizations of national variables, but only on lagged values of state variables. Because the impact of an individual state on national aggregates is small, S_{it} can be nearly exogenous with respect to the individual error term for state i.

We have the data to construct S_{it} only since 1929. For that reason, we also include the previously described variable $Agry_{i,t-T}$, as a separate influence. We include $Agry_{i,t-T}$ for all subperiods, although the results are similar if we omit this variable for the subperiods after 1929.

When the two variables, $Agry_{i,t-T}$ and S_{it}, are included in the regressions, the principal new finding is that the estimates of $\hat{\beta}$ are much more stable across periods. The greater stability arises because we hold constant the shocks (for some subperiods) that are correlated with initial per capita income as well as hold constant those that affect groups of states in common. For example, agriculture suffered relative to other sectors in the 1920s.[14] Because agricultural states had below-average per capita income in 1920, we estimate negative β coefficients for the 1920–30 subperiod in the first two columns. But, once we hold constant the differences in agricultural shares, $Agry_{i,t-T}$, we estimate a β coefficient for this subperiod that is similar to those found for the other subperiods. The joint estimate for the nine subperiods is now $\hat{\beta} = 0.0224$ (s.e. $= 0.0022$) and we accept the hypothesis of coefficient stability at the 5 percent level. Thus, as noted before, the results suggest β convergence at a rate somewhat above 2 percent a year.[15]

The estimates of β convergence shown in the last columns of the table are net of compositional effects from shifts of persons out of agriculture and toward higher productivity jobs in industry and services.[16] These effects are held constant by the initial agricultural shares, $Agry_{i,t-T}$, which are included as regressors. In particular, if we add the change in the agricultural share, $Agry_{it} - Agry_{i,t-T}$, to the regressions, the joint estimate of β is virtually unchanged from that shown in the last equation. In general, industry-mix effects matter for the results if shifts in income shares among sectors with different average levels of productivity are correlated with initial levels of per capita income. It is unclear that we would want to filter out this kind of effect in measuring β convergence, but, in any event, our examination of productivity data from the post–World War II period suggests that shifts between agriculture and nonagriculture would be the principal effect of this type.

We have also computed regression estimates that parallel those in the last equation of table 6.1 but exploit only the between-region variation in growth rates. Because we have four regions and nine subperiods, we now have thirty-six observations of per capita growth rates. (With a single β coefficient, this system has twenty-five independent variables and therefote eleven degrees of freedom.) The joint estimate of β is 0.0187 (s.e. $= 0.0069$), which does not differ greatly from the joint estimate shown in the last equation of table 6.1. Thus, as noted before, the between-region β convergence is similar to the within-region convergence. We would not get this similarity if the states in the four regions differed substantially (after holding constant the regional differences in $Agry_{i,t-T}$ and S_{it}) in terms of the steady-state values, x_i^* and $\hat{y}_i^*$, in equation (1). Thus, the findings suggest that the regions are converging toward similar steady-state behavior of per capita income.

Dispersion of Personal Income

Figure 6.4 shows the unweighted cross-sectional standard deviation, σ_t, for the log of per capita personal income for forty-eight U.S. states from 1880 to 1988. (The observation for 1880 applies to 47 states or territories. The data are plotted for 1880, 1900, 1920, 1929, 1930, 1940, 1950, and annually since 1955.) We concentrate for now on the data that exclude government transfers, which are the figures that we have used thus far.

Figure 6.4 shows that the dispersion of personal income declined from 0.54 in 1880 to 0.33 in 1920, but then rose to 0.40 in 1930. This rise reflects the adverse shock to agriculture during the 1920s; the effect on σ_t is pronounced because the agricultural states were already below average in per capita income before the shock. After 1930, σ_t fell to 0.35 in 1940, 0.24 in 1950, 0.21 in 1960, 0.17 in 1970, and reached a low point of 0.14 in 1976. The sharp decline during the 1940s reflects the favorable experience of agriculture.[17] The pattern of long-term decline in σ_t reversed after the mid-1970s, and σ_t rose to 0.15 in 1980 and 0.19 in 1988. We think that the increase in σ_t after the mid-1970s relates to oil shocks. A later section discusses these effects in the context of comparing the results for personal income with those based on gross state product.

The broad observation from figure 6.4 is a long-term decline in σ_t from a value above 0.5 to a plateau around 0.15–0.20. This pattern accords with the σ convergence predicted by the neoclassical growth model if the states began, in 1880, with a dispersion that was well above the steady-state value, σ. If we use the observed values, $\sigma_{1880} = 0.545$ and $\sigma_{1988} = 0.194$, and the previous estimate, $\beta = 0.02$ a year, then we can estimate the

Income dispersion[a]

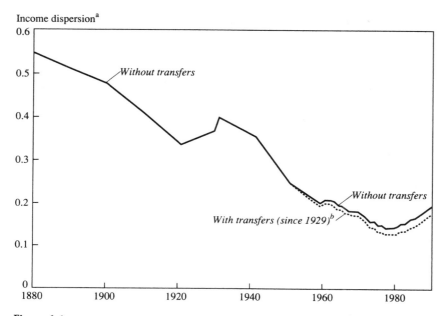

Figure 6.4
Dispersion of personal income across U.S. states, 1880–1988. Sources: Authors' own calculations using Bureau of Economic Analysis (1984), Easterlin (1960a, 1960b), and *Survey of Current Business*, various issues. The data are for the continental U.S. states, except the 1880 figure, which excludes Oklahoma. The data are plotted for 1880, 1900, 1920, 1929, 1930, 1940, 1950, and annually since 1955.
a. Income dispersion is measured by the unweighted cross-sectional standard deviation of the log of per capita personal income.
b. Data on the dispersion of per capita personal income inclusive of government transfer payments are included since 1929, although the effect of including transfer payments is negligible before 1950.

standard deviation, σ_u, of the annual error term as 0.037. This value implies that the steady-state dispersion is 0.18.[18]

One aspect of the high dispersion in 1880 is the low per capita incomes of southern states relative to nonsouthern states, a pattern that can be traced back to the Civil War. As discussed in our 1990 study, in 1840 the average income in the South was not very much below that in the non-South, but in 1880 it was about 50 percent of that in the non-South. Another element is that the western states, which resembled new territories in 1880, had relatively high per capita incomes at the start of the sample. Some of this high income represented temporary opportunities in mining.

Figure 6.4 also shows the values of σ_t computed from personal income inclusive of government transfer payments.[19] (Our data on transfers do not separate the amounts received from the federal government from those received from state and local governments.) As might be expected, government transfers reduce the dispersion of personal income, since many of these transfers aim to supplement the income of lower-income individuals. The ratio of transfers to personal income exclusive of transfers is substantially negatively correlated with the log of personal income exclusive of transfers. For example, the correlation between the transfer ratio and the log of personal income exclusive of transfers is -0.76 in 1987. On the other hand, the time pattern for σ_t is similar with and without transfers. The quantitative effect of the transfer component has been increasing over time. It is negligible in 1950, but by 1987 σ_t exclusive of transfers is 0.187, whereas σ_t inclusive of transfers is 0.165.

When personal income dispersion (excluding transfers) is computed across regions rather than states, the time path is very similar to that in figure 6.4. Figure 6.5 shows the underlying data on average per capita income for the four regions. This figure shows clearly that the average

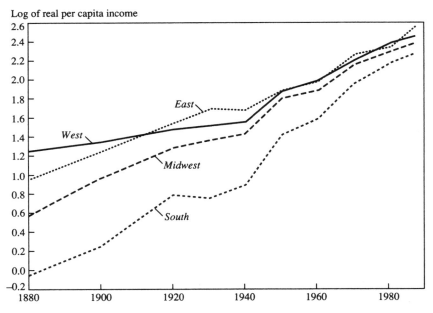

Figure 6.5
Personal income of U.S. regions, 1880–1988. Sources: Authors' own calculations using Bureau of Economic Analysis (1984), Easterlin (1960a, 1960b), and *Survey of Current Business*, various issues. The data are plotted for 1880, 1900, 1920, every ten-year interval that follows, and 1988.

incomes in each region have gotten much closer over time.[20] The main inference from figure 6.5 is that a lot of the long-term reduction in σ_t reflects the typical southern and western state becoming more like the typical eastern and midwestern state.

Figure 6.6 shows the patterns for σ_t within each of the four regions. The long-term decline in income dispersion among the western states is apparent, but the other patterns are less straightforward. One clear result, however, is that the values of σ_t within each of the four regions are essentially the same toward the end of the sample.

The regional patterns highlight the distinction between σ and β convergence that was discussed earlier. With respect to σ convergence, the narrowing of the gap in average incomes across regions is a central element of the story, and the changes within regions are a sideshow. In contrast, the estimated speeds of β convergence between and within regions are virtually

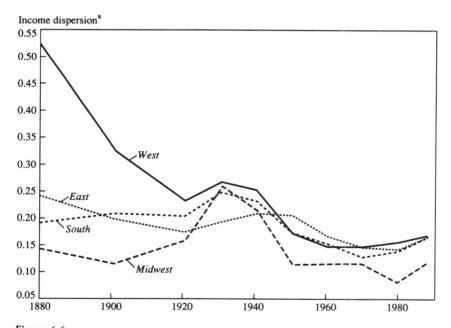

Figure 6.6
Dispersion of personal income within U.S. regions, 1880–1988. Sources: Authors' own calculations using Bureau of Economic Analysis (1984), Easterlin (1960a, 1960b), and *Survey of Current Business*, various issues. The data are plotted for 1880, 1900, 1920, every ten-year interval that follows, and 1988.
a. Income dispersion is measured by the unweighted cross-sectional standard deviation of the log of per capita personal income.

identical. That is, relatively poor eastern states (such as Maine and Vermont in 1880) tended to catch up to relatively rich eastern states (Massachusetts and Rhode Island in 1880) about as fast as the poor southern state tended to catch up to the better off western or eastern state. These findings are consistent with the underlying model if the initially high values of σ_t reflected temporary disturbances that affected entire regions (such as the Civil War and the opening of territories in the West).

6.3 Net Migration across U.S. States

This section, which extends the work of Sala-i-Martin, examines the migration of persons among the U.S. states in the context of the process of growth and convergence that we have been considering.[21] As already mentioned, the process of convergence is quickened by movements of people out of areas where ratios of capital to workers are low—and hence wage rates and levels of per capita income are also low—to areas where they are high. We investigate whether the flows of net migration accord with this story and whether these flows are a substantial force in the convergence we have estimated for the U.S. states.

Modeling Net Migration

Suppose that people (and hence workers) are identical and that states offer the same amenities, government policies, and so on. Suppose that places differ by initial ratios of physical capital to labor, and hence by wage rates, and that existing capital cannot move. Then, people are motivated to move from low-wage to high-wage areas.

If moving were costless, the migration of persons would equalize per capita incomes instantaneously according to the model. In truth, however, moving entails costs, which include direct outlays for transportation, costs of familiarizing oneself with new jobs and surroundings, psychic costs of leaving acquaintances, and so on. If we allow for heterogeneity among persons, then the costs of moving differ in accordance with age, family status, occupation, and other characteristics that affect the direct and indirect costs of moving or preferences about moving. Therefore, not all persons in low-wage areas are motivated to leave at a given point in time. This conclusion is reinforced if we allow for heterogeneity of jobs and workers so that wage rates and employment involve features of a matching problem.

Furthermore, the costs of moving into an area may depend on the aggregate flow of persons into that area. This rate of flow could influence job-search costs (which would show up in properly defined wage rates of new entrants) and housing costs. Thus, even if we abstract from matching considerations, these elements imply that not all migrants will go to the same place at a given point in time.

In addition to moving costs, other factors enter into an empirical analysis of net migration. If places differ in the amenities that affect utility or production, such as climate, natural resources, and government policies, then the long-run equilibrium described by Jennifer Roback entails a range of wage rates for identical workers, along with a range of population densities and land prices.[22] Although wage rates differ across places, these variations perfectly compensate for differences in land prices and amenities; hence people will have no incentive to move. In terms of the reduced form, the equilibrium wage rate and population density for state i, w_i^* and π_i^* respectively, are determined along with the land prices by the underlying amenities, denoted θ_i. We can think, as an approximation, of people having an incentive to move to state i if $\pi_i < \pi_i^*$ (θ_i), so that $w_i > w_i^*$ (θ_i). With costs to moving, the rate of migration into state i would be a positive function of the gap $w_i - w_i^*$ (θ_i). The derivative of this function would be finite.

The analysis is more complicated with variable capital stocks. We are especially interested in analyzing their effects in the context of our data set, which includes information about per capita incomes (which we take as proxies for wage rates) and population densities, but not about capital stocks. If starred variables denote steady-state values, then a place with a temporarily high intensity of physical capital could have $w_i > w_i^*$ (θ_i) and $\pi_i > \pi_i^*$ (θ_i). In this case, for a given $w_i - w_i^*$ (θ_i), a higher $\pi_i - \pi_i^*$ (θ_i) signals that current capital intensity is higher and hence that capital intensity and wage rates will decline over time. In particular, the greater $\pi_i - \pi_i^*$ (θ_i) is, the shorter the expected persistence of the gap between w_i and w_i^* (θ_i) and hence the lower the incentive to migrate into the state.

The above reasoning leads us to write a function for m_{it}, the net rate of migration into state i between years $t - T$ and t, as

$$m_{it} = f(y_{i,t-T}, \theta_i, \pi_{i,t-T}, \text{ and variables that depend on } t \text{ but not on } i), \quad (3)$$

where the partial effects of $y_{i,t-T}$ and θ_i are positive (if a higher θ_i means more amenities) and the partial effect of $\pi_{i,t-T}$ is negative.[23] We assume that θ_i—an exogenous characteristic like climate or geography—does not change over time. (Thus, the analysis would have to be modified for exhaustible resources like silver and oil that are depleted over time and also modified for changing government policies.) The set of variables that depend on t but not i includes any elements that influence the national averages of per capita income and population density; that is, $y_{i,t-T}$ and $\pi_{i,t-T}$ in equation (3) involve comparisons among locations at time t. The set also includes effects like technological progress in heating and air conditioning, which affect people's attitudes about climate and other components of the amenities, θ_i.

We have found empirically that a simple functional form of equation (3) does reasonably well in explaining net migration into state i:

$$m_{it} = a + b \cdot \log(y_{i,t-T}) + c_1 \cdot \theta_i + c_2 \cdot \pi_{i,t-T} + c_3 \cdot (\pi_{i,t-T})^2 + v_{it}, \qquad (4)$$

where v_{it} is an error term, b is positive, and the functional form allows for a quadratic in population density, $\pi_{i,t-T}$.[24] The marginal effect of $\pi_{i,t-T}$ on m_{it} is negative if $c_2 + 2c_3$ is negative. Although there is an extensive literature about variables to include in θ_i,[25] the present analysis includes only the log of average heating-degree days, denoted $\log(Heat_i)$, which is a disamenity so that c_1 is negative. The variable $\log(Heat_i)$ has a good deal of explanatory power for net migration—we did explore different functional forms as well as the addition of cooling-degree days as an explanatory variable, but the alternative functional forms did not fit as well as the one described in equation (4) and the cooling-degree days variable is insignificant.[26] Including other variables in θ_i would be important for a fuller study of migration. It would also be useful to introduce migration for retirement, a mechanism that likely explains some outliers like Florida. However, these-kinds of modifications probably would not change our basic findings about the relation between net migration and state per capita income and the interaction between migration and the convergence results.

Empirical Results

Figure 6.7 shows the simple, long-term relation between in-migration and initial per capita income. The variable on the vertical axis is the average annual in-migration rate for each state from 1900 to 1987.[27] The horizontal axis plots the log of state per capita personal income in 1900. The figure shows a positive relationship (with a correlation of 0.51), but the relation is not nearly as clear-cut as that seen for long-term per capita growth in figure 6.1. Figure 6.8 shows the partial relation between the long-term in-migration rate and the log of initial per capita income—after holding constant the values of the right-side variables (at their 1900 levels) con-

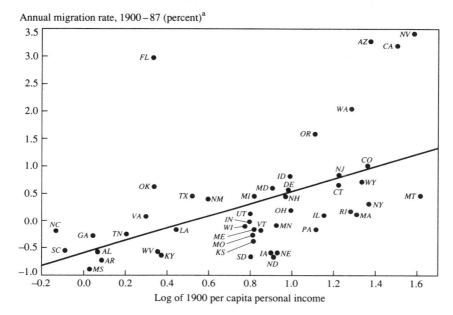

Annual migration rate, 1900–87 (percent)[a]

Log of 1900 per capita personal income

Figure 6.7
Migration and initial state income, 1900–87. Sources: Bureau of the Census (1975, 1990).
The postal abbreviation for each state is used to plot the figure.
a. The variable is the average of the rates for the subperiods, 1900–20, 1920–30, ...,
1970–80, and 1980–87, weighted by the length of the subperiod. The rate for each
subperiod is the annual average of net migration, divided by state population at the
start of the subperiod.

tained in equation (4), the regional dummies, and the agricultural-share
variable. The partial correlation is positive and equal to 0.45.

Table 6.2 shows regression results, in the form of equation (4), for net
migration into U.S. states.[28] The results are for eight subperiods beginning
with 1900–20.[29] The dependent variable, m_{it}, is the ratio of migrants
(annual average over each subperiod) to state population at the start of the
subperiod.[30] Hence, the dependent variable approximates the contribution
of net migration to the state's rate of population growth over the subperiod.

The equations include period-specific coefficients for $\log(y_{i,t-T})$ and
$\log(Heat_i)$, but single coefficients for the two population-density variables,
$\pi_{i,t-T}$ (thousands of persons per square mile of total area) and $(\pi_{i,t-T})^2$.
The regressions also include period-specific coefficients for the regional
dummies, the agriculture share in personal income, $Agry_{i,t-T}$, and (for
subperiods that start in 1930 or later) the structure variable, S_{it}. These
variables are the ones used in the last equation of table 6.1. (The estimated

Annual migration rate, 1900–87 (percent)[a]

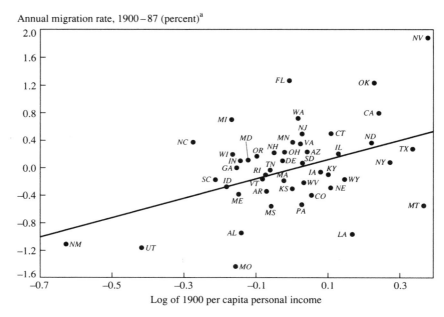

Figure 6.8
Partial Relation between migration and initial state income, 1900–87. Sources: Bureau of the Census (1975, 1990). The figure plots the residuals from an equation explaining the migration rate with the variables in equation 4 against the residuals from an equation explaining the log of 1900 per capita income with the same variables. The postal abbreviation for each state is used to plot the figure.
a. The variable is the average of the rates for the subperiods, 1900–20, 1920–30, ..., 1970–80, and 1980–87, weighted by the length of the subperiod. The rate for each subperiod is the annual average of net migration, divided by state population at the start of the subperiod.

coefficients of these other variables—not shown in table 6.2—are sometimes statistically significant but play a relatively minor role overall.) The hypothesis that the coefficient for the population-density variables is stable over time is accepted at the 5 percent level, and the other results change little if period-specific coefficients on these variables are introduced. The hypothesis of stability over the subperiods in the coefficients of $\log(Heat_i)$ is rejected at the 5 percent level, although the estimated coefficients, $\hat{b}$, on $\log(y_{i,t-T})$ change little if only a single coefficient is estimated for the heat variable.

The estimated coefficients of $\log(Heat_i)$ in table 6.2 are all negative and most are significantly different from zero. These results indicate that, all else being equal, people prefer warmer states. For population density, $\pi_{i,t-T}$, the

Table 6.2
Regressions for Net Migration into U.S. states, 1900–87

Period	Personal income[a]	Heating-degree days[a]	Population density[b]	Square of population density[b]	$R^2[\hat{\sigma}]$
1900–20	0.0335	−0.0066	−0.0452	0.0340	0.70
	(0.0075)	(0.0037)	(0.0077)	(0.0092)	[0.0112]
1920–30	0.0363	−0.0124	−0.0452	0.0340	0.61
	(0.0078)	(0.0027)	(0.0077)	(0.0092)	[0.0079]
1930–40	0.0191	−0.0048	−0.0452	0.0340	0.71
	(0.0037)	(0.0014)	(0.0077)	(0.0092)	[0.0042]
1940–50	0.0262	−0.0135	−0.0452	0.0340	0.83
	(0.0056)	(0.0022)	(0.0077)	(0.0092)	[0.0065]
1950–60	0.0439	−0.0205	−0.0452	0.0340	0.76
	(0.0085)	(0.0031)	(0.0077)	(0.0092)	[0.0091]
1960–70	0.0436	−0.0056	−0.0452	0.0340	0.70
	(0.0082)	(0.0025)	(0.0077)	(0.0092)	[0.0069]
1970–80	0.0240	−0.0076	−0.0452	0.0340	0.73
	(0.0091)	(0.0024)	(0.0077)	(0.0092)	[0.0071]
1980–87	0.0177	−0.0075	−0.0452	0.0340	0.73
	(0.0057)	(0.0018)	(0.0077)	(0.0092)	[0.0049]
Eight periods combined[c]	0.0261	. . .	−0.0447	0.0329	. . .
	(0.0023)		(0.0078)	(0.0093)	

Sources: Authors' own calculations using Bureau of Economic Analysis (1984), Easterlin (1960a, 1960b), Bureau of the Census (1990), and *Survey of Current Business*, various issues. All regressions are for the continental states. The regressions use iterative, weighted least squares to estimate equations of the form:

$$m_{it} = a + b\log(y_{i,t-T}) + c_1 \log(Heat_i) + c_2 \pi_{i,t-T} + c_3(\pi_{i,t-T})^2 + \text{other variables},$$

where m_{it} is the average annual net migration into state i between years $t - T$ and t, expressed as a ratio to the state's population in year $t - T$; $y_{i,t-T}$ is real per capita personal income at the beginning of the subperiod as described in table 6.1; $Heat_i$ is the average number of heating-degree days for state i, formed as an average for available cities in the state; $\pi_{i,t-T}$ is the population density (thousands of people per square mile of area) of state i at the beginning of the subperiod; and the other variables are the regional dummies, the share of agriculture in personal income, and the sectoral composition variable. Standard errors are in parentheses. The standard errors of the regression are in brackets.

a. The logarithms of initial personal income, $y_{i,t-T}$, and the number of heating-degree days, $Heat_i$, are used in the regression.

b. The coefficients on the population-density variables, c_2 and c_3 in the above equation, are constrained to be the same for all subperiods.

c. The combined regression restricts the value of b to be the same across all eight subperiods. This regression includes separate coefficients for $\log(Heat_i)$ for each subperiod. The likelihood ratio statistic for equal b's is 17.0 and the p-value is 0.017. The 0.05 χ^2 value with seven degrees of freedom is 14.1.

jointly estimated linear term is significantly negative, -0.0452, and the square term is significantly positive, 0.0340. These point estimates imply that, all else being equal, the marginal effect of population density on in-migration is negative except for a few observations with the highest densities (New Jersey and Rhode Island since 1960 and Massachusetts since 1970). Since the implied marginal effect of population density for these outliers is small and since we are fitting a quadratic approximation, the true effect of population density could be negative throughout.

Although figures 6.7 and 6.8 show that the long-term relation between migration rates and initial income is positive but not very strong, the regression results, which are conditioned on the values of $\log(y_{i,t-T})$ and $\pi_{i,t-T}$ at the beginning of each subperiod, are considerably clearer. The estimated coefficient, $\hat{b}$, on $\log(y_{i,t-T})$ is significantly positive for every subperiod shown in table 6.2. The joint estimate, $\hat{b}$, for the eight subperiods is 0.0261 (s.e. $= 0.0023$), which implies a t-value over 11. Thus, the regressions provide strong statistical evidence that, all else being equal, higher per capita income leads to a greater rate of net in-migration. The estimates in table 6.2 do, however, reject at the 5 percent level the hypothesis of stability in the b coefficients across the subperiods (p-value $= 0.02$).

Recall that we do not use individual state deflators for personal income. We can, however, interpret the population-density variable as a proxy for housing costs; the differences in these costs are a major source of variation in the cost of living across states . Thus, the estimated coefficients of per capita personal income in table 6.2 likely represent effects for given costs of housing. It turns out, however, that the jointly estimated coefficient of $\log(y_{i,t-T})$ is significantly positive (with a t-value of 9), even if the only other regressors in the equations are period-specific constant terms. Thus, the results suggest that the measured differences in nominal per capita personal income across states reflect variations in *real* per capita income.

Although the relation between the rate of in-migration and lagged per capita income is positive and highly significant (holding fixed our measure of amenities, population density, and some other variables), the magnitude of the relation is small. For example, the joint estimate for b implies that, all else being equal, a 10 percent increase in a state's per capita personal income raises net in-migration only by enough to raise the state's rate of population growth by 0.26 percentage points a year. The slow adjustment through net migration means that unless there is a substantial response of a state's fertility or mortality, population densities do not adjust rapidly to differences in per capita income adjusted for amenities. Our previous results suggest that differences in per capita income tend themselves to be elimi-

Annual migration rate, 1940–87 (percent)

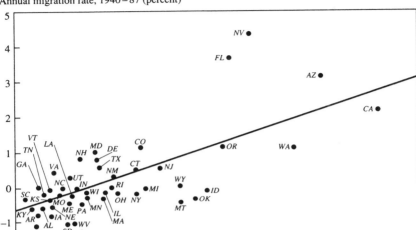

Figure 6.9
Persistence of migration rates across U.S. states, 1900–87. Sources: Bureau of the Census (1975, 1990).

nated over time, but only at a rate of about 2 percent a year. Thus, disparities in per capita income also persist for a long time. Putting these results together, the implication is that net migration rates are highly persistent over time. The data accord with this conclusion. For example, the correlation of the average net migration rate from 1900 to 1940 with that from 1940 to 1987 is 0.70. Figure 6.9 depicts the pattern of persistence.

Migration and Convergence

As discussed, the migration of raw-labor from poor to rich states speeds up the convergence of per capita income. That is, the estimated coefficients, $\hat{\beta}$, shown in table 6.1, include the impact of migration. To quantify the effect of migration on the convergence coefficient, we can relate the estimated response of migration to $\log(y_{i,t-T})$—$\hat{b} = 0.026$ from table 6.2—with the estimate, $\hat{\beta} = 0.0210$, which comes from the last equation of table 6.1 when estimated for the eight subperiods used in table 6.2. We have modified the neoclassical growth model to include endogenous migration as a source of linkage between population growth and the log of per capita income. (We neglect here any endogeneity of fertility or mortality.) The effect of migration on the rate of convergence depends in the model on the underlying parameters of preferences and technology and on the quantity of human capital that migrants possess. We use parameter values that are consistent with the estimated values of β and b and with information from other studies.[31] If we assume, unrealistically, that migrants have zero human capital, then—depending on the specification of the underlying parameters—we calculate that β without migration would have been between 0.014 and 0.016, instead of the estimated value, 0.0210. Thus, migration can account for as much as a third of the estimated rate of convergence if we neglect the human capital of migrants. The role of migration is, however, considerably less if we allow for migrants' human capital. For example, if the typical migrant's human capital is half the total capital stock per person in the destination state, then the computed β without migration is between 0.018 and 0.019. Hence, if we allow for a reasonable amount of human capital, migration cannot explain much more than 10 percent of the estimated rate of convergence.

We now attempt to get a direct estimate of the effect of migration on convergence by entering migration rates into the growth-rate regressions . The expectation is that exogenous in-migration will have a negative effect on the per capita growth rate and that the addition of the migration rate as a regressor will lower the estimated β coefficient We first enter the contemporaneous migration rate, m_{it}, into regressions of the type presented in the last equation of table 6.1. We drop the first subperiod (1880–1900) and consider only the eight subperiods that begin in 1900. If we restrict the coefficient on m_{it} to be the same for the eight subperiods, the estimated coefficient on m_{it} is *positive* and significant: 0.098 (s.e. = 0.029). The joint estimate of β, 0.0250 (s.e. = 0.0027), is actually somewhat higher than the value that arises when the migration rate is excluded from the regression. Thus, contrary to expectations, the estimated β convergence does not diminish if we hold net migration rates constant. If we allow for separate coefficients on m_{it} for each subperiod, all eight point estimates are positive, and the hypothesis of coefficient stability over the subperiods is accepted at the 5 percent level. In any event, the resulting joint estimate of β, 0.0256 (s.e. = 0.0027), is about the same as that with a single coefficient for m_{it}.

A state's per capita growth rate and net migration rate are simultaneously determined. Suppose, for example, that a state is known to have favorable prospects for growth, but that these prospects are not adequately captured by the explanatory variables that we have included in the regressions for growth and migration. Then the residuals in each equation would tend to be positive; the positive residual in the migration equation reflects the response of migrants to the favorable growth opportunities that are not controlled for by the included regressors. It seems likely that the positive estimated coefficients for m_{it} in the growth-rate regressions reflect this type of interaction.

We have also estimated by an instrumental variables procedure the growth-rate equations that include m_{it} as an explanatory variable. Aside from the predetermined variables that enter into the growth-rate equations in table 6.1, we include as instruments the additional variables that influence the net migration rate in table 6.2: $\log(Heat_i)$, $\pi_{i,t-T}$, and $(\pi_{i,t-T})^2$.[32] If the coefficients on m_{it} in the growth-rate equations are restricted to be the same over the eight subperiods, the estimated coefficient of m_{it} is 0.010 (s.e. = 0.047), which differs insignificantly from zero. The joint estimate of β, 0.0214 (s.e. = 0.0030), is close to the value found when the migration rate is omitted from the regression. The findings are basically the same if we allow for separate coefficients on m_{it} for each subperiod. In particular, the joint estimate of β is 0.0209 (s.e. = 0.0032). These results suggest that exogenous shifts in net migration rates do not have a strong contemporaneous interaction with per capita growth: if we hold net migration rates constant, we estimate about the same rate of β convergence as we did before.

The empirical conclusion—that migration plays a small part in β convergence—should be compared with the values of β that we expect to find when we hold migration rates constant. Recall that removing the effects of migration gives an estimate of β between 0.014 and 0.016 if migrants have zero human capital and between 0.018 and 0.019 if human capital per migrant is half the total capital stock per person in the destination state. The differences between the estimated coefficient, 0.0209, and the predicted coefficients are small and statistically insignificant for the values that allow for human capital. Thus, the results are consistent with the modified neoclassical growth model that includes endogenous migration.

To summarize the main points on migration, we find that, all else being equal, per capita income has a highly significant positive effect on net migration rates into a state. Thus, we verify the predicted response of net migration to economic opportunity. We find, however, little contemporaneous interplay between net migration and economic growth. Specifically, we observe little change in the estimated β coefficients when we hold net migration rates constant. These results are consistent with a modified neoclassical growth model that allows for endogenous migration; in particular, given the estimated response of migration to per capita income, the modified model predicts that migration would explain only a small part of β convergence.

6.4   Gross State Product

Data on gross state product (GSP) for forty-eight states are available from 1963 to 1986.[33] GSP, analogous to gross domestic product, refers to the payments to the factors that produce goods within a state, whereas personal income pertains to the returns to the factor owners, who may reside in other states. The main distinction between GSP and personal income arises in the case of income from physical capital.

Table 6.3 shows regressions for per capita GSP for four subperiods: 1963–69, 1969–75, 1975–81, and 1981–86. Real GSP in this table is the nominal aggregate for the state divided by the national deflator for GSP.[34]

These figures reflect the current returns to factors of production and are therefore relevant for decisions on investment, migration, and so on. However, the measured growth rates pick up a combination of changes in quantities produced and changes in relative prices across sectors. The effects of the relative-price changes, which interact with the composition of production within a state, can be viewed as part of the error term, u_{it} in equation (1), that is filtered out by the structural-composition variable, S_{it}. For GSP, the variable S_{it} is based on a division of production into 54 sectors. Thus, the breakdown is much finer than the nine-sector construct used for personal income in table 6.1.

Overall, the results on β convergence for GSP are similar to those for personal income from table 6.1. If we exclude the structure variable and include only lagged GSP (the first equation of table 6.3) or if we add regional dummies (the second equation), then the estimated β's are unstable. The estimates are far more stable when we add the explanatory variable S_{it} in the last equation. The joint estimate of β for the four subperiods is 0.0216, and the hypothesis of stability in the β coefficients over the four subperiods is accepted at the 5 percent level.

Figure 6.10 shows a plot of the average growth rate of per capita GSP from 1963 to 1986 against the log of per capita GSP in 1963. The downward-sloping relation is clear, although the fit is not as good as that for the longer-period relation for personal income shown in figure 6.1. The main difference relates to the sample period and not to the distinction between GSP and personal income.

Table 6.4, which extends an analysis by Sala-i-Martin, breaks down the results by sector for the period 1963–86.[35] We look at GSP per worker

Table 6.3
Regressions for gross state product across U.S. states, 1963–86

Period	Basic equation $\hat{\beta}$	$R^2[\hat{\sigma}]$	Equation with regional dummies $\hat{\beta}$	$R^2[\hat{\sigma}]$	Equation with regional dummies and sectoral variables $\hat{\beta}$	$R^2[\hat{\sigma}]$
1963–69	0.0317 (0.0067)	0.36 [0.0070]	0.154 (0.0060)	0.63 [0.0056]	0.0157 (0.0060)	0.63 [0.0056]
1969–75	0.0438 (0.0166)	0.16 [0.0138]	0.0406 (0.0162)	0.41 [0.0120]	0.0297 (0.0101)	0.74 [0.0081]
1975–81	−0.0159 (0.0133)	0.03 [0.0145]	−0.0285 (0.0134)	0.17 [0.0139]	0.0258 (0.0108)	0.78 [0.0072]
1981–86	0.1188 (0.0294)	0.39 [0.0205]	0.1130 (0.0251)	0.62 [0.0168]	0.0238 (0.0091)	0.92 [0.0079]
Four periods combined[a]						
β restricted	0.0335 (0.0057)	...	0.0211 (0.0053)	...	0.0216 (0.0042)	...
Likelihood-ratio statistic[b]	75.6	...	32.1	...	1.7	...
P-value	0.000		0.000		0.637	

Sources: Authors' own calculations using Renshaw, Trott, and Friedenberg (1988). All regressions are for the continental states. The regressions use nonlinear least squares to estimate equations of the form:

$$(1/T)\log(y_{it}/y_{i,t-T}) = a - [\log(y_{i,t-T})](1 - e^{-\beta T})(1/T) + \text{other variables},$$

where $y_{i,t-T}$ is per capita gross state product (GSP), divided by the national deflator for GSP, in state i at the beginning of the subperiod; y_{it} is the real GSP at time t; T is the length of the interval; and the other variables are regional dummies and the structural composition variable described in the text. Standard errors are in parentheses. The standard errors of the regression are in brackets.

a. The combined regression restricts the value of β to be the same across all four subperiods. The restricted β are estimated using iterative, weighted, nonlinear least squares.
b. The likelihood ratio test is based on the null hypothesis that the β are the same across subsamples. It follows a chi-squared (χ^2) distribution; the 0.05 χ^2 value with three degrees of freedom is 7.8.

Annual growth rate, 1963–86 (percent)

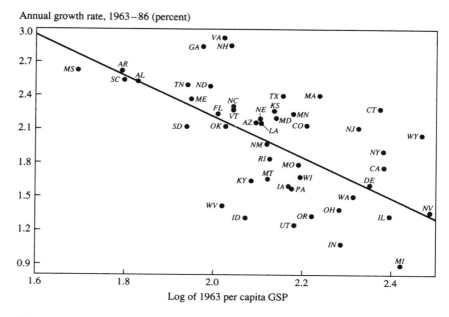

Figure 6.10
Convergence of gross state product across U.S. states: 1963 GSP and GSP growth from
1963 to 1986. Sources: Renshaw, Trott, and Friedenberg (1988). The postal abbreviation
for each state is used to plot the figure. Alaska and Hawaii are excluded from the analysis.

originating in eight standard nonagricultural sectors: mining; construction;
manufacturing; transportation; wholesale and retail trade; finance, insurance,
real estate (FIRE); services; and government.[36] We have omitted the agricultural sector because data on agricultural employment are not comparable to
those for the nonagricultural sectors. The first two columns of the table
show the shares of each sector in U.S. aggregate GSP at the beginning and
end of the period. The main patterns in the shares, which are well known,
are the declines in manufacturing and agriculture (the latter is measured by
the increase in the sum of the other eight sectors) and the increases in
services and FIRE.

The third column of table 6.4 shows positive estimates of β for each of
the eight sectors, although not all of the estimates are statistically significant. (Each of these regressions includes a constant, the log of the sector's
productivity in 1963, and the regional dummies.) Basically, the $\hat{\beta}$ values for
the four service-type sectors—wholesale and retail trade, FIRE, services,
and government—are similar and fall in a range from 0.009 to 0.016. The
$\hat{\beta}$ values are higher for the other four sectors, especially for manufacturing,

Table 6.4
Regressions for sectors of gross state product, 1963–86

Sector	Sector share[a] 1963	Sector share[a] 1986	$\hat{\beta}$	R^2	Standard error[b]
Mining	0.023	0.022	0.0240 (0.0074)	0.49	0.0134
Construction	0.048	0.047	0.0169 (0.0203)	0.20	0.0110
Manufacturing	0.284	0.199	0.0460 (0.0082)	0.73	0.0041
Transportation	0.092	0.094	0.0257 (0.0176)	0.15	0.0045
Wholesale and retail trade	0.164	0.169	0.0093 (0.0064)	0.24	0.0030
Finance, insurance, and real estate	0.145	0.167	0.0150 (0.0062)	0.43	0.0046
Services	0.105	0.166	0.0149 (0.0077)	0.27	0.0036
Government	0.102	0.115	0.0161 (0.0039)	0.55	0.0032
Eight sectors combined[c]	0.963	0.978	0.0213 (0.0024)	...	...

Sources: Authors' own calculations using Renshaw, Trott, and Friedenberg (1988) and Bureau of Labor Statistics (various years). Each sectoral regression has observations for the continental states, except mining, which only has 42 observations. The regressions use nonlinear least squares to estimate equations of the form:

$$(1/T)\log(y_{it}/y_{i,t-T}) = a - [\log(y_{i,t-T})](1 - e^{-\beta T})(1/T) + \text{regional dummies},$$

where y_{it} is the ratio of the sector's contribution to state i's gross state product (GSP) to the employment in the sector for that state at time t, with T equal to 23 years. The agricultural sector is omitted because of unreliable data on employment. Standard errors are in parentheses.

a. The share of the sector in aggregate GSP in 1963 and 1986 is shown.

b. The standard error of the regression is shown.

c. Iterative, weighted, nonlinear least squares is used to estimate the eight-sector joint regression with a single value for β. The likelihood-ratio statistic for equal β is 22.4, and the p-value is 0.002. The 0.05 χ^2 value with seven degrees of freedom is 14.1.

where the estimate is 0.0460. It is only this high and precisely estimated value for manufacturing that leads to rejection of the hypothesis that the β coefficients are the same across the sectors. The joint estimate of β for the eight sectors is 0.0213, but we reject at the 5 percent level the hypothesis that the individual β's are the same. We would accept the hypothesis that the β coefficients are the same for the seven sectors other than manufacturing —the estimate is $\hat{\beta} = 0.0164$ (s.e. $= 0.0024$) and the p-value for the test of equality for the coefficients is 0.77.

The main inference that we draw from table 6.4 is that β convergence applies within sectors in a manner that is broadly similar to that found in tables 6.1 and 6.3 for state aggregates of personal income and gross state product. Thus, an important part of the overall process of convergence across the states involves adjustments of productivity levels within sectors.

Figure 6.11 shows the dispersion of GSP across U.S. states, measured by the unweighted cross-sectional standard deviation, σ_t, for the log of per

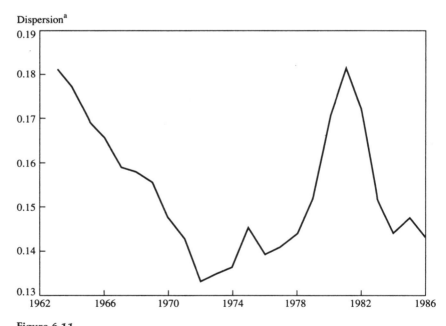

Figure 6.11
Dispersion of gross state product across U.S. states, 1963–86. Sources: Authors' own calculations using Renshaw, Trott, and Friedenberg (1988). Alaska and Hawaii are excluded from the analysis.
a. Dispersion of GSP is measured by the unweighted cross-sectional standard deviation of the log of per capita GSP.

capita GSP from 1963 to 1986. The decline of σ_t from 0.18 in 1963 to a low point of 0.13 in 1972 accords with the behavior for personal income shown in figure 6.4. We think that the rise in σ_t to a peak of 0.18 in 1981 reflects the behavior of oil prices. Especially in the 1979–81 period, the oil shocks benefited those states that already had above-average per capita GSP, thereby leading to an increase in σ_t. After 1981, the decline in σ_t reflects the normal pattern of a convergence, reinforced later by a fall in oil prices.

The different patterns from 1973 to 1986 in σ_t based on GSP versus σ_t based on personal income reflect, at least in part, differences in the relation between shares of product or income originating in oil-related industries and the levels of per capita product or income. The correlation of the log of per capita GSP with the share of GSP originating in crude oil and natural gas rises because of the oil shocks from 0.1 in 1973 to 0.4 in 1975 and 0.7 in 1981, and then falls with the decline in oil prices to 0.1 in 1986. In contrast, the correlation of the log of per capita personal income with the share of personal income originating in oil and natural gas is -0.3 in 1970 and 0.0 in 1980. These divergent patterns reflect the distinction between the location of oil and gas facilities and the ownership of these facilities.

From 1973 to 1981 the oil shocks have less of an effect on σ_t for personal income than for GSP because the increases in oil prices do not particularly harm the states with already low levels of per capita personal income, but they do harm states with lower levels of GSP. Similarly, a possible reason why σ_t for personal income does not decline later in the 1980s is that, unlike for GSP, the declines in oil prices do not particularly benefit the states with low per capita incomes.

6.5 Convergence across Regions of Europe

We now apply the analysis to the behavior of gross domestic product (GDP) in the regions of seven European countries. We have data on GDP and a few other variables for 73 regions: 11 in Germany, 11 in the United Kingdom, 20 in Italy, 21 in France, 4 in the Netherlands, 3 in Belgium, and 3 in Denmark.[37] Table 6.5 lists the regions.

Data for 1950, 1960, and 1970 are from Willem Molle.[38] Data for 1966 (missing France and Denmark), 1970 (missing Denmark), 1974, 1980, and 1985 are from Eurostat. The nominal figures on GDP are expressed using current exchange rates in terms of a common currency unit. It is unnecessary to deflate the nominal values for the purposes of the cross-section equations that we consider: any common deflation affects only the constant terms in the regressions.[39] Aside from GDP and population, the data set includes a breakdown of employment into three sectors—agriculture, in-

Table 6.5
Regions of Europe

Germany	*France*
1. Schleswig-Holstein	43. Region Parisienne
2. Hamburg	44. Champagne-Ardenne
3. Niedersachsen	45. Picarde
4. Bremen	46. Haute Normandie
5. Nordrhein-Westfalen	47. Centre
6. Hessen	48. Basse Normandie
7. Rheinland-Pfalz	49. Bourgogne
8. Saarland	50. Nord–Pas-de-Calais
9. Baden-Württemberg	51. Lorraine
10. Bayern	52. Alsace
11. Berlin (West)	53. Franche-Comte
United Kingdom	54. Pays de la Loire
12. North	55. Bretagne
13. Yorkshire-Humberside	56. Poitou-Charentes
14. East Midlands	57. Aquitaine
15. East Anglia	58. Midi-Pyrénées
16. South-East	59. Limousin
17. South-West	60. Rhône-Alpes
18. North-West	61. Auvergne
19. West Midlands	62. Languedoc-Roussillon
20. Wales	63. Provence, Alpes, Côte d'Azur, Corse
21. Scotland	*Netherlands*
22. Northern Ireland	65. Noord
Italy	66. Oost
23. Piemonte	67. West
24. Valle d'Aosta	68. Zuid
25. Liguria	*Belgium*
26. Lombardia	69. Vlaanderen
27. Trentino–Alto Adige	70. Wallonie
28. Veneto	71. Brabant
29. Friuli-Venezia, Giulia	*Denmark*
30. Emilia-Romagna	72. Sjaelland-Lolland-Falster-Bornholm
31. Marche	73. Fyn
32. Toscana	74. Jylland
33. Umbria	
34. Lazio	
35. Campania	
36. Abruzzi	
37. Molise	
38. Puglia	
39. Basilicata	
40. Calabria	
41. Sicilia	
42. Sardegna	

Sources: Molle (1980) and Eurostat (various years). Because GDP data from Eurostat for Corse were combined with those for Provence, Alpes, and Côte d'Azur, region 64 has been eliminated leaving a total of 73 regions.

Relative growth rate, 1950–85 (percent)[a]

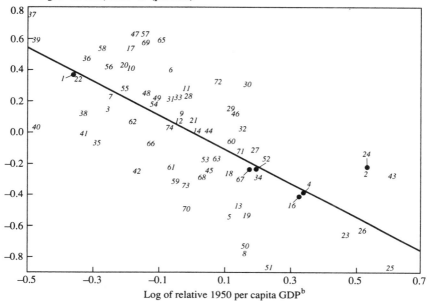

Log of relative 1950 per capita GDP[b]

Figure 6.12
Convergence of gross domestic product across European regions: 1950 GDP and GDP
growth from 1950 to 1985. Source: Molle (1980) and Eurostat (various years). Current
exchange rates were used to convert nominal GDP figures to a common currency. The
numbers in the figure correspond to the regional numbers in table 6.5 and figure 6.13.
a. Growth is measured by the deviation of the average per capita growth rate of GDP for
each region from 1950 to 1985 from the average growth rate for the country over the
same period.
b. The log of initial regional income is measured relative to the respective country mean.

dustry, and services—for 1950, 1960, and 1970, as well as a breakdown of
GDP into the same three sectors for 1966 (missing France and Denmark),
1970, 1974, 1980, and 1985. (The sectoral data for Denmark are available
only for 1974.)

Figure 6.12 shows the relation of the growth rate of per capita GDP from
1950 to 1985 to the log of per capita GDP in 1950 for the 73 European
regions. (The numbers of the regions correspond to those in table 6.5. See
figure 6.13 for a map of the regions.) The values are all measured relative
to the means of the respective countries. The figure shows the type of
negative relation that is familiar from the study of the U.S. states. The
correlation between the growth rate and the log of initial per capita GDP
in figure 6.12 is −0.70.

Figure 6.13
Regions of Europe. Source: Map is adapted from Molle (1980, p. 20). See table 6.5 for
names of regions.

Because the underlying numbers are expressed relative to own-country means, the relation in figure 6.12 pertains to β convergence within countries rather than between countries. For the seven countries that we are considering, the estimates of β convergence between countries turn out to be similar to those within the countries. Previous research has considered β and σ convergence among larger groups of countries.[40] Since the seven-country data set considered here provides much less information about behavior across countries, we shall focus our attention on the within-country results.

Analysis of β Convergence

Table 6.6 shows regressions for the European regions over four subperiods: 1950–60, 1960–70, 1970–80, and 1980–85. The form of the analysis parallels that for the U.S. states in tables 6.1 and 6.3. The regressions in the first equation of table 6.6 include only a constant and $\log(y_{i,t-T})$ as independent variables. The estimated coefficients, $\hat{\beta}$, are positive but unstable across the periods. The pattern of results over the subperiods is similar to that found for the U.S. states, and the joint estimate is slightly smaller than that found for the United States. The hypothesis of a constant β coefficient is again rejected at the 5 percent level.

The second equation of table 6.6 adds country dummies, which have enormous explanatory power for the growth rates of European regions. We think of the country dummies, which are analogous to the regional dummies that we used for the United States, as proxies for the steady-state values, x_i^* and $\hat{y}_i^*$, and for countrywide fixed effects in the error term, u_{it}. The addition of the country dummies makes the estimates of β in equation (1) markedly more stable across the subperiods, but the joint estimate is very close to that shown in the first column. (This joint estimation includes period-specific country dummies.) The results in the second equation still reject at the 5 percent level the hypothesis of equal β coefficients across the subperiods.

The results with country dummies show within-country β convergence and are analogous to that shown in figure 6.12. In contrast, the results from the first equation show a combination of within- and between-country β convergence. The joint estimates of β in the two sets of columns are similar because the rates of within- and between-country β convergence are nearly the same in this seven-country sample. We can also estimate β by using only the data on country aggregates (as we did for the U.S. regions). Over the same time period, the jointly estimated β coefficient is 0.0183 (s.e. = 0.0029), virtually the same as the value shown in the second equation.

Table 6.6
Regressions for gross domestic product across European regions, 1950–85

Period	Basic equation $\hat{\beta}$	Basic equation $R^2[\hat{\sigma}]$	Equation with country dummies $\hat{\beta}$	Equation with country dummies $R^2[\hat{\sigma}]$	Equation with country dummies and structural variables[a] $\hat{\beta}$	Equation with country dummies and structural variables[a] $R^2[\hat{\sigma}]$
1950–60	0.0106	0.06	0.0105	0.78	0.0206	0.80
	(0.0051)	[0.0155]	(0.0038)	[0.0077]	(0.0078)	[0.0076]
1960–70[b]	0.0367	0.39	0.0279	0.92	0.0241	0.92
	(0.0066)	[0.0149]	(0.0036)	[0.0057]	(0.0062)	[0.0058]
1970–80[b]	0.0035	0.01	0.0184	0.43	0.0139	0.44
	(0.0035)	[0.0098]	(0.0049)	[0.0078]	(0.0082)	[0.0078]
1980–85	0.0953	0.60	0.0116	0.95	0.0111	0.96
	(0.0122)	[0.0212]	(0.0048)	[0.0077]	(0.0060)	[0.0070]
Four periods combined[c]						
β restricted	0.0183	...	0.0186	...	0.0178	...
	(0.0029)		(0.0021)		(0.0034)	
Likelihood ratio statistic[d]	70.9	...	13.3	...	2.6	...
P-value	0.000		0.004		0.457	

Sources: Data up through 1970 are from Molle (1980). Data for and after 1970 are from Eurostat (various years). Each regression has observations for the 73 European regions listed in table 6.5. The regressions use nonlinear least squares to estimate equations of the form:

$$(1/T)\log(y_{it}/y_{i,t-T}) = a - [\log(y_{i,t-T})](1 - e^{-\beta T})(1/T) + \text{other variables,}$$

where $y_{i,t-T}$ is per capita gross domestic product (GDP) in region i at the beginning of the subperiod; y_{it} is per capita GDP at time t; T is the length of the interval; and the other variables are country dummies and the shares of agriculture and industry in employment or GDP at the start of the time period (see note a). Standard errors are in parentheses. The standard errors of the regression are in brackets.

a. The additional variables in this column are the shares of agriculture and industry in employment at the start of the subperiod, based on a three-way division of employment into agriculture, industry, and services, for the subperiods 1950–60, 1960–70, and 1970–80. The regression for the subperiod 1980–85 includes the shares of agriculture and industry in GDP in 1980.

b. We have two alternative sources of GDP for 1970, Molle (1980) and Eurostat (various editions); they do not coincide. We computed the figures for the 1960–70 subperiod from Molle and those for 1970–80 from Eurostat. Since the correlation between the two measures of the levels of per capita GDP in 1970 is 0.988, this discrepancy should not be important.

c. The combined regression restricts the value of β to be the same across all four subperiods. The restricted β are estimated using iterative, weighted, nonlinear least squares.

d. The likelihood-ratio test is based on the null hypothesis that the β are the same across all subperiods. It follows a chi-squared (χ^2) distribution. The 0.05 χ^2 value with three degrees of freedom is 7.8.

Note that the first value, for country aggregates, is an estimate of β convergence between countries, whereas the second, with regional dummies, is an estimate within countries.

The last equation of table 6.6 adds the shares of agriculture and industry in total employment at the start of the subperiod for the 1950–60, 1960–70, and 1970–80 subperiods. The regression for the 1980–85 subperiod adds the shares in overall GDP at the start of the period. These share variables are analogous to the agricultural share and structural composition variables that we used for the United States. In effect, the share variables for the European regions are as close as we can come with our present data to the structural variable, S_{it}.

The main new result from adding these variables is the acceptance of the hypothesis of stability in the β coefficients at the 5 percent level. (These results allow for period-specific coefficients on the share variables and the country dummies.) The joint estimate, $\hat{\beta} = 0.0178$, does not change much from that shown in the second equation. This point estimate—showing β convergence at slightly below 2 percent a year—is somewhat less than the corresponding value, 0.0216, found for the U.S. states in table 6.3.

We have also estimated the joint system with individual β coefficients for the seven countries. This system corresponds to the four-period regression shown in the last equation of table 6.6 except that the coefficient β is allowed to vary over the countries (but not over the subperiods). Thus, the system contains period-specific country dummies and the agricultural and industrial share variables (with coefficients that vary over the subperiods but not across the countries). The resulting estimates for β follow.

Country	Estimate (standard error)
Germany (11 regions)	0.0230 (0.0061)
United Kingdom (11 regions)	0.0337 (0.0093)
Italy (20 regions)	0.0118 (0.0036)
France (21 regions)	0.0097 (0.0059)
Netherlands (4 regions)	0.0496 (0.0202)
Belgium (3 regions)	0.0237 (0.0164)
Denmark (3 regions)	0.0018 (0.0211)

The likelihood-ratio statistic for equality of the β coefficients across the seven countries is 12.6, which coincides with the 5 percent critical value from the chi-squared distribution with six degrees of freedom. We could try to come up with reasons why the regions in the Netherlands and the United Kingdom have higher than average β convergence, whereas those

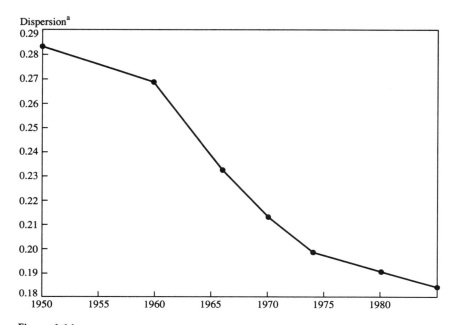

Figure 6.14
Dispersion of gross domestic product across European regions, 1950–85. Source: Authors' own calculations using Molle (1980) and Eurostat (various years). The 73 regions listed in table 6.5 are included in the analysis.
a. Dispersion is measured by the unweighted cross-sectional standard deviation of the log of per capita GDP, relative to the country mean.

in Denmark, France, and Italy have lower than average convergence. But, since the differences are only marginally significant in a statistical sense, the main conclusion is that similar rates of β convergence are consistent with the data.

Analysis of σ Convergence

Figure 6.14 shows the unweighted standard deviation, σ_t, for the log of per capita GDP (expressed relative to the mean for the respective country) for the seventy-three European regions. (The data point for 1966 is based on partial coverage because figures for France and Denmark are unavailable.) Since the regional data are expressed relative to country means, the values shown in the figure refer to σ convergence for regions within countries and not across countries. The principal observation is that σ_t for the European regions declined from 0.28 in 1950 to 0.18 in 1985. The value for Europe

Dispersion[a]

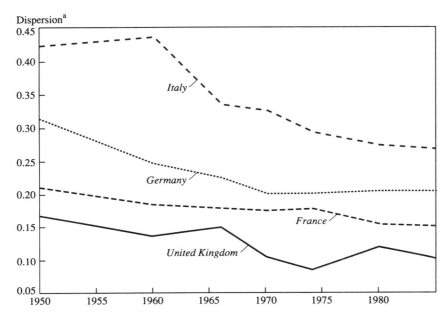

Figure 6.15
Dispersion of gross domestic product within four European countries, 1950–85. Source:
Authors' own calculations using Molle (1980) and Eurostat (various years). See table 6.5
for a list of regions in each country.
a. Dispersion is measured by the unweighted cross-sectional standard deviation of the log
of per capita GDP.

in 1985 is still somewhat above the 0.14 value for U.S. GSP in 1986 (or the
low point of 0.13 in 1972).

Figure 6.14 shows that the fall in σ_t for the European regions moderated
from 1974 to 1985. We found somewhat similar behavior for σ_t based on
U.S. GSP in figure 6.11, although the U.S. results showed a substantial rise
in σ_t from the mid-1970s to the early 1980s. For the United States, we think
we can explain part of the pattern in σ_t after the mid-1970s as an effect of
oil shocks; a similar story may account for the behavior of σ_t for Europe in
figure 6.14. (Although the United Kingdom is the only oil producer among
the seven countries, the regions of Europe can still vary substantially in
their sensitivity to oil shocks.)

Figure 6.15 shows the behavior of σ_t for the regions within the four
largest European countries in the sample: Germany, the United Kingdom,
Italy, and France. The rank order among these countries does not change
over the period: dispersion is highest in Italy, followed by Germany, France,

and the United Kingdom. The overall pattern shows declines in σ_t over time for each country, although little net change occurs since 1970 for Germany and the United Kingdom. In particular, the rise in σ_t from 1974 to 1980 for the United Kingdom—the one oil producer in the European sample—likely reflects the effects of oil shocks. In 1985, the values of σ_t are 0.26 for Italy, 0.20 for Germany, 0.15 for France, and 0.10 for the United Kingdom, compared with 0.15 for U.S. GSP. Thus, although σ_t for Italy has fallen from 0.42 in 1950, Italy still has a way to go to attain the regional dispersion of per capita GDP that is characteristic of the other countries.

The high value of σ_t for Italy especially reflects the spread between the prosperous north and the poor south. A popular view is that the backward regions of southern Italy will always lag behind the advanced regions of northern Italy (and vice versa for the United Kingdom). Our overall findings do not accord with this type of story since we find substantial evidence of β and σ convergence across the regions of Europe. For example, with respect to the β convergence seen in figure 6.12, many of the observations with the highest initial per capita GDP (relative to the own-country mean) are for northern Italy, whereas many with the lowest per capita GDP are for southern Italy (see table 6.5 and the map in figure 6.13). These observations scatter reasonably well around the regression line: as predicted, the initially poorer regions in Italy generally grow faster than the initially richer.

Table 6.7 shows the full array of data for the averages of four prosperous regions in northern Italy and seven poor regions in southern Italy. The northern regions began in 1950 with per capita GDP 70 percent above the mean for Italy, whereas the southern regions began 32 percent below the mean. As predicted, the northern regions grew from 1950 to 1985 at a below-average rate—0.71 percent a year below the mean—whereas the southern regions grew at an above-average rate—0.39 percent a year above the mean. Accordingly, in 1985, the northern regions were only 38 percent above the mean, whereas the southern regions were only 25 percent below the mean. The relative growth performances from 1950 to 1985 correspond well to the predicted behavior implied by the jointly estimated value from the last equation of table 6.6. That value implies that the northern regions should have grown on average at a rate 0.70 percent a year below the mean, whereas the southern regions should have grown on average at a rate 0.51 percent a year above the mean. Thus, there is nothing surprising in the relative performances of the regions of northern and southern Italy. The south of Italy has not yet caught up because it

Table 6.7
Relative gross domestic product and growth in the north and south of Italy and the
United Kingdom, 1950–85

Variable	Italy		United Kingdom	
	North	South	North	South
Relative GDP, 1950[a]	0.532	−0.385	−0.002	0.003
Relative growth, 1950–60[b]	−0.0014	0.0002	−0.0002	0.0003
Relative GDP, 1960	0.518	−0.383	−0.004	0.006
Relative growth, 1960–70	−0.0155	0.0080	−0.0027	0.0041
Relative GDP, 1970[c]	0.363	−0.303	−0.031	0.047
Relative GDP, 1970[d]	0.404	−0.344	−0.044	0.066
Relative growth, 1970–80	−0.0075	0.0042	0.0021	−0.0031
Relative GDP, 1980	0.329	−0.302	−0.023	0.035
Relative growth, 1980–85	−0.0011	0.0023	−0.0016	0.0024
Relative GDP, 1985	0.324	−0.290	−0.031	0.047

Sources: Data up through 1970 are from Molle (1980). Data after 1970 are from Eurostat
(various years). The four northern regions for Italy are Piemonte (number 23 in table 6.5),
Valle d'Aosta (24), Liguria (25), and Lombardia (26). The seven southern regions for Italy
are Campania (35), Abruzzi (36), Molise (37), Puglia (38), Basilicata (39), Calabria (40), and
Sicilia (41). The six northern regions for the United Kingdom are North (12), Yorkshire-
Humberside (13), North-West (18), West Midlands (19), Wales (20), and Scotland (21).
Northern Ireland is excluded here. The four southern regions for the United Kingdom are
East Midlands (14), East Anglia (15), South-East (16), and South-West (17).
a. The variable is regional relative to national per capita GDP, calculated as the ratio of logs.
Both regional and national data are unweighted means of the disaggregated data.
b. The variable is regional relative to the national annual growth rate of per capita GDP.
Both regional and national data are unweighted means of the disaggregated data.
c. Data are from Molle (1980).
d. Data are from Eurostat (various years).

started far behind the north, and the rate of β convergence is only about 2
percent a year.

Table 6.7 also shows comparable statistics for the north and south of the
United Kingdom. (The region for Northern Ireland—a substantial outlier
for the United Kingdom—is excluded from these calculations.) One immediate observation is that the magnitude of the dispersion between the north
and south of the United Kingdom is trivial relative to that between the
north and south of Italy. In any event, because the six northern and four
southern regions began in 1950 with similar averages for per capita GDP,
the theory predicts that subsequent growth rates would also be similar. In
fact, the northern regions grew by 0.05 percent a year below the mean,
whereas the southern ones grew at 0.07 percent a year above the mean.
Therefore, in 1985, the average level of per capita GDP in the north was

about 3 percent below the mean, whereas that in the south was about 5 percent above the mean. Although the theory does not predict this outcome, these results can likely be explained by sectoral disturbances that affected the regions differentially (and in a way that was uncorrelated with the initial levels of per capita GDP).

6.6 The Implications of β Convergence

A striking aspect of our findings is the similarity in the estimated rates of β convergence in different contexts. We first summarize the elements of this empirical regularity, then assess the similarity in the estimates from a theoretical perspective, and finally show the significance of the results by applying them to developments in recently unified Germany.

We find ample evidence that poorer regions within a country tend to grow faster than richer regions, a property that we call β convergence. For U.S. per capita personal income from 1880 to 1988, we estimate the speed of convergence, β, to be around 2 percent a year whether we look within or across the four major geographical regions. We also get similar estimates of β when we examine per capita gross state product from 1963 to 1986. For the output measure, β convergence appears within eight standard nonagricultural sectors of production (mining; construction; manufacturing; transportation; wholesale and retail trade; finance, insurance, real estate; services; and government), although the size of β for manufacturing is substantially higher than those for the other sectors.

The results for seventy-three regions of seven European countries (Germany, the United Kingdom, Italy, France, the Netherlands, Belgium, and Denmark) apply to per capita gross domestic product from 1950 to 1985. The estimated rates of β convergence are similar to those found for the United States; in particular, we see no evidence that poor regions, such as those in southern Italy, are being systematically left behind in the growth process. For the seven countries considered in this study, the cross-country estimates of β are similar to the within-country estimates.

We have, in other recent work, obtained estimates of β for a broader cross section of countries in the post–World War II period: one sample contains twenty OECD countries and another comprises a less homogeneous group of ninety-eight countries.[41] If we examine only the simple relation between the per capita growth rate and initial per capita product, then the estimates of β are around 1 percent a year for the OECD sample and near 0 for the larger sample. Recall, however, that the neoclassical growth model summarized by equation (1) predicts a conditional form of convergence in which differences in per capita product enter relative to differences in steady-state positions, $\hat{y}_i^*$ and x_i^*. If we hold constant additional variables that we interpret as proxies for differences across countries in steady-state positions, then we again obtain estimates of β in the neighborhood of 2 percent a year.[42] These results suggest that the ranking of the divergence in the steady-state values goes from the heterogeneous collection of ninety-eight countries at the top to the relatively homogeneous OECD countries to the still more homogeneous regions within the United States or within the seven European countries. In the regional context, our long-period estimates of β depend little on whether we hold constant the proxies for steady-state values, a result that suggests little regional variation of steady-state values within the countries that we have studied.

The neoclassical growth model does not imply that the convergence coefficient, β, would be the same in all times and places. The coefficient depends, as we discussed before, on the underlying parameters of technology and preferences, but not on differences in technologies or government policies that can be represented as proportional effects on the production function, that is, as variations in the parameter A in the function, $Af(\hat{k})$. These A-type effects have important influences on steady-state output per worker, $\hat{y}_i^*$, but not on the speed with which an economy approaches its steady state. Therefore, economies that differ greatly in some respects may nevertheless exhibit similar rates of β convergence.

We noted that a greater degree of labor mobility leads theoretically to a higher convergence coefficient. This effect means that the rates of β convergence would be higher for the regions within countries than for across countries. Direct estimates for the effect of net migration across the U.S. states indicate, however, that this effect is small. In particular, the magnitude of the effect is not large enough to generate a statistically detectable gap between the β coefficients for regions and countries.

Capital mobility also tends to be greater across regions within a country than across countries. The effects of capital mobility on β convergence are, however, difficult to pin down. With identical technologies, capital mobility speeds up convergence for per capita product but slows down convergence for per capita income. Our results for the U.S. states show little distinction in the dynamics of product and income, an observation that leads us to deemphasize capital mobility. Also, if technologies (including government policies) differ across economies, then capital may move from poor to rich economies and thereby lead to divergence of per capita product. Thus, it is not obvious that greater capital mobility across regions than across countries would lead to higher rates of β convergence for regions than for countries.

Suppose that, despite the theoretical ambiguities, we take it as an empirical regularity that the rate of β convergence is roughly 2 percent a year in a variety of circumstances. We can highlight the potential significance of this finding by showing how it applies to the recent unification of East and West Germany.[43] Suppose that the ratio of the West's per capita income to the East's in 1990 is two, the order of magnitude suggested by George Akerlof and his coauthors. Then a β coefficient of 2 percent a year implies that the East's per capita income would grow initially by 1.4 percent a year higher than the West's.[44] The half-life of this convergence process is thirty-five years; that is, it would take thirty-five years for half of the initial East-West gap to be eliminated. Thus, the results extrapolated from our findings for regions of the United States and Europe and for a variety of countries imply that East Germany's achieving "parity" in the short run is unimaginable.

Table 6A.1
Personal income data for U.S. states, 1880–1988

Variable	Year(s)	Mean	Standard deviation
Log of income[a]	1880[b]	0.478	0.545
	1900	0.719	0.465
	1920	0.995	0.327
	1930	1.026	0.401
	1940	1.170	0.356
	1950	1.661	0.244
	1960	1.805	0.208
	1970	2.112	0.168
	1980	2.262	0.150
	1988	2.425	0.194
Growth of income[c]	1880–1988[b]	0.0181	0.0045
	1880–1900[b]	0.0126	0.0083
	1900–20	0.0138	0.0105
	1920–30	0.0030	0.0140
	1930–40	0.0144	0.0090
	1940–50	0.0492	0.0147
	1950–60	0.0143	0.0065
	1960–70	0.0308	0.0063
	1970–80	0.0150	0.0067
	1980–88	0.0204	0.0141

Table 6A.1 (continued)

Variable	Year(s)	Mean	Standard deviation
Share of agriculture[d]	1880[b]	0.307	0.184
	1900	0.273	0.150
	1920	0.211	0.120
	1930	0.134	0.087
	1940	0.122	0.084
	1950	0.117	0.087
	1960	0.058	0.050
	1970	0.040	0.040
	1980	0.020	0.019
Structural composition variable[e]	1930–40	0.0164	0.0012
	1940–50	0.0393	0.0020
	1950–60	0.0103	0.0082
	1960–70	0.0254	0.0028
	1970–80	0.0044	0.0026
	1980–88	0.0464	0.0058
Regional dummies			
East	...	0.229	...
South	...	0.292	...
Midwest	...	0.250	...
West	...	0.229	...

Sources: Bureau of Economic Analysis (1984), Easterlin (1960a, 1960b), and *Survey of Current Business*, various issues. Except where noted, all figures include observations for the continental states.

a. The log of income is the log of real per capita personal income in state i at time t, or $\log(y_{it})$, where y_{it} is nominal personal income in thousands of nominal dollars per person, divided by the overall CPI (1982 as base year).

b. Oklahoma is excluded from the 1880 data. Wyoming is excluded from the 1880 data on the share of personal income originating in agriculture.

c. The variable is the average annual growth rate of real per capita personal income in state i between years $t - T$ and t: $(1/T)\log(y_{it}/y_{i,t-T})$.

d. The variable is the share of personal income originating in agriculture in state i at time t: $Agry_{it}$.

e. The structural composition variable, S_{it}, described in the text is based on the division of production into nine sectors.

Table 6A.2
Gross state product data, 1963–86

Variable	Year(s)	Mean	Standard deviation
Log of GSP[a]	1963	2.138	0.181
	1969	2.360	0.155
	1975	2.456	0.145
	1981	2.580	0.181
	1986	2.659	0.142
Growth of GSP[b]	1963–86	0.0227	0.0050
	1963–69	0.0370	0.0087
	1969–75	0.0159	0.0149
	1975–81	0.0207	0.0146
	1981–86	0.0159	0.0260
Structural composition variable[c]	1963–69	0.0282	0.0037
	1969–75	0.0053	0.0060
	1975–81	0.0156	0.0080
	1981–86	0.0158	0.0112
Growth of sectoral productivity[d]			
Construction	1963–86	−0.0223	0.0117
Mining[e]	1963–86	−0.0082	0.0178
Manufacturing	1963–86	0.0282	0.0076
Transportation	1963–86	0.0230	0.0047
Trade	1963–86	0.0105	0.0033
FIRE	1963–86	0.0006	0.0058
Services	1963–86	−0.0053	0.0041
Government	1963–86	−0.0062	0.0045
Log of sectoral productivity[d]			
Construction	1963	2.233	0.172
Mining[e]	1963	2.727	0.505
Manufacturing	1963	2.213	0.224
Transportation	1963	2.631	0.076
Trade	1963	2.065	0.087
FIRE	1963	3.494	0.190
Services	1963	1.996	0.118
Government	1963	1.840	0.216
Log of sectoral productivity[d]			
Construction	1986	3.697	0.282
Mining[e]	1986	4.353	0.456
Manufacturing	1986	3.737	0.119
Transportation	1986	4.300	0.109
Trade	1986	3.318	0.096
FIRE	1986	4.750	0.153
Services	1986	3.325	0.114
Government	1986	3.285	0.161

Table 6A.2 (continued)
Source: Renshaw, Trott, and Friedenberg (1988). Except where noted, all figures include observations for the continental states.
a. The log of GSP is the log of real per capita GSP in state i at time t, or $\log(y_{it})$, where y_{it} is nominal GSP in thousands of nominal dollars per person, divided by the national deflator for GSP (1982 as base year).
b. The variable is the average annual growth rate of real per capita GSP between years $t - T$ and t: $(1/T)\log(y_{it}/y_{i,t-T})$.
c. The structural composition variable for GSP is based on a division of production into 54 sectors.
d. Sectoral productivity is defined as the contribution of the sector to real GSP per worker.
e. Connecticut, Delaware, Maine, Massachusetts, New Hampshire, and Rhode Island, which have negligible mining, are excluded from the analysis.

Table 6A.3
Data for European regions, 1950–85

Variable	Year(s)	Mean	Standard deviation
Log of GDP[a]	1950	. . .	0.395
	1960	. . .	0.387
	1970[b]	. . .	0.306
	1970[c]	. . .	0.334
	1980	. . .	0.337
	1985	. . .	0.234
Growth of GDP[a]	1950–85	. . .	0.0088
	1950–60	. . .	0.0159
	1960–70	. . .	0.0190
	1970–80	. . .	0.0098
	1980–85	. . .	0.0331
Sectoral shares in employment			
Agriculture	1950	0.319	0.199
	1960	0.231	0.165
	1970	0.142	0.110
Industry	1950	0.373	0.125
	1960	0.412	0.106
	1970	0.430	0.080
Sectoral shares in GDP[d]			
Agriculture	1970	0.076	0.051
	1980	0.050	0.035
	1985	0.045	0.030
Industry	1970	0.430	0.079
	1980	0.403	0.066
	1985	0.362	0.065
Country dummies			
Germany	. . .	0.151	. . .
Italy	. . .	0.274	. . .
United Kingdom	. . .	0.151	. . .
France	. . .	0.288	. . .

Table 6A.3 (continued)

Variable	Year(s)	Mean	Standard deviation
Netherlands	...	0.055	...
Belgium	...	0.041	...
Denmark	...	0.041	...

Sources: Data up through 1970 are from Molle (1980). Data after 1970 are from Eurostat (various years).
a. The levels of per capita GDP for different years are based on noncomparable indexes.
b. Data are from Molle (1980).
c. Data are from Eurostat (various years).
d. Three regions of Denmark are excluded from the sectoral share in GDP data. For the regressions the 1980 values for Denmark were approximated from the available data for 1974.

Table 6A.4
Migration data for the U.S. states, 1880–1987

Variable	Year(s)	Mean	Standard deviation
Net migration rate[a]	1900–87	0.0034	0.0107
	1900–40	0.0051	0.0119
	1940–87	0.0019	0.0113
	1900–20	0.0107	0.0187
	1920–30	−0.0002	0.0115
	1930–40	−0.0086	0.0069
	1940–50	0.0004	0.0140
	1950–60	0.0009	0.0167
	1960–70	0.0009	0.0112
	1970–80	0.0055	0.0123
	1980–87	0.0020	0.0086
Population density[b]	1880[c]	0.0388	0.0521
	1900	0.0559	0.0797
	1920	0.0771	0.1145
	1930	0.0906	0.1342
	1940	0.0935	0.1379
	1950	0.1062	0.1553
	1960	0.1247	0.1817
	1970	0.1416	0.2081
	1980	0.1504	0.2099
$Heat_i$	...	5.033	2.116
$Log(Heat_i)$	...	8.407	0.539

Source: Bureau of the Census (1975, 1990). Except where noted, the figures include observations for the continental states.
a. The variable is the average annual rate of net in-migration, m_{it}.
b. Population density, π_{it}, is thousands of people per square mile of total area.
c. Oklahoma is excluded from the 1880 data.

Notes

Reproduced with permission from *Brookings Papers on Economic Activity*, no. 1, 1991. Our research has benefited from support by the National Science Foundation and the Bradley Foundation. We appreciate comments on this and related research from members of the Brookings Panel and from Gary Becker, Olivier Blanchard, Paul David, Steve Durlauf, Susan Guthrie, Carol Heim, Anne Krueger, Edward Lazear, Bob Lucas, Greg Mankiw, Kevin M. Murphy, Danny Quah, Sergio Rebelo, and Gavin Wright. We also appreciate research assistance from Michael Kremer and Casey Mulligan.

1. Barro and Sala-i-Martin (1990).

2. Barro and Sala-i-Martin (1990).

3. Solow (1956); Cass (1965); Koopmans (1965).

4. See discussion in Rebelo (1990).

5. Barro and Sala-i-Martin (1991, chap. 1).

6. Barro and Sala-i-Martin (1990) discusses some implications of capital mobility.

7. Some of the counterfactual results of open-economy models with perfect capital markets disappear if we assume that people become less patient as they raise assets and consumption; see Uzawa (1968). This form of preferences is introspectively unappealing. but Blanchard (1985) shows that the aggregation across individuals makes overall economies act this way. In particular, the initially most patient economy stops short of owning everything in the long run, and the less patient economies do not tend toward zero consumption per effective worker. Assets are, however, still likely to become negative for less patient economies.

8. Cohen and Sachs (1986); Barro and Sala-i-Martin (1991, chap. 2).

9. Convergence can be less rapid if immigrants to rich economies are substantially above average in human capital. See Borjas (1990) for a discussion of the characteristics of immigrants.

10. See Nelson and Phelps (1966) for an early model of technological diffusion.

11. Quah (1990) discusses β and σ convergence in terms of Galton's fallacy: the observation that heights of persons in a family regress to the mean across generations (a form of β convergence) does not imply that the dispersion of heights across the population diminishes over time (an example of σ convergence). None of this makes β convergence uninteresting, as Quah seems to suggest; it just points out that β and σ convergence are different concepts. One example of the Quah-Galton effect is the ordinal rankings of teams in a sports league. Although σ_t is constant by definition (so σ convergence cannot apply), we can still think of β convergence in terms of how rapidly teams at the bottom of the ranking tend to rebound toward the middle or how quickly champions tend to revert to mediocrity. The sports example also leads naturally to the issue of overshooting: is a currently weak team or country likely to be in a better position than a currently strong team or country at some future date? In the Quah-Galton context, if person 1 is taller than person 2, would we predict that the offspring of person 2 would eventually be taller than

those of person 1? This type of overshooting cannot occur in the standard neoclassical growth model, which generates a first-order differential equation that is approximated in the linear log-difference form of equation (1). Thus, if x_i^* and $\hat{y}_i^*$ are the same for all i, then if economy 1 starts out ahead of economy 2 we would predict that economy 1 would still be ahead of economy 2 at any date in the future. Our conjecture is that heights also satisfy this property, although we have not examined the data. The possibility of overshooting seems more likely for the rankings of sports teams; in fact, this area may be the best place to apply models of overshooting. For an overview of these models, see Schools Brief (1990).

12. The data on personal income are from Bureau of Economic Analysis (1984), recent issues of *Survey of Current Business*, and Easterlin (1960a, 1960b). See our 1990 study for a discussion . There are no data for Oklahoma for 1880 (which preceded the Oklahoma land rush) and we exclude Alaska, Hawaii, and the District of Columbia throughout the analysis. We use nominal income figures deflated by the overall consumer price index (CPI). If the price level is the same for all states at each point in time, then we can just as well use nominal income figures in our cross-sectional analysis. If prices differ across states at a point in time—that is, if there are departures from purchasing-power parity—then it would be preferable to use individual-state deflators. We think, however, that the available price indexes across states do not improve on the assumption of a common price level. (The analysis requires only constant relative prices for growth rates but equal levels of prices for levels of real income.)

13. These results come from an iterative, weighted, nonlinear least squares method, which allows for heteroskedasticity across the subperiods but not for correlation of the error terms over the subperiods. We have also estimated systems that allow for the correlation by using seemingly unrelated regression, or SURE. In most cases, the results of hypothesis tests are similar. In some cases, however, we had difficulty getting the estimates to converge because of the interaction of the nonlinearity in the model with the large number of parameters introduced by the SURE procedure. Probably it would be better to estimate parsimonious representations that allow for a restricted form of serial correlation in the errors, rather than an arbitrary pattern across the subperiods.

14. The ratio of the wholesale price index (WPI) for farm products to the CPI for all items fell at an annual rate of 3.5 percent from 1920 to 1930. Over that period, the average growth rate of real per capita farm income—nominal income divided by the CPI and farm population—was -2.7 percent a year. In contrast, the average growth rate of real per capita nonfarm personal income was 0.8 percent a year. The data are from Bureau of Economic Analysis (1973) and Bureau of the Census (1975).

15. It is well known that temporary measurement error in y_{it} can lead to an overestimate of the convergence coefficient, β. In previous research we have taken several approaches to assessing the likely magnitude of this effect. See Barro (1991) and Barro and Sala-i-Martin (1990). In one approach we related the growth rate of income between $t - T$ and t, $(1/T) \cdot \log(y_{it}/y_{i,t-T})$, to income at a date prior to $t - T$, say to $\log(y_{i,t-T-\tau})$. If measurement error does not persist over an interval

greater than T' (which we took to be five or ten years), then with a plausible magnitude for β, the asymptotic bias in this form is in the direction opposite to that in the original form. Because the empirical estimates of β from the two forms did not differ greatly, we argued that the effects of measurement error were unlikely to be major.

16. We do not have reliable data on agricultural employment, but the data on farm population suggest that this productivity differential is large, at least in earlier years. We measure farm productivity as farm national income divided by farm population and measure nonfarm productivity as nonfarm national income divided by nonfarm population. Using these concepts of productivity, the ratio of nonfarm to farm productivity was 4.0 in 1889. 2.7 in 1899, 2.3 in 1909, 2.9 in 1920, 3.6 in 1930, 3.7 in 1940, 2.4 in 1960, 1.8 in 1970, 1.6 in 1980, and 1.5 in 1988. The data are from Bureau of Economic Analysis (1973) and Bureau of the Census (1975, 1990). One shortcoming of these measures of productivity is that they do not adjust for differences in family size between farm and nonfarm populations.

17. The ratio of the WPI for farm products to the CPI for all items grew at an average annual rate of 9.5 percent from 1940 to 1950. Over this period, the average growth rate of real per capita farm income (nominal income divided by the CPI and farm population) was 7.8 percent a year, compared to 2.9 percent a year for real per capita nonfarm personal income. The data are from Bureau of the Census (1975).

18. To estimate σ_u we use the first-difference equation for σ_t^2, derived in our 1990 study: $\sigma_t^2 = \sigma_u^2/(1 - e^{-2\beta}) + [\sigma_0^2 - \sigma_u^2/(1 - e^{-2\beta})]e^{-2\beta t}$. The steady-state variance, σ^2, equals the first term in this formula, $\sigma_u^2/(1 - e^{-2\beta})$.

19. The data on transfers come from the Commerce Department and only begin in 1929. Since the amounts of transfers for earlier years are small, the behavior of σ_t with and without transfers would be similar before 1929.

20. See Easterlin (1960a) and Borts and Stein (1964, chap. 2) for related analyses of the regional dispersion of per capita personal income.

21. Sala-i-Martin (1990, chap. 5).

22. Roback (1982).

23. See Mueser and Graves (1990) for a related model of migration.

24. Population density is the ratio of state population to total area (land and water). The data on area are from Bureau of the Census (1990).

25. See, for example, Blomquist, Berger, and Hoehn (1988). Some of the variables that they consider, such as criminal activity, are, however, not exogenous in the same sense as climate or geography.

26. The data on heating- and cooling-degree days refer to average temperatures from 1951 to 1980 and are from Bureau of the Census (1990).

27. The variable is the average of the rates for the subperiods, 1900–20, 1920–30, and so forth through to the final subperiod 1980–87, weighted by the lengths of each interval. The rate for each subperiod is the annual average of net migration divided by state population at the start of the subperiod.

28. The regressions use an iterative, weighted least squares procedure.

29. The overall results do not change greatly if we add the subperiod 1880–1900. This subperiod includes some enormous rates of in-migration, which correspond to the opening of new territories. Because our simple functional form does not fit well in these years, we decided to exclude this subperiod from the present analysis.

30. The data on migration are from Bureau of the Census (1975). Recent figures are computed from data on population, births, and deaths from Bureau of the Census (1990).

31. See Barro and Sala-i-Martin (1990).

32. The assumption here is that the instrumental variables, $\log(Heat_i)$ and $\pi_{i,t-T}$, do not directly influence per capita growth.

33. The data are from Renshaw, Trott, and Friedenberg (1988). See Barro and Sala-i-Martin (1990) for a discussion .

34. Individual-state deflators are unavailable. Since we use a common deflator at each point in time, the particular deflator that we use affects only the constant term in the regressions.

35. Sala-i-Martin (1990, chap. 3).

36. The data on employment by sector are from the Bureau of Labor Statistics (various years).

37. We lost one region for France because some of the data on Corse are combined with those for Provence-Alpes-Côte d'Azur.

38. Molle (1980). We appreciate Carol Heim's suggestion to look at these data.

39. Departures from purchasing-power parity across countries would not affect our main results, which filter out own-country effects. The growth rates for regions within countries involve the same kind of sensitivity to changes in relative prices that applied to GSP for the U.S. states.

40. See Baumol (1986), De Long (1988), Dowrick and Nguyen (1989), and Barro (1991).

41. Barro and Sala-i-Martin (1991, table 5).

42. See Barro and Sala-i-Martin (1991, table 5).

43. A paper by Akerlof and others (1991) explores the issue of German unification.

44. We can also use the findings for the United States (table 6.2) to estimate net migration from Germany's East to its West. The resulting estimate for 1991 (which allows for the differences in per capita income and population density, but not for differences in amenities) is that 1.2 percent, or 203,000, of the people residing in the East would migrate to the West. Akerlof and others (1991, table 9) show that the net out-migration from the East averaged about 22,800 a month, or 274,000 at an annual rate, over the three months since unification in July 1990. Although this rate exceeds our estimate of 203,000, the extrapolation of the U.S. experience to Germany does provide a reasonable order of magnitude.

References

Akerlof, George A., and others. 1991. "East Germany in from the Cold: The Economic Aftermath of Currency Union." *BPEA, 1:1991*, 1–87.

Barro, Robert J. 1991. "Economic Growth in a Cross Section of Countries." *Quarterly Journal of Economics* 106:407–43.

Barro, Robert J., and Xavier Sala-i-Martin. 1990. "Economic Growth and Convergence across the United States." Working Paper 3419. Cambridge, Mass.: National Bureau of Economic Research (August).

Barro, Robert J., and Xavier Sala-i-Martin. 1991. *Economic Growth*. Manuscript, Harvard University.

Baumol, William J. 1986. "Productivity Growth, Convergence, and Welfare: What the Long-Run Data Show." *American Economic Review* 76:1072–85.

Blanchard, Olivier J. 1985. "Debt, Deficits, and Finite Horizons." *Journal of Political Economy* 93:223–47.

Blomquist, Glenn C., Mark C. Berger, and John P. Hoehn. 1988. "New Estimates of Quality of Life in Urban Areas." *American Economic Review* 78:89–107.

Borts, George H., and Jerome L. Stein. 1964. *Economic Growth in a Free Market*. New York: Columbia University Press.

Borjas, George J. 1990. *Friends or Strangers: The Impact of Immigrants on the U.S. Economy*. New York: Basic Books.

Bureau of the Census. 1975. *Historical Statistics of the United States, Colonial Times to 1970, Bicentennial Edition, Parts 1 and 2*. Washington: U.S. Department of Commerce.

Bureau of the Census. 1990. *Statistical Abstract of the United States: 1990*. Washington: U.S. Department of Commerce.

Bureau of Economic Analysis. 1973. *Long Term Economic Growth, 1860–1970*. Washington: Government Printing Office.

Bureau of Economic Analysis. 1984. *State Personal Income by State: Estimates for 1929–1982, and a Statement of Sources and Methods*. Washington: U.S. Department of Commerce.

Bureau of Labor Statistics. Various years. *Employment and Earnings, States and Areas*. Washington: U.S. Department of Labor.

Cass, David. 1965. "Optimum Growth in an Aggregative Model of Capital Accumulation." *Review of Economic Studies* 32:233–40.

Cohen, Daniel, and Jeffrey Sachs. 1986. "Growth and External Debt under Risk of Debt Repudiation." *European Economic Review* 30:526–60.

De Long, J. Bradford. 1988. "Productivity Growth, Convergence, and Welfare: Comment." *American Economic Review* 78:1138–54.

Dowrick, Steve, and Duc-Tho Nguyen. 1989. "OECD Comparative Economic Growth 1950–85: Catch-Up and Convergence." *American Economic Review* 79: 1010–30.

Easterlin, Richard A. 1960a. "Regional Growth of Income: Long Run Tendencies." In *Population Redistribution and Economic Growth, United States, 1870–1950. II: Analyses of Economic Change*, edited by Simon Kuznets, Ann Ratner Miller, and Richard A. Easterlin. Philadelphia: The American Philosophical Society.

Easterlin, Richard A. 1960b. "Interregional Differences in Per Capita Income, Population, and Total Income, 1840–1950." In *Trends in the American Economy in the Nineteenth Century. A Report of the National Bureau of Economic Research, New York.* Princeton: Princeton University Press.

Eurostat. Various years. *Basic Statistics of the Community: A Comparison with Some European Countries, Canada, the USA, Japan, and the USSR.* Luxembourg: Statistical Office of the European Communities.

Koopmans, Tjalling C. 1965. "On the Concept of Optimal Economic Growth." In *Study Week on the Econometric Approach to Development Planning.* Pontificiae Academiae Scientiarum Scripta Varia, no. 28. Chicago: Rand McNally.

Molle, Willem. 1980. *Regional Disparity and Economic Development in the European Community.* Farnborough, England: Saxon House.

Mueser, Peter R., and Philip E. Graves. 1990. "Examining the Role of Economic Opportunity and Amenities in Explaining Population Redistribution." Working Paper 90–4. University of Missouri-Columbia (October).

Nelson, Richard R., and Edmund S. Phelps. 1966. "Investment in Humans, Technological Diffusion, and Economic Growth." *American Economic Review, Papers and Proceedings* 56:69–75.

Quah, Danny. 1990. "Galton's Fallacy and Tests of the Convergence Hypothesis.' Manuscript, Massachusetts Institute of Technology (May).

Rebelo, Sergio T. 1990. "Long Run Policy Analysis and Long Run Growth." Working Paper 3325. Cambridge, Mass.: National Bureau of Economic Research (April).

Renshaw, Vernon, Edward A. Trott, Jr., and Howard L. Friedenberg. 1988. "Gross State Product by Industry, 1963–1986." *Survey of Current Business* 68 (May): 30–46.

Roback, Jennifer. 1982. "Wages, Rents, and the Quality of Life." *Journal of Political Economy* 90:1257–78.

Sala-i-Martin, Xavier. 1990. "On Growth and States." Ph.D. diss., Harvard University.

Schools Brief. 1990. "Why Currencies Overshoot." In *The Economist*, December 1, pp. 89–90. Brief on "Expectations and Exchange Rate Dynamics," by Rudiger Dornbusch, in *Journal of Political Economy* 84:1161–76.

Solow, Robert M. 1956. "A Contribution to the Theory of Economic Growth." *Quarterly Journal of Economics* 70:65–94.

Uzawa, Hirofumi. 1968. "Time Preference, the Consumption Function, and Optimum Asset Holdings." In *Value, Capital, and Growth: Papers in Honour of Sir John Hicks*, edited by J. N. Wolfe. Chicago: Aldine Publishing Company.

7 Technology Adoption and the Mechanics of Economic Development

Stephen L. Parente and Edward C. Prescott

Why aren't all nations as rich as the United States? That is the fundamental problem of economic development. The prevailing view, and ours as well, is that most of the variation in income levels is attributed to differences in technologies. The fundamental question confronting the field of development therefore is why the technologies of all countries are not the same as that of the United States.

Lucas (1988) and others emphasize the difference in the incentives for individuals to acquire knowledge and the resulting difference in stocks of human capital in explaining the disparity in income levels. We are closer to Kuznets in that we emphasize the difference in the incentives for firms or organizations to adopt more advanced technologies and the resulting difference in the technologies used in explaining this disparity in income levels.[1]

The incentives to technology adoption are related to the returns firms expect to realize on the investments they must make in order to adopt a more advanced technology. We know from industry studies that some of this investment takes the form of new machines and equipment. We also know from these same studies that a substantial fraction of investment takes the form of intangible capital. Firms, for instance, devote substantial resources to training workers to use a new technology. Some of this knowledge is embodied in specific individuals; some is embodied within groups of individuals. There is evidence that some of these resources are spent trying to get workers to function within a group framework.

Our theme is that this return on investment is determined primarily by two factors: a country's current technology level relative to the current level of pure or disembodied knowledge in the world (i.e., scientific knowledge, blueprints, ideas—essentially anything that can be written down on a piece of paper), and what we identify as a country's institutional arrangements. The first factor is typically associated with the catch-up hypothesis that a poorer country will tend to grow faster than a richer country until differences in per capita incomes are eliminated. This is because a poorer country, being technologically behind, can adopt the more advanced technologies currently or previously used in richer countries. Furthermore, a technologically backward country need not invest as much as those countries that preceded it in adopting a particular technology because the technologically backward country is able to learn from the experiences of the other countries. This has the effect of increasing the return to technology adoption in these technologically backward countries.

This is the usual explanation given for Japan's spectacular growth over the postwar period. Indeed, several aspects of its experience accord well with this theory. Industry studies do show that much of Japan's success is attributed to its adoption of Western technologies, and Japan's growth rate of per capita output has slowed as the gap between its per capita income level and that of the United States' has narrowed.

But clearly technological backwardness cannot be a sufficient condition for rapid growth. While it is true that Japan technologically lagged behind the United States at the end of the war, it is also true that Japan was technologically backward relative to the United States before the war as well. If technological backwardness was all that mattered, why then did rapid growth in Japan not occur until after the war?

Japan did, of course, suffer significant human loss and destruction of capital as a result of the war. Given these losses and the technological advances that occurred in the United States, Japan may have actually been more technologically backward relative to the United States after the war than before it. But this still leaves unexplained why Japan's per capita income shows a tendency to converge to U.S. levels after the war and not before the war. One could possibly subscribe to those theories that predict that following the destruction of a country's physical capital stock, that country assumes a higher steady state (e.g., Becker, Murphy, Tamura 1990, Chamley 1990). We do not for several reasons. First, England, too, sustained considerable losses of physical capital during the war. Yet its growth rate over the twentieth century has been fairly constant. Second, the evidence does not support the hypothesis that the destruction of physical capital is the catalyst for rapid growth. If so, why was East Germany's performance so poor relative to West Germany's or North Korea's performance so poor relative to South Korea's?

Perhaps, the most overwhelming evidence against the catch-up hypothesis, though, is the failure of per capita income levels across countries to exhibit any tendency to converge. Over the 1950–1985 period, the standard deviation of the logarithm of per capita income increased by 17 percent. Most of this increase is attributed to the performance of the countries of sub-Saharan Africa. These countries, which were among the poorest in the world in 1950, not only stayed poor relative to the rest of the world but many actually experienced declines in real per capita income levels over the postwar period.

The reason technological backwardness is not a sufficient condition for rapid growth is that the return to technology adoption is not determined solely by a country's relative position in the world. Government policies as well as the actions of individuals or groups of individuals other than those making the adoption decision are known to substantially affect this return. The ways a society or components of a society affect the return that the individual or group of individuals adopting the more advanced technology earns on its investment are what we refer to as a country's *institutional arrangements*. Our view is that a backward country will experience rapid growth only if its institutional arrangements do not significantly reduce this return.

The ways by which this return may be reduced are numerous. Some policies and actions reduce this return by effectively increasing the cost of adopting more advanced technologies. The typical way that government increases this cost is by excessive regulation. Bribes are another common way that government increases this cost. This cost can also be raised deliberately by the actions of private individuals or private groups of individuals who either seek economic rents or desire to preserve economic rents. Through lobbying efforts, these private citizens and private groups have been known to delay the adoption of more advanced technologies and, in many cases, prevent outright their adoptions. Other ways this return is reduced are more in the nature of taxes. Through various tax laws, especially corporate tax codes and depreciation tax allowances. government affects the amount of return the adopter can keep. Redistributional coalitions as well, such as labor unions, can also tax away part of this return. This latter type of "tax" has been emphasized particularly by Olson (1982).

Once one considers the effect of these institutional arrangements, or changes in these institutional arrangements, in conjunction with a country's relative position in the world, it becomes easy to make sense of the experiences of most nations. The fact that Japan began to grow rapidly after the war and ever since appears to be converging to U.S. per capita income levels is clearly not coincidental. After its defeat and due to the U.S. presence there under the direction of General Douglas MacArthur, many of Japan's institutional arrangements were replaced with ones more closely resembling those in the United States. It is in this sense that we believe the war served as a catalyst for growth.

That the postwar experiences of South Korea and North Korea or West Germany and East Germany have been so different is really not surprising in light of the tremendous differences in institutional arrangements between the countries. South Korea, in particular, offers a unique example in that its government has taken unusual steps to ensure that the return of firms making the adoption decisions is not reduced significantly. From the end of the Korean War to its first democratic elections, the government outlawed all labor unions. Subsequent to democratic elections in 1961, labor unions have been legalized, but the government still maintains a close watch and tight control over them. On several occasions the government has been linked to the beating of union leaders and organizers. The government's policy of rewarding businesses that achieve specific production targets with cheap credit and tax breaks further serves to increase the returns that businesses can expect to realize. Of recent, the government, in an attempt to maintain South Korea's competitiveness in world markets, set a maximum rate of increase for wages. Interestingly enough, this rate was significantly below the rate that business leaders were willing to accept.

In contrast, governmental policies in many of the less-developed countries have been detrimental to technology adoption and growth. In fact, over the postwar period, government policies in most sub-Saharan African countries and several Central and South American countries have resulted in smaller and smaller returns being realized by those firms doing the technology adoptions. Krueger (1990) documents the increase in what she calls government failures in several less-developed countries over the postwar period. In Ghana, for example, the Cocoa Marketing Board started in 1947 with a government share of sales revenue equal to 3 percent, but by 1978 this share grew to 60 percent. According to Krueger, the increase in government's share of sales revenue in the 1970s alone was associated with a 50 percent reduction in real returns and output over that decade.

Given that such increasingly pervasive policies characterized the vast majority of the less-developed nations, it is not any wonder why many of these countries experienced a decline in real living standards over the postwar period. Ghana, which was one of the biggest losers in terms of the percentage decrease in per capita income over the postwar period, has begun to reverse its growth performance. Between 1983 and 1989, Ghana's average annual rate of growth has exceeded 5 percent. The reversal coincides with the many improvements in Ghana's institutional arrangements that have occurred subsequent to the 1979 military coup in that country.

In order to encourage domestic and foreign investment, for example, the government in 1985 revised the country's investment code to include guarantees against expropriation and for the repatriation of capital and dividends of foreigners. That rapid growth has been associated with such improvements in Ghana's institutional arrangements is exactly what our theory predicts.[2]

We emphasize the need for quantitative theories of growth; that is, theory that provides quantitative answers to specific questions. We think that a criterion for a theory of growth is how well it quantitatively answers the following three questions. The first, in the tradition of Solow (1970), is how well the theory accounts for U.S. steady-state observations. The second question is whether the theory can account for the postwar experience of Japan relative to the United States—in 1950 Japan's per capita income level was one sixth the 1950 U.S. level, and in 1985 it was three fourths the 1985 U.S. level. The third question is how much of the observed diversity in per capita incomes across countries can the model explain.

Much of the groundwork for this theory was laid by Parente (1990), however, his theory did not distinguish between capital and labor inputs. As such, that theory was unable to provide an answer to the first question. Essentially, what we do here is extend that model by introducing a version of the Lucas span-of-control model to the production technology to be able to distinguish between labor and capital inputs. This extension permits us to match the Parente model to the U.S. National Income and Product Account data.

Before proceeding, however, we think it important to note that this model is not one of endogenous growth. Savings rates in the model do not have growth rate effects. Differences in institutional arrangements between two countries in the model translate into different steady-state income levels but not different steady-state growth rates. This puts this theory in the minority of growth theories recently put forth. We do not, however, view this feature as a deficiency of the model. Rather, we see it as a virtue. Because our reasons may not be apparent to the reader, we postpone the description of the model by one section in order to explain ourselves.

7.1   Endogenous Models of Growth and the Data

Part of the reason endogenous growth models have gained such acceptance since Paul Romer brought them to the forefront in 1986 is the failure of neoclassical growth theory to adequately account for the huge disparity in per capita income levels across countries. In that model, of course, savings rates only have level effects. Lucas (1988) showed that these level effects were not large enough to account for the huge observed disparity in income levels. With these endogenous growth models, however, generating huge differences in per capita income levels is easy. Since differences in preference and policy parameters translate into different steady-state growth rates, all that is really needed to explain the huge differences in income levels is that a sufficient number of years have passed.

The major problem we see with these endogenous growth theories, however, is that they predict that the difference in the logarithm of per capita income between two nonidentical countries should increase without bound over time.[3] According to these models, not only should we see the distribution of income spreading out, but we should see for any arbitrary subset of countries its distribution spreading out as well. As noted in the introduction, the standard deviation of the logarithm of per capita income did increase by 17 percent over the 1950 to 1985 period, but most of this increase is attributed to the performance of the countries in the tail end of the distribution. Table 7.1 documents this feature of the data. It shows the standard deviation of the logarithm of per capita income for various subsets of countries in selected years where the subsets are determined by whether a country had a beginning level of per capita income at least x percent of the U.S. level in that year.[4] As can be easily seen by this table, for the higher income subsets there is no tendency for income levels to move apart. In fact, for the countries with an initial per capita income level at least 30 percent of the U.S.'s initial level, there is a slight tendency for income levels to converge.

Proponents of these endogenous growth models point to several cross-country growth regression studies that find robust correlations between certain policy parameters and growth rates (e.g., Barro 1991). In a thorough study of these regressions, Levine and Renelt (1991), however, find that almost all these "robust" correlations disappear when the list of explanatory variables in the regression is slightly altered. Using Laemer's extreme bound test, Levine and Renelt find that only a country's investment share of GDP and its initial level of income are robustly correlated with a country's growth rate of per capita income.[5] Such findings are entirely consistent with our model.[6]

By pointing out this failure of endogenous models of growth, we do not mean to imply, however, that we believe that no actions taken by individuals affect growth rates . We are just saying that over long periods of time, countries cannot be growing at different rates. It may be the case that some policies in some countries, (in particular, those policies that affect the rate

Table 7.1
Standard deviations of the logarithm of per capita income

Set of countries beginning with at least 0% of U.S. per capita income
Beginning years

	1950	1955	1960	1965	1970	1975
1950	.87	—	—	—	—	—
1955	.88	.88	—	—	—	—
1960	.90	.90	.98	—	—	—
1965	.93	.92	1.01	1.02	—	—
1970	.95	.95	1.04	1.04	1.07	—
1975	.97	.96	1.06	1.07	1.09	1.09
1980	1.00	1.01	1.11	1.12	1.13	1.13
1985	1.02	1.04	1.15	1.15	1.15	1.16
	(65)	(78)	(124)	(126)	(129)	(130)

Set of countries beginning with at least 15% of U.S. per capita income
Beginning years

	1950	1955	1960	1965	1970	1975
1950	.55	—	—	—	—	—
1955	.55	.56	—	—	—	—
1960	.59	.56	.66	—	—	—
1965	.59	.56	.64	.64	—	—
1970	.60	.56	.60	.60	.65	—
1975	.58	.53	.56	.56	.56	.60
1980	.60	.57	.56	.56	.56	.58
1985	.67	.62	.61	.61	.61	.60
	(44)	(48)	(63)	(64)	(69)	(71)

Set of countries beginning with at least 30% of U.S. per capita income
Beginning years

	1950	1955	1960	1965	1970	1975
1950	.33	—	—	—	—	—
1955	.30	.32	—	—	—	—
1960	.28	.30	.52	—	—	—
1965	.29	.30	.46	.47	—	—
1970	.28	.28	.41	.42	.50	—
1975	.28	.27	.37	.37	.44	.43
1980	.30	.29	.36	.36	.40	.43
1985	.37	.36	.42	.42	.42	.42
	(27)	(29)	(37)	(38)	(46)	(49)

* Number in parentheses at bottom of column denotes number of countries included in calculations of standard deviation.

of scientific advance), affect the growth rates of those countries, but because of spillovers, all countries average the same rate of growth. We do not consider this scenario here, however, as we treat pure knowledge as exogenous. An interesting extension of the model would allow for the level and growth rate of this knowledge to be endogenously determined.[7]

7.2 Model Economy

The Household

The household is assumed to value a composite commodity made up of a consumption good, c, and services generated by the stock of household durables, d. In addition to this composite commodity, the household is assumed to derive utility from a public good, which we denote by g. This good is viewed in the model as being local in nature (i.e., parks, libraries, fire and police services, et al.). In order to simplify the analysis, we assume that the household's utility is additively separable in the composite commodity and the public good.

The discounted stream of utility over a household's infinite lifetime is

$$\sum_{t=0}^{\infty} \beta^t \cdot \left[\frac{1}{1-\sigma} \cdot (c_t^\phi \cdot d_t^{1-\phi})^{1-\sigma} + U(g_t) \right] \tag{1}$$

where $0 < \phi < 1$, $0 < \beta < 1$, $\sigma > 1$, and U is strictly increasing in g. Leisure is suppressed from the household's utility as the labor-leisure decision is not that central to growth.

The time endowment of the household in every period is one. In addition the household is endowed at date 0 with a stock of durables d_o. This stock of durables is assumed to depreciate at a rate of δ_d. If x_{dt} denotes additions to a household's stock of durable goods at time t, then its stock in period $t+1$ is

$$d_{t+1} = (1 - \delta_d) \cdot d_t + x_{dt}. \tag{2}$$

The Firm

For each household there corresponds a firm, which at any date that household can manage if it chooses to do so.[8] The time requirement to manage a firm is 1 so that a household that manages a firm in period t cannot supply labor elsewhere in the economy. We index a household's managerial talent by μ. A manager at date t hires labor, N_t, and combines it with the firm's stock of tangible capital, K_t, and its technology level, A_t, to produce output, Y_t, according to the following production function

$$Y_t = \mu \cdot A_t \cdot K_t^{\theta} \cdot [\min(N_t, \bar{N})]^{1-\theta} \qquad 0 < \theta < 1, \bar{N} > 0. \qquad (3)$$

The function given by equation (3) is increasing and concave in K and N. Essentially, (3) is a version of the Lucas span-of-control model with the technology-level variable, A_t, added.

Besides choosing the amount of labor to hire, a manager at date t also chooses the firm's period $t + 1$ tangible capital stock and its level of technology. A firm's stock of tangible capital is assumed to depreciate at a rate δ_k. Let X_{kt} denote the amount of investment in tangible capital by a firm at time t. Then that firm's tangible stock of capital in period $t + 1$ is

$$K_{t+1} = (1 - \delta_k) \cdot K_t + X_{kt}. \qquad (4)$$

The increase in the firm's technology level resulting from an investment of X_A units of output depends on its current level of technology relative to the level of world technology at the time of investment. The world technology at time t is denoted by W_t. By world technology we mean the stock of pure or disembodied knowledge (i.e., blueprints, ideas, scientific knowledge, anything that can be written down on a piece of paper). All individuals in our model are assumed to have access to this knowledge. Thus, pure knowledge spills over to the entire world equally.[9]

For the purpose of this paper, W is assumed to be determined outside the model and to grow at the constant rate of γ_w. The law of motion that describes this is

$$W_{t+1} = W_t \cdot (1 + \gamma_W). \qquad (5)$$

Clearly, specific actions undertaken by individuals or groups of individuals affect the level of world technology and its rate of growth. This theory, however, is not intended to be a theory of world technology growth. We are interested in the problem of development, that is, why all countries are not as rich as the United States. For most countries in the world, especially the poorest, their policies would not seem to significantly affect this stock of knowledge.

Given the world technology at time t, and given a firm's current technology level A, the amount of investment needed to realize a technology level equal to A' in period $t + 1$ is

$$X_{At} = \int_A^{A'} \left(\frac{s}{W_t}\right)^{\alpha} ds \qquad \alpha \geq 0. \qquad (6)$$

There are at least two features of this investment technology worth emphasizing. The first is that given a firm's current technology level and a world technology level, there are diminishing returns to investment. The second, and the more important of the two in terms of the theme of this chapter, is that for a given amount of investment, the increase in technologies is larger the lower is the firm's current level of technology. A firm that in period t has a higher technology level than another firm but invests the same amount will in period $t + 1$ still have a higher technology level than the other firm, but the difference between the two firms' technologies will diminish.

The parameter α has important implications for the benefits associated with being technologically behind. Larger values for α imply larger increases in technologies for any given amount of investment X_A. Larger values for α also imply smaller differences in period $t + 1$ technologies between two firms with different technology levels in period t that make the same investment X_A.

Integration of (6) yields

$$(\alpha + 1) \cdot X_{At} = [A_{t+1}^{\alpha+1} - A_t^{\alpha+1}]/[W_o^\alpha \cdot (1 + \gamma_w)^{\alpha \cdot t}] \tag{7}$$

Without loss of generality, we set W_o equal to 1.

The only way any firm can raise its technology level from A to A' is if that firm makes the investment X_A given by equation (7). In this sense, technology is firm specific. We treat tangible capital in the model as being firm specific as well. Clearly, some fraction of a firm's tangible capital stock that consists of vehicles, buildings, and office equipment is not firm specific. Nevertheless, we make this assumption as it significantly simplifies the subsequent analysis. Because capital and technology are both firm specific, a firm that is not operated in some period cannot rent out its tangible capital stock or license its technology.

Feasibility requires that at each date the number of managers and the number of workers per firm equal the size of the work force. We denote the size of the work force in period t by L_t. In this chapter, we ignore population growth. Thus, L_t is assumed to equal L for all time. Because our emphasis is primarily on growth and not on the size and distribution of firms, we simply assume that there are $M = L/(\bar{N} + 1)$ households with managerial talent $\mu = \eta > 0$ and $L - M$ households with managerial talent $\mu = 0$. The implication of this assumption is that in equilibrium there will be M firms in the economy, each of which employs $\bar{N}$ units of labor at each date. Given that we assume all firms begin with the same technology level A_o and tangible capital stock K_o, in equilibrium the date t product of each firm will be

$$Y_t = \eta \cdot A_t \cdot K_t^\theta \cdot \overline{N}^{1-\theta}. \tag{8}$$

From (8) it is apparent that it is impossible for Y, A, and K to all grow at the same rate along a balanced growth path. However, if we define

$$Z_t = A_t^{\alpha+1}/(1 + \gamma_W)^{\alpha \cdot t} \qquad \text{and} \qquad X_{Zt} = X_{At}, \tag{9}$$

and make the corresponding change in variables, it is possible to define a steady-state solution where Y, K, X_k, Z, and X_Z all grow at the same rate γ. Variable Z will have the interpretation of a firm's stock of intangible or technology capital. In this Z-space, the date t product of a firm becomes

$$Y_t = \eta \cdot (1 + \gamma_W)^{\alpha \cdot t/(\alpha+1)} \cdot Z_t^{1/(\alpha+1)} \cdot K_t^\theta \cdot \overline{N}^{1-\theta} \tag{10}$$

and the investment technology (7) becomes

$$(\alpha + 1) \cdot X_{Zt} = (1 + \gamma_W)^\alpha \cdot Z_{t+1} - Z_t. \tag{11}$$

From (10) and (11) it follows that in order for Y, K, and Z to all grow at a rate of γ, the following relation between γ and γ_w must hold:

$$1 + \gamma = (1 + \gamma_W)^{\alpha/[\alpha - \theta \cdot (\alpha+1)]}. \tag{12}$$

As can be seen by (12), this model is not one of endogenous growth: there is no relation between a country's thriftiness and its growth rate of per capita income in steady state.

Because we wish to stay within the competitive equilibrium framework, we require that the coefficients on the two types of capital stocks sum to less than one. Labor in our model will receive the residual of output after both types of capital are paid their marginal products. If the sum of the coefficients on tangible and intangible capital were to exceed one, then payment of these factors' marginal product would more than exhaust output.

Institutional Arrangements

There are many ways by which a country's institutional arrangements can reduce the returns that a firm adopting a more advanced technology earns on its investment. In this chapter, we are not so much interested in how this return is reduced, but by how much it is reduced. A construct that has proved very useful in the public finance area is that of an effective tax rate.

The effective tax rate construct allows one to summarize all the effects of a tax system into a single measure. It is the tax rate on broad-based income that would lead to the same after-tax return that is actually observed.

The effective tax rate for tangible capital has been determined for some countries in several other papers. We believe that this same approach can be used to determine an effective tax rate for intangible capital as well. Of course, in determining the effective tax rate for intangible capital, we need to incorporate all the various ways a country's institutional arrangements reduce the return to technology adoption. We discuss the issue of an effective tax rate in greater detail at the end of the chapter.

Let τ_z and τ_k denote the effective tax rates on intangible and tangible capital income. Then the effective tax on intangible capital income is

$$\tau_z \cdot r_z \cdot Z_t \tag{13}$$

and the effective tax on tangible capital income is

$$\tau_k \cdot r_k \cdot K_t \tag{14}$$

The variable r_z is the steady-state marginal product of intangible capital. The variable r_z is the steady-state marginal product net of depreciation. An important distinction between the two types of capital is that tangible capital physically depreciates. In contrast, intangible capital depreciates only in the sense that over time, as the level of world technology increases, its price falls. For tax purposes only physical depreciation on tangible capital is taken into account. Alternatively, we could have used the marginal product of tangible capital in equation (14). In that case the effective tax rate would be adjusted to take the depreciation tax allowances into account. However, because we wished to make clear the difference in depreciations of the two types of capital, we chose to use the marginal product net of depreciation in (14).

It is very easy to think of ways in which these taxes are redistributed or dissipated. Some may be used by the government to provide infrastructure and services that increase private business productivity. We do not model the use of these taxes in this way, but it would be very easy to think of an extension of the model in the tradition of Barro (1990) where government services would also be an input in the firm's production function. Within the lesser-developed countries of the world, a large percentage of these tax receipts tend to be pocketed by government officials. Alternatively, we could model these tax receipts as being redistributed to a select subset of the population. This would, however, seem to complicate the notation and analysis without significantly enriching the results. What we do instead is assume that all such tax receipts are used to provide the local public good. The technology for producing this good is assumed to be such that one unit of tax revenue results in one unit of the public good.

In light of this redistributional scheme and the tax revenues given by equations (13) and (14), the resource constraint for our economy is

$$c_t + x_{kt} + x_{dt} + x_{zt} = (1 + \gamma_W)^{\alpha \cdot t/(\alpha+1)} \cdot k_t^\theta \cdot z_t^{1/(\alpha+1)} - \tau_z \cdot r_z \cdot z_t - \tau_k \cdot r_k \cdot k_t$$

(15)

and

$$g_t = \tau_z \cdot r_z \cdot z_t + \tau_k \cdot r_k \cdot k_t.^{10}$$

(16)

Here, and in subsequent notation, lowercase letters denote per capita values of variables.

The Competitive Equilibrium

A household at each date either manages a firm or supplies work elsewhere in the economy. We permit households to go from being managers to workers and vice versa between any two periods. However, since capital is firm specific, a firm that is not managed in a given period is assumed to lose both its tangible and intangible capital stocks. Furthermore, we assume that a firm's capital stocks can only be increased if a manager is on hand in the preceding period to make the investments. Thus, any time a firm is started up again by its manager, its output in that period is zero. Let m_t indicate whether a firm is or is not managed in period t. A value of 1 for m_t indicates that the firm is managed in period t while a value of 0 indicates that the firm is not managed in period t. The problem facing a manager-firm given the institutional arrangements of the country in which it resides is to maximize it present value

$$V(K_0, Z_0) = \text{maximize} \left\{ \sum_{t=0}^{\infty} m_t \cdot p_t \cdot [Y_t - w_t \cdot (N_t + 1) - X_{kt} - X_{zt}] \right.$$

$$\left. - r_k \cdot \tau_k \cdot K_t - r_z \cdot \tau_z \cdot Z_t] \right\}$$

(17)

subject to equations (4), (10), and (11), subject to constraints $K_{t+1} = Z_{t+1} = 0$ whenever $m_t = 0$, and given initial capital stocks K_0 and Z_0. Here, $\{p_t\}_{t=0}^{\infty}$ are the Arrow-Debreu prices of the composite commodity and $\{w_t\}_{t=0}^{\infty}$ are the real wages. Both $\{p_t\}_{t=0}^{\infty}$ and $\{w_t\}_{t=0}^{\infty}$ are taken as given by the manager-firm.

The problem facing the household is to choose a path for consumption and the stock of durables that maximizes

$$\sum_{t=0}^{\infty} \beta^t \cdot \frac{1}{1-\sigma} \cdot (c_t^\phi \cdot d_t^{1-\phi})^{1-\sigma} \qquad (18)$$

subject to the constraint that a household is either a manager or worker at each date, subject to consumer durable constraints (2), subject to the budget constraint

$$\sum_{t=0}^{\infty} p_t \cdot [c_t + x_{dt} - w_t] \leqslant V_0, \qquad (19)$$

and given an initial capital stock d_0. Here, the variable V_0 denotes the household's wealth. The household, like the manager-firm, takes $\{p_t\}_{t=0}^{\infty}$ and $\{w_t\}_{t=0}^{\infty}$ as given.

Steady-State Analysis

We exploit the fact that the competitive equilibrium allocation solves a particular programming problem to find the competitive equilibrium. Because preferences are homothetic, equilibrium prices and market clearing quantities will be the same whether wealth is distributed evenly or unevenly. To be specific and to keep the notation to a minimum, we assume that all households have the same wealth V_0 and initial stock of durables d_0.

Each manager owns the firm it operates so that any manager whose firm has a sufficiently large present value must have debts at date 0 just large enough so that its wealth is V_0. Any household that never manages and any manager whose firm has a sufficiently small present value conversely is assumed to have claims at date 0 just large enough so that their individual wealths are also V_0. A consistency requirement is that aggregate wealth $L \cdot V_0$ satisfy

$$L \cdot V_0 = \sum V(K_0, Z_0). \qquad (20)$$

Given the assumption of equal wealth, the relevant programming problem which the competitive equilibrium solves is

$$\text{maximize } \sum_{t=0}^{\infty} \beta^t \cdot \frac{1}{1-\sigma} \cdot (c_t^\phi \cdot d_t^{1-\phi})^{1-\sigma} \qquad (21)$$

subject to

$$c_t + x_{kt} + x_{dt} + x_{zt} = (1+\gamma_w)^{\alpha \cdot t/(\alpha+1)} \cdot k_t^\theta \cdot z_t^{1/(\alpha+1)} - \tau_z \cdot r_z \cdot z_t - \tau_k \cdot r_k \cdot k_t \qquad (22)$$

$$k_{t+1} = (1 - \delta_k) \cdot k_t + x_{kt} \qquad (23)$$

$$d_{t+1} = (1 - \delta_d) \cdot d_t + x_{dt} \qquad (24)$$

$$(1 + \gamma_W)^\alpha \cdot z_{t+1} = z_t + (1 + \alpha) \cdot x_{zt} \qquad (25)$$

given z_0, d_0, k_0, τ_k, and τ_z. The date t decision variables for this problem are c_t, k_{t+1}, d_{t+1}, and z_{t+1}. The amount of local public good g_t is not a decision variable. The amount of the public good consumed each period is simply determined by the amount of tax revenues collected in each period. Thus, the choices of k_{t+1}, d_{t+1}, z_{t+1}, and c_t are not affected by g_t.

There are two special features of the problem that result in the competitive allocation being the one that solves this program. The first is that preference orderings of households on private consumptions are independent of public consumptions. The second is that taxes on capital stocks can be treated as if they were features of the technology. The taxes paid by a firm depend only on its stocks and not the stocks of other firms.

In finding the steady-state solution, we first substitute constraints (23)–(25) into constraint (22), and then substitute constraint (22) for c_t in equation (21). We then take derivatives with respect to k_{t+1}, z_{t+1}, and d_{t+1}. In taking these derivatives, we treat r_k and r_z parametrically. Next we substitute into these first-order necessary conditions the marginal product of intangible capital for r_z and the marginal product of tangible capital net of depreciation of tangible capital for r_k, both of which are functions of k and z. Last, we invoke the steady-state condition that $k_{t+1} = k_t \cdot (1 + \gamma)$, $d_{t+1} = d_t \cdot (1 + \gamma)$, and $z_{t+1} = z_t \cdot (1 + \gamma)$ for all time and then solve for k_t, d_t, and z_t.

Off-Steady-State Analysis

The system given by (21)–(25) is a well-behaved, deterministic, discounted dynamic program with returns bounded from above (note $\sigma > 1$). Consequently (see Stokey, Lucas, and Prescott 1989, Theorems 4.2 and 4.14), successive approximations to optimality equation, beginning with a bounded initial approximation, converge to the optimal return function. This optimal return function can be used to find an optimal policy rule that is a stationary Markov policy in the state variable (d, k, z). Indeed, this policy rule generates the unique optimal sequence. The uniqueness of the optimal policy sequence follows from the strict concavity of the return function in (c, d), the strict concavity of the production function in (k, z), and the fact that the return function is strictly increasing in c.

7.3   Model Calibration

This section contains the quantitative theoretic analysis of the first two questions posed in the introduction. As we have now described the model fully, it is possible to be more exact with respect to these questions. More precisely defined, the first question is how well the steady-state values of the model match their corresponding counterparts in the U.S. National Income and Product Accounts. The second question is that if we assume that the effective tax rates between the United States and Japan are the same, and all other technology and preference parameters are the same as well, (the only difference, therefore, that we assume is that the United States in 1950 was on its steady-state growth path but Japan was not), does the path of per capita output implied by the model Japan coincide with Japan's actual path? For actual Japan, per capita income in 1950 was one-sixth the U.S. 1950 level, and in 1985 Japan's per capita income was three-fourths the U.S. 1985 level.

To provide answers to these questions, the model is calibrated to 1987 U.S. National Income and Product Accounts and to the postwar experience of Japan relative to the United States. In doing so, we use a period length of one year. Our source for the U.S. National Income and Product Accounts is *The Economic Report of the President 1990*. The observations pertaining to the postwar experiences of Japan and the United States are from the Summers and Heston data set.

The assumption that the institutional arrangements of the United States and Japan were the same over the 1950–1985 period is certainly subject to debate. After the war, many of Japan's institutions were modeled after those of the United States. This may not mean that the effective tax rates on the returns to technology adoption were the same in the two countries. Clearly, research is needed in order to determine the extent to which these effective tax rates may have differed, but for now we proceed under the assumption that the two countries' institutional arrangements were identical.

We note before describing in greater detail the calibration experiment that we stress the postwar institutional change in Japan and not the destruction and loss of capital that occurred during the war as the reason for Japan's rapid growth. That is the theme of this chapter and the point of this particular experiment. The differences in initial capital stocks matters precisely because both countries are assumed to have the same institutions. The destruction of capital only meant that Japan was further behind relative to the United States, and this translated into more spectacular growth after its institutions became more like those of the United States.

Because some variables in our model do not correspond exactly to those measured in either the National Income and Product Accounts or the Summers and Heston survey, adjustments are required. First, U.S. National Income and Product Accounts do not measure the stock of intangible capital and investment in that capital. For this reason, we need to reduce output in our model by the amount of investment in intangible capital. Second, since we treat residential structures as part of household capital, we reduce GNP by the amount of housing services. Given that final real estate services product is approximately 10 percent of GNP, measured output in our model, y-x_z, is .90 $\cdot$ GNP. Third, we separate consumption expenditures on durables from consumption expenditures on nondurables and services and include the former in the category of investment in household capital. Fourth, we remove residential investment from gross private investment and add it to the category of investment in household capital. Fifth, we assign 10 percent of government purchases to investment in tangible business capital. We do this because public investments in infrastructure increase private business productivity. The remaining fraction of government purchases is identified with household consumption of the local public good in the model.

Our economy is a closed system. Therefore, there is the question of how to treat net exports listed in the National Income and Product Accounts. We simply choose to increase real GNP by the amount of net exports and assume that for each expenditure category, the expenditure on net exports increases the expenditure category by the same percentage as net exports increase GNP.

After making such adjustments, the ratio of consumption to measured GNP for the United States in 1987 is .54, the ratio of investment in durables to measured GNP is .15, the ratio of investment in tangible capital to measured GNP is .14, and the ratio of consumption of the public good to measured GNP is .17. In addition to these statistics, the model is calibrated to the ratio of nonhousehold tangible capital to measured GNP, to the ratio of household capital to measured GNP, to the U.S. steady-state growth rates of per capita consumption and output, to the real return on equity in the United States over the postwar period, and to tangible business capital's share of output less investment in intangible business capital.

Using the Summers and Heston data, the average annual growth rate of both per capita output and consumption in the United States over the 1950–1985 period is approximately 2 percent. The real return on equity in the United States over the postwar period is 6.5 percent. The ratio of tangible business capital to measured GNP in the United States is approximately 1.25. With the capital of the government, we believe a ratio of 1.75 for nonhousehold tangible capital to measured GNP is reasonable. The ratio of the stock of household capital to measured GNP for the United States is approximately 1.25. The share parameter for tangible capital s_k for our model economy is

$$s_k = (r_k + \delta_k) \cdot k / (y - x_z) \tag{26}$$

To compute the counterpart of this statistic for the U.S. economy, we estimate the numerator of (26) by subtracting from $.90 \cdot$ GNP our estimates of payments to labor. In payments to labor we include all compensation of employees, fraction $1 - s_k$ of entrepreneur income, fraction $1 - s_k$ of surplus on government enterprises, and 50 percent of indirect business taxes. Our resulting estimated value of s_k is .25.

Discussion of Calibration Parameters

The preference parameters whose values are selected to match these steady-state observations are the relative rate of risk aversion, σ, the consumption share parameter in the utility function, ϕ, and the subjective time discount factor, β. The technology parameters whose values are to be chosen are the growth rate of world technology, γ_w, the coefficient on tangible capital in the production function, θ, the annual depreciation rates of business and household capital, δ_k and δ_d, and α. In addition to these parameters, the effective tax rates, τ_k and τ_z, must be chosen.

For most parameters, there are a sufficient number of micro and growth studies that can guide us in our selections. For some, namely α, γ_w, and τ_z, there are not. For the effective tax rate on intangible capital, we arbitrarily select it to the effective tax rate on tangible capital. Using Lucas's (1989) estimate for the ratio of total revenues from all tangible capital taxation to total tangible capital income in 1985, this effective tax rate is approximately 1/3.

U.S. steady-state observations do not tie down values for all parameters. With respect to α and γ_w, either one or the other is free. In steady state, γ_w, α, and θ, together with the growth rate γ, must satisfy equation (12). The value for θ, in effect, is determined by matching the model with tangible capital's share of output in the United States so that if a value for α is specified, a value for γ_w is automatically determined, and vice versa.

There are many values for γ_w and α consistent with U.S. steady-state growth. Almost all, however, are inconsistent with the spectacular growth experience of Japan over the postwar period. With larger values of α, technology capital becomes less important and the adjustment to steady state too rapid. For smaller values of α, technology capital becomes more important and the adjustment to steady state too slow.

Because we require that the sum of the coefficients on the two types of capital in the production function be less than one, α must be greater than $\theta/(1 - \theta)$. For the limiting case where $\alpha = +\infty$, the model is essentially the neoclassical theory with optimal capital accumulation. For the other limiting case where $\alpha = \theta/(1 - \theta)$, the model is essentially Lucas's (1988). The problems associated with too large and too small values for α in accounting for the postwar experience of Japan relative to the United States within our model point out some of the failures of these models. The neoclassical growth model predicts that the difference in per capita incomes between the United States and Japan should have been eliminated well before 1980.[11] The Lucas model cannot generate the spectacular growth of postwar Japan.

Computational Experiments

The computational experiments involve the following steps. First, a set of parametric values for the model is chosen. Once this selection is made, the steady-state solution is calculated and this solution is compared to the steady-state ratios for the United States listed earlier. If a solution is not inconsistent with these statistics, we then proceed to determine whether the model, with that particular set of parametric values, can account for the postwar experience of Japan.

To do this we employ the methods of dynamic programming. We find the optimal policy functions corresponding to the system and then trace out the optimal path for a country that begins with roughly one-sixth of its steady-state income in 1950. If we find that after a 36-year period the per capita income level for this artificial economy is not approximately three-fourths of its steady-state level, we consider a new set of parametric values and begin the experiments again.

The parametric values that seem to provide the best fit to the U.S. steady-state observations and the postwar experience of Japan are listed in table 7.2. Table 7.3 compares the steady-state solution of the model with the observation for the United States, while figure 7.1 plots the off-steady-state path traced by the model to the actual path for Japan. As both table 7.3 and figure 7.1 demonstrate, the model's fit is quite good.

Table 7.2
Model parameters

Preference parameters	$\sigma = 1.120$	$\beta = 0.960$	$\phi = 0.725$
Technology parameters	$\alpha = 1.155$ $\theta = 0.217$	$\delta_k = 0.080$ $\delta_d = 0.080$	$\gamma_w = 0.012$
Tax rates	$\tau_k = .333$	$\tau_z = .333$	

Table 7.3
Steady-state calibrations

	Model economy	U.S. economy (1987)
c/y	0.50	0.54
g/y	0.22	0.17
x_k/y	0.14	0.14
x_d/y	0.13	0.15
x_z/y	0.15	—
k/y	1.46	1.75
d/y	1.36	1.25
z/y	4.81	—

Note: The variable y is measured output which does not include x_z.

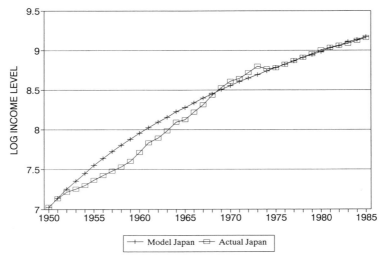

Figure 7.1
Log income level.

Table 7.4
Level effects

		Steady-state relative outputs					
τ_k	.33	.43	.53	.63	.73	.83	.93
τ_z							
.33	21.90	20.60	19.00	17.00	14.50	11.30	6.51
.43	17.70	16.60	15.30	13.70	11.70	9.12	5.26
.53	13.60	12.70	11.80	10.60	9.05	7.03	4.05
.63	9.80	9.21	8.49	7.61	6.52	5.06	2.91
.73	6.30	5.92	5.46	4.90	4.19	3.25	1.87
.83	3.24	3.05	2.81	2.52	2.15	1.67	0.97
.93	0.87	0.82	0.76	0.68	0.58	0.45	0.26

7.4   Level Effects

The most striking feature of the data is the tremendous diversity in per capita income levels that exists across countries. A crucial test of a theory of growth is whether it can account for this diversity. Our theme is that this diversity is the result of the differences in "taxes" imposed by a country's institutional arrangements on the return to the investment of firms adopting a more advanced technology. Obviously, we want to know how large, according to the model, must the differences in effective tax rates be across countries to account for the observed disparity in per capita income levels.

To determine the level effects associated with a country's institutional arrangements, we simply calculate the steady-state solution to the model for various tax rates, keeping all other parameters to their values of section 7.3. Table 7.4 reports the steady-state income levels for pairs of effective tax rates (τ_k, τ_z). As can be seen from the table, differences in the taxes imposed by a country's institutional arrangements can result in large differences in steady-state income levels. Differences in tax rates, for example, of a factor 3 can lead to differences in steady-state per capita output of a factor 84.

As the table also indicates, the tax on the return to intangible capital is associated with much larger level effects than the tax on the return to tangible capital. Holding the tax rate on tangible capital fixed and changing the tax rate on intangible capital by roughly a factor 3 result in level effects of roughly a factor 25 Holding the tax rate on intangible capital fixed and changing the tax rate on tangible capital by a factor 3, however, only result in level effects of roughly a factor 3.

The level effects associated with these differences in effective tax rates decrease with the size of α. If the value for α was 1.0 (keeping all other parameters to their values reported in table 7.2), then differences in tax rates of a factor 3 are associated with differences in steady-state income levels of a factor greater than 200. Smaller values for α, of course, imply slower rates of convergence to steady state so when $\alpha = 1.0$, the model cannot replicate the postwar growth experiences of Japan and the United States.

7.5 Effective Tax Rates

To test this theory, the effective tax rates of countries need to be determined, and these rates then must be compared to those predicted by the model. While this is beyond the scope of this chapter, we do briefly outline here how they might be calculated. Most of the existing work on effective tax rates is based on a production function with a single capital input; see Jorgenson and Hall (1967). For this standard case, the firm's problem is to maximize its present value by maximizing

$$V(K_0) = \sum_{t=0}^{\infty} (1 + r)^{-t}\{(1 - \tau) \cdot [F(K_t, N_t) - w_t \cdot N_t] - (1 - \Delta_k) \cdot q_k \cdot X_{kt}\}$$

(27)

subject to

$$K_{t+1} = (1 - \delta_k) \cdot K_t + X_{kt},$$

(28)

by choosing a path for N_t and X_{kt}. Here the parameter τ denotes the corporate tax rate, the parameter Δ_k denotes the sum of the investment tax credit plus the present value of the discounted stream of depreciation allowances, and the parameter q_k denotes the price of the capital good. Differentiating the system with respect to K_{t+1} yields the familiar optimality condition

$$F_k(K_t, N_t) = q_k \cdot (r + \delta_k) \cdot (1 - \Delta_k)/(1 - \tau).$$

(29)

To determine the effective tax rate on tangible capital, τ_k, the question that is normally asked is what tax rate on the firm's true economic income would have to be in effect when the investment tax credit is eliminated and depreciation allowances are at their true economic rate δ_k so as to leave the investment incentives the same as before. Implicitly, τ_k is defined by

$$q_k \cdot [r/(1 - \tau_k) + \delta_k] = q_k \cdot (r + \delta_k) \cdot (1 - \Delta_k)/(1 - \tau).$$

(30)

The extension of this standard model to include a second type of capital and the calculation of an effective tax rate on that capital are straightforward. Instead of (27) and (28), the firm's problem would be to maximize its present value by maximizing

$$V(K_0, Z_0) = \sum_{t=0}^{\infty} (1 + r)^{-t} \{(1 - \tau) \cdot [F(K_t, Z_t, N_t) - w_t \cdot N_t]$$

$$- (1 - \Delta_k) \cdot q_k \cdot X_{kt} - (1 - \Delta_z) \cdot q_z \cdot X_{zt}\} \tag{31}$$

subject to

$$K_{t+1} = (1 - \delta_k) \cdot K_t + X_{kt} \tag{32}$$

and

$$Z_{t+1} = (1 - \delta_z) \cdot Z_t + X_{zt}.^{12} \tag{33}$$

Differentiating the system given by (31)–(33) with respect to Z_{t+1} yields the condition

$$F_z(K_t, Z_t, N_t) = q_z \cdot (r + \delta_z) \cdot (1 - \Delta_z)/(1 - \tau). \tag{34}$$

The effective tax rate on this second capital stock would then be calculated by asking the question just stated.[13]

Our theme in this chapter is that the incentives to investment are greatly affected by a country's institutional arrangements. The preceding calculations of effective tax rates are based only on those institutional arrangements of a country that correspond to its tax system. We want the calculations of effective tax rates to reflect among other things the amount of bribes, the costs imposed by government regulations, the costs imposed by individuals or groups of individuals trying to either preserve economic rents or trying to seek economic rents, and the amount of the return that is taxed away by redistributional coalitions.

Incorporating these institutional arrangements into the calculation of an effective tax rate is actually quite simple. Government regulations and the actions by individuals or groups of individuals attempting to either seek economic rents or preserve economic rents would affect the price of intangible capital q_z. Bribes are essentially a negative tax credit so that they would affect the size of the term Δ_z, (unless they were based on a per unit of investment basis, and then they would affect the price of intangible capital). The actions of redistributional coalitions that effectively tax away part of this return would simply add to the tax rate τ.[14]

This then leaves the issue of actually calculating the increase in the price of capital resulting from government regulations, rent seeking or preservation of rents activity, the amount of bribes, and the amount of the return taken away by redistributional coalitions. While a tremendous amount of work needs to be done in this area, several studies exist that measure some of these institutional arrangements in various countries. De Soto (1989), for one, documents some of the costs associated with Peru's burdensome business and legal codes as well as the amount of bribes to government officials. Levy (1991), for another, compares the regulatory and financing constraints as well as the use of bribes in small and medium-sized firms in Sri Lanka and Tanzania. In addition, there are numerous studies that compare the wage differential between union and nonunion workers.

7.6   Conclusion

Our theme is that differences in effective tax rates on the returns to technology adoption are fundamental to understanding the huge diversity in per capita incomes across countries. Following a permanent decrease in its effective tax rate, a country will grow at a rate above the world average for a sustained but not permanent period of time. This growth will be higher for poorer countries that experience such changes as a given advance in technologies is cheaper the lower a country's current technology level is relative to world level. Our model, calibrated to the postwar growth experiences of the United States and Japan, can account for this tremendous diversity with what we think is an entirely plausible implied range of tax rates.

Clearly, what is needed is systematic measurement of the τ_k's and τ_z's across countries. If after measuring these effective tax rates it is found that they are inconsistent with the theory's prediction as to how large they must be in order to account for the diversity in per capita incomes, we would have to abandon or revise this theory. Many factors determine these effective tax rates, and while measurement may be difficult, it should not be impossible. Case studies that measure some of the institutional arrangements already exist. Our hope is that this research will stimulate effort in this area.

Notes

The views expressed herein are those of the authors and not necessarily those of the Federal Reserve Bank of Minneapolis, the University of Minnesota, the Federal Reserve System or Northeastern University.

1. The standard measurement of human capital is the number of years of education. We do not mean to imply here that we think education does not matter. Indeed, we believe there is some minimum level of education that is necessary for technology adoption to be important to growth. Implicitly, we assume such a level in our theory. We do not, however, believe that increases in the level of education beyond this minimum level are that important for growth. Japan, for instance, more than doubled its per capita income between 1960 and 1970, yet the number of years of schooling increased by far less than that. Kyriacou (1991) estimates that the average years of schooling of the Japanese labor force was 7.23 in 1965, 7.68 in 1970, 8.318 in 1975, 8.89 in 1980, and 9.47 in 1985. (Estimates are not provided for earlier years.)

2. Last year, Ghana's average annual growth fell to 2.7 percent. Several experts on that economy attribute the slowdown in growth to the failure of Ghana's government to further improve the country's institutional arrangements. For examples of some of the growth-inhibiting institutional arrangements that still exist in that country, see Paul (1989).

3. The exact preference and policy parameters that affect these growth rates differ somewhat between models, so it may be the case that within a particular model countries that differ with respect to some parameter(s) may grow at the same rate. The point here is that within all these models there are some parameters by which if countries differ, they will grow at different rates.

4. The source of this data is Summers and Heston [1988]. Because observations for all countries in that data set do not begin with year 1950, the subsets of countries we use to calculate the standard deviations are also determined by the beginning year we consider. That is why at the top of each column in the table we list an initial year. The standard deviations for the subset of countries with incomes at least x percent of the United States and with observations available in that beginning year are read by columns.

5. The correlation with investment's share of GDP is positive. The correlation with initial level of income is negative. The negative correlation with initial income is found for the 1960–1989 period when investment and a measure of initial human capital are included in the regression equation.

6. In the computational experiments, countries that began below their steady states always grew at rates above the steady-state growth rate. These higher growth rates were also associated with higher investment shares of output. As these countries' income levels approached their steady states, growth rates and investment's share of output decreased. This we found to be the case even when assuming complete reversibility of capital stocks.

7. For an interesting paper in which agent's decisions affect growth rates but all countries grow at the same rate, see Krusell (1990).

8. For simplicity, we assume that a single manager operates a firm. For an extension to coalition management, see Prescott and Boyd (1987).

9. This is literally not the case. The amount of spillover would clearly depend upon movement of individuals between profit centers.

10. Aggregation across firms in the economy implies the following aggregate per capita production relation: $y_t = \eta \cdot \varphi \cdot (1 + \gamma_w)^{\alpha \cdot t/(\alpha+1)} \cdot \bar{N}^{1-\theta} \cdot k_t^\theta \cdot z_t^{1/(\alpha+1)}$, where $\varphi = (1 + \bar{N})^{\theta + 1/(\alpha+1) - 1}$. To arrive at the reduced per capita production function that appears in the right-hand side of equation (14), the value for managerial ability, η, was selected so that $\eta \cdot \varphi \cdot \bar{N}^{1-\theta} = 1$. Since our interest is in the ratios of variables to output, the values for η and $\bar{N}$ are not central to our experiments so that such a simplification makes sense.

11. This failure has been noted by King and Rebelo (1989), Christiano (1989), and Parente (1990).

12. In our model, $q_k = 1$, $q_z = (1 + \gamma_w)^\alpha/(\alpha + 1)$, and $(1 - \delta_z) = 1/(1 + \gamma_w)^\alpha$.

13. Actually, the effective tax rate on intangible capital in (17) is not exactly the one that is implied by this question. The effective tax rate on intangible capital that corresponds to this question is implicitly defined by $q_z \cdot [(r/(1 - \tau_z) + \delta_z] = q_z \cdot (r + \delta_z) \cdot (1 - \Delta_z)/(1 - \tau)$. The one represented in (17) is implicitly defined by $q_z \cdot (r + \delta_z)/(1 - \tau_z) = q_z \cdot (r + \delta_z) \cdot (1 - \Delta_z)/(1 - \tau)$.

14. For a discussion of how some other policies would be incorporated into a measure of effective tax rates, see for example Auerbach (1990).

References

Auerbach, Allan J. 1990. The cost of capital and investment in developing countries. Policy, Research, and External Affairs Working Paper Series 410. Washington, D.C.: The World Bank.

Barro, Robert J. 1990. Government spending in a simple model of endogenous growth. *Journal of Political Economy* 98:103–125.

Barro, Robert J. 1991. Economic growth in a cross section of countries. *Quarterly Journal of Economics* 106:407–443.

Becker, Gary S., Murphy, Kevin M., and Tamura, Robert. 1990. Human capital, fertility, and growth. *Journal of Political Economy* 98:12–37.

Chamley, Christophe. 1990. The last shall be first: foreign borrowing and growth with human capital in an open economy. Manuscript.

Christiano, Lawrence J. 1989. Understanding Japan's savings rate: the reconstruction hypothesis. *Federal Reserve Bank of Minneapolis Quarterly Review* 13:10–25.

De Soto, Hernando. 1989. *The Other Path*. New York: Harper and Row.

Jorgenson, Dale and Hall, Robert E. 1967. Tax policy and investment behavior. *American Economic Review* 57:391–414.

King, Robert and Rebelo, Sergio. 1989. Transitional dynamics and economic growth in the neoclassical model. Rochester Center for Economic Research Working Paper #206. Rochester, N.Y.: Rochester Center for Economic Research.

Krueger, Anne O. 1990. Government failures in development. NBER Working Paper #3340.

Krusell, Per. 1990. Dynamic, firm-specific increasing returns and the long-run performances of growing economies. Manuscript.

Kyriacou, George A. 1991. Level and growth effects of human capital: a cross-country study of the convergence hypothesis. Economic Research Reports RR #91-26. New York, NY: C.V. Starr Center for Applied Economics.

Levine, Ross and Renelt, David. 1991. A sensitivity analysis of cross-country growth regressions. Policy, Research, and External Affairs Working Paper Series 609. Washington, D.C.: The World Bank.

Levy, Brian. 1991. Obstacles to developing small and medium-sized enterprises: an empirical assessment. Policy, Research, and External Affairs Working Paper Series 588. Washington, D. C.: The World Bank.

Lucas, Robert E. 1989. Supply-side economics: an analytical review. *Oxford Economic Papers—New Series* 42:293–316.

Lucas, Robert E. 1988. On the mechanics of economic development. *Journal of Monetary Economics* 22:3–42.

Lucas, Robert E. 1976. On the size distribution of business firms. *The Bell Journal of Economics* 9:508–523.

Nasar, Sylvia. 1991. Industrial policy the Korean way. *New York Times*, Section D2. July 12.

Noble, Kenteh B. 1991 Ghana, after hard-won growth is faltering. *New York Times*, Section D2. June 24.

Olson, Mancur. 1982. *The Rise and Decline of Nations*. Oxford: Oxford University Press.

Parente, Stephen L. 1990. Economic institutions and external factors: implications for the replacement of inferior technologies and growth Manuscript.

Parente, Stephen L. and Prescott, Edward C. 1991. Technology adoption and growth. Manuscript.

Paul, Samuel. 1989. Private Sector Assessment of Pilot Exercise in Ghana. PPR Working Paper No. WPS 199. The Woris Bank.

Prescott, Edward C. and Boyd, John H. 1987. Dynamic coalitions, growth, and the firm." In Edward C. Prescott and Neil Wallace (eds.). *Contractual Arrangements of Intertemporal Trade*. Minneapolis: University of Minnesota Press.

Reynolds, Lloyd G. 1983. The spread of economic growth to the third world. *Journal of Economic Literature* 21:941–980.

Romer, Paul M. 1986. Increasing returns and long-run growth. *Journal of Political Economy* 94:1002–1037.

Solow, Robert M. 1956. A contribution to the theory of economic growth. *Quarterly Journal of Economics* 70:65–94.

Solow, Robert M. 1970. *Growth Theory: an Expository*. Oxford: Oxford University Press.

Stokey. N. L. and Lucas. R. E., Jr., with Prescott. E. C. 1989. *Recursive Methods in Economic Dynamics*. Cambridge, MA: Harvard University Press.

Summers, Robert and Heston, Alan. 1988. A new set of international comparisons of real product for 130 countries. *Review of Income and Wealth* 34:1–25. (Data reproduced on diskette by Prospect Research Corporation, New Haven, CT 1987, 1988).

III

Business Cycles within Politico-Economic Frameworks

8

Macroeconomic Policy and Elections in OECD Democracies

Alberto Alesina,
Gerald D. Cohen, and
Nouriel Roubini

Do politicians manipulate economic policy in order to win elections? For many economists, political scientists, and laypeople, the answer to this question is obvious: of course they do! In a very influential paper, Nordhaus (1975) formalized and clarified the idea of an opportunistic "political business cycle." According to this model, politicians stimulate aggregate demand before elections in order to create fast growth and reduce unemployment. The inflationary consequences of this policy are eliminated by a postelectoral contraction.

Surprisingly, the empirical literature generated by the Nordhaus paper yielded, at best, mixed results. Partly as a reaction to these empirical rejections and partly in response to the "rational expectation" critique, in the late eighties a new generation of "rational political business cycles models" emerged. This line of research includes work by Cukierman and Meltzer (1986), Rogoff and Sibert (1988), and Rogoff (1990). These models have empirical implications that differ somewhat from those of Nordhaus's (1975) model.

The purpose of this chapter is to examine in detail the evidence of political business cycle (PBC) models on a large sample of eighteen OECD economies using both the Nordhaus model and the new rational models as a guide to our study. Our results can be summarized as follows:

1. We find very little evidence of preelectoral effects on economic outcomes—in particular, on GDP growth and unemployment, as implied by the Nordhaus model.

2. We see some evidence of "political monetary cycles"; that is, expansionary monetary policy in election years.

3. We also observe indications of "political budget cycles," or "loose" fiscal policy prior to elections.

4. Inflation exhibits a postelectoral jump, which could be explained by either the preelectoral loose monetary and fiscal policies and/or by an opportunistic timing of increases in publicly controlled prices or indirect taxes.

It should be emphasized that this evidence on monetary and fiscal policy is statistically significant but not extremely strong. Our interpretation of these results is that preelectoral manipulation of economic policy occurs frequently, but not always, and is constrained by the politicians' concern about their reputation. These results support modeling efforts that emphasize the constraints imposed on policymakers by economic agents' and voters' rationality.

In this chapter we do not consider the "partisan" model of political cycles (Hibbs 1977, 1987, Alt 1985, and Alesina 1987), which emphasizes systematic differences in macroeconomic policymaking between the "unemployment averse" left and the "inflation averse" right. However, in concluding we offer a synthesis and discussion of the results of the present chapter in light of previous research that has found strong support for the partisan model.

The chapter is organized as follows. In section 8.1 we briefly review the theory of opportunistic political business cycles. In section 8.2 we review previous empirical results. Section 8.3 describes our data. Section 8.4 explores the extent of political business cycles on growth and unemployment; this section extends earlier results by Alesina and Roubini (1990). Section 8.5 presents the results on inflation. Section 8.6 discusses the evidence for monetary policy. Section 8.7 considers fiscal policy—namely, budget deficits, spending, and taxes. The final section suggests an interpretation of our results in the broader context of the literature on political cycles.

8.1   The Theory of Opportunistic Political Cycles

The original model by Nordhaus (1975) is based upon the following assumptions:

1. The economy can be described by an "expectations augmented" Phillips curve.

2. Expectations are adaptive.

3. Politicians control a policy instrument that directly affects aggregate demand.

4. Politicians are opportunistic: they only care about holding office.

5. Voters are naive and retrospective: they judge the incumbent government by evaluating positively high growth, low unemployment, and low inflation. They heavily discount past observations and do not understand the economic model that relates inflation and unemployment.

6. The timing of elections is exogenously fixed.

Based upon these hypotheses, Nordhaus obtains well-known empirical implications: (a) every incumbent government expands the economy immediately before each election by taking advantage of the favorable short-run Phillips curve; (b) inflation increases around election time as a result of this expansion;[1] (c) inflation is reduced by a postelectoral contraction of aggregate demand that leads to a downturn or recession; (d) the economy exhibits an "inflation bias," that is, inflation is higher than "socially optimum."

This chapter is concerned with the first three implications. In fact, although the experience of the past twenty-five years suggests that an inflation bias may indeed exist, other models are consistent with this observation. In particular an inflation bias is the central implication of the "time consistency" literature originated by Kydland and Prescott (1977) and Barro and Gordon (1983a,b).

Rational Models

The application of game theory to macroeconomics has led to a reformulation of the insight of the political business cycle model in a rational expectations framework. This result was originally achieved by Cukierman and Meltzer (1986), Rogoff and Sibert (1988), and Rogoff (1990). Persson and Tabellini (1991) later provided interesting extensions along the same lines. In these models, governments have the same utility function as private agents (i.e., they care about unemployment, inflation, and government spending in the same way that private agents do), but they are also "opportunistic." That is, governments care about winning elections, get welfare from being in power, and do not have "partisan" motivations. These papers share two basic ingredients: different governments are characterized by different degrees of competency, and the government is more informed than the voters are about its own level of competency.

In Cukierman and Meltzer (1986), different governments are characterized by differing abilities to forecast. In Rogoff and Sibert (1988) and Rogoff (1990), "competency" is referred to as the government's efficiency in reducing "waste" in the budget process. That is, more competent governments can produce more public goods for given fiscal revenues. Persson and Tabellini (1991) apply Rogoff's competency model to the Phillips curve case; more competent governments can achieve higher growth with less unexpected inflation. In all of these models, the incumbent government has an incentive to "signal" its competence by engaging in preelectoral manipulations of policy instruments.

In the present chapter we will focus specifically on the monetary and budget cycles studied by Rogoff and Sibert (1988) and Rogoff (1990). In the former paper, an equilibrium with signaling looks as follows: incumbents reduce taxes and/or increase spending before elections to appear "competent" since, needless to say, voters prefer competent governments to less competent ones. Preelectoral deficits are monetized, but the effects of monetization on inflation and on the seigniorage tax are perceived by the voters only with a lag, thus *after* the election. Although voters are rational and aware of the policymakers' incentives, preelectoral deficits for signaling purposes still occur.[2]

Rogoff (1990) presents a nonmonetary model in which he focuses upon government spending on "consumption" (or transfers) and "investments." Signaling, in this model, takes the form of preelectoral surges in immediately visible expenditures for consumption and cuts in investment expenditure. Although the decrease in investment is harmful for both productivity and efficiency, these results are observable by voters only with lags. Thus, budget cycles take the form of distortions in the allocation of resources across public spending programs.

In summary, this body of research has made two important points:

1. "Opportunistic" cycles survive in rational models, with substantially different features than the original Nordhaus formulation. In a rational model one is not likely to observe regular multiyear cycles on GDP or unemployment.[3] Rational behavior of voters and economic agents would make these cycles impossible or counterproductive for the politicians. "Rational cycles" should thus take the form of short-run manipulations of policy instruments around elections. In other words, politicians may find it much easier and electorally rewarding to "mail some checks" before elections, print money, and postpone tax increases ("read my lips"), than to reduce the rate of unemployment in the election year.

2. "Retrospective voting" is not inconsistent with rational behavior, that is, it is a rational strategy for the voters to judge the incumbent's performance based upon preelectoral economic conditions. This is, of course, a key element for the existence of opportunistic cycles.

Notice that, while the first implication concerning "signaling" crucially rests upon the assumption of asymmetric information over the government's competence, the second does not. In fact, one can observe rational retrospective voting even without asymmetric information, as long as competence is serially correlated (see Alesina, Londregan, and Rosenthal 1990). That is, rational retrospective voting emerges even in a model where the voters and the government have the same information about the government's competence, as long as the latter is serially correlated.

8.2 Review of Previous Empirical Results

Tests of opportunistic political business cycles can be divided into two categories: tests on policy outcomes—namely, output growth, unemployment, and inflation—and tests on policy instruments such as money growth, taxes, transfers, and government spending. The first set of tests (on policy outcomes), in our view, overwhelmingly rejects the political business cycle hypothesis. The second set of tests (on policy instruments) has yielded mixed results.

Soon after the publication of Nordhaus's (1975) paper, McCallum (1978) and Golden and Poterba (1980) rejected Nordhaus's model on economic outcomes, using U.S. data. Paldam (1979) obtained similar negative results on a sample of OECD economies. Further rejection of the political business cycle model on GNP and unemployment in the United States were presented more recently by Hibbs (1987) and Alesina (1988). For a large sample of OECD economies, similar rejections were obtained by Alesina (1989) and Alesina and Roubini (1990).

Haynes and Stone (1989) claim to have found support for the Nordhaus hypothesis on GNP in the United States. However, in our view, a careful analysis of their results suggests that they have found evidence of partisan effects rather than of opportunistic cycles. The same criticism applies to results presented by Nordhaus (1989). For an exposition of this critical observation, see Alesina's (1989) comment on Nordhaus.[4]

The evidence on manipulation of policy instruments is more favorable to the political business cycle model. Tufte (1978) presents evidence of manipulation of the timing of fiscal instruments, in particular transfers, and evidence of "monetary cycles." His evidence is, however, confined to a few American elections. Results in line with those of Tufte (1978) on fiscal transfers are also reported in Alesina (1988). Bizer and Durlauf (1990) report results on the dynamics of taxes in the United States that claim to support a political budget cycle.[5] Both Tufte (1978) and Hibbs (1987) find evidence of political business cycles on disposable income. This observation, coupled with the lack of similar evidence on GNP, suggests the presence of "fiscal cycles."

Recently, McDonald (1991) has found evidence of public expenditure cycles by examining state level evidence in the United States. Alesina (1989) presents some qualitative evidence that does not rule out the existence of budget cycles in OECD economies. This evidence is, however, weak and very far from conclusive. Finally, Grier (1987, 1989) reports interesting results that identify a monetary cycle in a sample from the early sixties to the very early eighties in the U.S. However, when the sample is extended to include more of the eighties, the results tend to vanish (see Grier 1989 and section 8.6 of this chapter).

8.3   Data

We consider all the OECD economies that have been democracies for the sample period which is, for most of our regressions, 1960 to 1987. The countries included in our study are Australia, Austria, Belgium, Canada, Denmark, Finland, France, Germany, Japan, Ireland, Italy, the Netherlands, New Zealand, Norway, Sweden, Switzerland, the United Kingdom, and the United States. Our data set for output, GDP, unemployment, and inflation is the same one used in Alesina and Roubini (1990). Inflation is defined as the yearly rate of change of the consumer price index (CPI) from the International Monetary Fund, *International Financial Statistics* (IMF, IFS). Output growth is defined as the yearly rate of change of real GDP (or GNP) from IMF, IFS. Unemployment is obtained from OECD; we consider the total standardized unemployment rate. More details on country-specific data issues can be found in table A-1 of Alesina and Roubini (1990). Data for money supply are also obtained from IMF, IFS, with money growth defined as the yearly rate of change of M1. Our data for the fiscal variables used in section 8.7 are the same as those used by Roubini and Sachs (1989).[6] Sources of election dates and of electoral results are Alt (1985) and Banks (1987, 1989). The same data set for elections used in Alesina and Roubini (1990) is adopted here. See table 8A.1 in the appendix for a description of the political data.

8.4   Political Business Cycles, GDP, and Unemployment

In this section we review and extend results obtained by Alesina and Roubini (1990).

A simple but powerful test of the PBC is obtained by running the following panel regression of time series cross-section data, for instance on output growth:[7]

$$y_{it} = \alpha_0 + \alpha_1 y_{it-1} + \alpha_2 y_{it-2} \cdots + \alpha_n y_{it-n} + \alpha_{n+1} yw_{it} + \alpha_{n+2} PBC_{it} + \varepsilon_{it} \tag{1}$$

where y_{it} is the rate of output growth for country i at time t; this rate of growth is defined as $y_{it} = \dfrac{x_{it} - x_{it-4}}{x_{it-4}} \cdot 100$ where x_{it} is the level of real GDP in country i at time t. yw_{it} is a proxy for the growth of the world economy; this proxy is obtained as the average growth of the seven largest economies in our sample, weighted by each country's share of GDP over the total.[8] PBC is a "dummy" that captures the dynamic implication of the theory. Several different definitions of the dummy are used. In addition, we introduce country dummies in the regressions to correct for country-specific effects. The autoregressive specification for the dependent variable is chosen as the "best" using standard techniques.[9]

Table 8.1 reports the results for two regressions on GDP growth, which differ in the specification of the political dummy. The two dummies, PBCN, with $N = 4$ and $N = 6$ reported in the first and second column respectively, are defined as follows:

Table 8.1
Panel regressions on GDP growth, dependent variable: Y

Variable*	1 Coefficient (*t*-statistic)	2 Coefficient (*t*-statistic)
Constant	−0.0001 (−0.004)	0.130 (0.52)
$Y(-1)$	0.713 (28.82)	0.732 (29.49)
$Y(-2)$	−0.055 (−2.34)	−0.059) (−2.48)
YW	0.396 (13.73)	0.344 (12.03)
PBC4	−0.001 (−0.64)	—
PBC6	—	−0.110 (−0.97)
R^2	0.67	0.65

* The estimated regressions include country-fixed effects that are not reported in the table.

Table 8.2
Panel regressions on unemployment, dependent variable: U^{DIF}

Variable*	1 Coefficient (t-statistic)	2 Coefficient (t-statistic)
Constant	0.035 (3.10)	0.167 (3.77)
$U^{DIF}(-1)$	1.334 (49.10)	1.323 (50.98)
$U^{DIF}(-2)$	−0.333 (−12.07)	−0.335 (−12.79)
PBC4	−0.003 (−0.13)	—
PBC6	—	−0.014 (−0.80)
R^2	0.99	0.99

* The estimated regressions include country-fixed effects that are not reported in the table.

$$\text{PBCN} = \begin{cases} 1 \text{ in the } (N-1) \text{ quarters before an election and in the election quarter} \\ 0 \text{ otherwise} \end{cases}$$

In the sample we have 144 elections.[10] The country dummies are not reported but were included in the regressions. In both regressions the political dummy has the sign *opposite* from the theoretical prediction, although the coefficients are insignificantly different from zero.

Table 8.2 reports analogous results for unemployment. The dependent variable is U^{DIF}, defined as the difference between the domestic unemployment rate and the proxy for the OECD unemployment rate, defined analogously to the world average GDP growth. In evaluating results on unemployment, one must be aware of problems of "unit roots," (see, for instance, Blanchard and Summers 1986). By taking the difference from the world average, rather than using levels as the dependent variable and the world average as a regressor, unit roots problems are somewhat, although far from completely, mitigated. In any event, the results of table 8.2 are essentially identical as far as the political dummies are concerned to those obtained by using the world average as a regressor. In table 8.2 the coefficients on PBC4 and PBC6 have the correct sign, but they are insignificantly different from zero.

Several different specifications of the regressions in these two tables were tried, also leading to no support for the theory. First, we tried to hold

Table 8.3
Political business cycle theory, dependent variable: Y (t-statistics in parentheses)

Country	Constant	Y_{t-1}	Y_{t-2}	PBC(J)		YW	R^2
US	0.247	1.139	−0.384	0.334	(6)	0.101	0.780
	(0.83)	(12.21)	(−4.20)	(1.22)		(1.31)	
UK	−0.062	0.517	−0.099	0.737	(6)	0.317	0.450
	(−0.16)	(5.03)	(−1.05)	(1.72)		(3.16)	
Austria	−0.392	0.863	−0.168	0.129	(4)	0.484	0.623
	(−0.423)	(8.565)	(−1.734)	(0.135)		(2.363)	
Denmark	0.112	0.758	−0.150	−0.105	(6)	0.330	0.657
	(0.323)	(1.739)	(−1.601)	(−0.334)		(3.739)	
Norway	0.964	0.847	−0.144	−0.006	(6)	0.086	0.613
	(3.043)	(8.450)	(−1.437)	(−0.027)		(1.602)	
Canada	0.401	0.742	−0.258	0.081	(6)	0.510	0.720
	(1.24)	(7.73)	(−3.03)	(0.25)		(5.15)	
Belgium	−1.774	0.628	−0.073	−0.287	(4)	0.873	0.690
	(−2.930)	(6.594)	(−0.845)	(−0.470)		(5.630)	
Germany	−0.961	0.463	0.051	0.905	(6)	0.555	0.660
	(−2.37)	(4.58)	(0.58)	(2.56)		(5.47)	
Italy	0.246	0.948	−0.238	−0.100	(4)	0.284	0.646
	(0.356)	(9.638)	(−2.368)	(−0.153)		(2.145)	
Netherlands	−1.579	0.506	−0.159	−0.256	(6)	0.839	0.760
	(−2.95)	(4.97)	(1.71)	(−0.51)		(6.06)	
Australia	0.884	0.569	0.028	−0.806	(6)	0.327	0.590
	(1.72)	(5.71)	(0.30)	(−2.12)		(3.39)	
New Zealand	−0.253	0.790	−0.012	0.780	(4)	0.154	0.760
	(−0.86)	(7.74)	(0.12)	(2.885)		(2.46)	
Finland	0.194	0.431	0.205	1.071	(4)	0.240	0.330
	(0.23)	(3.27)	(−1.53)	(1.28)		(1.50)	
Sweden	0.405	0.528	0.024	0.660	(4)	0.096	0.330
	(0.80)	(4.10)	(0.19)	(1.22)		(0.81)	
Ireland	−0.710	0.588	−0.148	0.512	(4)	1.203	0.600
	(−0.55)	(3.58)	(0.95)	(0.34)		(2.86)	
France	0.498	0.317	0.270	−0.720		0.308	0.420
	(0.95)	(2.80)	(2.52)	(−1.28)		(2.741)	
Japan	0.147	0.835	0.031	0.627	(6)	0.124	0.811
	(0.350)	(8.297)	(0.322)	(1.775)		(1.343)	
Switzerland	−1.201	0.614	0.144	0.501	(4)	0.499	0.696
	(−2.252)	(5.062)	(1.235)	(0.788)		(3.968)	

"partisan effects" constant, by distinguishing (with appropriate dummies) "left-" and "right-wing" governments. As reported in Alesina and Roubini (1990), we found substantial evidence of partisan effects, but the PBCN dummies remained insignificant. Second, we ran the regressions without correcting for the "world variable." One may argue that voters are so naive that they do not account for the world economic cycle when they evaluate the state of their economy. Once again no evidence of political business cycles was found. All these results are not reported but are available upon request.

Tables 8.3 and 8.4, which are borrowed from Alesina and Roubini (1990), display country-by-country results on growth and unemployment respectively. In these tables, for each country we report the "best," in terms of the t-statistic of the coefficient on the PBCN dummy, of the two regression with PBC4 and PBC6. This procedure is, of course, very generous to the theory.

Not surprisingly, given our panel regressions, our country results are mixed at best. In the growth regressions in only four countries, that is, the United Kingdom, Germany, New Zealand, and Japan, the coefficient has the sign predicted by the theory and is statistically significant (or borderline) at standard levels. The regressions on unemployment exhibit a majority of "correct" signs on the coefficient of the PBCN variable, but none of them is statistically significant. New Zealand is not included for lack of quarterly data on unemployment.

8.5 Political Business Cycles on Inflation

According to Nordhaus's model, the counterpart of the preelectoral expansion is a surge of inflation immediately before and/or after the election, depending on the exact specification of the lag structure in the Phillips curve. The Rogoff and Sibert's (1988) budget cycle model has a similar implication for inflation but no implications for growth and unemployment.

In table 8.5 we display panel regressions on the inflation rate (π) where the "world average," πW, is obtained analogously to the world average growth. We present two regressions, one using PBCX and the second one with PB̂C4, which are defined as follows:

$$PBCX = \begin{cases} 1 \text{ in the two quarters preceding and following an} \\ \text{ election, and in the election quarter} \\ 0 \text{ otherwise} \end{cases}$$

Table 8.4
Political business cycle, dependent variable: U^{DIF} (t-statistics in parentheses)

Country	Constant	$U^{DIF}(-1)$	$U^{DIF}(-2)$	$U^{DIF}(-3)$	PBC4	PBC6	R^2	D.W.
Australia	-0.026 (-0.52)	1.243 (11.50)	-0.273 (-2.49)			0.075 (0.99)	0.944	2.090
Austria	-0.422 (-2.89)	1.082 (8.83)	-0.200 (-1.79)			-0.011 (-0.16)	0.878	2.020
Belgium	0.064 (1.61)	1.55 (18.64)	-0.549 (-6.53)		-0.077 (-1.18)		0.995	2.142
Canada	0.097 (1.65)	1.312 (14.23)	-0.363 (-3.90)			-0.010 (-0.16)	0.935	1.999
Denmark	0.0524 (0.93)	1.445 (12.96)	-0.480 (-4.35)		-0.011 (-0.12)		0.975	1.989
Finland	-0.066 (-1.10)	1.412 (15.83)	-0.469 (-5.28)		-0.075 (-0.88)		0.944	2.057
France	0.003 (0.078)	1.504 (14.34)	-0.516 (-4.73)			0.077 (1.06)	0.972	1.925
Germany	0.009 (0.22)	1.610 (17.13)	-0.619 (-6.40)			-0.010 (-0.22)	0.984	1.870
Ireland	0.101 (1.18)	1.705 (13.74)	-0.710 (-5.42)			-0.066 (-0.79)	0.993	1.981
Italy	0.138 (1.66)	1.168 (11.83)	-0.230 (-2.32)			-0.035 (-0.37)	0.889	2.106
Japan	-0.124 (-1.89)	1.567 (17.33)	-0.592 (-6.53)	-0.142 (-1.04)	0.049 (1.00)		0.982	1.974
Netherlands	0.270 (2.22)	0.918 (6.79)	0.220 (1.21)			-0.247 (-1.21)	0.974	1.914

Table 8.4 (continued)

Country	Constant	$U^{DIF}(-1)$	$U^{DIF}(-2)$	$U^{DIF}(-3)$	PBC4	PBC6	R^2	D.W.
Norway	-0.346 (-1.61)	1.018 (7.27)	-0.101 (-0.72)			-0.001 (-0.01)	0.857	1.981
Sweden	-0.106 (-1.26)	1.431 (15.24)	-0.466 (-4.90)			-0.034 (-0.63)	0.959	1.954
Switzerland	-0.276 (-1.46)	1.507 (13.72)	-0.550 (-5.10)			0.099 (1.62)	0.960	1.967
UK	0.063 (1.33)	1.307 (13.62)	-0.310 (-3.11)			-0.101 (-1.19)	0.965	2.040
US	0.226 (3.15)	1.492 (18.15)	-0.594 (-7.07)			-0.029 (-0.48)	0.918	1.929

Table 8.5
Panel regressions on inflation, dependent variable: π

Variable*	1 Coefficient (*t*-statistic)	2 Coefficient (*t*-statistic)
Constant	−0.009 (−0.72)	−0.129 (−1.06)
$\pi(-1)$	1.085 (47.06)	1.078 (46.93)
$\pi(-2)$	−0.115 (−3.41)	−0.114 (−3.40)
$\pi(-3)$	−0.118 (−5.43)	−0.111 (−5.17)
πW	0.141 (13.06)	0.141 (13.12)
PBCX	0.110 (1.76)	—
PB̂C4	—	0.263 (4.67)
R^2	0.93	0.93

* The estimated regressions include country-fixed effects that are not reported in the table.

$$
PB̂C4 = \begin{cases} 1 \text{ in the three quarters following an election and in the election quarter} \\ 0 \text{ otherwise} \end{cases}
$$

Table 8.5, which extends earlier results by Alesina and Roubini (1990), shows that the dummy PB̂C4 has a very significant coefficient. On the other hand, the coefficient on PBCX is much smaller and not significant at the 5 percent confidence level. Further sensitivity analysis using various pre- and postelectoral dummies (available upon request) confirm that the surge in inflation is short-lived (lasts about a year) and immediately follows, rather than precedes, the election.

Table 8.6, reproduced from Alesina and Roubini (1990), reports country-by-country results on inflation using the dummy PB̂C4, which appears to be the most significant of the panel regressions. This table shows that in almost all of the countries the coefficient on PB̂C4 is positive, as predicted by the theory; in half of the countries the *t*-statistic on the coefficient is above one, and in Denmark, France, Germany, Italy, and New Zealand the coefficient is borderline significant at the 10 percent level or better. Hence, the PBC effect on inflation, although not very strong in any country, is

Table 8.6
Political business cycle theory, dependent variable: π (t-statistics in parentheses)

Country	Constant	πW	$\pi(-1)$	$\pi(-2)$	$P\hat{B}C4$	R^2	D.W.
Australia	0.104	0.122	1.158	−0.273	0.066	0.945	2.05
	(0.47)	(2.69)	(11.78)	(−2.94)	(0.31)		
Austria	0.513	0.132	0.853	−0.118	−0.108	0.829	1.92
	(2.20)	(3.52)	(8.65)	(−1.25)	(−0.57)		
Belgium	−0.070	0.142	1.130	−0.285	0.172	0.952	1.94
	(−0.45)	(4.49)	(11.92)	(−3.30)	(1.17)		
Canada	−0.011	0.134	1.158	−0.293	0.079	0.974	2.08
	(−0.10)	(4.47)	(12.45)	(−3.46)	(0.620)		
Denmark	0.934	0.263	0.843	−0.194	0.514	0.816	2.04
	(2.57)	(3.66)	(8.57)	(−2.08)	(1.64)		
Finland	0.249	0.183	1.217	−0.385	0.111	0.937	2.08
	(1.01)	(3.82)	(13.59)	(−4.65)	(0.48)		
France	0.119)	0.198	1.126	−0.311	0.306	0.968	1.69
	(0.80)	(5.55)	(12.29)	(−3.88)	(2.13)		
Germany	0.042	0.049	1.079	−0.196	0.216	0.923	1.96
	(0.35)	(2.35)	(11.15)	(−2.03)	(1.92)		
Ireland	−0.050	0.544	0.662	0.31	−0.503	0.929	1.99
	(−0.16)	(6.55)	(6.97)	(0.38)	(−1.43)		
Italy	−0.220	0.235	1.234	−0.357	0.417	0.967	1.97
	(−0.89)	(4.12)	(13.55)	(−4.33)	(1.52)		
Japan	0.148	0.040	1.174	−0.267	0.430	0.878	2.11
	(0.43)	(0.75)	(12.44)	(−2.80)	(1.35)		
Netherlands	0.197	0.111	0.835	−0.004	−0.098	0.84	1.94
	(0.73)	(2.58)	(8.43)	(−0.004)	(−0.40)		
New Zealand	0.006	0.115	1.323	−0.419	0.690	0.948	1.85
	(0.02)	(2.47)	(15.50)	(−4.94)	(2.62)		
Norway	0.398	0.139	1.075	−0.256	0.293	0.890	2.13
	(1.54)	(3.44)	(11.54)	(−2.90)	(1.26)		
Sweden	0.406	0.203	0.836	−0.067	0.118	0.883	1.98
	(1.45)	(4.45)	(8.68)	(−0.76)	(0.52)		
Switzerland	0.371	0.024	1.201	−0.312	−0.173	0.892	2.02
	(2.11)	(0.91)	(12.69)	(−3.37)	(−1.02)		
UK	−0.167	0.310	1.224	−0.421	0.365	0.957	2.03
	(−0.70)	(4.65)	(14.40)	(−5.33)	(1.22)		
US	0.059	0.051	1.390	−0.469	0.088	0.966	2.15
	(0.44)	(1.67)	(15.36)	(−5.49)	(0.65)		

rather widespread across countries and therefore appears in the panel results quite strongly.

The evidence presented in the past two sections, viewed together, can now be summarized as follows:

1. Two countries, Germany and New Zealand, show effects on both a "real" variable, GDP growth, and inflation that are consistent with the Nordhaus model. One other country, Japan, exhibits borderline results, particularly on inflation.[11] All of the other countries show either no evidence of cycles or evidence for only one of the two variables.

2. There seems to be a much more widespread electoral cycle on inflation than on growth and unemployment. This finding is inconsistent with the Nordhaus model, but it is consistent with models that emphasize cycles on policy instruments.

The finding that Germany has political business cycles is somewhat surprising, given the fact that the Bundesbank is one of the most, if not *the* most, independent central bank in the world.

In the next two sections we look directly at evidence on policy instruments.

8.6   Monetary Policy and Elections

If one expects to observe some type of electoral business cycle, then one should detect electoral manipulation of either, or both, of the macroeconomic policy instruments—monetary and fiscal policy. The focus of this section is to analyze the implications of the opportunistic political business cycle on monetary policy. Again we note that politicians of different countries may be severely constrained in their monetary policy manipulation by the autonomy of the central bank.

Our tests adopt methodology analogous to the output, unemployment, and inflation regressions used by Alesina and Roubini (1990), which were extended earlier in this chapter. A similar technique was also used by Grier (1987, 1989) for the United States.

The procedure used to test the PBC for both the pooled cross-section, time-series regressions, as well as the country-by-country regressions, was as follows:

$$m_{it} = \beta_0 + \beta_1 m_{it-1} + \beta_2 m_{it-2} + \cdots + \beta_n m_{it-n} + \beta_{n+1} \text{PBCN}_{it} + \varepsilon_t \qquad (2)$$

where m_{it} is the rate of growth of money for country i at time t. PBCN_{it} is the electoral "dummy" variable discussed earlier, which takes on a positive value the last three or five quarters before the election and during the quarter of the election. The PBC theory implies that the coefficient on $PBCN_{it}$ should be positive and significantly different from zero, indicating that money growth is higher immediately before an election. Our sample of quarterly data includes all eighteen countries listed above, and the sample period is 1958–1987.[12]

Money growth is defined as the yearly rate of change of M1. This definition is used to remove seasonality from the money data. Tests with the quarterly rate of change of M1, as well as other methods of seasonally adjusting the data, reveal no change in the results. The autoregressive specification for the dependent variable is chosen as the best using standard techniques. This is found to be an AR(9); however, the results are not dependent on the lag specification of the model. For brevity, the coefficients on the lags are not displayed.

The top of table 8.7, labeled PBC Test, reports the results of the panel regressions for PBC4 and PBC6. The table, which includes specifications

Table 8.7
Panel data money growth, dependent variable: m

Description*	No country dummies		With country dummies	
PBC Test	Coeff.	R^2	Coeff.	R^2
	(t-stat.)	N Obs.	(t-stat.)	N Obs.
PBC4	0.477	0.73	0.480	0.73
	(2.49)	1887	(2.50)	1887
PBC6	0.356	0.73	0.355	0.73
	(2.03)	1852	(2.01)	1852

Partisan test	Coefficient (t-statistic)	Coefficient (t-statistic)
PBC4–Left	0.415	0.411
	(1.42)	(1.40)
PBC4–Right	0.527	0.531
	(2.09)	(2.09)
Difference Test4	−0.112	−0.120
	(−0.29)	(−0.31)
PBC6–Left	0.403	0.409
	(1.52)	(1.52)
PBC6–Right	0.323	0.314
	(1.39)	(1.33)
Difference Test6	0.080	0.095
	(0.23)	(0.27)

* The estimated regressions include lags of the dependent variable, which are not reported the table.

with and without country dummies (for conciseness the coefficients on these dummies are not reported), indicates that the coefficient on the electoral dummy is both the correct sign and significantly different from zero. This outcome supports the implications of the PBC model. Thus, *ceteris paribus*, money growth is higher for the year to year and a half before an election. All of the reported results were found to be invariant to tests of robustness such as leading or lagging the political dummy, or excluding individual countries that might be believed to be driving the results. In addition, including a world average money growth variable, obtained analogously to the world average output growth, did not change the results.[13] Tests employing Grier's sinusoidal electoral dummy yielded no change in the results. It was felt that this symmetric V-shaped variable—which has its maximum value the period of the election, declines until the midpoint between elections (when it reaches its minimum), and then increases until the election—constrained the dynamic implications of the theory, and thus the PBCN political dummy was the preferred variable.

The country-by-country results reported in table 8.8 are not as compelling. Although, for PBC4, a vast majority of the countries in the sample (thirteen out of eighteen) have a coefficient greater than zero, we cannot reject the hypothesis that the coefficient is positive and significantly different from zero (at the 5 percent level) for only two countries, Australia and New Zealand. In addition, we cannot reject for Germany at the 10 percent level, and three other countries have a t-statistic greater than one.

It is not surprising that New Zealand, which until recently had one of the least autonomous central banks (see Alesina 1989 and Grilli, Masciandaro, and Tabellini 1991), shows the most significant evidence of an electoral cycle. Conversely, it is quite surprising that Germany, with one of the most independent central banks, displays some form of political manipulation of its monetary policy. Finally, our results for the United States differ from those of Grier (1987, 1989). However, further study of this matter reconciles these differences. If we split our sample in the early eighties, we discover that Grier's findings of an opportunistic PBC in the United States does in fact hold for his sample period of the early sixties to the early eighties. After the early eighties, the model does not perform as well. One explanation may be that policy manipulation was ineffectual and thus not utilized after 1980 due to the well-documented instability of the money demand equation in the United States.[14]

We can also note that for both the panel and the country-by-country data sets the outcomes of the PBC6 regressions are weaker. This result may be explained as follows. Opportunistic PBC models indicate that the office

Table 8.8
Country money growth PBC test, dependent variable: m

Country*	PBC4		PBC6	
	Coefficient (t-statistic)	R^2 N Obs.	Coefficient (t-statistic)	R^2 N Obs.
Australia	0.945 (1.73)	0.87 108	0.376 (0.71)	0.87 106
Austria	−0.207 (−0.36)	0.78 108	−0.146 (−0.28)	0.79 106
Belgium	0.104 (0.22)	0.75 108	0.153 (0.35)	0.75 106
Canada	0.563 (0.39)	0.82 64	0.571 (0.45)	0.79 62
Denmark	−0.607 (−0.67)	0.61 108	0.553 (0.64)	0.62 106
Finland	0.840 (0.77)	0.65 108	0.176 (0.17)	0.67 106
France	0.401 (0.39)	0.46 108	−0.398 (−0.45)	0.46 106
Germany	0.596 (1.46)	0.82 108	0.520 (1.37)	0.83 106
Ireland	−0.047 (−0.05)	0.71 108	0.724 (0.85)	0.71 106
Italy	0.552 (1.19)	0.85 108	0.381 (0.91)	0.85 106
Japan	0.604 (0.95)	0.89 108	0.647 (1.06)	0.89 106
Netherlands	0.777 (1.20)	0.75 108	−0.092 (−0.16)	0.74 106
New Zealand	2.235 (2.03)	0.70 108	1.575 (1.52)	0.70 106
Norway	0.226 (0.26)	0.54 107	0.425 (0.57)	0.56 106
Sweden	1.825 (1.13)	0.64 96	0.823 (0.53)	0.64 94
Switzerland	−0.034 (−0.04)	0.73 108	0.578 (0.71)	0.74 106
United Kingdom	−0.156 (−0.22)	0.85 108	−0.500 (−0.79)	0.84 106
United States	0.144 (0.53)	0.87 108	−0.109 (−0.47)	0.85 106

* The estimated regressions include lags of the dependent variable, which are not reported in the table.

holder wishes to pump up the economy right before the election, without any concurrent inflation. Given the long run inflationary implication of monetary policy, expansionary monetary policy too far in advance will result in an a boom too early, and high levels of inflation before the election.

We also investigated a "partisan/opportunistic" interaction term. As emphasized by Lindbeck (1976) and Alesina (1989), preelectoral opportunistic behavior for left-wing governments may be different than that of right-wing governments. More specifically, left-wing governments, who at the beginning of their administration pursued expansionary monetary policies to lower unemployment, may be reducing money growth at the end of their terms, to bring down the inflation caused by their initial policies. An opportunistic left-wing government may want to emphasize their antiinflation policies to appeal to the median voter in election years. Conversely, right-wing governments, who undertook contractionary monetary policy to lower inflation, may be expanding money at the end of their administrations to enter elections during a period of expansion.

A formal test of this hypothesis can made by running the following panel and country-by-country regressions:

$$m_{it} = \gamma_0 + \gamma_1 m_{it-1} + \gamma_2 m_{it-2} + \cdots + \gamma_n m_{it-n}$$
$$+ \gamma_{n+1} \text{DUML}_{it} + \gamma_{n+2} \text{PBCNL}_{it} + \gamma_{n+3} \text{PBCNR}_{it} + \varepsilon_t \qquad (3)$$

DUML_{it} is a dummy that identifies left-wing governments, and PBCNL_{it} and PBCNR_{it} are interaction terms between PBCN and the left- and right-wing government dummies respectively.[15] If partisan/opportunistic political manipulation of monetary policy exists, one expects the coefficients on the left- and right-wing interaction terms to be different. The strong form of this theory, as described above, suggests that the coefficients should in fact be of opposite sign.

The bottom of table 8.7, labeled Partisan Test, reports the results for the panel regressions. For PBC4, we find that the coefficient for right-wing governments is significantly different from zero at the 5 percent level while that of left-wing governments is not. However, we cannot reject the hypothesis that they are of the same magnitude. This test, which has the correct negative sign, is displayed in table 7 as Difference Test4.

The panel results for PBC6 are less compelling. We find that the coefficients for both left- and right-wing governments are not significantly different from zero. In addition, the difference test has the incorrect sign. This again may be attributed to the longer length of the political dummy, which is picking up more than just the preelectoral dynamics.

Table 8.9
Country money growth partisan test, dependent variable: m

Country*	PBC4–Left Coefficient (t-statistic)	PBC4–Right Coefficient (t-statistic)	Diff. Test4 Coefficient (t-statistic)
Australia	1.448 (1.00)	1.073 (1.82)	0.375 (0.25)
Austria	−1.223 (−1.50)	0.914 (1.05)	−2.137 (−1.75)
Belgium	0.285 (0.27)	−0.013 (−0.02)	0.298 (0.21)
Denmark	−0.702 (−0.63)	−0.269 (−0.16)	−0.432 (−0.21)
Finland	1.684 (1.33)	−1.365 (−0.65)	3.048 (1.23)
France	−2.161 (−0.83)	0.997 (0.85)	−3.158 (−1.07)
Germany	0.379 (0.67)	0.872 (1.42)	−0.493 (−0.61)
Ireland	−0.625 (−0.37)	0.178 (0.16)	−0.803 (−0.40)
Italy	0.240 (0.47)	1.802 (1.63)	−1.562 (−1.29)
Netherlands	1.961 (1.57)	0.242 (0.30)	1.718 (1.12)
New Zealand	−2.338 (−0.88)	3.080 (2.69)	−5.418 (−1.93)
Norway	−1.289 (−1.14)	2.668 (1.89)	−3.957 (−2.09)
Sweden	3.139 (1.61)	−1.437 (−0.47)	4.576 (1.24)
United Kingdom	−0.052 (−0.04)	−0.220 (−0.24)	0.168 (0.12)
United States	−0.097 (−0.24)	0.393 (0.96)	−0.490 (−0.82)

* The estimated regressions include lags of the dependent variable, which are not reported in the table.

Thus, for the country-by-country regressions, we present only the outcomes of the PBC4 regressions, which can be found in table 8.9.[16] These results indicate that only nine out of fifteen countries exhibit the expected negative sign for the difference test.[17] Some of the countries with the incorrect sign possess difference tests that are nearly significant.

In the sample of countries that exhibit the expected behavior, three, Austria, New Zealand, and Norway, cannot reject the hypothesis that their political parties pursue different monetary policies before elections, at the 5 percent level. In addition, two countries, France and Italy, have t-statistics for the difference test less than minus one. Finally, for Australia and Germany, we cannot reject the hypothesis that the coefficient on right-wing governments is positive and significantly different from zero (at the 5 percent and 10 percent levels respectively), whereas we can reject the same hypothesis for their left-wing governments.

Thus, the results of the partisan/opportunistic tests are somewhat ambiguous; however, they do move in the expected direction. For the PBC model the pooled cross-section, time-series results are more compelling than the country-by-country results, indicating that political monetary cycles occur frequently but not systematically.

8.7   Fiscal Policy, Budget Deficits, and Elections

In this section we will consider the effects of elections on fiscal policy. Both traditional and recent rational PBC models imply that we should observe fiscal deficits before elections. However, these theories are vague about whether the preelectoral fiscal expansion will occur through a reduction in taxes, or an increase in government spending, or both. In principle, the actual combination of preelectoral tax cuts and fiscal spending increases might change over time and across countries. We therefore start our analysis of preelectoral budget cycles by concentrating on the fiscal deficits of the public sector.

In analyzing the effects of elections on fiscal deficits, one needs a structural model of budget deficits in order to control for the economic determinants of budget deficits. We rely upon the structural model of budget deficits used by Roubini and Sachs (1989) to study the effects of political instability on budget deficits. The data sample available for this section of the chapter is smaller than the one used before. The size of the sample is limited by the availability of consistent OECD data on public debt (see Roubini and Sachs 1989). The countries (and sample periods) included are as follows: Austria (1970–1985), Belgium (1960–1985), Canada (1961–

1985), Denmark (1971–1985), France (1960–1985), Finland (1970–1985), Germany (1960–1985), Italy (1964–1985), the Netherlands (1970–1985), Norway (1970–1985), Sweden (1970–1985), the United Kingdom (1960–1985), and the United States (1960–1985).

The specification of our model is consistent both with elements of optimizing approaches to fiscal deficits (such as the "tax smoothing" model of Barro 1979) and with traditional Keynesian models of fiscal deficits. In fact, both theories imply that fiscal deficits are countercyclical; i.e., fiscal deficits will emerge during periods of recession and growth slowdown. In the tax-smoothing approach, recessions lead to fiscal deficits as optimizing governments try to minimize the deadweight losses from distortionary taxation; since they will stabilize tax rates, a recession will lead to a reduction of the tax base and a shortfall in revenues. Similarly, transitory shocks to government spending should also be financed through budget deficits.

In this sense, the sudden and sharp increase in budget deficits after 1973 in many OECD countries can be linked directly to the sudden slowdown in OECD growth and the corresponding sudden rise in unemployment after 1973. These shocks reduced revenues and increased government spending on what appeared to be a *cyclical* basis. Since it was widely expected then that the growth slowdown and the rise in unemployment would have been transitory, these deficits in the mid-seventies could have been consistent with the tax-smoothing equilibrium view.[18]

In addition to the tax-smoothing hypothesis, the tendency toward deficits after a slowdown in growth is exacerbated for two additional reasons. First, many major areas of public spending (e.g., unemployment compensation, social welfare expenditure, early retirement benefits, job retraining, and subsidies for ailing firms) are inherently countercyclical, so that portions of government spending actually tend to rise automatically when growth slows down and unemployment increases. The second reason is the intentional implementation in some countries of Keynesian aggregate demand policies in the face of a growth slowdown. The equilibrium model explicitly rejects the links of spending or taxes to the level of output and employment via aggregate demand, but many governments believed (and many still do so) in these links. Right or wrong, many governments reduce taxes or increase government spending during recessions.

In considering the economic determinants of budget deficits, one should also include the effects of real interest rate shocks. For example, after 1979 the increase in world real interest rates significantly and unexpectedly raised most governments' costs of debt servicing. One useful measure of the budgetary costs of higher interest rates is given by the debt-to-GDP ratio multiplied by the change in the differential between real interest rates and growth rates. Between 1979 and 1981, this measure rose by several percent of GDP in most of the industrial economies, thereby greatly adding to the fiscal burden.[19]

Given the above discussion of the determinants of fiscal deficits, as in Roubini and Sachs (1989), we estimate a pooled cross-section, time series regression where the left-hand side variable is the annual deficit, measured as the change in the debt-GDP ratio, $d(b_{it})$. The basic explanatory variables are: (1) the lagged deficit, $d(b_{it-1})$; (2) the *change* in the unemployment rate, $d(U_{it})$; (3) the *change* in the GDP growth rate, denoted $d(y_{it})$; (4) the *change* in the real interest rate minus the growth rate, multiplied by the lagged debt-GDP ratio, $d(r_t - n_t)^*b_{it-1}$; (5) a dummy for political instability, POL_{it}, first used in Roubini and Sachs (1989) (and to be described); (6) an electoral dummy ELE_{it}, to be defined; and (7) an error term, v_{it}. The basic structure of the pooled regression model is the following (*i* denotes country, *t* denotes time, and $d(x)$ denotes the change in variable x):

$$d(b_{it}) = \delta_0 + \delta_1 d(b_{it-1}) + \delta_2 d(U_{it}) + \delta_3 d(y_{it}) + \delta_4 d(r_t - n_t)b_{it-1}$$
$$+ \delta_5 POL_{it} + \delta_6 ELE_{it} + v_{it} \tag{4}$$

According to our discussion, we expect the following: $0 < \delta_1 < 1$ (to allow for any slow adjustment and persistence of budget deficits); $\delta_2 > 0$ (since a rise in the unemployment rate raises government spending above its permanent value in the short term); $\delta_3 < 0$ (since a rise in GDP growth lowers government spending below its permanent value in the short term and may raise tax revenues); and $\delta_4 > 0$ (since a rise in $r - n$ directly raises $(r - n)b_{it-1}$, which, if transitory, should be accommodated by a temporary rise in the budget deficit).

Before introducing and discussing the political and electoral determinants of budget deficits, in column 1 of table 8.10 we present the results of the regression when we include only the economic variables. This specification provides a rather successful account of the role of economic shocks in inducing budget deficits in the industrial countries. In particular, a rise in unemployment (denoted by DUB) raises the budget deficit; a rise in the debt-servicing cost (denoted by DRB) raises the budget deficit; and an acceleration of GDP growth (denoted by DGR) lowers the budget deficit, indicating that the deceleration of GDP growth after 1973 contributed to the rise in budget deficits. Note that the variable measuring this slowdown in growth is highly significant.[20] Finally, the lagged deficit (DBYL) enters

Table 8.10
Panel data regression of deficit with political variables, dependent variable: DBY

Regressors	Equation (1)	Equation (2)	Equation (3)	Equation (4)	Equation (5)
Constant	−0.002	0.006	−0.007	−0.004	−0.0037
	(−1.19)	(−2.73)	(−3.28)	(−1.97)	(−1.98)
DBYL	0.74	0.71	0.72	0.74	0.70
	(17.0)	(16.0)	(16.2)	(17.2)	(14.0)
DUB	0.23	0.18	0.19	0.24	0.24
	(2.98)	(2.32)	(2.51)	(3.15)	(3.17)
DRB	0.56	0.61	0.56	0.51	0.50
	(2.66)	(2.91)	(2.71)	(2.46)	(2.38)
DGR	−0.47	−0.45	−0.46	−0.48	−0.47
	(−8.49)	(−8.31)	(−8.50)	(−8.69)	(−8.49)
DUJAP*	1.82	2.75	2.62	1.76	1.70
	(1.46)	(2.16)	(2.07)	(1.42)	(1.38)
ELE	—	—	0.0065	0.0072	0.0063
			(2.17)	(2.41)	(2.04)
POL	—	0.0042	0.0039	—	—
		(2.77)	(2.57)		
DBYLELE	—	—	—	—	0.13
					(1.55)
R^2	0.65	0.66	0.67	0.66	0.66

t-statistics in parentheses.
* The regressor DUJAP is a country-specific dummy for DUB for Japan. This is the only country for which a country-specific effect was found in the data: its positive estimate implies that an increase in Japanese unemployment has a much stronger effect on budget deficits than in any other countries. The results, however, do not depend in any way on the inclusion of this variable.

with a coefficient of about 0.70, suggesting that about 70 percent of the lagged budget deficit persists to the next period.

In order to test the hypothesis that governments manipulate fiscal policies before elections in order to maximize their reelection probabilities, in column 3 we add to the basic regression a dummy ELE that takes value 1 in election years and 0 otherwise. In constructing the variable ELE we need to consider that, since our data on deficits are on a yearly basis, the exact time of an election during a year might be important for assessing the effects of elections on fiscal deficits. More specifically, if an election occurs toward the end of the year t, we can expect that an opportunistic government would run a fiscal deficit during that year. However, if the election occurs toward the beginning of year t, it is more reasonable to assume that the fiscal expansion will occur in year $t - 1$ so as to be timed with the early election time in year t. In practice, in constructing the variable ELE we assign value 1 to the dummy in the preelectoral year $t - 1$ if the election will occur in the first and second quarters of year t; we assign value 1 in the electoral year t if the election occurs in the third or fourth quarter of year t. As an additional check on the model, we also run regressions using a slightly different electoral dummy (ELX instead of ELE). ELX takes the value 1 in the election year regardless of whether the election occurs in the first or second half of the year.

In addition to the electoral variable, we also add to the regression the political variable successfully used by Roubini and Sachs (1989) to study the effect of government fragmentation on budget deficits. The hypothesis in that paper was that multiparty coalition governments, especially those with a short expected tenure, are poor at reducing budget deficits.[21] We therefore add to the regression the Roubini-Sachs index (denoted POL_{it} for country i at time t), which measures the degree of political cohesion of the national government. The index is constructed as follows:[22]

$$
POL = \begin{cases}
0 & \text{one-party majority parliamentary government; or a} \\
& \text{presidential government, with the same party in the} \\
& \text{majority in the executive and legislative branches} \\
\\
1 & \text{coalition parliamentary government with two coalition} \\
& \text{partners; or presidential government, with different parties} \\
& \text{in control of the executive and legislative branches} \\
\\
2 & \text{coalition parliamentary government with three or more} \\
& \text{coalition partners} \\
\\
3 & \text{minority parliamentary government}
\end{cases}
$$

The results of the estimations are shown in columns 2–4 in table 8.10. Several different versions of the regression are shown, involving different ways of including the variables ELE and POL, either jointly or separately. In column 2, we introduce the political instability variable and, as in Roubini and Sachs (1989), we find that (after controlling for the economic determinants of deficits) a greater degree of political instability (as proxied by the index POL) leads to higher budget deficits.[23] In column 3, we add our electoral dummy ELE to the regressors used in column 2; we find that, after controlling for the economic determinants, both POL and the electoral dummy, ELE, have the right sign and are statistically significant at the 5 percent confidence level. In other words, real fiscal deficits are higher in the year leading to an election. In column 4, we drop the POL variable and consider the effect of ELE alone; we again find a statistically significant coefficient.

The effect of elections on budget deficits is significant both statistically and economically; the estimated coefficient on ELE in columns 3 and 4 implies that, after controlling for other determinants of fiscal balances, real fiscal deficits will be higher in election years by more than 0.6 percent of GDP. We also ran the panel regressions in table 8.10 using the electoral dummy ELX instead of ELE (ELX takes the value 1 in the election year regardless of whether the election occurs in the first half of the year or the second half). As expected, ELX works less well than ELE, since this dummy variable does not correspond to the timing of elections. However, in these regressions ELX has the right sign and is statistically significant at the 10 percent confidence level. These results are available upon request.

In column 5, we investigate an interaction term of the electoral variable with the lagged deficit (termed DBYLELE), with the view that the speed of adjustment to an inherited level of the deficit, $d(b_{it-1})$ might be lower in election years. When we introduce the interaction variable DBYLELE in column 5, we find that the sign is the expected positive one (deficits are more persistent in election years, that is, the fiscal adjustment to past deficits is slower during election periods) but it is only borderline significant (the t-statistic is equal to 1.55).

The results in table 8.10 provide some evidence that during an election year fiscal policy is "loose." It would be interesting to investigate which countries exhibit more pronounced electoral budget cycles. However, such a test is difficult for two reasons. First, since the OECD data on public debt (from which we derived the real deficits measures) are available only on a yearly basis, the sample period for each country is quite small (ranging from 22 data points for the United States to 14 for Denmark). Second, elections are infrequent events, and the data set for each country does not include more than four electoral observations. These small sample problems severely constrain the possibility of running meaningful country-by-country regressions. Keeping in mind these important caveats and limitations, we ran the basic deficit equation for each country separately. We found the coefficient on the electoral dummy to be of the right sign in eight countries (Germany, Belgium, Japan, Austria, Netherlands, Norway, Finland, Denmark) but statistically significant (at the 10 percent confidence level) in only one (the Netherlands).[24] While the sample period constraints might account for these weak results, the inability to find strong electoral effects at the country level would suggest caution in arguing for a strong electoral budget cycle effect in this OECD sample.

Now that we have established some evidence in favor of fiscal manipulation, we can ask, does the electoral budget cycle found in the results displayed in table 8.10 derive from increased spending before elections or reduced taxes? The available theoretical models of electoral budget cycles do not provide a clear answer to such a question. Empirically, the issue is ambiguous as well. First, the choice of whether to reduce taxes or increase spending in any single country may vary over time and over different elections. Second, different countries may differ in the way they expand fiscal policy before elections: some may reduce taxes and others increase spending. Given the above observations, we do not necessarily expect to find a strong effect of elections on government spending or taxes in a large panel of countries.

Despite these caveats, we attempted to test whether there are any electoral cycles in government spending or revenues but found little evidence of any effects.[25] These outcomes are consistent with our prior that results of this kind are difficult to detect. We therefore leave attempts to systematically test whether particular subcomponents of spending and/or revenues have more pronounced electoral cycles to future research.

8.8   Discussion and Conclusions

The results of this chapter, viewed in the context of the literature on political cycles, suggest some general conclusions. Previous empirical findings suggest that partisan effects on both policy instruments and economic outcomes are quite widespread in OECD economies.[26] In particular, left-wing governments, when elected, favor expansionary demand policies leading to a temporary increase in growth and reduction in unemployment. These policies lead to an acceleration in inflation that often persists (because of credibility problems) even after the initial real expansion has disappeared. According to this view, left-wing governments often face new elections in a situation of high inflation; in this case, any further attempt to expand, as predicted by the Nordhaus model, would be counterproductive. In fact, the left may need to signal its competence in dealing with inflation by pursuing a "cautious" monetary policy. Conversely, when right-wing governments are appointed, they are willing to incur the costs of an immediate recession or downturn, in order to reduce inflation. After the initial downturn, the economy returns to its natural level of activity and inflation remains low. Thus, when the next election approaches, right-wing governments have "room" to pursue expansionary policies, yielding a Nordhaus-type political business cycle.

In addition to having these partisan goals, politicians are opportunistic. That is, they prefer being in office rather than out. In addition, partisan goals can be implemented only if elections are won. Thus, even partisan politicians, regardless of their ideology, may engage in opportunistic behavior if by doing so they can increase their chances of reelection (see Nordhaus 1989).

Our results of the panel regressions are quite suggestive (we tend to emphasize these panel regressions above the country-by-country regressions because the former are not affected by the very common problem in this literature of scarcity of degrees of freedom). The panel results reject the Nordhaus formulation of the PBC but do *not* reject the "rational political budget cycles" of Rogoff and Sibert (1988). In fact, even though at the panel level we found no evidence of cycles on GDP and unemployment, we observed evidence of electoral cycles on monetary and fiscal policy instruments and on inflation. This result is consistent with the notion that it is easy to manipulate policy instruments, while it is more difficult to control policy outcomes.[27] The country-by-country results suggest, however, that although these cycles are not strong in any particular country, they occur at least occasionally in many of the OECD democracies.

Our interpretation of these results is that, in general, politicians try to avoid restrictive monetary and fiscal policies in election years, and occasionally they are openly expansionary. This view is consistent with the overall significance of the electoral dummy in the full sample of countries and with its lack of significance in many subsamples (i.e., specific countries). In summary, our results suggest that monetary and budget cycles occur frequently, and in several countries, but in no country (with the possible exception of New Zealand) do they occur in every election, nor are they of very large dimensions.

Only two countries, Germany and New Zealand, do not reject the Nordhaus model. The findings for Germany are somewhat surprising. This is the country with the most independent central bank, thus one would expect very little preelectoral manipulation of monetary policy. One possible explanation of these somewhat puzzling results is Germany's ability to take advantage of its favorable short-term unemployment/inflation trade-off. Due to its strong commitment to price stability, yielding a flat short-run Phillips curve, one would expect even small manipulations of monetary policy to have large effects on outcomes.[28] The case of New Zealand is much more convincing. The recent institutional reform in this country that significantly increased the degree of independence of the central bank may have been a step taken to limit electoral manipulation of monetary policy.

In our view, the results of this chapter support the "rational" approach to modeling political cycles. In fact, if voters were very naive, and politicians could manipulate the economy very easily, one should observe pre-electoral manipulations of instruments and outcomes that are much more widespread, easily detectable, and larger in magnitude than our findings suggest. Instead, we ascertain that fiscal and monetary cycles probably occur frequently, but not in every election, and are of relatively moderate intensity. It would be quite interesting to pursue this analysis further to study *when* one is more likely to observe opportunistic manipulations of policy instruments. Perhaps they tend to occur when incumbents are unsure of reappointment and need an extra electoral boost, as suggested by Frey and Schneider (1978). Conversely, political cycles may not be observed when incumbents are "safe," and do not need to engage in any signaling of competence.

Table 8A.1
Election and regime change, E = Election; CH L = Change Left; Ch R = Change Right

Australia: Endogenous timing, 3 yrs				Austria: Endogenous timing, 4 yrs			
1961:4	E	RIGHT	a	1959:2	E	RIGHT	c
1963:4	E			1962:4	E		
1966:4	E			1966:1	E	CH R	
1969:4	E			1970:1	E	CH L	
1972:4	E	CH L		1971:4	E		(*)
1974:2	E		(*)b	1975:4	E		
1975:4	E	CH R		1979:2	E		
1977:4	E			1983:2	E	CH R	c
1980:4	E			1986:4	E	CH R	
1983:1	E	CH L					
1984:4	E		(*)				
1987:3	E						

Belgium: Endogenous timing, 4 yrs				Canada: Endogenous timing, 5 yrs			
1961:1	E	RIGHT		1962:2	E	RIGHT	
1965:2	E			1963:2	E	CH L	(*)
1968:1	E	CH L		1965:4	E		
1971:4	E			1968:2	E		
1973:1		CH R		1972:4	E		
1974:1	E			1974:3	E		(*)
1977:2	E	CH L		1979:2	E	CH R	
1978:4	E		(*)	1980:1	E	CH L	(*)
1981:4	E	CH R		1984:3	E	CH R	
1985:4	E	CH L					
1987:4	E						

Table 8A.1 (continued)

Denmark: Endogenous timing, 4 yrs			
1960:4	E	LEFT	
1964:3	E		
1966:4	E		
1968:1	E	CH R	(*)
1971:3	E	CH L	
1973:4	E	CH R	
1975:1	E	CH L	(*)
1977:1	E		
1979:4	E		
1981:4	E		
1982:3		CH R	
1984:1	E		
1987:3	E		

Finland: Endogenous timing, 4 yrs			
1962:1	E	LEFT	
1963:4		CH R	
1966:1	E	CH L	
1970:1	E		
1972:1	E		
1975:3	E	CH R	
1977:2		CH L	
1979:1	E		
1983:1	E	CH R	
1987:1	E	CH R	

France: Endogenous timing, 5 yrs			
1962:4	E	RIGHT	
1967:1	E		
1968:2	E		(*)
1973:1	E		
1978:1	E		
1981:2	E	CH L	
1984:3		CH R	
1986:1	E	CH R	

Germany: Endogenous timing, 4 yrs			
1961:3	E	RIGHT	
1965:3	E		
1966:4		CH L	c
1969:3	E	CH L	
1972:4	E	CH R	
1976:4	E		
1980:4	E		
1982:4		CH R	
1983:1	E		
1987:1	E		

Ireland: Endogenous timing, 5 yrs			
1961:4	E	RIGHT	
1965:2	E		
1969:2	E		
1973:1	E	CH L	
1977:2	E	CH R	
1981:2	E	CH L	
1982:1	E	CH R	(*)
1982:4	E	CH L	(*)
1987:1	E		

Italy: Endogenous timing, 5 yrs			
		RIGHT	
1962:4		CH L	
1963:2	E		
1968:2	E		
1972:2	E		
1974:4		CH R	
1976:2	E	CH L	
1979:2	E		
1983:2	E		
1987:2	E		

Japan: Endogenous timing, 4 yrs			
1960:4	E	RIGHT	
1963:4	E		
1967:1	E		
1969:4	E		
1972:4	E		
1976:4	E		
1979:4	E		
1980:2	E		(*)
1983:4	E		
1986:3	E		

Netherlands: Endogenous timing, 4 yrs			
1959:1	E	RIGHT	
1963:2	E		
1965:2		CH L	
1967:1	E	CH R	
1971:1	E		
1972:4	E		(*)
1973:2		CH L	
1977:2	E		
1977:4		CH R	
1981:2	E	CH L	
1982:3	E	CH R	(*)
1986:2	E		

Table 8A.1 (continued)

New Zealand: Endogenous timing, 3 yrs			Norway: Endogenous timing, 4 yrs		
1960:4	E	RIGHT	1961:3	E	LEFT
1963:4	E		1965:3	E	CH R
1966:4	E		1969:3	E	
1969:4	E		1971:4		CH L
1972:4	E	CH L	1972:4		CH R
1975:4	E	CH R	1973:3	E	CH L
1978:4	E		1977:3	E	
1981:4	E		1981:3	E	CH R
1984:3	E	CH L	1985:3	E	
1987:3	E		1986:2		CH L

Sweden: Exogenous timing, 3 yrs since late 60s, constitutional reform			Switzerland: Exogenous timing, 4 yrs		
1960:3	E	LEFT	1959:4	E	RIGHT
1964:3	E		1963:4	E	
1968:3	E		1967:4	E	
1970:3	E		1971:4	E	
1973:3	E		1975:4	E	
1976:3	E	CH R	1979:4	E	
1979:3	E		1983:4	E	
1982:3	E	CH L	1987:4	E	
1985:3	E				

UK: Endogenous timing, 5 yrs				US: Exogenous timing, 4 yrs		
1959:4	E	RIGHT		1960:4	E	RIGHT
1964:4	E	CH L		1964:4	E	CH L
1966:1	E		(*)	1968:4	E	
1970:2	E	CH R		1972:4	E	CH R
1974:1	E			1976:4	E	
1974:3	E	CH L	(*)	1980:4	E	CH L
1979:2	E	CH R		1984:4	E	CH R
1983:2	E					
1987:2	E					

a. RIGHT or LEFT indicates the type of government in power at the beginning of the sample which is 1959:1. We also indicate for each country whether elections dates are endogenous or exogenous and the official number of years between two elections.

b. Elections denoted with an asterisk "*" are not included in tests of the political business cycle theory because they are too close (less than two years) to previous elections. They are however included in tests of the opportunistic endogenous election model.

c. Both Germany and Austria had grand coalitions of Left and Right parties. Thus, a finer administration variable was used in the RPT inflation and partisan (Hibbs) regressions. This also explains the occurence of a rightward shift from an already central Right-leaning party.

Sources: Election dates are obtained from Banks (1989); dates of changes of government and their classification of "Right" and "Left" are obtained from Alt (1985) and Banks (1989).

Notes

Prepared for the Sapir Conference on "The Political Economy of Business Cycles and Growth," Tel Aviv University, June 2–3, 1991. We thank our discussants, Alex Cukierman and Ron Shachar, and several conference participants for very useful comments. Alesina's work was supported by a Sloan Research Fellowship.

1. In Nordhaus's (1975) original model, inflation was supposed to begin to increase *before* the election. However, by an appropriate choice of the lag structure in the Phillips curve, one can build a model in which inflation increases *after* the election, without affecting the basic results (see Lindbeck (1976)).

2. To be precise, in Rogoff and Sibert (1988) the budget is always balanced, in the sense that the difference between spending and taxes is covered by seigniorage.

3. Electoral cycles are not regular for several reasons. First, in a separating equilibrium, only competent governments would try to signal their competence by expanding output before elections. Second, pooling equilibria in which both competent and incompetent governments follow the same policy are possible; in this case regular electoral cycles would again be less likely. (See Persson and Tabellini (1991) for more on this point.)

4. In a nutshell the point is the following. The "partisan theory" with rational expectations in a wage-contracts model as originally formulated in Alesina (1987) implies that at the beginning of a right-wing government (i.e., Republican administration in the United States), one should observe a downturn or recession due to an antiinflationary policy. Later in their term of office, the economy recovers and returns to its "natural" level of economic activity. The opposite pattern is followed by Democratic administrations. Thus, the empirical implications of the Nordhaus model and of this "partisan" model are similar for right-wing governments, but *opposite* for left-wing governments. Both Haynes and Stone (1989) and Nordhaus (1989) find "evidence" of political business cycles only for Republican administrations, which suggests that, in fact, they are not rejecting a partisan model.

5. However, a careful examination of their results suggests that their time dummies are significant in the second and third years of an administration. Conversely, an electoral dummy assuming the value of 1 in the two years preceding each election is insignificant.

6. See Roubini and Sachs (1989) tables 3 and 4 and their data appendix for more information.

7. See Alesina and Roubini (1990) for a discussion of this econometric approach.

8. The seven largest countries are (in 1987 order) United States, Japan, Germany, France, the United Kingdom, Italy, and Canada. An analogous definition is used to construct proxies for OECD unemployment, inflation, and money growth.

9. See Alesina and Roubini (1990) for further discussions of this fixed effect model.

10. We have adopted the convention of excluding elections that were held less than eight quarters after the preceding one. This convention eliminates cases in which

very early elections were called to solve deadlocks caused by lack of a clear majority in the legislature resulting from the previous balloting.

11. Ito (1990a,b) finds evidence of a strategic choice of election timing in Japan. Early elections tend to be called when the economy is doing well. Alesina and Roubini (1990) confirm this result for Japan.

12. There are two exceptions: because of data problems the sample for Canada is 1969.1 to 1987.4 and for Sweden is 1961.1 to 1987.3.

13. These results are available upon request.

14. See Friedman and Kuttner (1989) for an in-depth discussion of the instability of the money demand equation in the 1980s. Also, Grier (1989) notes, in a footnote, this difference between pre- and post-1980 results of the political monetary cycle.

15. This was found to be the correct specification of the model after estimating the equations on the left- and right-wing governments separately. The coefficients on the lag money growth variables were found to be virtually identical.

16. The results for PBC6, which are similar to those of PBC4, are available upon request.

17. During our sample period, no left-wing governments held power in Switzerland and Japan. For Canada, its smaller sample and our convention of excluding elections that were held less than eight quarters after the preceding one required its exclusion from the sample.

18. By the early 1980s, however, it had become clear that the shocks had considerable persistence (to the point of spawning the new "hysteresis" theory of unemployment), and many governments began reducing their budget deficits. In broad terms, the equilibrium approach is much less successful in accounting for the *persistence* of budget deficits throughout the 1980s in many OECD countries. See Roubini and Sachs (1989) for more tests on the equilibrium approach to fiscal policy.

19. This rise was particularly large, of course, in countries such as Belgium, Ireland, and Italy, which had already accumulated a large stock of debt. As with the unemployment increase and the growth slowdown, the effects of higher interest rates have turned out to be more persistent than many policymakers expected in the early 1980s.

20. Its magnitude suggests that each 1 percentage point slowdown in GDP growth initially raises the budget deficit relative to GDP by 0.45 percentage points.

21. See Alesina and Tabellini (1990) and Tabellini and Alesina (1990) for a formal model of the effects of political instability and conflict on budget deficits.

22. Details on the construction of the index for each particular country can be found in the text and data appendix of Roubini and Sachs (1989).

23. The magnitude of the coefficient on the POL variable, 0.004, signifies that the difference *ceteris paribus* between a majority government and a minority govern-

ment ($p = 0$ versus $p = 3$), is 0.012, or 1.2 percentage points of added budget deficit per year.

24. These results are available upon request.

25 These results are available upon request.

26. See Hibbs (1977), Alt (1985), Alesina (1989), Paldam (1989a,b), and Alesina and Roubini (1990).

27. This finding that the PBC instruments have little influence on the real variables whereas inflation is strongly affected is also consistent with theories of the "dynamic inconsistency of monetary policy." (See Barro and Gordon 1983a and Persson and Tabellini 1991 for surveys of this subject.)

28. We are grateful to Alex Cukierman for suggesting this point. (See Lucas 1973 for more on this subject.)

References

Alesina, Alberto. 1989. Politics and Business Cycles in Industrial Democracies. *Economic Policy* 8:55–98.

Alesina, Alberto. 1988. Macroeconomics and Politics. NBER Macroeconomic Annual. Cambridge, MA: MIT Press. 13–52.

Alesina, Alberto. 1987. Macroeconomic Policy in a Two-Party System as a Repeated Game. *Quarterly Journal of Economics* 102:651–678.

Alesina, Alberto., Londregan, John, and Rosenthal, Howard. 1990. A Political-Economy Model of the United States. NBER Working Paper no. 3611.

Alesina, Alberto and Rosenthal, Howard. 1989. Ideological Cycles in Congressional Elections and the Macroeconomy. *American Political Science Review* 83:373–398.

Alesina, Alberto and Roubini, Nouriel. 1990. Political Business Cycles in OECD Economies. NBER Working Paper no. 3478.

Alesina, Alberto and Summers, Lawrence. 1990. Central Bank Independence and Macroeconomic Performance: Some Comparative Evidence. Manuscript.

Alesina, Alberto and Tabellini, Guido. 1990. A Political Theory of Fiscal Deficits and Government Debt in a Democracy. *The Review of Economic Studies* 57:403–414.

Alt, James. 1985. Political Parties, World Demand, and Unemployment: Domestic and International Sources of Economic Activity. *American Political Science Review* 79:1016–1040.

Banks, Arthur 1987, 1989. Political Handbook of the World. State University of New York at Binghamton: CSA Publications.

Barro, Robert. 1979. On the Determination of the Public Debt. *Journal of Political Economy* 87:940–947.

Barro, Robert and Gordon, David. 1983a. Rules, Discretion, and Reputation in a Model of Monetary Policy. *Journal of Monetary Economics* 12:101–122.

Barro, Robert and Gordon, David. 1983b. A Positive Theory of Monetary Policy in a Natural Rate Model. *Journal of Political Economy* 31:589–610.

Bizer, David S., and Durlauf, Steven N. 1990. Testing the Positive Theory of Government Finance. *Journal of Monetary Economics* 26:123–141.

Blanchard, Olivier and Summers, Lawrence. 1986. Hysteresis and the European Unemployment Problem. NBER Macroeconomic Annual. Cambridge, MA: MIT Press. 15–78.

Cukierman, Alex and Meltzer, Allan. 1986. A Positive Theory of Discretionary Policy, The Cost of a Democratic Government and The Benefit of a Constitution. *Economic Inquiry* 24:367–388.

Friedman, Benjamin M. and Kuttner, Kenneth N. 1989. Money, Income and Prices After the 1980s. NBER Working Paper no. 2852.

Frey, Bruno and Schneider, Frederich. 1978. An Empirical Study of Politico-Economic Interaction in the United States. *The Review of Economics and Statistics* 60:174–183.

Golden, David and Poterba, James. 1980. The Price of Popularity: The Political Business Cycle Reexamined. *American Journal of Political Science* 71:696–714.

Grier, Kevin B. 1987. Presidential Elections and Federal Reserve Policy: An Empirical Test. *Southern Economic Journal* 54:475–486.

Grier, Kevin B. 1989. On the Existence of a Political Monetary Cycle. *American Journal of Political Science* 33:376–389.

Grilli, Vittorio, Masciandaro, Donato, and Tabellini, Guido. 1991. Political and Monetary Institutions and Public Finance Policies in the Industrial Democracies. *Economic Policy*. forthcoming.

Haynes, Steve and Stone, Joe. 1989. Should the Political Business Cycle Be Revived?" Unpublished Manuscript.

Hibbs, Douglas. 1977. Political Parties and Macroeconomic Policy. *The American Political Science Review* 71:1467–1487.

Hibbs, Douglas. 1987. The American Political Economy. Cambridge, MA: Harvard University Press.

Ito, Takatoshi. 1990a. The Timing of Elections and Political Business Cycles in Japan. *Journal of Asian Economics* 1:135–146.

Ito, Takatoshi. 1990b. International Impacts on Domestic Political Economy: A Case of Japanese General Elections. Manuscript.

Kydland, Finn and Prescott, Edward. 1977. Rules Rather Than Discretion: The Inconsistency of Optimal Plans. *Journal of Political Economy* 85:473–490.

Lindbeck, Assar. 1976. Stabilization Policies in Open Economies with Endogenous Politicians. *American Economic Review* Papers and Proceedings: 1–19.

Lucas, Robert E. 1973. Some International Evidence on Output-Inflation Tradeoffs. *American Economic Review* 63:326–334.

McCallum, Bennett. 1978. The Political Business Cycle: An Empirical Test. *Southern Economic Journal* 44:504–515.

McDonald, Matthew. 1991. Political Budget Cycles: Evidence from the States. Harvard University Senior thesis.

Nordhaus, William. 1989. Alternative Models to Political Business Cycles. *Brookings Papers on Economic Activity* No. 2.

Nordhaus, William. 1975. The Political Business Cycle. *Review of Economic Studies* 42:169–190.

Paldam, Martin. 1989a. Politics Matter After All: Testing Alesina's Theory of RE Partisan Cycles. Aarhus University Working Paper.

Paldam, Martin. 1989b. Politics Matter After All: Testing Hibbs' Theory of Partisan Cycles. Aarhus University Working Paper.

Paldam, Martin. 1979. Is There An Electoral Cycle? *Scandinavian Journal of Economics* 81:323–342.

Persson, Torsten and Tabellini, Guido. 1991 Macroeconomic Policy, Credibility and Politics. New York, NY: Harwood Academic Publishers.

Rogoff, Kenneth. 1990. Equilibrium Political Budget Cycles. *American Economic Review* 80:21–36.

Rogoff, Kenneth and Sibert, Anne 1988. Equilibrium Political Business Cycles. *Review of Economic Studies* 55:1–16.

Roubini, Nouriel and Sachs, Jeffrey. 1989. Political and Economic Determinants of Budget Deficits in the Industrial Democracies. *European Economic Review* 33:903–933.

Tabellini, Guido and Alesina, Alberto. 1990. Voting on the Budget Deficit. *American Economic Review* 80:37–52.

Tufte, Edward. 1978. Political Control of the Economy. Princeton, N.J.: Princeton University Press.

9

Should Prices Be Decontrolled Gradually or in a Big Bang?

Sweder van Wijnbergen

There is a disturbing discrepancy between theory and practice in the economics of reform. Theorists have tended to argue for instantaneous removal of distorting policy intervention. On the other hand, public finance considerations argue for a partial, but not gradual, removal of tariff protection for example. But practice has been more complicated than theory would have one expect. Opposition to rapid reforms is often strong even if the need to reform eventually is granted. And where rapid reform has been implemented, benefits have been slow to materialize, for reasons that are not yet well understood.

Much recent work on the latter problem has focused on the importance of credibility. In particular investment response to structural reforms should be expected to be small or even negative if there is considerable doubt about whether the reform process can be sustained or whether old policies will be reversed. Capital investment is irreversible, so in periods of uncertainty more liquid assets such as foreign exchange acquire an option value in excess of their expected rate of return (van Wijnbergen 1985).

Such insights explain why credibility problems delay adjustment, but shed no light on why credibility problems persist, or arise to begin with. Practitioners invariably point to the political process as one of the sources of credibility problems. Reform processes are vulnerable to political pressure for reversal, particularly in their early phase when benefits have yet to materialize. It is this aspect, the impact of the political process on the dynamics of reform, that is at the core of this chapter.

The interaction between politics and economic reform is analyzed within the context of a particular reform effort that is of substantial current interest because of developments in Eastern Europe: price decontrol. But the same issue arises in the aftermath of the so-called "heterodox" stabilization programs, in which price controls play an important role.

How should countries such as Poland or the former USSR move toward price flexibility—gradually or in a "big bang"? Why is it that governments committed to eventual price flexibility so often seem unable to let go of "temporary" controls? How can one explain that following early price increases in a program of price controls one often sees output rise while at the same time shortages seem to increase as well (Bresser 1987, Ortiz 1990)? This chapter argues that intertemporal speculation, hoarding, and the political economy of price reform go a long way toward providing answers to these questions.

Two factors complicate the issue and are at the core of this chapter. In many cases price controls focus on commodities such as basic grains, commodities that are eminently storable and can thus be used in intertemporal speculation. This seems to have been acute in Brazil, for example, where in 1985 a series of price controls were introduced that where very much seen as temporary. Bresser (1987), who was the finance minister at the time, states, "There was shortage of merchandise in stores at the [same] time that stocks were accumulating in the factories." The second factor is that opposition to rapid dismantling of controls is often based on claims of low supply response and is greatly bolstered if a strong supply response indeed fails to materialize. This is especially relevant in Eastern Europe, where experience with price responsive markets is limited.

We show the difficulties that these two factors create for gradual decontrol of prices. We endogenize the probability of a collapse of the reform program along the lines of the recent literature about the impact of political considerations on economic policy (see Alesina and Cukierman 1990). Our core result is a forceful argument against gradual decontrol: we show that the smaller the initial price increase, the lower the *observed* supply elasticity and the greater the probability that the program of reform will in fact be abandoned.

9.1 Intertemporal Speculation and Supply Response

The Basic Model

We assume the simplest intertemporal structure possible, a two-period set up (period 1 and period 2).[1] Moreover, within each period, two types of goods are produced, traded and nontraded. Consumers have to decide how much to save (spend tomorrow rather than today), and, for given intertemporal allocation, how much to spend on either type of good in each period. Producers have to decide how much to produce in each period and, in period 1, how much of production should be sold today and how much put in storage for sale in period 2.

The government intervenes in the pricing of nontraded goods: initially, prices are set at P_0, which by assumption is below the market clearing price. We analyze two different reform programs. In a cold turkey reform, price controls are abolished immediately and permanently. In a gradual program, controlled prices are raised in period 1 to P_g, but only abolished in period 2. The market clearing price in period 1 (2) is P^* (p^*).

In both cases, the government has to face the voters at the beginning of period 2, before the period 2 program can be implemented. Voters choose between keeping the government in place and continuation of the reform program versus voting the "old guard" back in. In the latter case controls will be reimposed (the cold turkey case) or maintained (in the gradualism case), contrary to the reformist period 1 government's announcements. Thus economic agents in period 1 face uncertainty with respect to period 2 prices due to the uncertain outcome of the midreform elections. Call ρ the probability that the decontrol program will be abandoned and the old guard voted in power. In the next section we will derive ρ endogenously by linking it to aggregate shortages.

Consumers
The consumer chooses between traded (T) and nontraded (NT) goods each period and allocates expenditure over today and tomorrow. Aggregate consumer behavior is described by an expenditure function; in the absence of rationing, this function gives the minimum level of expenditure to reach welfare level U at given intra- and intertemporal relative prices:

$$E = E(\Pi(P^*, 1), \delta\pi(p^*, 1), U) \tag{1}$$

The derivatives of E with respect to prices yield the Hicksian demand functions (Dixit and Norman 1980). Π and π are exact price indices for current and future consumption corresponding to the utility structure underlying (1). We assume that Π and π are compatible with the assumption of unchanging static preferences accross periods.

However, when price controls are binding, consumer demand is not met at quoted prices. For that case we define *virtual* prices, which are the prices at which consumers would willingly consume the rations allocated to them (see Neary and Roberts 1980):

$$P_v : \frac{\partial E(\Pi(P_v, 1), \ldots)}{\partial P} = A_R^h$$

$$p_v : \frac{\partial E(\ldots, \pi(p_v, 1), U)}{\partial p} = a_r^h \tag{2}$$

where A_R^h is the ration allocated in period 1 and a_r^h the ration allocated in period 2. Clearly the following inequalities obtain:

$$P_g < P^* < P_v; \qquad p_g < p^* < p_v \tag{3}$$

Consumer behavior is furthermore restricted by the intertemporal budget constraint consumers face:

$$Y_T + P(Y - S) - C + \delta(\mathscr{C}p(y + s) - c) = E \tag{4}$$

Under gradualism, $P = P_g$, and under a cold turkey approach $P = P^*$. Y_T is output in the traded good sector.

The welfare gain due to an increase in the controlled price equals:

$$E_U \frac{dU}{dP_o} = -A_R^h + (P^v - P_o)\frac{dA_R^h}{dP_o}$$

$$= -A_R^h + (P_v - P_o)\alpha \tag{5}$$

For given ration size, price increases unambiguously *lower* welfare as there is only a negative income effect. However, higher prices may increase aggregate supply, which increases welfare at given prices as long as virtual prices exceed posted prices, hence the second term in (5).

Producers
The traded sector uses labor only, and at constant returns to scale; thus the real wage is fixed in terms of traded goods at say w. In the nontraded sector, production technology exhibits decreasing returns to scale because there is a fixed factor in the background (say land); unit costs are therefore an increasing function of output. There are a large number of producers in the NT sector, so that each individual producer has a negligible impact on the price, or, in the case of operative price controls, on aggregate shortages. Producer i's output today equals Y_i, and output tomorrow y_i. Labor is the only variable factor. Each producer faces exactly the same technology and prices; there is complete symmetry. The cost function for current (future) production equals C (c):

$$C = C(w, Y_i); \qquad C_w > 0, C_Y > 0$$

$$c \equiv (w, y_i); \qquad c_w > 0, c_y > 0 \tag{6}$$

Capital letters represent first-period variables and lowercase letters second-period variables. Decreasing returns imply increasing marginal costs, therefore C_{YY} and c_{yy} are both strictly positive.

Output produced today (Y_i) can be sold today or stored for sale tomorrow. Since there are only two periods, output produced tomorrow (y_i) will be fully sold tomorrow. Goods put in storage today (S_i) lead to goods available from storage in period 2 according to the storage technology ϕ:

$$s_i = \varphi(S_i); \qquad \varphi(0) = 0, 0 < \varphi' \leqslant 1, \varphi'' < 0 \qquad (7)$$

The assumption $\phi' < 1$ implies positive marginal storage costs: part of the goods stored goes to waste due to factors such as spoilage, pests, and so on. Moreover we assume that these storage costs increase with the amount stored: it becomes harder and harder to protect supplies from animals, pests, spoilage, or theft as they become bulkier ($\phi'' < 0$).

The producer has to choose today's output Y and level of inventories S before knowing whether the government will implement its announcements for period two or whether the program will collapse halfway.[2] However, second-period output can be chosen after period 2 government policies have become clear. The second-period production decision is thus a simple static optimization problem where S is inherited from period one. In period one, producers have to choose output Y and the part of output placed in storage S, knowing that in period two they will follow the solution to the static optimization problem just referred to. Setting up and solving the Lagrangean problem leads to the following optimality conditions (cf van Wijnbergen [1991] for derivation):

$$C_Y = P_g + \mu - P_g + \delta\varphi'\mathscr{C}_g p + \lambda - \mu = 0 \qquad (8)$$

δ is the market discount factor: $\delta = 1/(1 + r)$ with r the real interest rate in terms of traded goods. δ is exogenous as we assume open international capital markets. $\mathscr{C}$ is the expectations operator. In general $p_g^* \neq p_{ct}^*$, but we omit the subscript where this does not lead to confusion.

The first-order conditions in (8) indicate that output will be increased until its marginal cost equals the value of an extra unit of output. This latter value equals the price plus, in the first period only, any additional shadow price picked up by inventories if they are constrained by the fact that additions to inventories cannot exceed total production. Inventories are increased or decreased so as to equalize the value of an extra unit of output today (P_g) with the discounted value of an extra unit tomorrow $(\delta\phi'\mathscr{C}_g p)$, incorporating losses due to storage costs. Of course if inventories reach a corner solution (0 or Y), that equality cannot be brought about and either λ or μ becomes positive, driving a wedge between the marginal benefit of an extra sale today versus an extra sale tomorrow. The analysis for cold turkey decontrol follows along similar lines; just replace P_g by P^* and $\mathscr{C}_g$ by $\mathscr{C}_{ct}$ throughout.

For given collapse probability ρ (which will be endogenized in the next section), the model is closed in each period by either an equation defining virtual prices if price controls are operating (cf (2)), or by a market-clearing equation for the NT market in case market prices prevail:

$$Y - S = \frac{\partial E}{\partial P}$$

$$y + \varphi(s) = \frac{\partial E}{\partial p}$$

(9)

If controls operate in one period, and market prices in the other, the appropriate subequations from (2) and (9) need to be selected.

Hoarding, Aggregate Supply Response, and Price Decontrol

Differentiating the first-order conditions (8) indicates the relation between price decontrol, credibility, and net aggregate supply. Figure 9.1 helps in understanding the solution to these first-order conditions. The diagram illustrates the relation between net aggregate supply changes (production increases minus increased hoarding) as a function of the collapse probability ρ.

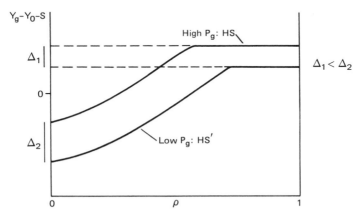

Figure 9.1
Net aggregate supply and the probability of collapse.

Consider first the case where an interior solution for S, say S^*, obtains ($\lambda = \mu = 0$). Van Wijnbergen (1991) shows that if there is an interior solution (S^* larger than 0 and smaller than Y), it is unique. At that interior solution S^*, the rate of return on inventories (inclusive of physical losses in storage and any expected capital gain or loss due to expected changes in nontraded goods prices) equals the rate of interest on world capital markets.

Differentiating (8) indicates the relation between the optimal level of hoarding S^* and the collapse probability ρ:

$$\left.\frac{dS}{d\rho}\right|_{\delta\varphi'\mathscr{C}_g p/P_g=1} = \frac{\varphi'(p^* - P_g)}{\varphi''\mathscr{C}_g p} < 0 \tag{10}$$

If there is a collapse, anticipated capital gains will not materialize, because in that case controls remain in place. Therefore a greater likelihood of collapse implies a greater likelihood of no price rise between today and tomorrow, and thus reduced hoarding incentives. On the other hand, reduced storage (lower S) reduces marginal storage costs and thus increases the return on inventory holding. As credibility declines and ρ moves up, hoarding declines and thus the observed supply response $Y - S$ actually increases. This is indicated by the upward sloping line labeled HS (for hoarding schedule) in figure 9.1. In fact if credibility is low enough, a corner solution may be reached where no intertemporal speculation is profitable and the corner solution associated with $\lambda > 0$ is reached (the flat segment in figure 9.1). This is clearly the case for the extreme outcome of no credibility at all ($\rho = 1$). At $\rho = 1$, prices are in fact not expected to rise at all; there will therefore not be any hoarding, and the HS curve intersects the $\rho = 1$ axis at Y_g.

Next, compare two different stabilization programs, each "gradualist," but with one program more gradualist than the other in that the initial price response is smaller (low P_g versus high P_g). First of all, a higher first-period control price P_g increases the optimal level of first period output for given incentives to hoard, because $C_{YY} > 0$. This means that the flat part of the hoarding schedule (where hoarding is zero and output at Y_g), shifts up by the increase in Y_g:

$$\Delta_1 = \frac{dY_g}{dP_g} = C_{YY}^{-1} > 0 \tag{11}$$

Also, higher initial prices mean lower percentage capital gains once the market is liberalized. Thus the incentive to hoard will, *ceteris paribus*, decline as P_g increases:

$$\frac{dS}{dP_g}\bigg|_{\rho \, cst} = \frac{(\rho + \mathscr{C}_g p/P_g)\varphi'}{\varphi''\mathscr{C}_g p} < 0 \tag{12}$$

Therefore:

$$\Delta_2 = \Delta_1 - \frac{dS}{dP_g}\bigg|_{\rho \, cst} > \Delta_1$$

$\Delta_2 > \Delta_1$ means that the curved segment of the diagram in fact shifts up more than the flat part. This implies that the point where hoarding becomes unprofitable moves to the left (cf figure 9.3, move from the low P_g schedule HS toward the high P_g schedule HS'). Also, with a higher P_g, there will be less first period rationing, and hence less spillover into the market for second-period home goods (note that $E_{pP} > 0$). Thus p^* will be lower, further reducing hoarding incentives; hence the area where $\lambda = 0$ shifts further to the left. The main result is that, for given collapse probability ρ, bolder decontrol programs (larger initial price increases) will lead to less hoarding, larger increases in output, and as a consequence, fewer problems with shortages.

However, this result is conditional on a given collapse probability and thus carries little weight as long as we do not know what happens to the collapse probability in response to a bolder program of price decontrol. This question is taken up in the next section.

9.2   Shortages and the Probability of Reform Failure

In most of the literature, credibility of stabilization programs, or more generally of policy reforms, is kept exogenous (Calvo 1988, van Wijnbergen (1985, 1988). But assuming exogenous credibility clearly limits the usefulness of the analysis severely, since the impact of any policy will most likely depend on whether it is going to be sustained or not.

Persson and van Wijnbergen (1989) and Vickers (1986) use the signaling equilibrium approach, which goes to the other extreme by only considering policies that from an incentive compatibility viewpoint are fully credible. In their approach a corner solution is reached, in a separating equilibrium: full credibility or none at all. However, the Mexican experience with extreme fiscal orthodoxy backed up in a later stage by more "heterodox" elements (cf Ortiz 1990) suggests that the clean solution promised by their separating equilibria is in fact hard to achieve.

In pioneering papers, Ize and Ortiz (1987) and Dornbusch (1989) attempted to endogenise credibility in a macroeconomic setting, linking credibility to various macroeconomic variables. The equilibria they consider have many prima facie plausible features. But their reliance on what is basically an arbitrary relation between program credibility and macro variables makes one wonder whether that relation itself, for all its empirical plausibility, would not be affected by economic policy. In this chapter we break new ground by drawing on recent innovations in the analysis of the impact of political considerations on economic policy to endogenise collapse probabilities in a more rigorous and explicit manner.

Intuition suggests a link between aggregate shortages in the early stages of the program and the likelihood that the program will be abandoned halfway. There are of course many ways in which a reform program can be aborted. Government officials may be bribed by lobbyists seeking the rents created by the price controls. A balance of payments crisis may make it impossible to continue the exchange rate policy on which many such decontrol programs are built. The political opposition may gather strength if the initial results are disappointing. Here we focus on the latter mechanism.

At the beginning of period 2, before the government can implement the second stage of its reform program, it has to face a vote that will determine whether it can continue or whether the opposition takes over. Alternatively, in a less democratic interpretation, the government may be forced to change its course of economic policy if unrest due to economic discontent becomes too widespread. Call the probability that this happens ρ. What determines ρ, the probability that the reform government will lose the elections?

Assume that voters are divided in their assessment of whether free markets will indeed outperform a controlled economy in supplying goods to consumers. Price rises will, on the one hand, have a negative impact effect proportional to the ration received. On the other hand, they will be beneficial to the extent they raise supply, since at the margin, marginal utility of one extra unit (P_v) exceeds the posted price P_0 (cf (5)). We parameterize the divergence of views by assuming that voters have different priors on the aggregate supply elasticity in the NT sector (The traded sector is not really an issue since there what is not supplied domestically can be imported).[3] Equation (5) can be used to solve for the value of α at which price changes yield no welfare impact either way, α_c:

$$\alpha_c = \frac{A_R^h}{(P_v - P_0)} \tag{A.2}$$

Welfare maximizing voters will vote yes or no depending on whether their posterior α_{po} is greater or smaller than α_c. Compensation programs offsetting the negative income effects of the higher price at which the original ration has to be purchased after the reform could bring α_c down to zero. Such programs have been implemented, for example, in Mexico prior to increases in maize prices in late 1990.

There is a continuum of voters, indexed by s. For analytical convenience, we assume that each voter's prior can be represented by the normal/inverted-Γ distribution commonly used in Bayesian analysis. This distribution retains its structure as new data are used to update it (i.e., it is a natural conjugate distribution).

Define $\alpha = (d(Y - S)/dP)^4$, and call the prior and posterior density function of voter s $p_{pr}(\alpha(s))$ and $p_{po}(\alpha(s))$ respectively. α_{pr} is the prior's mean and α_{po} the mean of the posterior distribution. Voters enter period one with a particular prior distribution, formed in periods before, and observe output response in period 1. They use that information to update their prior into the posterior distribution used to form (rational) expectations about the likely election outcome in period 2. Voters are ranked in ascending order of α_{pr}. Voters for whom $\alpha(s) > \alpha_c$ vote in favor of the government, and voters for whom $\alpha(s) \leqslant \alpha_c$ vote against it.

There is straight majority voting, and voters' preferences over the various alternatives are single peaked. Therefore the median voter, s_m, casts the decisive vote.[5] Voters know their own view on the supply elasticity α and form rational expectations about economic aggregates, but they do not know every other voter's views. In particular they do not know the magnitude of $\alpha(s_m)$, the median voter's estimate of the supply elasticity. Voters' beliefs on the magnitude of $\alpha(s_m)$ can be summarized by a density function f. We assume f to be the same accross voters.[6] Since the median voter determines the election outcome, the probability that the government will be voted out before it can implement the second part of its gradual decontrol program equals the probability that $\alpha(s_m) < \alpha_c$:

$$\rho(\alpha_c) = Pr(\alpha_{sm} < \alpha_c) = \int_{\alpha_{gm}=-\infty}^{\alpha_c} f(\alpha_{sm})d\alpha_{sm} \tag{15}$$

All voters use Bayes' rule to update their priors. Thus if a supply response different from a voter's prior is observed in the first stage of the program, voters revise their prior:

$$\alpha_{po} = \alpha_{pr} + (1 - \psi)\left(\left(\frac{Y_g - Y_o - S}{P_g - P_o}\right) - \alpha_{pr}\right) \tag{16}$$

with $0 < \Psi < 1$. Ψ gives the relative weight of old and new information in forming the posterior and depends on the subjective relative variances in the prior distribution and the likelihood function. Note that the voter will not assume a zero variance in the likelihood function for the period 1 events even though all uncertainty in the model refers to period 2. The absence of any information about producer inventory behavior makes the voter consider only current price information in assessing the period 1 supply response, so, because of this limited information problem, the voter will still observe what looks to the econometrician as positive variance, as inventory fluctuations trigger prediction errors in a static producer model.

To assess how hoarding in period 1 affects the probability of collapse of the program of price decontrol, we need to focus on how the updating process will affect $f(\alpha_m)$. After all, while voters do not know each other's individual preferences, they do know from each other that each voter updates using equation (16). With Bayesian updating, updating will shift $f(\alpha_m)$ such that f contracts towards the voter who has a prior mean equal to the α actually observed in period 1.

But the voter with prior mean α_c is more relevant, since α_c is the switch-off point for the voting. Equation (16) shows that the voter at α_c will shift up, down, or remain as is depending on whether the observed supply elasticity α in period 1 is larger, smaller, or equal to α_c. All voters whose prior mean exceeds the supply elasticity observed with hoarding revise their estimate of the supply elasticity downward. Thus if enough hoarding takes place to make the net supply response α *smaller than* α_c, f shifts to the left (i.e., its mean falls) and more weight is concentrated in the part of f defined over $(-\infty, \alpha_c)$. This will happen a priori if the supply response is negative (i.e., hoarding exceeds the increase in production). A supply response α *in excess of* α_c leads to an upward revision of α_{prior} by at least all voters whose prior was below α_c. In that case the integral of $f(\alpha_s)$ from minus infinity to α_c decreases. A downward revision of ρ after a net supply response below α_c, but an upward revision of ρ after a net supply response above α_c, leads to the negative relation between ρ and net aggregate supply response represented by the schedule VDS, for voters dissatisfaction schedule, in figure 9.2 (a formal presentation of this argument is given in van Wijnbergen [1991]).

Which way will this locus shift when a more gradual reform is implemented (i.e., a smaller price increase $(P_g - P_o)$ in period 1)? Consider the voter with zero prior mean first. Assume that in response to the smaller price increase enough hoarding takes place to just offset the increase in output (which itself is smaller than under the larger price increase). Equation (16) indicates that the zero prior mean voter will then not change his prior. This means that after a small price increase the VDS' will go through the

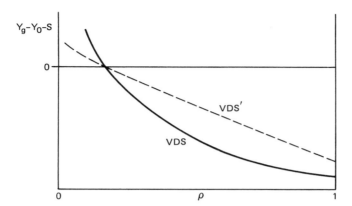

Figure 9.2
Impact of aggregate supply response on collapse probability.

same point at zero net supply response as it will after a large price increase (compare VDS and VDS' in figure 9.2).[7]

For any given net supply response larger than zero, the same quantity response to a smaller price change implies a larger elasticity and thus a larger upward revision from any given prior. This in turn implies a larger shift to the right of the probability density function f and hence a steeper decline in ρ (see the part of VDS' above 0 in figure 2). A similar line of reasoning applies to the case of negative supply response. Any given negative response represents a more negative supply elasticity than the corresponding one for the high P_g case since for the same quantity response the price change is smaller. This implies a larger shift to the left (downward revision of prior means) and thus a *higher* collapse probability in the low P_g case than in the high P_g case. All this makes for a counterclockwise rotation of the VDS schedule, to VDS' in figure 9.2, in response to a more gradualist (lower P_g) decontrol program.

9.3 Gradualism, Intertemporal Speculation, and the Political Economy of Price Reform

With the two building blocks (the hoarding schedule HS and the voters dissatisfaction schedule VDS) derived, we are ready to examine the consequences on credibility and aggregate supply response of a gradual price decontrol program (figure 9.3).

HS in figure 9.3 indicates, for given collapse probability ρ, how much producers choose to hoard. A higher collapse probability leads to lower

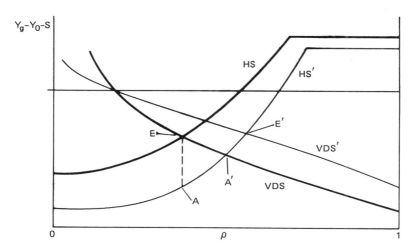

Figure 9.3
Hoarding, collapse probabilities and price decontrol: A rational expectations equilibrium.

expected future prices and thus gives less of an incentive to hoard. The HS locus therefore slopes up. But more hoarding lowers the *perceived* supply elasticity and therefore the voters' assessment that the program is failing; this in turn increases the probability that the government will be voted out. Thus the political economy schedule VDS slopes downward.

Rationality requires that the probability of program collapse used in producers' hoarding decisions will indeed come out if those hoarding decisions are in fact implemented. This will be the case at E, the intersection of the HS and the VDS. Thus E represents a rational expectations equilibrium for a given gradual decontrol policy that sets first period prices at P_g and promises to liberalize in period 2. At ρ_E, producers hoard S_E for a total (negative) supply response $Y_{g,E} - Y_o - S_E$. In turn, such a negative supply response leads to a private revision of the collapse probability that exactly matches ρ_E. Thus E is an internally consistent equilibrium: producers take intertemporal decisions based on an assessment of the collapse probability that is in fact consistent with the likely political response to initial reform failure given those producers' decisions.

The equilibrium at E has many plausible features. Output in fact rises in the early phases of a gradual decontrol program, as current prices do increase.[8] Thus the initial unemployment costs of such a decontrol will be quite small or even absent. However, in spite of increased output and higher prices, net supply actually reaching the market declines as producers in-

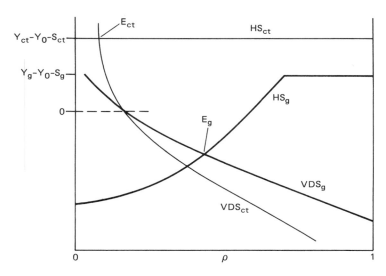

Figure 9.4
Cold Turkey versus gradual price control.

crease inventories, hoping for later capital gains. As a consequence, shortages develop, to the point that the net *observed* supply elasticity is in fact
negative. This in turn generates pressure against the decontrol policy,
increasing the probability that the program will have to be abandoned
for a prolonged period of controls before the final deregulation phase is
reached.

This machinery can be used to assess cold turkey decontrol approaches
(figure 9.4). Under a cold turkey approach, prices are liberalized immediately. Thus if the approach is maintained, prices will be market determined
in both periods. Under the assumptions made, the first period free market
price P^* will equal the second period price p^*. Thus without credibility
problems, there would be no hoarding, as waiting for tomorrow will not
bring higher prices to offset storage and interest costs.

Credibility problems in fact strengthen this result. If $\rho > 0$, there is a
positive probability that second-period prices will be *lower* than first-period
prices, in case controls get reimposed, which would lead to capital *losses*
rather than gains on inventories carried into period 2. Thus with a cold
turkey approach, hoarding incentives work the other way: there are strong
disincentives to hoard.

Therefore, a cold turkey approach leads to a larger observed net supply
response than gradualism. This is because with a cold turkey approach, if
there is any credibility problem at all, goods will in fact be pulled out of

inventories for sale today rather than tomorrow. But reversal of hoarding is not possible in our setup, so under cold turkey decontrol the case with zero inventory buildup ($\lambda = 0$) will always obtain. This means that the line labeled HS_{ct} in figure 9.4, a horizontal line at $Y_{ct} - Y_o > Y_g - Y_o > 0$, represents the cold turkey case. Thus the first result on the comparison between cold turkey and gradualism: there will be no hoarding under the cold turkey approach.

The second clear result relates to credibility (the equilibrium value of ρ). Since $P^* > P_g$, the VDS schedule rotates further, clockwise and still crossing the same zero point (compare VDS_{ct} with VDS_g in figure 9.4). The cold turkey equilibrium is at the intersection of VDS_{ct} and HS_{ct}, at E_{ct}. Since there is no hoarding under a cold turkey approach, there will be a high *observed* supply elasticity and thus a low probability of program collapse ρ_{ct}.

For comparison of the cold turkey decontrol strategy with a gradualist approach, consider two possible configurations for the latter. Assume first that, for the lower ranges of ρ, the increase in hoarding actually exceeds the increase in production, leading to a negative initial supply response (HS cuts the left vertical axis below 0, as in figure 9.4). Then the cold turkey equilibrium is to the left of $\rho(0)$ while the gradualism equilibrium is to the right of $\rho(0)$. Therefore the collapse probability under gradualism will always be higher in this case (cf figure 9.4).

If the initial distortion is so small, or the price increase brings prices so close to P^* that there would be no hoarding at all in the gradual case (i.e., $\lambda = 0$ and net supply equals Y_g), the additional assumption of $C_{YYY} < 0$ (i.e., marginal costs are increasing since $C_{YY} < 0$, but are bounded) implies a smaller supply response per unit of price increase than observed under the cold turkey approach. This in turn implies a larger assessed probability of collapse. So even if there is no hoarding under gradualism (mild initial distortions and $\lambda = 0$), gradual programs will still be less credible than cold turkey programs if $C_{YYY} < 0$.

Thus cold turkey programs will unambiguously be more credible than gradual programs that actually cause increasing shortages in their initial phase ($\rho_{Eg} > \rho(0)$); and even if gradual programs do not cause increasing shortages ($\rho_{Eg} \leqslant \rho(0)$), cold turkey decontrol programs will still be more credible if $C_{YYY} < 0$.

9.4 Conclusion

This chapter abstracts from the question of why price controls are used. Instead it asks a different question, one of great practical importance.

Assume that, for reasons good or bad, price controls are in place. How should they be terminated—cold turkey, or can a case be made for gradualism? The issue is in fact of much wider importance than the reference to stabilization programs suggests; all of Eastern Europe has been living under price controls, imposed for a very different reason. How should countries like Poland or the former USSR move toward price flexibility, gradually or in a "big bang"?

We endogenise the probability of a collapse of the reform program along the lines of the recent literature about the impact of political considerations on economic policy and show that such endogeneity in the presence of intertemporal speculation leads to a strong case *against* gradualism. Our core result is a forceful argument against gradual decontrol: we show that the smaller the initial price increase is, the lower the *observed* supply elasticity and the greater the probability that the program of reform will in fact be abandoned.

These results imply that the policy that makes most sense from a microeconomic point of view (decontrol immediately) is also advisable from a macroeconomic point of view. Credibility problems, which are at the core of the transitional output losses that characterize most stabilization programs, will be much less under a cold turkey approach and, therefore, so will transitional unemployment.

Notes

I am indebted to the Center for Economic Research at Tilburg University, where this paper was written, for their hospitality. The views expressed in this paper do not necessarily coincide with those of the institutions I am affiliated with.

1. The analysis that follows draws on van Wijnbergen (1991).

2. Subscripts *i* are omitted in what follows.

3. This supply elasticity is an attribute of producer behavior; producers can thus reasonably be expected to know this parameter exactly. We assume that there are many more consumers than producers and that this point can therefore be ignored.

4. Presentational reasons make it convenient to define α as $d(Y - S)/dP$ instead of as the elasticity $(P/(Y - S))^*d(Y - S)/dP$. For lack of a better word we will occasionally use the word elasticity when referring to α.

5. It is not implausible to assume that a vote early in a major reform program is going to be dominated by whether voters do or do not support the program. With such a single issue contest, median voter models are thought to be plausible descriptions of how voting mechanisms are likely to work (cf Enelow and Hinnich 1984 or Hillman 1990).

6. A similar device to introduce uncertainty about election outcomes is used in Alesina and Cukierman (1990).

7. The fact that VDS rotates around the intersection with the $\alpha = 0$ line hinges on the additional simplifying assumption that the variance of f does not change over time, for example, because it is known (van Wijnbergen 1991).

8. See Ortiz (1990), Bresser (1987), and Helpman (1988), covering respectively Mexico, Brazil, and Israel. The Brazilian and Mexican stabilization programs of 1986 and 1988 fit the assumptions made here particularly well: there were substantial price increases at the beginning of what was announced as a temporary use of price controls (Bresser 1987, Ortiz 1990).

References

Alesina, A. and A. Cukierman. 1990. "The Politics of Ambiguity," *Quarterly Journal of Economics* 4 : 829–851.

Bresser, T. 1987. "Inertial Inflation and the Cruzado Plan," *World Development* 15 : 1035–1044.

Calvo, G. A. 1988. "Credibility and Economic Policy," presented at the conference *Spain and the European Monetary System*.

Dixit, A. and V. Norman. 1980. *Theory of International Trade,* Cambridge: Cambridge University Press.

Dornbusch, R. 1989. "Credibility and Stabilization," NBER working paper 2790.

Enelow and Hinnich. 1984. *Advances in Spatial Theory of Voting,* Cambridge: Cambridge University Press.

Helpman, E. 1988. "Macroeconomic Effects of Price Controls: the Role of Market Structure," *Economic Journal* 98 : 340–355.

Hillman, Arye. 1990. *The Political Economy of Protection,* New York: Gordon and Breach.

Ize, A. and G. Ortiz. 1987. "Fiscal Rigidities, Public Debt and Capital Flight," *IMF Staff Papers* 34 : 311–331.

Neary, P. and K. Roberts. 1980. "Theory of Household Behavior under Rationing," *European Economic Review* 13 : 25–42.

Ortiz, G. 1990. "Mexico beyond the Debt Crisis: Towards Sustainable Growth with Price Stability," in M. Bruno (ed.), *Lessons on Economic Stabilization and its Aftermath,* Cambridge, MA. MIT Press.

Persson, T. and S. van Wijnbergen. 1989. "Signalling, Wage Controls and Monetary Disinflation Policy," NBER Working Paper 2939.

Vickers, John. 1986. "Signalling in a Model of Monetary Policy with Incomplete Information," *Oxford Economic Papers* 38 : 443–455.

Wijnbergen, S. van. 1985. "Trade Reform, Capital Flight and the Value of Information," *Economic Letters* 38:369–372.

Wijnbergen, S. van. 1988. "Monopolistic Competition, Credibility and the Output Costs of Disinflation Programs: an Analysis of Price Controls," *Journal of Development Economics* 29:375–398.

Wijnbergen, S. van. 1991. "Intertemporal Speculation, Shortages and the Political Economy of Price Decontrol," CEPR Working Paper no. 510.

IV

Business Cycles within Purely Economic Frameworks

10

Optimal Fiscal and Monetary Policy: Some Recent Results

V. V. Chari,
Lawrence J. Christiano,
and Patrick J. Kehoe

A fundamental question in macroeconomics is, how should fiscal and monetary policy be set over the business cycle? In three recent papers (Chari, Christiano, and Kehoe 1990a,b,c), we have analyzed various aspects of this question. In this chapter, we summarize our findings. In our models, optimal fiscal and monetary policy have four properties:

• Tax rates on labor are roughly constant over the business cycle.

• Capital income taxes are close to zero on average.

• The *Friedman rule* is optimal: Nominal interest rates are zero.

• Monetary policy responds to shocks: Money is countercyclical with respect to technology shocks and procyclical with respect to government consumption.

Our framework combines features of two distinguished traditions in economics: a public finance tradition and a more recent tradition of business cycle theory. The public finance tradition we follow stems from Ramsey (1927), who considers the problem of choosing an optimal tax structure when only distorting taxes are available. The business cycle tradition we follow stems from Kydland and Prescott (1982) and Long and Plosser (1983), who, along with others in this tradition, analyze the quantitative role of shocks to technology and government consumption in generating fluctuations in output and employment. We extend this framework to a monetary business cycle model using the cash-credit good construct of Lucas and Stokey (1983).

Merging these traditions allows us to develop a quantitative framework to analyze fiscal and monetary policy. We model policy choice by assuming that a technology exists through which the government can commit to a sequence of state-contingent policies. An *optimal* policy is one such sequence that maximizes the welfare of the representative agent subject to the constraint that the resulting outcomes constitute a competitive equilibrium.

We analyze fiscal and monetary policy in several closely related models. We specify the parameters for preferences and technology to be similar to those used in the public finance and business cycle literature. The stochastic processes for technology shocks and government consumption are chosen to mimic those in the postwar U.S. economy. With these specifications, we show that the optimal policies for our model economies have the four properties listed previously.

In terms of the properties of fiscal policy, optimal tax policies should smooth distortions over time and states of nature. This involves running a surplus in "good times" and a deficit in "bad times." In our models, good times are associated with above-average technology shocks and below-average government consumption; bad times, with the converse. For reasonable parameter values, smoothing tax distortions turns out to imply that the tax rates on labor (or consumption) should be essentially constant. Smoothing tax distortions also implies that capital tax rates should be close to zero on average, a result reminiscent of one in the deterministic literature (Judd 1985 and Chamley 1986).[1]

In terms of the properties of monetary policy, if the models had lump-sum taxes, then following the Friedman rule would be optimal. Phelps (1973) argues that in models with distorting taxes, it is optimal to tax all goods, including the liquidity services derived from holding money. Hence, Phelps argues that in such models the Friedman rule is not optimal. In our monetary model, however, even though the government has distorting taxes, the Friedman rule turns out to be optimal. In our model, deviating from the Friedman rule amounts to taxing a subset of consumption goods, called *cash goods*, at a higher rate than other consumption goods. Optimality requires that all types of consumption goods be taxed at the same rate; thus, optimality requires following the Friedman rule.

The cyclical properties of optimal monetary policy amount to requiring that the government inflate relatively in bad times and deflate relatively in good times. In effect, then, such a policy allows the government to use nominal government debt as a shock absorber. In the model, the government would like to issue real state-contingent debt in order to insure itself from having to sharply raise and lower tax rates when the economy is hit with shocks. The government achieves this outcome by issuing nominal noncontingent debt and then inflating or deflating to provide the appropriate ex post real payments. In bad times, inflating is optimal, so the real debt payments are relatively small. In good times, deflating is optimal, so the real debt payments are relatively large.

The plan of this chapter is as follows. Section 10.1 outlines a simple version of Lucas and Stokey's (1983) model without capital or money and describes the basic theoretical framework underlying the analysis. Section 10.2 develops a model with capital and derives its implications for fiscal policy. Section 10.3 develops a monetary model without capital and derives its implications for monetary policy. Section 10.4 discusses the scope and applicability of the analysis.

10.1   A Real Economy

Consider a simple production economy populated by a large number of identical infinitely lived consumers. In each period $t = 0, 1, \ldots$, the economy experiences one of finitely many events s_t. We denote by $s^t = (s_0, \ldots, s_t)$ the history of events up through and including period t. The probability, as of period zero, of any particular history s^t is $\mu(s^t)$. The initial realization s_0 is given. This suggests a natural commodity space in which goods are differentiated by histories.

In each period t, there are two goods: labor and a consumption good. A constant returns-to-scale technology is available to transform one unit of labor $l(s^t)$ into one unit of output. The output can be used for private consumption $c(s^t)$ or government consumption $g(s^t)$. Throughout, we will take government consumption to be exogenously specified. Feasibility requires that

$$c(s^t) + g(s^t) = l(s^t). \tag{1}$$

The preferences of each consumer are given by

$$\sum_{t,s^t} \beta^t \mu(s^t) U(c(s^t), l(s^t)) \tag{2}$$

where the discount factor $0 < \beta < 1$ and U is increasing in consumption, decreasing in labor, strictly concave, and bounded.

Government consumption is financed by proportional taxes on the income from labor $\tau(s^t)$ and by debt. Government debt has a one-period maturity and a state-contingent return. Let $b(s^t)$ denote the number of units of debt issued at state s^t and $R_b(s^{t+1})b(s^t)$ denote the payoff at any state $s^{t+1} = (s^t, s_{t+1})$. The consumer's budget constraint is

$$c(s^t) + b(s^t) \leq (1 - \tau(s^t))l(s^t) + R_b(s^t)b(s^{t-1}). \tag{3}$$

Let b_{-1} denote the initial stock of debt. Consumer purchases of government debt are bounded above and below by some arbitrarily large constants. Let $x(s^t) = (c(s^t), l(s^t), b(s^t))$ denote an allocation for consumers at s^t, and let $x = (x(s^t))$ denote an allocation for all s^t.

The government sets tax rates on labor income and returns for government debt to finance the exogenous sequence of government consumption. The government's budget constraint is

$$b(s^t) = R_b(s^t)b(s^{t-1}) + g(s^t) - \tau(s^t)l(s^t). \tag{4}$$

Let $\pi(s^t) = (\tau(s^t), R_b(s^t))$ denote the government policy at s^t, and let $\pi = (\pi(s^t))$ denote the policy for all s^t.

Note that for notational simplicity we have not explicitly included markets in private claims. Since all consumers are identical, such claims will not be traded in equilibrium; hence, their absence will not affect the equilibrium. Thus, we can always interpret this model as having complete contingent private claims markets.

Consider now the policy problem faced by the government. Suppose an institution or a commitment technology exists through which the government can bind itself to a particular sequence of policies once and for all at period zero. We model this by having the government choose a policy $\pi = (\pi(s^t))$ at the beginning of time and then having consumers choose their allocations. Since the government needs to predict how consumer allocations and prices will respond to its policies, consumer allocations and prices are described by rules that associate allocations with government policies. Formally, allocation rules are sequences of functions $x(\pi) = (x(s^t|\pi))$ that map policies π into allocations x. We then have this definition:

A *Ramsey equilibrium* is a policy π and an allocation rule $x(\cdot)$ that satisfy

• *Government maximization*: The policy π maximizes

$$\sum_{t,s^t} \beta^t \mu(s^t) U(c(s^t|\pi), l(s^t|\pi))$$

subject to (4) with allocations given by $x(\pi)$.

• *Consumer maximization*: For every π', the allocation $x(\pi')$ maximizes (2) subject to the bounds on debt purchases and to (3) evaluated at the policy π'.

The allocations in a Ramsey equilibrium solve a simple programming problem called the *Ramsey allocation problem*. For convenience, let $U_c(s^t)$ and $U_l(s^t)$ denote the marginal utilities of consumption and labor at state s^t. We have, then,

Proposition 1 (The Ramsey Allocations). The consumption and labor allocations in the Ramsey equilibrium solve the Ramsey allocation problem

$$\sum_{t,s^t} \beta^t \mu(s^t) U(c(s^t), l(s^t)) \tag{5}$$

subject to

$$c(s^t) + g(s^t) = l(s^t) \tag{6}$$

$$\sum_{t,s^t} \beta^t \mu(s^t) [U_c(s^t) c(s^t) + U_l(s^t) l(s^t)] = U_c(s_0)[R_b(s_0) b_{-1}]. \tag{7}$$

Proof. In the Ramsey equilibrium, the government must satisfy its budget constraint taking as given the allocation rule $x(\pi)$. These requirements impose restrictions on the set of allocations the government can achieve by varying its policies. We claim that these restrictions are summarized by constraints (6) and (7). We first show that these restrictions imply (6) and (7). To see that the restrictions imply (6), note that (3) holds with equality under the allocation rule $x(\cdot)$. We can add (3) and (4) to get (6); thus, these requirements imply that feasibility is satisfied. We next show that these requirements imply (7). Consider the allocation rule $x(\pi)$. For any policy π, we describe the necessary and sufficient conditions for c, l, and b to solve the consumer's problem. Let $p(s^t)$ denote the Lagrange multiplier on constraint (3). Then, by Weitzman's (1973) theorem, these conditions are constraint (3) together with first-order conditions for consumption and labor:

$$\beta^t \mu(s^t) U_c(s^t) \leqslant p(s^t), \qquad \text{with equality if } c(s^t) > 0 \tag{8}$$

$$\beta^t \mu(s^t) U_l(s^t) \leqslant -p(s^t)(1 - \tau(s^t)), \qquad \text{with equality if } l(s^t) > 0; \tag{9}$$

first-order conditions for bonds:

$$\left[p(s^t) - \sum_{s^{t+1}} p(s^{t+1}) R_b(s^{t+1}) \right] b(s^t) = 0; \tag{10}$$

and the transversality condition. This condition specifies that, for any infinite history s^∞,

$$\lim p(s^t) b(s^t) = 0 \tag{11}$$

where the limits are taken over sequences of histories s^t contained in the infinite history s^∞. Multiplying (3) by $p(s^t)$, summing over t and s^t, and using (10) and (11) gives

$$\sum_{t,s^t} p(s^t)[c(s^t) - (1 - \tau(s^t)) l(s^t)] = p(s_0) R_b(s_0) b_{-1}. \tag{12}$$

Using (8) and (9), we can rewrite (12) as

$$\sum_{t,s^t} \beta^t \mu(s^t)[U_c(s^t)c(s^t) + U_l(s^t)l(s^t)] = U_c(s_0)[R_b(s_0)b_{-1}]. \tag{13}$$

Thus, (6) and (7) are implied by the requirements that the government must satisfy its budget constraint and that allocations are consistent with the allocation rule $x(\cdot)$.

Next, given any set of allocations c and l that satisfy (6) and (7), we can construct sequences of bond holdings, returns on debt, and sequences of tax rates on labor income such that these allocations are consistent with the allocation rule $x(\cdot)$ and the government's budget constraint. Construct the bond allocation $b(s^r)$ as follows. In equilibrium, (3) holds with equality. Multiply this equation by $p(s^t)$ and sum over all dates and states following s^r; then use (8)–(11) to obtain

$$b(s^r) = \sum_{t=r+1}\sum_{s^t} \beta^{t-r}\mu(s^t|s^r)[U_c(s^t)c(s^t) + U_l(s^t)l(s^t)]/U_c(s^r). \tag{14}$$

Construct the tax rates on labor income by noting that the consumer's first order conditions imply that

$$1 - \tau(s^t) = -\frac{U_l(c(s^t), l(s^t))}{U_c(c(s^t), l(s^t))}. \tag{15}$$

The returns on debt can be found by substituting (14) and (15) into (3). Therefore, (6) and (7) completely characterize the restrictions imposed on allocations by the requirements that when choosing a policy the government must satisfy its budget constraint and the resulting allocations are determined by the allocation rule $x(\cdot)$. Since in the Ramsey equilibrium the government chooses a policy that maximizes the welfare of consumers, it follows that the allocations in the Ramsey equilibrium solve (5). □

For convenience later, write the Ramsey allocation problem as

$$\max \sum_{t,s^t} \beta^t \mu(s^t) W(c(s^t), l(s^t), \lambda) \tag{16}$$

subject to (6). Here λ is the Lagrange multiplier on constraint (7), which is called the *implementability constraint*. Note that the function W simply incorporates the implementability constraint into the maximand. For $t \geq 1$,

$$W(c(s^t), l(s^t), \lambda) = U(c(s^t), l(s^t)) + \lambda[U_c(s^t)c(s^t) + U_l(s^t)l(s^t)] \tag{17}$$

and for $t = 0$, W equals the right side of (17), evaluated at s_0, minus $\lambda U_c(s_0)[R_b(s_0)b_{-1}]$. The first order conditions for this problem imply that

$$-\frac{W_l(c(s^t), l(s^t), \lambda)}{W_c(c(s^t), l(s^t), \lambda)} = 1. \tag{18}$$

Notice that (18) together with (6) implies that the allocations for consumption and labor depend only on the current realization of government consumption, not separately on the entire history of realizations. Thus, in a Ramsey equilibrium, $c(s^t) = \bar{c}(g_t)$ and $l(s^t) = \bar{l}(g_t)$, where $g_t = g(s^t)$. We are interested in the implications of this feature of the Ramsey allocations for tax rates. To develop these, note that the consumer's first order conditions imply that (15) holds in a Ramsey equilibrium. Since the allocations depend only on the current realization of government consumption, so do the tax rates. Hence, Ramsey tax rates satisfy $\tau(s^t) = \bar{\tau}(g_t)$. Since the Ramsey tax rates depend only on the current level of government consumption, these rates inherit the persistence properties of the process on government consumption. For example, if the process on government consumption is i.i.d., then so are the tax rates; if this process is highly persistent, then so are the tax rates.

From a quantitative standpoint, an important question is, How responsive should tax rates be to shocks? For a plausibly parameterized version of the model considered here, it turns out that optimal tax rates on labor are essentially constant. (See also the model in the next section.) In particular, the revenues from labor taxation are much smoother than government consumption. The government keeps its revenues smoother than its consumption by using debt policy as a shock absorber. In periods of high consumption, for example, the government accomplishes this by both selling more debt and lowering the return on inherited debt. Such a debt policy lets the government smooth tax distortions while satisfying its budget constraint.

The idea that governments should sell more debt in periods of higher-than-average consumption is common to many models. The rather novel idea that in such periods the government should also lower the rate of return on inherited debt is due to Lucas and Stokey (1983). To see how this idea works, suppose that government shocks follow a two-state Markov process, and interpret the states as wartime and peacetime. Suppose the economy starts in wartime with no inherited debt. It is easy to show that since the shocks are Markov, the value of the inherited debt $R_b(s^t)b(s^{t-1})$ depends only on the current state s_t. Thus, the value of the inherited debt is the same in any period of war as it was at the initial date, namely, zero. Since it can be shown that the debt issued into a state of war is not zero, the return on debt R_b in wartime is zero.

The intuition for this result is as follows. In the initial period, there is a war, and to smooth tax distortions, the government issues debt. If the war continues, the government cancels the debt. If peace breaks out, the government pays a relatively high rate of return on the debt to compensate debt holders for the losses they suffered in wartime. Such a state-contingent return policy for the debt lets the government run a deficit in wartime and a surplus in peacetime and yet still maintain a stationary pattern for the debt.

In this model, the government implements the state-contingent return policy by directly changing the ex post return on the debt. Another way for the government to implement a state-contingent return policy is to issue nominal debt and use inflation to alter the real rates of return appropriately. We explore this way of implementing the shock absorber role for debt in section 10.3.

Here we have shown that optimal labor tax rates inherit the persistence properties of the underlying shocks and that debt acts as a shock absorber. These results are quite different from received wisdom. Following Barro (1979), many macroeconomists—including Mankiw (1987) and Judd (1989) —have argued that tax rates should follow a random walk regardless of the persistence properties of the underlying shocks. These arguments have been based on partial equilibrium models that assume a constant rate of return on debt and a loss function for the government that depends directly on the tax rates rather than on the allocations. One conjecture is that if we restrict the government to issue only real state-noncontingent debt, then our general equilibrium model will also produce tax rates close to a random walk. For an analysis of this conjecture and a general discussion of the random walk theory of taxation, see Chari, Christiano, and Kehoe 1990a.

10.2   A Real Economy with Capital

Now consider modifying the economy in section 10.1 to incorporate a constant returns-to-scale technology that transforms labor $l(s^t)$ and capital $k(s^{t-1})$ into output by a production function $F(k(s^{t-1}), l(s^t), s_t)$. Notice that the production function incorporates a stochastic shock. The output can be used for private consumption $c(s^t)$, government consumption $g(s^t)$, and new capital $k(s^t)$. Feasibility requires that

$$c(s^t) + g(s^t) + k(s^t) = F(k(s^{t-1}), l(s^t), s_t) + (1 - \delta)k(s^{t-1}) \qquad (19)$$

where δ is the depreciation rate on capital. The preferences of each consumer are as before.

Government consumption is financed by proportional taxes on the income from labor and capital and by debt. Let $\tau(s^t)$ and $\theta(s^t)$ denote the tax rates on the income from labor and capital. Government debt has a one-period maturity and a state-contingent return. Let $b(s^t)$ denote the number of units of debt issued at state s^t and $R_b(s^{t+1})b(s^t)$ denote the payoff at any state $s^{t+1} = (s^t, s_{t+1})$. The consumer's budget constraint is

$$c(s^t) + k(s^t) + b(s^t) \leqslant (1 - \tau(s^t))w(s^t)l(s^t) + R_b(s^t)b(s^{t-1}) + R_k(s^t)k(s^{t-1})$$

(20)

where $R_k(s^t) = 1 + [1 - \theta(s^t)](r(s^t) - \delta)$ is the gross return on capital after taxes and depreciation and $r(s^t)$ and $w(s^t)$ are the net before-tax returns on capital and labor. Competitive pricing ensures that these returns equal their marginal products, namely, that $r(s^t) = F_k(s^t)$ and $w(s^t) = F_l(s^t)$, where $F_k(s^t)$ and $F_l(s^t)$ denote the marginal products of capital and labor at state s^t. Consumer purchases of capital are constrained to be nonnegative, and the purchases of government debt are bounded above and below by some arbitrarily large constants. Let $x(s^t) = (c(s^t), l(s^t), k(s^t), b(s^t))$ denote an allocation for consumers at s^t, and let $x = (x(s^t))$ denote an allocation for all s^t.

In this economy, the government sets tax rates on labor and capital income and returns for government debt to finance the exogenous sequence of its consumption. The government's budget constraint is

$$b(s^t) = R_b(s^t)b(s^{t-1}) + g(s^t) - \tau(s^t)w(s^t)l(s^t) - \theta(s^t)(r(s^t) - \delta)k(s^{t-1}).$$

(21)

Let $\pi(s^t) = (\tau(s^t), \theta(s^t), R_b(s^t))$ denote the government policy at s^t, and let $\pi = (\pi(s^t))$ denote the policy for all s^t.

A Ramsey equilibrium for this economy is defined analogously to that in section 10.1. As is well known, in the Ramsey equilibrium the government has an incentive to set the initial tax rate on capital income to be as large as possible. To make the problem interesting, we adopt the convention that the initial tax rate $\theta(s_0)$ is fixed at some rate, say, zero. Then the consumption, labor, and capital allocations in the Ramsey equilibrium solve this Ramsey allocation problem:

$$\sum_{t,s^t} \beta^t \mu(s^t) U(c(s^t), l(s^t))$$

subject to (19) and

$$\sum_{t,s^t} \beta^t \mu(s^t)[U_c(s^t)c(s^t) + U_l(s^t)l(s^t)] = U_c(s_0)[R_k(s_0)k_{-1} + R_b(s_0)b_{-1}].$$

(22)

(For details, see Chari, Christiano, and Kehoe 1990b.)

For convenience later, write the Ramsey allocation problem as

$$\max_{t,s^t} \sum \beta^t \mu(s^t) W(c(s^t), l(s^t), \lambda) \tag{23}$$

subject to (19). Here λ is the Lagrange multiplier on the implementability constraint (22). For $t \geq 1$,

$$W(c(s^t), l(s^t), \lambda) = U(c(s^t), l(s^t)) + \lambda[U_c(s^t)c(s^t) + U_l(s^t)l(s^t)] \tag{24}$$

and for $t = 0$, W equals the right side of (22), evaluated at s_0, minus $\lambda U_c(s_0)[R_k(s_0)k_{-1} + R_b(s_0)b_{-1}]$. The first order conditions for this problem imply that

$$-W_l(s^t)/W_c(s^t) = F_l(s^t) \tag{25}$$

and

$$1 = \sum_{s^{t+1}} \beta\mu(s^{t+1}|s^t)(W_c(s^{t+1})/W_c(s^t))[1 - \delta + F_k(s^{t+1})]. \tag{26}$$

We begin our analysis of optimal fiscal policy for this model by considering a nonstochastic version of the model in which the stochastic shock in the production function is constant. Government consumption is also constant, so $g(s^t) = g$. Suppose that under the Ramsey plan the allocations converge to a steady state. In such a steady state, W_c is constant. Thus, from (26),

$$1 = \beta[1 + F_k - \delta]. \tag{27}$$

The consumer's intertemporal first-order condition is

$$U_{ct} = \beta U_{ct+1}[1 + (1 - \theta_{t+1})(F_{kt+1} - \delta)]. \tag{28}$$

In a steady state, U_c is a constant, so (28) reduces to

$$1 = \beta[1 + (1 - \theta)(F_k - \delta)]. \tag{29}$$

Comparing (27) and (29), we can see that in a steady state the optimal tax rate on capital income, θ, is zero. This result is due to Chamley (1986).

In Chari, Christiano, and Kehoe 1990b, we show that an analogous result holds in stochastic economies; namely, the value of tax revenue across states of nature is approximately zero in a stationary equilibrium. However, the state-by-state capital taxes are not uniquely determined and can be quite different from zero. A review of some features of the model in section 10.1 will help explain why. In that model, state-contingent government debt plays a key role in smoothing tax distortions over time and over states of nature. One way to implement the required state-contingency of debt payments is to use state-contingent taxes on private assets, which in that model are the same as government debt. In this model, private assets include capital as well as government debt. In it both state-contingent taxes on capital and state-contingent debt play analogous roles in smoothing tax distortions over time and over states of nature. Arbitrage conditions require that the ex ante rates of return on both types of assets be equalized. However, the pattern of ex post tax rates on capital and the rates of returns on bonds can be structured in many ways and still meet the ex ante arbitrage conditions and raise the same revenue in each state of nature. We will focus on just one of these ways. We suppose that the government is restricted to making capital tax rates not contingent on the current state. Under this assumption, the policy is uniquely determined and government debt is the only shock absorber.

In Chari, Christiano, and Kehoe 1990b, we explore the quantitative properties of optimal policy in a parameterized version of the model. We consider preferences of the form

$$U(c, l) = [c^{1-\gamma}(L - l)^\gamma]^\psi/\psi \tag{30}$$

where L is the endowment of labor. This class of preferences has been widely used in the literature (Kydland and Prescott 1982; Christiano and Eichenbaum 1990; Backus, Kehoe, and Kydland 1991). The production technology is given by

$$F(k, l, z, t) = k^\alpha[e^{\rho t+z}l]^{(1-\alpha)}. \tag{31}$$

Notice that the production technology has two kinds of labor augmenting technological change. The variable ρ captures deterministic growth in this

Table 10.1
Parameter values for the real models

Models	Parameters and values			
Baseline model				
Preferences	$\gamma = 0.80$	$\psi = 0$	$\beta = 0.97$	$L = 5,475$
Technology	$\alpha = 0.34$	$\delta = 0.08$	$\rho = 0.016$	
Markov Chains for government				
consumption	$g_l = 350$	$g_h = 402$	$\phi = 0.95$	
Technology shock	$z_l = -0.04$	$z_h = 0.04$	$\pi = 0.91$	
High risk aversion model				
Preferences	$\psi = -8$			

Source: Chari, Christiano, and Kehoe 1990b.

change. The variable z is a technology shock that follows a symmetric two-state Markov chain with states z_l and z_h and transition probabilities $\text{Prob}(z_{t+1} = z_i | z_t = z_i) = \pi$, $i = l, h$. Government consumption is given by $g_t = ge^{\rho t}$, where ρ is the deterministic growth rate and g follows a symmetric two-state Markov chain with states g_l and g_h and transition probabilities $\text{Prob}(g_{t+1} = g_i | g_t = g_i) = \phi$, $i = l, h$. Notice that without technology or government consumption shocks, the economy has a balanced growth path along which private consumption, capital, and government consumption grow at rate ρ and labor is constant.

We consider two parameterizations of this model. (See table 10.1.) Our *baseline* model has $\psi = 0$ and thus has logarithmic preferences. Our *high risk aversion* model has $\psi = -8$. The rest of the parameters for preferences and the parameters for technology are the annualized versions of those used by Christiano and Eichenbaum (1990). We choose the three parameters of the Markov chain for government consumption to match three statistics of the postwar U.S. data: the average value of the ratio of government consumption to output, the variance of the detrended log of government consumption, and the serial autocorrelation of the detrended log of government consumption. We construct the Markov chain for the technology parameters by setting the mean of the technology shock equal to zero and use Prescott's (1986) statistics on the variance and serial correlation of the technology shock to determine the other two parameters.

For each setting of the parameter values, we simulate our economy starting from the steady state of the deterministic versions of our models. In table 10.2 we report some properties of the fiscal variables for our baseline model. The table shows that tax on labor income fluctuates very little. For example, if the labor tax rate were approximately normally distributed, then 95 percent of the time the tax rate would fluctuate between 27.89 percent and 28.25 percent. The tax on capital income is zero. This is to be expected from the analytic results in Chari, Christiano, and Kehoe 1990b since with $\psi = 0$ the utility function is separable between consumption and leisure and homothetic in consumption. For such preferences, this chapter shows that the tax on capital is zero in all periods but the first.[2] In the baseline model, the tax on private assets has a large standard deviation.

In table 10.2 we also report some properties of the fiscal policy variables for the high risk aversion model. Here, too, the tax rate on labor fluctuates very little. The tax rate on capital income has a mean of -0.13 percent, which is close to zero. We find this feature interesting because it suggests that our analytical result approximately holds for the class of utility func-

Table 10.2
Properties of the real models and the U.S. economy

	Models		U.S. economy
Tax rates	Baseline	High risk aversion	
Labor			
Mean	28.07	33.67	24.76
Standard deviation	.09	.20	2.39
Autocorrelation	.83	.91	.77
Capital			
Mean	.00	−.13	28.28
Standard deviation	.00	3.82	8.75
Autocorrelation	—	.85	.74
Private assets			
Mean	.15	.22	.00
Standard deviation	4.12	4.70	.73
Autocorrelation	.02	.04	−.32

Notes: All statistics are based on 400 simulated observations. The means and standard deviations are in percentage terms. For the U.S. economy, the labor tax rate is measured by the average marginal tax rate of Barro and Sahasakul (1983), the capital tax rate is measured by the effective corporate tax rate of Jorgenson and Sullivan (1981), and the tax on private assets is constructed as described by Chari, Christiano, and Kehoe (1990b). For the baseline model, the capital tax rate is zero; thus, its autocorrelation is not defined.

tions commonly used in the literature. This feature also suggests that Chamley's (1986) result on the undesirability of the taxation of capital income in a deterministic steady state approximately holds in stochastic steady states of stochastic models. As in the baseline model, we find here that the standard deviation of the tax on private assets is large.

To gain an appreciation of the magnitudes of some of the numbers for our model economies, we compute analogous numbers for the U.S. economy. In table 10.2, we report these as well. For the labor tax rate, we use Barro and Sahasakul's (1983) estimate of the average marginal labor tax rate. The standard deviation of this rate is 2.39 percent, which is approximately twenty-five times the standard deviation in our baseline model. For the tax rate on capital income, we use Jorgenson and Sullivan's (1981) estimate of the effective corporate tax rate. This number probably underestimates the ex ante rate since it ignores the taxation of dividends and capital gains received by individuals. The mean effective rate in the data is 28.28 percent whereas our baseline model has an ex ante tax rate of zero. Finally, the standard deviation of the innovation in the tax on private assets in the baseline model is about six times that in the data.[3]

10.3   A Monetary Economy

Now we study the properties of the optimal inflation tax using a version of Lucas and Stokey's (1983) cash-credit goods model. We study both the mean inflation rate and its cyclical properties. Friedman (1969) has argued that monetary policy should follow a rule: set nominal interest rates to zero. For a deterministic version of our economy, this would imply deflating at the rate of time preference. Phelps (1973) argues that Friedman's rule is unlikely to be optimal in an economy with no lump-sum taxes. His argument is that optimal taxation generally requires using all available taxes, including the inflation tax. Thus, Phelps argues that the optimal inflation rate is higher than the Friedman rule implies.

In sections 10.1 and 10.2, we have shown how real state-contingent debt can serve a useful role as a shock absorber. Here we allow the government to issue only nominal state-noncontingent debt. We examine how the government should optimally use monetary policy to make this debt yield the appropriate real state-contingent returns.

Consider, then, a simple production economy with three goods. The goods are labor l and two consumption goods: a cash good c_1 and a credit good c_2. A stochastic constant returns-to-scale technology transforms labor into output according to

$$c_1(s^t) + c_2(s^t) + g(s^t) = z(s^t)l(s^t) \tag{32}$$

where $z(s^t)$ is a technology shock and, again, $g(s^t)$ is government consumption. The preferences of each consumer are given by

$$\sum_t \sum_{s^t} \beta^t \mu(s^t) U(c_1(s^t), c_2(s^t), l(s^t)) \tag{33}$$

where U has the usual properties.

In period t, consumers trade money, assets, and goods in particular ways. At the start of period t, after observing the current state s_t, consumers trade money and assets in a centralized securities market. The assets are one-period state-noncontingent nominal claims. Let $M(s^t)$ and $B(s^t)$ denote the money and nominal bonds held at the end of the securities market trading. Let $R(s^t)$ denote the gross nominal return on these bonds payable in period $t + 1$ in all states s^{t+1}. After this trading, each consumer splits into a worker and a shopper. The shopper must use the money to purchase cash goods. To purchase credit goods, the shopper issues nominal claims that are settled in the securities market in the next period. The worker is paid in cash at the end of each period.

This environment leads to this constraint for the securities market:

$$M(s^t) + B(s^t) = R(s^{t-1})B(s^{t-1}) + M(s^{t-1}_*) - p(s^{t-1})c_1(s^{t-1})$$

$$- p(s^{t-1})c_2(s^{t-1}) + p(s^{t-1})(1 - \tau(s^{t-1}))z(s^{t-1})l(s^{t-1}).$$

$$(34)$$

The left side of (34) is the nominal value of assets held at the end of securities market trading. The first term on the right side is the value of nominal debt bought in the preceding period. The next two terms are the shopper's unspent cash. The next is the payments for credit goods, and the last is the after-tax receipts from labor services. Besides this constraint, we will assume that the real holdings of debt, $B(s^t)/p(s^t)$, are bounded below by some arbitrarily large constant. Purchases of cash goods must satisfy a cash-in-advance constraint:

$$p(s^t)c_1(s^t) \leq M(s^t). \tag{35}$$

Money is introduced into and withdrawn from the economy through open market operations in the securities market. The constraint facing the government in this market is

$$M(s^t) - M(s^{t-1}) + B(s^t) = R(s^{t-1})B(s^{t-1}) + p(s^{t-1})g(s^{t-1})$$

$$- p(s^{t-1})\tau(s^{t-1})z(s^{t-1})l(s^{t-1}). \tag{36}$$

The terms on the left side of this equation are the assets sold by the government. The first term on the right is the payments on debt incurred in the preceding period, the second is the payment for government consumption, and the third is tax receipts. Notice that government consumption is bought on credit.

The consumer's problem is to maximize (33) subject to (34) and (35) and the bound on debt. Money earns a gross nominal return of 1. If bonds earn a gross nominal return of less than 1, then the consumer can make infinite profits by buying money and selling bonds. Thus, in any equilibrium, $R(s^t) \geq 1$. The consumer's first-order conditions imply that $U_1(s^t)/U_2(s^t) = R(s^t)$; thus, in any equilibrium, this constraint must hold:

$$U_1(s^t) \geq U_2(s^t). \tag{37}$$

This feature of the competitive equilibrium constrains the set of Ramsey allocations.

A Ramsey equilibrium for this economy is defined in the obvious way. As is well known, if the initial stock of nominal assets held by consumers is positive, then welfare is maximized by increasing the initial price level to infinity. If the initial stock is negative, then welfare is maximized by setting the initial price level so low that the government raises all the revenue it needs without levying any distorting taxes. To make the problem interesting, we set the initial nominal assets of consumers to zero. Let $a(s_0)$ denote initial real claims that the government holds against private agents. As we show in Chari, Christiano, and Kehoe 1990c, the Ramsey allocation problem is

$$\max \sum_t \sum_{s^t} \beta^t \mu(s^t) U(c_1(s^t), c_2(s^t), l(s^t))$$

subject to (32), (37), and

$$\sum_t \sum_{s^t} \beta^t \mu(s^t)[U_1(s^t)c_1(s^t) + U_2(s^t)c_2(s^t) + U_3(s^t)l(s^t)] = U_2(s_0)a(s_0). \quad (38)$$

For convenience in studying the properties of the Ramsey allocation problem, let

$$W(c_1, c_2, l, \lambda) = U(c_1, c_2, l) + \lambda[U_1 c_1 + U_2 c_2 + U_3 l] \quad (39)$$

where λ is the Lagrange multiplier on the implementability constraint (38). The Ramsey allocation problem is, then, to maximize

$$\sum_t \sum_{s^t} \beta^t \mu(s^t) W(c_1(s^t), c_2(s^t), l(s^t), \lambda)$$

subject to (32) and (37). Consider utility functions of the form

$$U(c_1, c_2, l) = h(c_1, c_2)v(l) \quad (40)$$

where h is homogenous of degree k and the utility function has the standard properties. We then have the following:

Proposition 2 (the Optimality of the Friedman Rule). For utility functions of the form (40), the Ramsey equilibrium has $R(s^t) = 1$ for all s^t.

Proof. Consider for a moment the Ramsey problem with constraint (37) dropped. A first-order condition for this problem is

$$W_1(s^t)/W_2(s^t) = 1. \quad (41)$$

For utility functions of the form (40),

$$W = hv + \lambda[c_1 h_1 v + c_2 h_2 v + lhv'].$$

Since h is homogenous of degree k, $c_1 h_1 + c_2 h_2 = kh$. Thus, $W = h(c_1, c_2)Q(l, \lambda)$ for some function Q. Combining this feature with (41) gives

$$1 = W_1/W_2 = U_1/U_2. \tag{42}$$

Since the solution to this less-constrained problem satisfies (37), it is also a solution to the Ramsey problem. Then the consumer's first order condition $U_1(s^t)/U_2(s^t) = R(s^t)$ implies that $R(s^t) = 1$. $\square$

In Chari, Christiano, and Kehoe 1990c, we show that the Friedman rule is optimal for more general utility functions of the form

$$U(c_1, c_2, l) = V(h(c_1, c_2), l)$$

where h is homothetic. We also show that the Friedman rule is optimal for money-in-the-utility-function economies and transaction cost economies that satisfy a similar homotheticity condition.

The intuition for this result is as follows. In this economy, the tax on labor income implicitly taxes consumption of both goods at the same rate. A standard result in public finance is that if the utility function is separable in leisure and the subutility function over consumption goods is homothetic, then the optimal policy is to tax all consumption goods at the same rate (Atkinson and Stiglitz 1972). If $R(s^t) > 1$, the cash good is effectively taxed at a higher rate than the credit good since cash goods must be paid for immediately but credit goods are paid for with a one-period lag. Thus, with such preferences, efficiency requires that $R(s^t) = 1$ and, therefore, that monetary policy follow the Friedman rule.

This intuition is not complete, however. As we mentioned earlier, the Friedman rule turns out to be optimal even in many models with money in the utility function or with money facilitating transactions. In such models, money and consumption goods are taxed at different rates. Specifically, money is not taxed at all while consumption goods are. Thus, the Phelps (1973) argument turns out to be more tenuous than it first appears. (For analyses of optimality of the Friedman rule in various deterministic models of money with distorting taxes, see Kimbrough 1986, Faig 1988, and Woodford 1990.)

We turn now to some numerical exercises that examine the cyclical properties of monetary policy in our model. In these exercises, we consider preferences of the form

$$U(c, l) = [c^{1-\gamma}(L - l)^\gamma]^\psi/\psi$$

where L is the endowment of labor and

$$c = [(1 - \sigma)c_1^\nu + \sigma c_2^\nu]^{1/\nu}.$$

The technology shock z and government consumption both follow the same symmetric two-state Markov chains as in the model in section 10.2.

For preferences, we set the discount factor $\beta = 0.97$, we set $\psi = 0$, which implies logarithmic preferences between the composite consumption good and leisure, and we set $\gamma = 0.8$. These values are the same as those in Christiano and Eichenbaum 1990. The parameters σ and v are not available in the literature, so we estimate them using the consumer's first-order conditions. These conditions imply that $U_{1t}/U_{2t} = R_t$. For our specification of preferences, this condition can be manipulated to be

$$\frac{c_{2t}}{c_{1t}} = \left(\frac{\sigma}{1-\sigma}\right)^{1/1-v} R_t^{1/1-v}. \tag{43}$$

With a binding cash-in-advance constraint, c_1 is real money balances and c_2 is aggregate consumption minus real money balances. We measure real money balances by the monetary base, R_t by the return on three-month treasury bills, and consumption by consumption expenditures. Taking logs in (43) and running a regression using quarterly data for the period 1959–89 gives $\sigma = 0.57$ and $v = 0.83$.

Our regression turns out to be similar to those used in the money demand literature. To see this, note that (43) implies that

$$\frac{c_{1t}}{c_{1t} + c_{2t}} = \left[1 + \left(\frac{\sigma}{1-\sigma}\right)^{1/1-v} R_t^{1/1-v}\right]^{-1}. \tag{44}$$

Taking logs in (44) and then taking a Taylor's expansion yields a money demand equation with consumption in the place of output and with the restriction that the coefficient of consumption is 1. Our estimates imply that the interest elasticity of money demand is 4.94. This estimate is somewhat smaller than estimates obtained when money balances are measured by M1 instead of the base.

Finally, we set the initial real claims on the government so that, in the resulting stationary equilibrium, the ratio of debt to output is 44 percent. This is approximately the ratio of U.S. federal government debt to GNP in 1989. For the second parameterization, we set $\psi = -8$, which implies a relatively high degree of risk aversion. For the third, we make both technology shocks and government consumption i.i.d.

In table 10.3 we report the properties of the labor tax rate, the inflation rate, and the money growth rate for our monetary models. In all three, the labor tax rate has the same properties it did in the real economy with capital:

Table 10.3
Properties of the monetary models

| | Models | | |
	Baseline	High risk aversion	I.I.D.
Labor tax			
Mean	20.05	20.18	20.05
Standard deviation	.11	.06	.11
Autocorrelation	.89	.89	.00
Correlation with government consumption	.93	−.93	.93
Technology shock	−.36	.35	−.36
Output	.03	−.06	.02
Inflation			
Mean	−.44	4.78	−2.39
Standard deviation	19.93	60.37	9.83
Autocorrelation	.02	.06	−.41
Correlation with government consumption	.37	.26	.43
Technology shock	−.21	−.21	−.70
Output	−.05	−.08	−.48
Money growth			
Mean	−.70	4.03	−2.78
Standard deviation	18.00	54.43	3.74
Autocorrelation	.04	.07	.00
Correlation with government consumption	.40	.28	.92
Technology shock	−.17	−.20	−.36
Output	.00	−.07	.02

it fluctuates very little, and it inherits the persistence properties of the underlying shocks.

Consider next the inflation rate and the money growth rate. Recall that for these monetary models the nominal interest rate is identically zero. If government consumption and the technology shock were constant, then the price level and the money stock would fall at the rate of time preference, which is 3 percent. In a stochastic economy the inflation rate and the money growth rate vary with consumption. Therefore, the mean inflation rate depends not only on the rate of time preference, but also on the covariance of the inflation rate and the intertemporal marginal rate of substitution. This effect causes the inflation rate and the money growth rate to rise with an increase in the coefficient of risk aversion.

In the monetary models, the autocorrelations of the inflation rate are small or negative. Thus, they are far from a random walk. The correlations of inflation with government consumption and with the technology shock have the expected signs. Notice that these correlations have opposite signs, and in the baseline and high risk aversion models, this leads to inflation having essentially no correlation with output. The most striking feature of the inflation rates is their volatility. In the baseline model, for example, if the inflation rate were normally distributed, it would be higher than 20 percent or lower than − 20 percent approximately a third of the time. The inflation rates for the high risk aversion model are even more volatile. The money growth rate has essentially the same properties as the inflation rate.

Note that our results are quite different from those of Mankiw (1987). Using a partial equilibrium model, he argues that optimal policy implies that inflation should follow a random walk. It might be worth investigating whether there are any general equilibrium settings that rationalize Mankiw's argument.

10.4   Conclusions

In this chapter we have summarized four properties of optimal fiscal and monetary policy in a particular class of models. We have obtained sharp quantitative properties of such policies using reasonable parameter values of standard models of macroeconomics and public finance. These models abstract from a host of issues, including income distribution, heterogeneity, and externalities. The monetary models also abstract from intermediation and nominal rigidities. Thus, these models focus attention on intertemporal efficiency. We think that the forces driving our results will be present in dynamic models generally.

We have focused on calculating the optimal policies in quantitative models. But, as Lucas and Stokey (1983, 87) point out, "a policy or policy rule that is optimal in a theoretical model that is an approximation to reality, can only be approximately optimal applied in reality." Furthermore, simple policy rules are preferable to complicated state-contingent policies. These considerations suggest that, in practice, we should look for policy rules that are simple approximations to the complicated optimal policies and that continue to perform well for minor perturbations of the model. We think the quantitative framework summarized here will be useful in comparing the performance of simple policy rules. Clearly, a lot more work needs to be done with serious quantitative models before the models can be used to make practical policy proposals. However, we think that the research summarized here represents a step toward a quantitative analysis of optimal policy design and that the general methodology will be useful in more elaborate studies.

Notes

This is an edited version of a paper that was prepared for a November 1990 conference sponsored by the Federal Reserve Bank of Cleveland and published in a special issue of the *Journal of Money, Credit, and Banking* 23, part 2, (6): 519–539 (August 1991). The paper appears here with the permission of the Federal Reserve Bank of Cleveland. © All rights reserved. The authors thank Nick Bull and George Hall for excellent research assistance. The views expressed here are those of the authors and not necessarily those of the Federal Reserve Bank of Minneapolis or the Federal Reserve System. Kehoe's research was partially supported by the National Science Foundation.

1. The public finance literature on various aspects of optimal capital income taxes is voluminous. It includes Atkinson 1971, Diamond 1973, Pestieau 1974, and Atkinson and Sandmo 1980. (See also the Auerbach 1985 and Stiglitz 1987 surveys.) These analyses primarily deal with overlapping generations models whereas we use a model with infinitely lived agents. For other analyses of optimal taxation in business cycle models, see King 1990 and Zhu 1990. For analyses of optimal taxation with human and physical capital in an infinite-lived agent model, see Bull 1990 and Jones, Manuelli, and Rossi 1990.

2. Separability between consumption and leisure and homotheticity in consumption are the well-known conditions under which the optimal policy is uniform consumption taxes in all periods except the first. (See Atkinson and Stiglitz 1972 for an analysis in a partial equilibrium setting.) In our model, uniform consumption taxes are equivalent to zero capital income taxes; thus, with $\psi = 0$, the result that capital income taxes are zero in a stochastic steady state is not surprising. More interesting is the result that, even for the high risk aversion model, which is not separable between consumption and leisure, the mean of the capital income tax is close to zero in a stochastic steady state.

3. We compute the tax on private assets by first constructing a value for total debt. Following Jorgenson and Sullivan (1981), we note that the present value of depreciation allowances is a claim on the government similar to conventional debt. We thus define total debt to be the sum of the market value of federal debt and the value of depreciation allowances. We compute an innovation in this sum by regressing it on two lags of these variables: federal government expenditures net of interest payments, Hansen's (1984) Solow residual series, and the sum itself. For further details, see Chari, Christiano, and Kehoe 1990b.

References

Atkinson, A. B. 1971. "Capital Taxes, the Redistribution of Wealth and Individual Savings." *Review of Economic Studies* 38 (April): 209–27.

Atkinson, A. B., and A. Sandmo. 1980. "Welfare Implications of the Taxation of Savings." *Economic Journal* 90 (September): 529–49.

Atkinson, A. B., and J. E. Stiglitz. 1972. "The Structure of Indirect Taxation and Economic Efficiency." *Journal of Public Economics* 1 (April): 97–119.

Auerbach, Alan J. 1985. "The Theory of Excess Burden and Optimal Taxation." In *Handbook of Public Economics*, vol. I, edited by Alan J. Auerbach and Martin Feldstein, pp. 61–127. Amsterdam: North-Holland.

Backus, David K., Patrick J. Kehoe, and Finn E. Kydland. 1991. "International Real Business Cycles." Research Department Working Paper 426R, Federal Reserve Bank of Minneapolis.

Barro, Robert J. 1979. "On the Determination of the Public Debt." *Journal of Political Economy* 87 (October): 940–71.

Barro, Robert J., and Chaipat Sahasakul. 1983. "Measuring the Average Marginal Tax Rate From the Individual Income Tax." *Journal of Business* 56 (October): 419–52.

Bull, Nicholas. 1990. "Optimal Taxation in an Endogenous Growth Model With Human Capital." Federal Reserve Bank of Minneapolis. Manuscript.

Chamley, Christophe. 1986. "Optimal Taxation of Capital Income in General Equilibrium With Infinite Lives." *Econometrica* 54 (May): 607–22.

Chari, V. V., Lawrence J. Christiano, and Patrick J. Kehoe. 1990a. "On the Random Walk Theories of Optimal Taxation." Federal Reserve Bank of Minneapolis. Manuscript.

Chari, V. V., Lawrence J. Christiano, and Patrick J. Kehoe. 1990b. "Optimal Fiscal Policy in a Business Cycle Model." Federal Reserve Bank of Minneapolis. Manuscript.

Chari, V. V., Lawrence J. Christiano, and Patrick J. Kehoe. 1990c. "The Friedman Rule in Economies with Tax Distortions." Federal Reserve Bank of Minneapolis. Manuscript.

Christiano, Lawrence J., and Martin Eichenbaum. 1990. "Current Real Business Cycle Theories and Aggregate Labor Market Fluctuations." Institute for Empirical Macroeconomics Discussion Paper 24, Federal Reserve Bank of Minneapolis.

Diamond, Peter A. 1973. "Taxation and Public Production in a Growth Setting." In *Models of Economic Growth*, edited by James A. Mirrlees and N. H. Stern, pp. 215–35. New York: Wiley.

Faig, Miquel. 1988. "Characterization of the Optimal Tax on Money When It Functions as a Medium of Exchange." *Journal of Monetary Economics* 22 (July): 137–48.

Friedman, Milton. 1969. "The Optimum Quantity of Money." In *The Optimum Quantity of Money and Other Essays*, pp. 1–50. Chicago: Aldine.

Hansen, Gary D. 1984. "Fluctuations in Total Hours Worked: A Study Using Efficiency Units." Working Paper, University of Minnesota.

Jones, Larry E., Rodolfo E. Manuelli, and Peter E. Rossi. 1990. "Optimal Taxation in Convex Models of Equilibrium Growth." Northwestern University. Manuscript.

Jorgenson, Dale W., and Martin A. Sullivan. 1981. "Inflation and Corporate Capital Recovery." In *Depreciation, Inflation and the Taxation of Income From Capital*, edited by C. R. Hulten. Washington, D.C.: Urban Institute Press.

Judd, Kenneth L. 1985. "Redistributive Taxation in a Simple Perfect Foresight Model." *Journal of Public Economics* 28 (October): 59–83.

Judd, Kenneth L. 1989. "Optimal Taxation in Dynamic Stochastic Economies: Theory and Evidence." Working Paper, Hoover Institution.

Kimbrough, Kent P. 1986. "The Optimum Quantity of Money Rule in the Theory of Public Finance." *Journal of Monetary Economics* 18 (November): 277–84.

King, Robert G. 1990. "Observable Implications of Dynamically Optimal Taxation." University of Rochester. Manuscript.

Kydland, Finn E., and Edward C. Prescott. 1982. "Time to Build and Aggregate Fluctuations." *Econometrica* 50 (November): 1345–70.

Long, John B., Jr., and Charles I. Plosser. 1983. "Real Business Cycles." *Journal of Political Economy* 91 (February): 39–69.

Lucas, Robert E., Jr., and Nancy L. Stokey. 1983. "Optimal Fiscal and Monetary Policy in an Economy Without Capital." *Journal of Monetary Economics* 12 (July): 55–93.

Mankiw, N. Gregory. 1987. "The Optimal Collection of Seigniorage: Theory and Evidence." *Journal of Monetary Economics* 20 (September): 327–41.

Pestieau, Pierre M. 1974. "Optimal Taxation and Discount Rate for Public Investment in a Growth Setting." *Journal of Public Economics* 3 (August): 217–35.

Phelps, E. S. 1973. "Inflation in the Theory of Public Finance." *Swedish Journal of Economics* 75 (March): 67–82.

Prescott, Edward C. 1986. "Theory Ahead of Business Cycle Measurement." *Federal Reserve Bank of Minneapolis Quarterly Review* 10 (Fall): 9–22.

Ramsey, Frank P. 1927. "A Contribution to the Theory of Taxation." *Economic Journal* 37 (March): 47–61.

Stiglitz, Joseph E. 1987. "Pareto Efficient and Optimal Taxation and the New New Welfare Economics." In *Handbook of Public Economics*, vol. II, edited by Alan J. Auerbach and Martin Feldstein, pp. 991–1042. Amsterdam: North-Holland.

Weitzman, Martin L. 1973. "Duality Theory for Infinite Horizon Convex Models." *Management Science* 19 (March): 783–89.

Woodford, Michael. 1990. "The Optimum Quantity of Money." In *Handbook of Monetary Economics*, vol. II, edited by Benjamin M. Friedman and Frank H. Hahn, pp. 1067–1152. Amsterdam: North-Holland.

Zhu, Xiaodong. 1990. "Optimal Fiscal Policy in a Stochastic Growth Model." Manuscript, University of Chicago.

11

The Allocation of Capital and Time over the Business Cycle

Jeremy Greenwood and Zvi Hercowitz

There are two striking facts regarding the accumulation of capital in the nonmarket or household sector: (1) The stock of household capital, defined as the combined stock of consumer durables and residential capital, is higher than the stock of business nonresidential capital. The average ratio between the two capital stocks in the 1954–1988 period is 1.13. (2) Investment in household capital is highly procyclical. As can be seen in figure 11.1, it moves together with and even leads movements in business investment. Figure 11.1 also shows the higher level of household investment, which is a reflection of observation 1.

The first observation indicates that household capital accumulation is quantitatively important. The second highlights its interesting cyclical behavior. The macroeconomic question that arises is, How is the allocation of capital between the business and household sectors over the business cycle determined? The purpose of this chapter is to address this question. A macroeconomic model that stresses the role of capital in household activities is developed to study the allocation of capital and time across the two sectors. The theoretical model constructed is parameterized and simulated to see whether it can rationalize the observations above, as well as other stylized facts for the postwar U.S. economy. In particular, a set of second moments for the model's variables—reflecting their variability, persistence, and pattern of comovement—is computed and compared with the corresponding set that characterizes U.S. business cycle fluctuations.

By and large, the business cycle literature is silent on the role of the capital stock held by households. However, some studies, such as Kydland and Prescott (1982) and Christiano (1988), do consider household capital by adding it to business capital and including its services in total consumption. The basic assumption underlying this aggregation procedure is that household and business capital are perfect substitutes For this reason, the composition of total capital investment between business and household

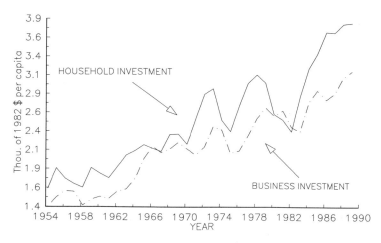

Figure 11.1
U.S. business and household investment: 1954–1989.

investment is indeterminate. Thus, this modeling strategy, which has been useful for the analysis of business fluctuations, is not well equipped to address the question at hand.

Another problem with the perfect substitution assumption arises when taxation of market activity is considered. Although both capital stocks are subject to property taxes, only business capital is subject to income taxation, which is far from being trivial (see Jorgenson and Yun 1986). This creates a significant distortion favoring the accumulation of household capital at the expense of business capital. This feature of the tax system, which is incorporated in the current analysis, is likely to be important for modeling the behavior of business and household investment. In a model with perfect substitution between the two capital stocks, business capital would be driven to zero.

Obviously then, a more complete analysis of capital accumulation requires a framework that assigns to household capital a distinct role from business capital. The main methodological issue involved here is the development of a framework to model household activities. In real business cycle models, as advanced by Kydland and Prescott (1982) and Long and Plosser (1983), the household sector is encapsulated in a utility function defined over consumption and leisure that is not affected by physical capital accumulation and technological progress. A simple extension of this approach to the problem at hand would be to include the services of household capital as an additional argument in the utility function. However, given that household activities involve approximately as much capital as business activities and three times as much (nonsleeping) time, it seems reasonable to conjecture, ex ante, that a more detailed treatment of the household sector could prove fruitful. In fact, ex post, such a treatment does provide a better rationalization of the observed pattern of cyclical fluctuations in household investment spending.

To provide a natural structure to this analysis, a Beckerian (1965) view of household production is adopted.[1] The similarities between market and home activities are stressed by following the extreme methodological strategy of symmetric treatment of both activities. There are two production functions, one for market activities and the other for nonmarket activities. In the first, labor interacts with market capital (equipment and structures) to produce market goods and services. In the second, the remaining time interacts with household capital (consumer durables and residence) to produce home goods and services. For example, watching TV, listening to music, or playing with a computer combines time with household capital to produce home goods (entertainment). Utility depends only on the consumption of market and home goods. Nonmarket time affects utility only via being an input in the production of home goods. The basic premise of this chapter is that considerations of capital accumulation and technological change are important for activities carried out at home as well as in business. As in the market sector, the productivity of time spent in nonmarket activities depends on the state of knowledge and the stock of capital in the household. The model does incorporate one asymmetry between the two sectors, however, capital goods can be produced in the market sector only. This feature is important in the present context since it affects the allocation of capital across the two sectors over time. Last, Benhabib, Rogerson, and Wright (1991) also study the macroeconomic implications of household production theory. The current research, which focuses on the allocation of capital over the business cycle, is a close cousin of their analysis, which stresses the allocation of time.

The chapter is organized as follows: Section 11.1 presents the model. Next, section 11.2 describes the parameterization of the model and the results from the quantitative analysis. Finally, some concluding comments are offered in section 11.3.

11.1 The Model and Solution Technique

The Economic Environment

Consider an economy in which the representative household maximizes its expected lifetime utility, as given by

$$E_0 \left[\sum_{t=0}^{\infty} \beta^t U(c_t, h_t) \right] \qquad 0 < \beta < 1, \tag{1}$$

where c_t is consumption of nondurable goods and services purchased in the market, and h_t is consumption of goods and services produced at home. The momentary utility function U, in addition to having the usual properties, is assumed to be homogeneous of degree q.

Market and home production technologies are described by

Market: $y_t = F(k_t, z_t l_t)$, \tag{2}

Home: $h_t = H(d_t, z_t(1 - l_t))$, \tag{3}

where k_t is the business capital stock, d_t is the household capital stock (consumer durables and residential capital stock), 1 is the household's (normalized) endowment of time, and l_t is the part of it allocated to market production. The production functions F and H are both assumed to be homogeneous of degree one. The variable z_t represents labor augmenting technological progress and it evolves according to

$$z_t = A z_{t-1} \varepsilon_t, \qquad A > 1, \tag{4}$$

where ε_t is a stationary random variable with unit mean drawn from the distribution $G(\varepsilon_t | \varepsilon_{t-1})$.[2]

Two examples may help to illustrate the economic environment being envisioned. A meal cooked at home combines food and beverages produced in the market, using capital and time with household cooking services that use capital and time at home, to create the end-good utility. Other utility-generating activities are engaged in outside the home but can be interpreted in a similar way. Golfing, for example, mixes services provided by the business sector, green and clubhouse facilities that use business capital and labor, with ones provided by the household using household capital—car, golf clubs—and time. In the spirit of Becker (1965), one can interpret $F(\cdot)$ and $H(\cdot)$ as producing intermediate goods, which are then used in $U(\cdot)$ to make the final product—utility. Time, like capital, has no intrinsic worth on its own in this framework, but instead derives its value from what can be done with it.

The two capital stocks evolve as

$$k_{t+1} = k_t(1 - \delta_k) + i_{kt}, \qquad 0 < \delta_k < 1, \tag{5}$$

and

$$d_{t+1} = d_t(1 - \delta_d) + i_{dt}, \qquad 0 < \delta_d < 1, \tag{6}$$

where δ_k and δ_d are the depreciation rates, i_{kt} is gross business investment in nonresidential market capital, and i_{dt} is household investment.

The constraint applying to market output is

$$c_t + i_{kt} + i_{dt} \leqslant y_t.$$

Note that this is the condition that breaks the symmetry between the two sectors. Capital goods can be produced by the business sector only.

Finally, there is a government present in the economy. It levies taxes on the market income earned by labor and capital at the rates τ_l and τ_k. The revenue raised by the government in each period t is rebated back to agents in the form of lump-sum transfer payments in the amount μ_t. The government's period-t budget constraint is

$$\mu_t = \tau_k r_t k_t + \tau_l w_t l_t, \tag{7}$$

where r_t represents the market return on capital and w_t the real wage rate.

Competitive Equilibrium

The competitive equilibrium for the economy under study will now be formulated. To this end, let the aggregate state-of-the-world be denoted by the vector (s, ε), where $s \equiv (d, k, z)$—time subscripts are dropped in standard fashion. Assume that the market wage and rental rates, w and r, and per capita transfer payments, μ, can all be expressed as functions of the aggregate state-of-the-world as follows: $w = W(s, \varepsilon), r = R(s, \varepsilon)$, and $\mu = M(s, \varepsilon)$. Likewise, suppose that k and d evolve in equilibrium according to the laws of motion $k' = K(s, \varepsilon)$ and $d' = D(s, \varepsilon)$. Also, in similar fashion, let the law of motion for z read $z' = Z(s, \varepsilon') \equiv Az\varepsilon'$. Thus, the movement in the vector s is governed by the transition function $s' = S(s, \varepsilon, \varepsilon'; K, D) \equiv (K(s, \varepsilon), D(s, \varepsilon), Z(s, \varepsilon'))$, where the adopted notation serves to emphasize that the function S depends upon the forms of the functions K and D.

Each period the "representative" household chooses its consumption of market goods, $\tilde{c}$, stocks of business and household capital, $\tilde{k}'$ and $\tilde{d}'$, and time allocated to market work, $\tilde{l}$, so as to solve the dynamic-programming problem (P1).[3]

$$V(\tilde{k}, \tilde{d}; s, \varepsilon) = \max_{(\tilde{c}, \tilde{k}', \tilde{d}', \tilde{l})} \{U(\tilde{c}, H(\tilde{d}, z(1 - \tilde{l})) + \beta V(\tilde{k}', \tilde{d}'; s', \varepsilon') dG(\varepsilon'|\varepsilon)\} \tag{P1}$$

subject to

$$\tilde{c} + \tilde{k}' + \tilde{d}' = (1 - \tau_k)R(s, \varepsilon)\tilde{k} + (1 - \tau_l)W(s, \varepsilon)\tilde{l} + (1 - \delta_k)\tilde{k}$$

$$+ (1 - \delta_d)\tilde{d} + M(s, \varepsilon), \tag{8}$$

and

$$s' = S(s, \varepsilon, \varepsilon'; K, D).$$

Similarly, the representative firm hires capital and labor, $\hat{k}$ and $\hat{l}$, in each period so as to maximize profits. Hence, it solves the problem (P2).

$$\max_{\hat{k}, \hat{l}} \{F(\hat{k}, z\hat{l}) - R(s, \varepsilon)\hat{k} - W(s, \varepsilon)\hat{l}\}. \tag{P2}$$

Needless to say, the firm earns zero profits each period due to the constant-returns-to-scale assumption.

The competitive equilibrium under study is now formally defined, where again $(s, \varepsilon) = (k, d, z, \varepsilon)$.

Definition: A competitive equilibrium is a set of allocation rules, $c = C(k, d, z, \varepsilon)$, $k' = K(k, d, z, \varepsilon)$, $d' = D(k, d, z, \varepsilon)$, $l = L(k, d, z, \varepsilon)$, and pricing and transfer functions, $r = R(k, d, z, \varepsilon)$, $w = W(k, d, z, \varepsilon)$, $\mu = M(k, d, z, \varepsilon)$, such that:[4]

(i) Households solve problem (P1), taking as given the aggregate state-of-the-world (k, d, z, ε) and the form of functions $R(\cdot)$, $W(\cdot)$, $M(\cdot)$, $K(\cdot)$, and $D(\cdot)$, with the solution to this problem having the form $\tilde{c} = C(k, d, z, \varepsilon)$, $\tilde{k}' = K(k, d, z, \varepsilon)$, $\tilde{d} = D(k, d, z, \varepsilon)$, and $\tilde{l} = L(k, d, z, \varepsilon)$.

(ii) Firms solve problem (P2), given (k, d, z, ε) and the functions $R(\cdot)$ and $W(\cdot)$, with the solution to this problem having the form $\tilde{k} = k$ and $\tilde{l} = L(k, d, z, \varepsilon)$.

(iii) The goods market clears each period implying that

$$c + k' + d' = F(k, zl) + (1 - \delta_k)k + (1 - \delta_d)d. \tag{9}$$

It is easy to deduce from the definition for a competitive equilibrium that the allocation rules for c, k', d', and l are implicitly defined by the system of equations (10), (11), and (12), in addition to the aggregate resource constraint (9).

$$U_1(c, h) = \beta \int U_1(c', h')[(1 - \tau_k)F_1(k', z'l') + (1 - \delta_k)]dG(\varepsilon'|\varepsilon). \tag{10}$$

$$U_1(c, h) = \beta \int U_1(c', h')[H_1(d', z'(1 - l'))$$

$$\times \frac{U_2(c', h')}{U_1(c', h')} + (1 - \delta_d)]dG(\varepsilon'|\varepsilon). \tag{11}$$

$$(1 - \tau_l)zF_2(k, zl) = \frac{U_2(c, h)}{U_1(c, h)}zH_2(d, z(1 - l)) \tag{12}$$

recall that $h = H(d, z(1 - l))$.

Equations (10), (11), and (12) combine the efficiency conditions associated with the household's problem (P1) together with those of the firm's problem (P2). The first-order conditions connected with (P1) govern the accumulation of business and household capital in addition to the allocation of time, given the rental and wage rates r and w, while the conditions from (P2) equate these rates to the marginal products of business capital and market time, $F_1(k, zl)$ and $zF_2(k, zl)$. Finally, note that the economy's resource constraint (9) can be obtained by substituting (7) into (8) while making use of parts (i) and (ii) of the definition for a competitive equilibrium.

In order to put the implications of the present framework for the allocation of time into perspective, consider the standard paradigm used in business cycle analysis. There, a homothetic momentary utility function $U(c, 1 - l)$ defined over consumption c and leisure $1 - l$ is used. The optimality condition governing the allocation of time appears as

$$\frac{U_2(c, 1 - l)}{U_1(c, 1 - l)} \equiv \Gamma\left(\frac{c}{1 - l}\right) = (1 - \tau_l)w, \tag{13}$$

with the form of the function Γ following from the assumed homotheticity of U. Note that for this paradigm to be consistent with secular increases in real wages and consumption on the one hand, and a stationary allocation of time to market work on the other, a unit elasticity of substitution between consumption and leisure is required.[5]

A related important implication of (13), which has played a crucial role in neoclassical macroeconomic thinking, is that for real wage movements to have strong effects on market labor, they should, at least partly, be transitory. Using equation (13) and intuitive reasoning from the permanent income hypothesis, when w increases only temporarily it has a minor effect on c. Hence, (13) implies an expansion of market work. For the case when w moves permanently, it has a stronger effect on c, which reduces the extent to which market labor reacts.

By contrast, from (12), the condition for optimal allocation of time in the present model is

$$zH_2[d, z(1 - l)]\frac{U_2(c, h)}{U_1(c, h)} = (1 - \tau_l)zF_2(k, zl) = (1 - \tau_l)w. \tag{14}$$

Here technological progress and capital accumulation, which affect market productivity and hence the real wage, also affect home productivity. Hence, stationarity of market hours does not restrict the elasticity of substitution in utility. It requires now that technological progress and capital accumulation affect the two marginal productivities of labor in a parallel way. For this to be the case, the two production functions should display constant returns to scale, the utility function over c and h be homogeneous of arbitrary degree, and technological progress be representable as labor augmenting. Observe that two new factors will now influence the allocation of time between market and nonmarket activities. The first is the relative price of household goods (in terms of market goods) $U_2(c, h)/U_1(c, h)$. The second is the degree of substitution between household capital, d, and (effective) nonmarket time, $z(1 - l)$, in home production.

11.2   Quantitative Analysis: Calibration and Simulation

In this section of the chapter, a parametric version of the model is calibrated, simulated, and evaluated. The dynamics of the simulated economy are compared with the behavior of annual U.S. data for the sample period 1954–1989. Specifically, the question addressed is whether the model is able to mimic the observed behavior of investment in household and market production, as well as other features of business fluctuations.

To impose some discipline on the simulation conducted, the calibration procedure advanced by Kydland and Prescott (1982) is adopted—for an introduction to this literature see Prescott (1986). An important feature of this approach is that as many model parameters as possible are set in advance based upon either (i) a priori information about their magnitudes, or (ii) so that along a deterministic balanced growth path the ratios for various endogenous variables in the model correspond to their average values for the U.S. postwar period. Hence prior information and the first moments of the data are stressed in setting parameter values. The implications of different values for free parameters—in the present case there will only be one—can be studied by simulating the model. The shocks to the system are the z-process, whose moments are set to match the sample moments observed for the corresponding productivity measures from the market data.

Specifically, the procedure is the following: First, the model is given a suitable parametric form and calibrated. Then it is transformed into a stationary representation. Next, the allocation rules for the stationary model are computed. Using these allocation rules, 5000 artificial samples of 36 observations (the number of years in the 1954–1989 sample) for each variable of interest are simulated. Each simulation corresponds to a randomly generated sample of 36 realizations of ε and the corresponding z-process. Then the data from the model are transformed back to their nonstationary form and detrended using the Hodrick-Prescott (H-P) filter.[6] The average moments over the 5000 samples are computed and compared to the corresponding moments of the actual H-P filtered U.S. data. The transformation procedure used, and the solution algorithm employed, are detailed in the appendix.

The unit of time for the quantitative analysis is a year. This time unit was chosen for two reasons. First, the stochastic process governing technological change in the household sector is identified in the current framework through the assumption that technological change in the business sector is governed by the same process. The implication that labor augmenting innovations in technology affect both sectors simultaneously is more realistic the longer the basic time period. While a year is probably too short in this regard, it is preferable to a quarter. Second, an additional benefit of this time unit in the current context, which stresses capital accumulation, is the implied one-year time to build for capital. Investment becomes part of the capital stock with a simple to model one-year delay. This implication of the time unit seems reasonable and is in line with the analysis of Kydland and Prescott (1982)—who used a quarterly model with a more elaborate time-to-build structure spread over four quarters.

Last, some care must be taken when matching up the theoretical constructs of the model with their counterparts in the U.S. data. U.S. GNP includes in it a measure of the service flow from the economy's housing stock. Gross housing product is made up of the value added from commercial residential renting plus an imputed value added from owner-occupied homes. For the purposes of the current analysis, the product from the economy's housing stock should be counted as part of nonmarket production and therefore netted out of GNP. Thus, in the data, market output is taken to be GNP less gross housing product. The data analogue for market consumption in the model is personal consumption expenditure on nondurable goods and services. Again, the value of services from housing is subtracted. The durable goods component of personal consumption expenditure is added to residential investment to obtain a measure of investment in household capital in the data. Similarly, business investment is represented by fixed nonresidential investment in equipment and structures.

Specification of the Economy

To begin with, let tastes and technology be specified in the following way:

$$U(c, h) = \frac{1}{1 - \gamma}[\theta c^\sigma + (1 - \theta)h^\sigma]^{(1-\gamma)/\sigma} - \frac{1}{1 - \gamma}, \tag{15}$$

$$F(k, zl) = k^{\alpha}(zl)^{1-\alpha}, \tag{16}$$

and

$$H(d, z(1-l)) = \{\omega d^{\lambda} + (1-\omega)[z(1-l)]^{\lambda}\}^{1/\lambda}, \tag{17}$$

where σ, $\lambda \leqslant 1$, $\gamma > 0$, and $0 < \alpha$, θ, $\omega < 1$. Preferences and household production have been given constant elasticity of substitution (CES) functional forms, while market production has a Cobb-Douglas characterization—i.e., a CES with unit elasticity of substitution. Note that under this specification the term $z^{1-\alpha}$ in (16) will correspond to the "Solow residual" as it is conventionally defined in the business cycle literature.

The stochastic structure of the model is described by a two-state Markov process. Specifically, in any given period the technology shock, ε, is assumed to be drawn from the time-invariant, two-point set $\varepsilon = \{e^{\xi_1}, e^{\xi_2}\}$. The distribution function governing next period's technology shock, ε', conditional on the current realization, ε, is defined by $\mathrm{prob}[\varepsilon' = e^{\xi_s}|\varepsilon = e^{\xi_r}] = \pi_{rs}$, where $0 \leqslant \pi_{rs} \leqslant 1$, for $r, s = 1, 2$.

Calibration Procedure and Benchmark Model Results

In the first stage of the quantitative analysis attention is directed to a special version of the model, with the following properties: (i) technological change does not play any role in decisions of the household sector, and (ii) the services from household capital enter the utility function in an additive manner. Hence, this version of the model can be seen as a straw man that downplays the household production structure, incorporating the minimal requirement for households to demand capital.

Features (i)–(ii) are achieved as follows: First, both preferences and household production are restricted to have unitary elasticity of substitution (i.e., $\sigma = \lambda = 0$), so that they assume the form

$$U(c, h) = \frac{1}{1-\gamma}(c^{\theta}h^{1-\theta})^{1-\gamma} - \frac{1}{1-\gamma}, \tag{18}$$

and

$$H[d, z(1-l)] = d^{\omega}[z(1-l)]^{1-\omega}. \tag{19}$$

Substituting (19) into (18) yields

$$\underline{U}(c, 1-l, d, z) = \frac{1}{1-\gamma}[c^{\theta}(1-l)^{(1-\omega)(1-\theta)}d^{\omega(1-\theta)}z^{(1-\omega)(1-\theta)}]^{1-\gamma} - \frac{1}{1-\gamma}. \tag{20}$$

The stock of household capital enters $\underline{U}$ in a similar way as in the utility function used by Macklem (1989) and others (see the references therein).

Second, γ is chosen to be one so that $\underline{U}$ becomes

$$\underline{U}(c, 1 - l, d, z) = \theta \ln c + (1 - \omega)(1 - \theta)\ln(1 - l) + \omega(1 - \theta)\ln d$$

$$+ (1 - \omega)(1 - \theta)\ln z. \tag{21}$$

Note that (21) satisfies the criteria (i)–(ii). The choice regarding l has the standard form (equation (13)) with unit elasticity of substitution between c and $(1 - l)$, and technological change in home production does not affect any household decisions.

In order to implement the benchmark model, values for the following parameters need to be chosen:

Utility	$\theta, \beta,$
Market production	$\alpha,$
Home production	$\omega,$
Depreciation rates	$\delta_k, \delta_d,$
Technology process	$A, \xi_1, \xi_2, \pi_{11}\pi_{22},$
Tax rates	$\tau_k, \tau_l.$

First, the number of parameters is reduced by imposing symmetry on the stochastic technology process. It is assumed that $\xi_1 = -\xi_2 = \xi$, and that $\pi_{11} = \pi_{22} = \pi$. Then, ξ is the standard deviation of the shock and $\rho = 2\pi - 1$ is the coefficient of serial correlation. In market production α is chosen to be 0.3, given that labor's share of GNP net of housing was about 70 percent during the 1954–1989 sample period. For utility since the time unit is a year, β is set equal to the standard value of 0.96.

The depreciation rate on market capital δ_k is chosen to be 7.8 percent, a value derived from the average service life of nonresidential structures and equipment for the period 1954–1985.[7] It is assumed that the average depreciation rate of household capital δ_d, which consists of components similar to the structures and equipment in business capital, is equal to δ_k.

The parameters of the z-process require the calculation of the Solow residuals from the U.S. data and their sample moments. This calculation was carried out using GNP (net of housing) for market output and data on net fixed nonresidential private capital and total man-hours employed for factor inputs. The average growth rate of z is 0.01; hence A was equated to 1.01. The first difference of the log of the Solow residual, corresponding to $\ln A + \ln \varepsilon$, has a standard deviation of 0.022 and an autocorrelation coefficient of 0.16, which is statistically insignificantly different from zero. Hence, $\xi = 0.022$ and ρ was set to zero, implying that $\pi = 0.5$.

The tax rate τ_k, applying in the model to gross capital income, was set equal to 0.25. On the deterministic balanced growth path, and given the values of δ_k and β described above, this corresponds to a tax rate on net capital income of about 50 percent. This figure is between the effective tax rates of 52 percent on corporate capital income and 40 percent on non-corporate capital income computed by Jorgenson and Yun (1986). Regarding the tax rate on labor income, prior to the Tax Reform Act of 1986 the marginal tax rates on personal income ranged from 11 percent to 50 percent. In this range $\tau_l = 0.25$ was picked.[8]

Two parameters, θ in utility and ω in home production, still remain. Two first moments computed from the U.S. data are relevant for the determination of these parameters: (a) the average ratio of total hours worked to total nonsleeping hours of the working age population (16 hours per day) is 0.24, and (b) the average ratio of household capital to market capital is 1.13.[9,10] The values of θ and ω were chosen so that these two first moments are satisfied along the model's balanced growth path.

Specifically, along the balanced growth path for the model all variables grow at the same rate as z, or at the gross rate A (see the appendix for more detail). Thus, $c'/c = k'/k = d'/d = z'l'/zl = z'(1 - l')/z(1 - l) = A$. Given the current parameterization for tastes and technology, the balanced growth path analogues to equations (10), (11), (12), and (9) are:

$$1 = \beta A^{-\gamma}(1 - \tau_k)[\alpha(k/zl)^{\alpha-1} + (1 - \delta_k)], \tag{22}$$

$$1 = \beta A^{-\gamma}\{\omega[(1 - \theta)/\theta]c/d + (1 - \delta_d)\} = \beta A^{-\gamma}\{\omega[(1 - \theta)/\theta](c/z)/(d/z)$$
$$+ (1 - \delta_d)\}, \tag{23}$$

$$(1 - \tau_l)(1 - \alpha)(k/zl)^{\alpha} = (1 - \omega)[(1 - \theta)/\theta]c/(z(1 - l)), \tag{24}$$

and

$$c = k^{\alpha}(zl)^{1-\alpha} - Ak + (1 - \delta_k)k, \tag{25}$$

which implies

$$c/z = (k/z)^{\alpha}(l)^{1-\alpha} - Ak/z + (1 - \delta_k)k/z.$$

The above two restrictions from the long-run data imply

$$l = 0.24, \tag{26}$$

and

$$d/k = (d/z)/(k/z) = 1.13. \tag{27}$$

Given values for β, A, γ, α, δ_k, δ_d, τ_k, and τ_l, this system of six equations can be thought of as determining a solution for the six unknowns k/z, d/z, l, c/z, θ, and ω. The parameter values obtained for ω and θ are 0.13 and 0.26, respectively.

The values for k/z, d/z, l, and c/z, as determined by (22), (23), (24), and (25), are sensitive to the tax parameters τ_k and τ_l. As one might expect, the taxation of the market income earned by labor and capital induces substitution toward nonmarket activity. For instance, if capital taxation is eliminated in the model the ratio of household to business capital drops from 1.13 to 0.80 and the ratio of nonmarket to market time falls from 3.2 to 3.0. The marginal welfare cost of capital taxation along the benchmark economy's balanced growth path is high, being 3.4 units of output in lossed welfare for each extra unit of output raised in revenue.[11] The corresponding figure for labor taxation is 0.92.

Finally, the model's balanced growth path can be used to compute the total amount of goods and services produced in the economy. The aggregate $F(k, zl) + [U_2(c, h)/U_1(c, h)] \times H(d, z(1 - l))$, where market goods are used as the numeraire, can be denoted Gross Economic Product (GEP). Along the model's balanced growth path the ratio of GEP to GNP is 2.9. The large size of this number follows from the fact that household production uses about 1.1 times the capital and 3.2 times the time of market production.

The results of the current simulation are shown in table 11.1 (under model 1) and in figure 11.2. By comparing the standard deviations of the variables for model 1 with those characterizing the U.S. data, one can see that, in general, the model generates too little variation. For example, the standard deviation of actual GNP around the H-P trend is 2.3 percent, while the model generates a corresponding 1.9 percent. The standard deviation of market labor is particularly low, 0.8 percent, relative to the actual figure of 1.7 percent. One cause of this result is the nature of the technology process. Since z is a random walk, changes in market opportunities for labor are permanent, and hence they generate a weak response of market labor effort. Also given the focus of this chapter, mechanisms that enhance labor's responsiveness to market opportunities were not incorporated, such as the intertemporal nonseparability of preferences in Kydland and Prescott (1982) or the indivisibility of market work in Hansen (1985) and Rogerson (1988).

Hours and output are even less variable when the model is transformed into the prototypical real business cycle model (with a Cobb-Douglas utility

Table 11.1
Summary statistics: U.S. economy and models

Variables	U.S. annual data 1954–1989			Model 1			Model 2		
	S.D.	A.C.	C.C.	S.D.	A.C.	C.C.	S.D.	A.C.	C.C.
Output	2.3	0.53	1.00	1.9	0.50	1.00	2.0	0.37	1.00
Consumption	1.4	0.61	0.80	1.0	0.51	0.92	1.0	0.54	0.92
Business investment	6.2	0.45	0.85	9.2	−0.05	0.69	4.1	0.45	0.99
Household investment	7.7	0.44	0.65	6.1	0.13	0.34	4.9	0.24	0.96
Market time	1.7	0.46	0.90	0.8	0.52	0.95	1.1	0.32	0.95

Note: The U.S. data were divided by the working age population (16–64) logged and Hodrick-Prescott (H–P) filtered. Output is GNP less gross housing product. Consumption is personal consumption expenditures on nondurables and services—excluding housing. Business investment is fixed non-residential private investment, and household investment is private residential investment plus personal consumption expenditure on durable goods. These quantities are in 1982 dollars. Market time is total hours from the Citibase Databank.
S.D. = standard deviations, measured in percent.
A.C. = first-order autocorrelations.
C.C. = cross correlations with output.

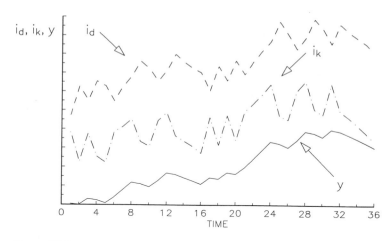

Figure 11.2
Behavior of investment and output: model 1.

function defined over consumption and leisure) by eliminating household capital from the home production function. The standard deviations of output and market hours drop to 1.6 and 0.4 percent in this case.[12] Given that only the stock of business capital needs to be adjusted following a shock, one can expect market time to react by less. Thus, the inclusion of household capital into real business cycle models increases the volatility of output and hours.

The behavior of investment in business and household capital for the benchmark model is shown in figure 11.2, which plots the variables i_k and i_d for an artificial sample of thirty-six years. It can be clearly seen that the two investments tend to react in opposite directions, with business investment moving much closer to output. Also, fluctuations in investment tend to be short-lived. Only when the fluctuations persist do the two investments begin to move together positively. The short nature of the fluctuations is reflected in the coefficients of serial correlation of i_k, which is slightly negative, -0.05, and of i_d, which is only weakly positive, 0.13. By contrast, in the U.S. data their coefficients of serial correlation are 0.45 and 0.44, respectively. Another lack of correspondence are the relative volatilities. Business investment is less volatile in the data with a standard deviation of 6.2 percent against 7.7 percent for household investment, while in model 1 the corresponding figures are 9.2 percent and 6.1 percent.

The negative comovement of the two investments, which stands in contrast with the positive one displayed by actual data (figure 11.1), has to

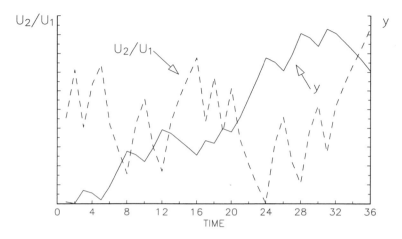

Figure 11.3
Behavior of the price of home goods and output: model 1.

do with the basic asymmetry between the two types of capital. Business capital can be used to produce household capital, but not the other way around. When an innovation to technology occurs, say a positive one, the optimal levels for both capital stocks increase. Given the asymmetry in the nature of the two capital goods, the tendency for the benchmark model is to build business capital first, and only then household capital. Capital investment requires abstention from consumption of market goods, but not (directly) from consumption of home goods. The induced short-run scarcity of market consumption goods in terms of nonmarket ones operates to reduce the benefit from immediate investment in household capital vis-à-vis business capital. The short-run scarcity of market consumption goods following a positive technology shock is reflected in the countercyclical behavior of the relative price of home goods (figure 11.3), which has a correlation with output of -0.81. The next section addresses this question in greater detail.

Departing from the Benchmark Model

In the benchmark model, market and home production functions were parameterized identically. Given the asymmetric role the two types of capital play in the paradigm and the poor outcome of the earlier simulation, it may be profitable to investigate whether relaxing the assumption of a unitary elasticity of substitution in home production, ($\lambda = 0$), can improve

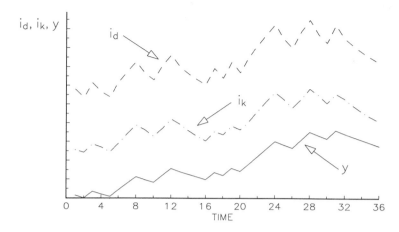

Figure 11.4
Behavior of investment and output: model 2.

the ability of the model to generate the pattern of investment behavior observed in the data. Note that higher values for $\lambda \in (-\infty, 1]$ in (17) imply greater substitutability between d and $z(1 - l)$ in household production.

It turns out that reducing the degree of substitution in home production, relative to the Cobb-Douglas case, has strong implications for the pattern of comovements between the two investments. The simulation results obtained when $\lambda = -1$ are reported under model 2 in table 11.1 and portrayed in figure 11.4.[13] The most striking outcome is that investments now become strongly positively correlated with output. This can be seen in table 11.1, where the correlations with output for market and household investment are 0.99 and 0.96, and in figure 11.4, which illustrates the strong positive comovement between the two types of investment.

To interpret this result, consider the following expression that appears in (11), the Euler equation associated with household capital:

$$H_1(d', z'(1 - l'))\frac{U_2(c', h')}{U_1(c', h')} = \omega\frac{d'^{\lambda-1}}{\omega d'^{\lambda} + (1 - \omega)z'^{\lambda}(1 - l')^{\lambda}}\frac{(1 - \theta)}{\theta}c'.$$

$$(28)$$

This term describes the marginal benefit from household investment (measured in terms of market goods). When a technological improvement hits the economy in the current period, z' is expected to rise since z follows a random walk. On the one hand, this tends to increase the marginal product of household capital, $H_1(d', z'(1 - l'))$. On the other hand, the shadow price of home goods, $U_2(c', h')/U_1(c', h')$, declines because of the induced desire to build up the capital stocks (resulting in a relative scarcity of market goods). Here technological change has two opposing effects on the marginal benefit of household investment.

In the Cobb-Douglas case, where $\lambda = 0$, these two effects cancel each other out, as can be seen in equation (28). It is not surprising then that in model 1, household investment falls following a positive shock since the latter only improves the marginal benefit of market investment. When $\lambda < 0$, the higher complementarity between d' and $z'(1 - l')$ in next period's household production implies a stronger impact of the shock on the marginal productivity of household capital, $H_1(d', z'(1 - l'))$. Observe that (28) is increasing in z' when $\lambda < 0$. Thus, in model 2, the marginal productivity effect becomes more important relative to the relative price effect, and this is the reason behind the more procyclical behavior of household investment.

On the volatility and serial correlation properties of the two investments, model 2 is better able to mimic the data than model 1. Household investment is now more volatile than business investment—standard deviations of 4.9 percent and 4.1 percent—and the serial correlation coefficients are larger, with business investment exhibiting stronger serial correlation. Also, the variability of market time is increased from 0.8 percent in model 1 to 1.1 percent, which is, however, still lower than in the actual data.[14]

The intuition behind the increase in the volatility of market time can be obtained by examining the expression shown below representing the marginal value of time *at home* (cf equation (12)):

$$zH_2(d, z(1 - l))\frac{U_2(c, h)}{U_1(c, h)} = \frac{(1 - \omega)z^\lambda(1 - l)^{\lambda-1}}{\omega d^\lambda + (1 - \omega)z^\lambda(1 - l)^\lambda}\frac{(1 - \theta)}{\theta}c. \tag{29}$$

Consider first the case where the household production technology is Cobb-Douglas ($\lambda = 0$). Here, when a positive technological innovation occurs, the marginal product of household time, $zH_2(d, z(1 - l))$, increases. This effect, by itself, operates to increase the amount of time spent at home. However, this is not the end of the story, as the relative price of home goods in terms of market goods, $U_2(c, h)/U_1(c, h)$, falls due to the scarcity of market resources—since investment is expanded. This effect works in the direction of increasing market time. In the Cobb-Douglas case, these two forces exactly cancel each other out, and the expression in (29) is independent of z. The upshot is that nonmarket time falls following a positive shock, since the marginal value of time has increased only in the market sector.

When λ is negative, the above expression is decreasing in z so that market time rises, a fortiori, in response to a positive innovation. As the degree of complementarity between time and capital in household production is increased, the effect of technological innovation on the marginal product of nonmarket time is dampened. (In the limiting case where $\lambda \to -\infty$, the household production function becomes Leontief and the effect that a positive shock has on nonmarket time's marginal product vanishes.)

The preceding discussion illustrates the relevance of technological complementarity in household production for the allocation of capital and time across sectors. The analysis suggests that within the CES family of production functions, the degree of substitution between time and capital in household production is less than the Cobb-Douglas case, in the sense that this hypothesis allows the model to mimic better the observed pattern of cyclical fluctuations in household investment.[15] Little independent evidence is available to assess the reasonableness of the value chosen for the elasticity of substitution between capital and time in household production. And it would seem difficult on theoretical grounds alone to argue about the appropriate value for this parameter—as indeed it would be for market production parameters too. Clearly, further empirical work is needed to gauge the value of this and other parameters governing household activity.

11.3   Concluding Comments

Two observations about investment in durable consumption goods and housing were stressed in the introduction: (1) its high level relative to nonresidential business investment and (2) its procyclical behavior, leading business investment. The aim of this chapter was to construct a model that treated the market and nonmarket sectors symmetrically, to see whether it could mimic both these observations as well as other important features of business fluctuations.

The first observation about the level of home investment (arising from the first moments of the U.S. data) was satisfied by adjusting the parameters of taste and technology. This was part of the calibration procedure that was followed. It may be noted that in spite of the high *level* of household capital in the United States the nonmarket sector is still strongly labor intensive. Capital in the household sector is about 1.1 times higher than in the business sector, but time spent in nonmarket activities is about 3 times greater than the time spent in market activities. (This is reflected in a higher value for α than for ω.)

In the model, the level of business capital is strongly related to taxation, which applies to business capital income but not to household capital productivity. This tax asymmetry shifts capital toward the nonmarket sector. Given the values of the parameters of the model, found under realistic tax rates, if the taxation of capital is eliminated (being replaced by lump-sum taxation), the ratio of household to business capital along the balanced growth path drops from 1.13 to 0.80.

The observation about the cyclical behavior of investment was analyzed by simulating the model. Of pivotal importance for the dynamics is the fact that capital goods can only be produced in the market sector. The ramifications of this asymmetry can be illustrated as follows. Suppose a positive technological innovation hits the economy. In response, the optimal levels of business and household capital increase. Given that capital goods are produced in the business sector only, the induced scarcity of market goods reduces the shadow price of home goods in terms of market goods. A shift of resources to the business sector, in terms of both time and capital, ensues. Hence, this mechanism implies a tendency for business capital to be built first, and then household capital. This effect operates to produce negative comovement between the two investments, in contrast with the positive covariation observed in the data. The mechanism just described is not a specific feature of this framework. It would be present in any general equilibrium model with household durables. Model 1, which downplays the household production structure, is an example.

In order to overcome the tendency for household investment to move out of phase with business investment, the degree of technical complementarity between time and capital in household production was increased (model 2). This strengthens the positive impact that a technological improvement has on the marginal value of household capital and weakens its effect on the marginal value of household time, thereby promoting an increase in household investment and a reallocation of time toward the market. As a result, household investment moved procyclically and market time became more volatile.

A feature that the present model fails to rationalize is household investment's lead over business investment. Strengthening the effect of shocks on the degree of substitution between labor and capital in home production (i.e., making λ more negative) does not affect this timing of events. The introduction of adjustment costs in business capital, which can be thought of as retarding business investment, does not produce the actual type of behavior. Such adjustment costs retard the entire build up of the two capital stocks, producing only a reduction in general volatility, including that of the two investments.

Given that investment in consumer durables and housing tends to lead other macroeconomic variables over the cycle, household capital plays an interesting macroeconomic role. It seems that a richer model is called for. Production in the business and household sectors may be modeled as requiring the input of services produced in the other sector. For example, households may produce commuting services to and from work, which represent an intermediate good in market production. This kind of interaction between the two sectors may be relevant for the cyclical behavior of household investment, since it involves an association between business activity and the demand for household capital. Also, it is well known that fluctuations in the amount of time households devote to the market are reflected mainly in the number of jobs rather than in the number of hours worked in existing ones. Hence, reallocation of time from home to market production may require purchases of new cars, homes, appliances, and so forth, at early stages of the business cycle. Further investigation of the role of nonmarket activities, especially their implications regarding housing and consumer durable goods, may contribute to the understanding of the origin and propagation of business cycles.

Finally, human capital evolved exogenously in the model. A potential extension would be to endogenize the process governing human capital accumulation (see Ben-Porath 1967). This would permit endogenous growth in the framework. Unlike physical capital, important components of human capital are produced in the household sector. It is easy to visualize a setting where human capital production requires the input of goods and services from both the market and nonmarket sectors. Such a framework could be useful for studying the cyclical behavior of investment in human capital and also the role of the household sector in long-run growth.

Appendix

Transformation to a Stationary Representation

The system of equations (9), (10), (11), and (12)—in conjunction with (3)—describes the model's general equilibrium, or provides a determination of c, k', d', and zl. Let $c = C(k, d, z; \varepsilon)$, $k' = K(k, d, z; \varepsilon)$, $d' = D(k, d, z; \varepsilon)$, and $zl = L(k, d, z; \varepsilon)$, represent the solution to (9), (10), (11), and (12), taking account of (3). These allocation rules are homogeneous of degree one in

(k, d, z). This is immediate from the system of equations implicitly defining the solution since U_1 and U_2 are homogeneous of degree $q - 1$, while F and H are homogeneous of degree one, and F_1, F_2, H_1, and H_2 are homogeneous of degree zero. Recall from (4) that z is growing across time. The model's variables can be rendered stationary by deflating them by the lagged value of z. By defining x^* by $x^* = x_t/z_{t-1}$, for $x = c$, k, and d, the above decision rules can be transformed to get $c^* = C(k^*, d^*, A\varepsilon; \varepsilon)$, $k^{*'} = K(k^*, d^*, A\varepsilon; \varepsilon)/A\varepsilon$, $d^{*'} = D(k^*, d^*, A\varepsilon; \varepsilon)/A\varepsilon$, and $l = L(k^*, d^*, A\varepsilon; \varepsilon)/A\varepsilon$. Now the model's solution is expressed in a stationary form. Observe that these transformed allocation rules will also satisfy (10), (11), and (12)—together with (3)—if β and z are changed to β^* and z^*, where $\beta^* \equiv \beta(A\varepsilon)^{q+1}$ and $z^* \equiv A\varepsilon$.[16]

Solution Algorithm

Let the system of equations (10), (11), and (12) defining a stationary solution to the model—once c^* and h^* been solved out for using (3) and (9)—be more compactly represented by

$$\Delta(k^*, d^*, k^{*'}, d^{*'}, l; \varepsilon) = \int \Lambda(k^{*'}, d^{*'}, l', k^{*''}, d^{*''}; \varepsilon, \varepsilon') d\varepsilon'. \tag{A1}$$

Here $\Delta: \mathbb{R}^6_+ \to \mathbb{R}^3_+$ and $\Lambda: \mathbb{R}^6_+ \to \mathbb{R}^3_+$. In order to simulate the model, a set of policy functions of the form $k^* = K(k^*, d^*; \varepsilon)$, $d^* = D(k^*, d^*; \varepsilon)$, and $l = L(k^*, d^*; \varepsilon)$ must be found that solves this system of integral equations. To do this, an algorithm proposed by Coleman (1988) is employed that approximates the true equilibrium allocation rules over a grid using a multilinear interpolation scheme.[17]

To begin with, assume that the technology shock, ε, is an element of the time invariant set $E = \{\varepsilon_1, \ldots, \varepsilon_p\}$. Next, restrict the permissible range of values for the stocks of capital and durables to lie in the closed intervals $[k_1, k_m]$ and $[d_1, d_n]$, respectively, and let $K = \{k_1, k_2, \ldots, k_m\}$ and $D = \{d_1, d_2, \ldots, d_n\}$ represent sets of monotonically increasing grid points that span these intervals. Now, make an initial guess for the value of the function $x = X(k^*, d^*, \varepsilon)$, for $x = k^{*'}$, $d^{*'}$, and l, at each of the $m \times n \times p$ points in the set $K \times D \times E$. Denote the value for the initial guess of the function X at the grid point (k_h, d_i, e_j) by $X^0(k_h, d_i, e_j)$. A guess for X at other points in its domain $[k_1, k_m] \times [d_1, d_n] \times E$ is then constructed through multilinear interpolation (see Press et al. 1986). Specifically, take some point $(k^*, d^*, \varepsilon_j) \in [k_1, k_m] \times [d_1, d_n] \times E$. The value of the function X^0 at the point or $(k^*, d^*, \varepsilon_j)$, or $X^0(k^*, d^*, \varepsilon_j)$, is defined as follows:

$$X^0(k^*, d^*, \varepsilon_j) = (1 - u)(1 - v)X^0(k_h, d_i, \varepsilon_j) + u(1 - v)X^0(k_{h+1}, d_i, \varepsilon_j)$$

$$+ uvX^0(k_{h+1}, d_{i+1}, \varepsilon_j) + (1 - u)vX^0(k_h, d_{i+1}, \varepsilon_j), \quad \text{(A2)}$$

where the weights u and v are given by

$$u = \frac{k^* - k_h}{k_{h+1} - k_h} \quad \text{and} \quad v = \frac{d^* - d_i}{d_{i+1} - d_i},$$

with the grid points k_h, k_{h+1}, d_i, and d_{i+1} being chosen such that $k_h \leqslant k^* \leqslant k_{h+1}$ and $d_i \leqslant d^* \leqslant d_{i+1}$. Thus, the interpolated value of X^0 at $(k^*, d^*, \varepsilon_j)$ is simply taken to be a weighted average of its values at the four nearest grid points. Note that the interpolated function X^0 is continuous on $[k_1, k_m] \times [d_1, d_n]$.

Given initial guesses for the functions, K, D, and L, denoted by K^0, D^0, L^0, respectively, it is straightforward to compute revised guesses, K^1, D^1, and L^1. In particular, for each grid point $(k_h, d_i, \varepsilon_j) \in K \times D \times E$, values for $K^1(k_h, d_i, \varepsilon_j)$, $D^1(k_h, d_i, \varepsilon_j)$, and $L^1(k_h, d_i, \varepsilon_j)$ can be computed by solving the following nonlinear system of equations for $k^{*\prime}$, $d^{*\prime}$, and l.

$$\Delta(k_h, d_i, k^{*\prime}, d^{*\prime}, l, \varepsilon_j) =$$

$$\sum_{r=1}^{p} \Lambda(k^{*\prime}, d^{*\prime}, L^0(k^{*\prime}, d^{*\prime}, \varepsilon_r), K^0(k^{*\prime}, d^{*\prime}, \varepsilon_r), D^0(k^{*\prime}, d^{*\prime}, \varepsilon_r); \varepsilon_j, \varepsilon_r). \quad \text{(A3)}$$

Given values for $k^{*\prime}$, $d^{*\prime}$, and l at each of the $m \times n \times p$ grid points in $K \times D \times E$, the functions K^1, D^1, and L^1 can be extended over the entire domain $[k_1, k_m] \times [d_1, d_n] \times E$ via interpolation, as was done previously. The functions K^1, D^1, and L^1 are then used as guesses on the next iteration, with the whole procedure being repeated until the allocation rules have converged.

Once the allocation rules have been obtained, the model can be simulated and various sample statistics for variables of interest computed. Variables need to be converted back to their nonstationary form when simulating the model. This merely requires multiplying the stationary value of a variable at a point in time by the lagged value of z. Thus, $x = x_t^* z_{t-1}$ for $x = c$, k, and d.

Notes

This chapter is reproduced with permission from the *Journal of Political Economy*, Vol. 99, No. 6, December 1991. Discussions with John Coleman and Edward Prescott have been extremely helpful in preparing this paper. Also, skillful research assistance from George Hall and comments made by two referees are gratefully acknowledged. The second author thanks the Foerder Institute for financial support.

The views expressed herein are those of the authors and not necessarily those of the Federal Reserve Bank of Minneapolis or the Federal Reserve System.

1. Gronau (1986) surveys the literature on household production.

2. Prescott (1986) states that "to a first approximation, the process on the percentage change on the technology process is a random walk with drift plus some serially uncorrelated measurement error" (p. 15). Another reasonable form for the technology process is $z_{t+1} = A^t z_t^\rho \varepsilon_t$, where $A > 1$ and $\rho \in (0, 1)$. As an empirical matter, it turns out to be hard to discriminate between these two technology processes. Benhabib, Rogerson, and Wright (1991) treat the second case while allowing the technology shock in the market and nonmarket sectors to be different —this latter feature of their analysis is discussed later.

3. It is straightforward to introduce irreversible investment into the analysis, albeit at some expense in notation. Let $p_k = P_k(s, \varepsilon)$ and $p_d = P_d(s, \varepsilon)$ represent the prices of business and household capital. When a capital good is being produced in the economy, its price must be unity, since any agent can freely transform output into capital. Thus, if $K(s, \varepsilon) > (1 - \delta_k)K$, then $P_k(s, \varepsilon) = 1$, and if $D(s, \varepsilon) > (1 - \delta_k)D$, then $P_d(s, \varepsilon) = 1$. If a capital good is not being produced, then its price must adjust to clear the used market for it. Consequently, if $K(s, \varepsilon) = (1 - \delta_k)K$, then $P_k(s, \varepsilon) \leqslant 1$, and if $D(s, \varepsilon) = (1 - \delta_k)D$, then $P_d(s, \varepsilon) \leqslant 1$. The household's budget constraint (8) now appears as

$$c + P_k(s, \varepsilon)k' + P_d(s, \varepsilon)d' = (1 - \tau_k)R(s, \varepsilon)k + (1 - \tau_l)W(s, \varepsilon)l + P_k(s, \varepsilon)(1 - \delta_k)k$$
$$+ P_d(s, \varepsilon)(1 - \delta_d)d + M(s, \varepsilon).$$

The classic treatment of this problem is contained in Sargent (1980). In the simulations undertaken, the irreversibility constraints, $K(s, \varepsilon) \geqslant (1 - \delta_k)K$ and $D(s, \varepsilon) \geqslant (1 - \delta_d)D$, are never binding for two reasons: first, the economy is growing over time, and second, the stock of old capital depreciates each period.

4. This definition presupposes that at the start of time the initial conditions $k = \hat{k}$ and $d = \hat{d}$ hold; that is, at the time the world begins, the aggregate stocks of business and household capital should coincide with the stocks of business and household capital held by the representative household.

5. Kydland (1984) shows that within the C.E.S. family of utility functions, only the specification corresponding to unitary elasticity (the Cobb-Douglas form) is consistent with balanced growth with stationary labor time. As shown in King, Plosser, and Rebelo (1988), the same holds with the more general structure

$$U(c, 1 - l) = \begin{cases} \dfrac{c^{1-\gamma}}{1 - \gamma} V(1 - l), & \text{if } 0 < \gamma \text{ and } \gamma \neq 1 \\ \text{and} \\ lnc + V(1 - l), & \text{if } \gamma = 1, \end{cases}$$

where $V(\cdot)$ is such that $U(\cdot)$ satisfies the standard properties.

6. For the reader unfamilar with the real business cycle literature, the H-P filter fits a smooth, slowly varying curve through time series data. See Prescott (1986) and Dantbine and Donaldson (1991) for more detail.

7. The source: *Fixed Reproducible Tangible Wealth in the United States, 1925–1985*, Bureau of Economic Analysis, U.S. Department of Commerce, June 1987.

8. This seems in line with the tax rates reported in Hausman and Poterba (1987).

9. The first average was calculated by taking the mean over the 1954–1989 sample period of (total weekly hours of work—from the Household Survey)/(16–64 population × 7 days × 16 hours per day).

10. Recall there is no notion of leisure in the model. This simplifies the quantitative analysis. Here time and capital are simply divided into their market and nonmarket components. Leisure could be incorporated into the model by subdividing nonmarket time into homework and leisure time. One man's recreation is another man's toil. Should household activities such as exercising, gardening, or renovating be counted as work or leisure, and similarly, should business activities such as entertaining be considered leisure or work? According to Becker (1965), "although the social philosopher might have to define precisely the concept of leisure, the economist can reach all his traditional results as well as many more without introducing it at all" (p. 504). Gronau (1986) provides an operational definition of leisure by defining work at home to be those activities for which one could hire someone else to do. He suggests that it is impossible to enjoy leisure vicariously. There is some cross sectional data that breaks down nonmarket time into homework and leisure time. More problematic for the questions being addressed here, though, would be undertaking the corresponding breakdown for the stock of household capital. The two hypotheses are likely to be observationally equivalent, suggests Gronau (1986). Indeed, Benhabib, Rogerson and Wright (1991) include leisure time in their study and arrive at similar conclusions to the current chapter.

11. Along a balanced growth path, the level of market goods, c, home goods, h, tax revenue, μ, and welfare, W, will be functions of the tax rates τ_k and τ_l (as well as the parameters describing taste and technology). It is straightforward to deduce (see appendix) that one can write $c = zc(\tau_k, \tau_l)$, $h = zh(\tau_k, \tau_l)$, and $\mu = z\mu(\tau_k, \tau_l)$, where $c(\cdot)$, $h(\cdot)$, and $\mu(\cdot)$ are time-invariant functions. Consequently, W can be expressed as $W = z^q W(\tau_k, \tau_l) \equiv z^q U(c(\tau_k, \tau_l), h(\tau_k, \tau_l))$, given the assumed homogeneity property of the momentary utility function. (By *trivially* modifying the line of argument being pursued here a constant term could be added to the momentary utility function, as in (15).) The marginal welfare cost of capital taxation is defined as

$$[z^q W_1(\tau_k, \tau_l)/z^{q-1} U_1(c(\tau_k, \tau_l), h(\tau_k, \tau_l))]/z\mu_1(\tau_k, \tau_l)$$

$$= [W_1(\tau_k, \tau_l)/U_1(c(\tau_k, \tau_l), h(\tau_k, \tau_l))]/\mu_1(\tau_k, \tau_l).$$

12. The findings for the model without household capital are:

	Standard deviation (Percent)	Autocorrelation	Correlation with output
Output	1.6	0.42	1.00
Consumption	1.1	0.48	0.98
Business investment	4.3	0.35	0.97
Market time	0.4	0.35	0.92

These results were obtained by setting $\omega = 0.0004$ in the benchmark model while dropping equation (27) from the calibration procedure.

13. Note that changing this parameter implies recalculating ω and θ using the steady-state equations for model 2. One now obtains $\omega = 0.11$ and $\theta = 0.26$. For the configuration of parameters values used in model 2, the marginal welfare cost of capital taxation is 2.6 and for labor taxation is 0.64.

14. Real business cycle models have some difficulty in accounting for the cyclical behavior of factor prices. In the U.S. data, real wages have a standard deviation of 1.1 percent and a correlation with output of 0.61. The corresponding numbers for the model are 1.1 and 0.95. The return on capital has a standard deviation of 6.9 percent and a correlation with output of 0.77 in the data, with the figures for the model being 1.9 percent and 0.49. Thus real wages are too procyclical in the model, and the return on capital not procyclical enough. Benhabib, Rogerson, and Wright (1991) address the wage rate observation by allowing the technology shock in the business and household sectors to be different. Ceterus paribus, a positive shock to household technology leads to a rise in the real wage rate but a fall in market output. Consequently, in a model with separate business and household technology shocks, the correlation between the wage rate and output will be reduced. An alternative strategy would be to assume that built into wage payments is an insurance component designed to protect workers against cyclical risk. This would operate to dampen the procyclical movement in wages and make the return on capital move more procyclically.

15. Some limited experimentation with other configurations of parameter values had little success in accounting for the stylized facts on investment. For instance, it may seem reasonable to conjecture that making capital and time more substitutable in market production (when adopting a more general C.E.S. form) would have the same affect as making them more complementary in home production. It didn't. To get household investment to move more procyclically, the benefit from investing in household capital (the term shown in (28)) must be made to do so too. Experimentation along the above lines had little direct influence on this return. In light of this, perhaps making market and home goods more substitutable in consumption could work by dampening the countercyclical movement in the relative price of home goods. (Observe that as $\sigma \to 1$, $U_2/U_1 \to (1 - \theta)/\theta$). This does make household investment move somewhat more procyclically, but at the expense of drastically cutting the volatility of market time and output. Now the return on market time (the term shown on the left-hand side of (29)) becomes less procyclical.

16. For the transformed model, the resource constraint (9) reads:

$$c^* + z^*k^{*\prime} + z^*d^{*\prime} = F(k^*, z^*l) + (1 - \delta_k)k^* + (1 - \delta_d)d^*$$

This is readily verified by dividing both sides of (9) through by the lagged value of z.

17. Coleman's (1988) technique is related to one developed by Baxter (1988) and Danthine and Donaldson (1990). In a nutshell, the principle difference between the method of Baxter (1988) and Danthine and Donaldson (1990) on the one hand, and Coleman (1988) on the other, is that the former restricts the range of the functions

describing the laws of motion for the state variables to lie on a grid while the latter does not.

References

Baxter, Marianne. 1988. Approximating Suboptimal Dynamic Equilibria: An Euler Equation Approach. Working Paper 139. Rochester, N.Y.: Rochester Center for Economic Research, University of Rochester.

Becker, Gary S. 1965. "A Theory of the Allocation of Time." *The Economic Journal* 229: (September) 493–517.

Benhabib, Jess; Rogerson, Richard; and Wright, Randall. 1991. Homework in Macroeconomics: Household Production and Aggregate Fluctuations. *Journal of Political Economy* 99: (December) 1166–1187.

Ben-Porath, Yoram. 1967. "The Production of Human Capital and the Life Cycle of Earnings." *Journal of Political Economy* 75: (August) 352–365.

Christiano, Lawrence J. 1988. "Why Does Inventory Investment Fluctuate so Much?" *Journal of Monetary Economics* 21: (March/May) 247–280.

Coleman, Wilbur John. 1988. Money, Interest, and Capital in a Cash-in-Advance Economy. International Finance Discussion Paper 323. Washington, D.C. Board of Governors of the Federal Reserve System.

Danthine, Jean-Pierre, and Donaldson, John B. 1990. "Efficiency Wages and the Business Cycle Puzzle." *European Economic Review* 34: (November) 1275–1301.

Gronau, Reuben. 1986. "Home Production—A Survey." In Orley Ashenfelter and Richard Layard, eds., *Handbook of Labor Economics*, Vol. 1. Amsterdam: Elsevier Science Publishers BV.

Hansen, Gary D. 1985. "Indivisible Labor and the Business Cycle." *Journal of Monetary Economics* 16: (November) 309–327.

Hausman, Jerry A., and Poterba, James M. 1987. "Household Behavior and the Tax Reform Act of 1986." *Journal of Economic Perspectives* 1: (Summer) 101–119.

Jorgenson, Dale W., and Yun, Kun-Young. 1986. "Tax Policy and Capital Allocation." *Scandinavian Journal of Economics* 88: (June) 355–377.

King, Robert E.; Plosser, Charles, I.; and Rebelo, Sergio T. 1988. "Production, Growth, and Business Cycles, I and II." *Journal of Monetary Economics* 21: (March/May) 195–232 and 309–341.

Kydland, Finn E., and Prescott, Edward C. 1982. "Time-to-Build and Aggregate Fluctuations." *Econometrica* 50: (November) 1345–70.

Kydland, Finn E. 1984. "Labor-Force Heterogeneity and the Business Cycle." *Carnegie-Rochester Conference Series on Public Policy* 21: (Autumn) 173–208.

Long, John B., and Plosser, Charles I. 1983. "Real Business Cycles." *Journal of Political Economy* 91: (February) 39–69.

Prescott, Edward C. 1986. "Theory Ahead of Business Cycle Measurement." *Federal Reserve Bank of Minneapolis Quarterly Review* 10: (Fall) 9–22.

Press, William H.; Flannery, Brian P.; Teukolsky, Saul A.; and Vetterling, William T. 1986. *Numerical Recipes: The Art of Scientific Computing.* Cambridge: Cambridge University Press.

Rogerson, Richard. 1988. "Indivisible Labor, Lotteries, and Equilibrium." *Journal of Monetary Economics* 21: (January) 3–16.

Sargent, Thomas J. 1980. "Tobin's q and the Rate of Investment in General Equilibrium." *Carnegie-Rochester Conference Series on Public Policy* 12: (Spring) 107–154.

12

Identification and the Liquidity Effect of a Monetary Policy Shock

Lawrence J. Christiano
and Martin Eichenbaum

Conventional wisdom holds that unanticipated expansionary monetary policy shocks cause transient but persistent decreases in real and nominal interest rates. However, there is virtually no formal econometric evidence in the literature to support this contention. (See Reichenstein 1987 for a review of the literature.) Indeed, many empirical studies have concluded that the data support the opposite view, namely, that unexpected shocks to monetary policy actually raise, rather than lower, short-term interest rates. (See, for example, Mishkin 1981, 1982 and R. King 1991.) This finding typically is rationalized as reflecting the weakness of liquidity effects associated with expansionary monetary policy and the relative strength of expected inflation effects on nominal interest rates. (See, for example, Mishkin 1981, 1982 or S. R. King 1983.) We argue here that an analysis of the data that pays particular attention to the problem of measuring monetary policy shocks reveals substantial support for the conventional wisdom. Existing results in the literature that purport to cast doubt on that wisdom are not robust to plausible changes in identifying assumptions or to alternative ways of measuring money.

Analysts of monetary policy must confront two problems. One is just which measure of money to use. After all, we have at our disposal a plethora of measures ranging from narrow, direct measures of open market operations such as nonborrowed reserves (NBR) to relatively broad aggregates such as M2. The choice of money measure has important implications for inference because different monetary aggregates interact in very different ways with short-term interest rates. The other problem is which set of identifying assumptions to adopt to measure the exogenous component (if any) of changes in monetary policy. Without such assumptions, causal inference is simply not possible. In practice, these two choices—of monetary aggregate and identifying assumptions—cannot be viewed as distinct problems because there is no reason to believe that any given set of identifying assumptions will be equally appropriate across different measures of money.

These difficulties notwithstanding, empirical work on the liquidity effects of monetary policy almost always uses high-order monetary aggregates like M1.[1] This choice of monetary aggregate is usually coupled with the identifying assumption that the monetary policy disturbance corresponds to the statistical innovation in money. Put differently, innovations to objects like M1 are entirely attributed to the actions of the monetary authority.[2] In our view, an alternative assumption is at least as plausible, namely, that innovations to NBR capture Fed policy shocks, while innovations to broader aggregates confound many other shocks, in addition to policy shocks.[3]

In contrast to the existing literature, in this chapter we use various measures of money and different identifying assumptions to measure unanticipated shocks to monetary policy.[4] For each measure of money considered (NBR, the monetary base, M0, and M1), we engage in a specification search across the elements of two classes of identifying assumptions. The first class, which we call *M-rules*, is defined by the assumption that unanticipated changes in monetary policy can be measured by some orthogonalized component of the innovation to the monetary aggregate. Each such component corresponds to a different assumption regarding the variables included in the contemporaneous portion of the Federal Reserve Open Market Committee's (FOMC's) reaction function for setting the monetary aggregate. While quite natural, this class of identifying assumptions is by no means noncontroversial. McCallum (1983), Sims (1986, 1991), and Bernanke and Blinder (1990) have argued that—at least for high-order aggregates like M1 and M2—unanticipated shocks to monetary policy are best measured as the innovation in the federal funds rate. For this reason, we consider a second class of identifying restrictions that is defined by the assumption that unanticipated changes in monetary policy can be measured by some orthogonalized component of the innovation to the federal funds rate. Each such component corresponds to a different assumption about the variables included in the contemporaneous portion of the FOMC's rule for setting the federal funds rate. We refer to this class of policy rules as *R-rules*.[5]

Our empirical analysis reveals that inference about the effects of monetary policy on interest rates hinges critically on both the identifying assumptions exploited and the measure of money used. Certainly we have found combinations of monetary aggregate and identification schemes that together generate challenges to the conventional view. But in every such instance the associated measure of unanticipated shocks to monetary policy generates seemingly implausible implications about things other than interest rates. When these combinations of monetary aggregates and identification schemes are eliminated, the remaining combinations all yield results that strongly support the conventional view. Specifically, using exactly identified vector autoregressions, we find that when identifying assumptions corresponding to M-rules are coupled with either M0 or M1, unanticipated changes in monetary policy generate increases in the federal funds rate. However, so identified, unanticipated expansionary monetary policy shocks generate sharp, persistent declines in aggregate output. Indeed, our point estimates indicate that, for M1, real gross national product (GNP) falls for over nine years. One cannot accept the interest rate implications of these measures of monetary policy shocks without also accepting these seemingly implausible aggregate output implications.[6]

Inference with M0 and M1 is greatly affected by moving to the class of identifying restrictions corresponding to R-rules. Under these circumstances, we find that unanticipated changes in monetary policy generate sharp, persistent declines in the federal funds rate. Moreover, when measured in this way, unanticipated expansionary monetary policy generates persistent increases in aggregate real output. We infer that if one insists on using high-order monetary aggregates to study the effects of monetary policy on interest rates, this class of identifying restrictions is preferable to the class of M-rules.

Interestingly, in sharp contrast to results based on M0 or M1, inference about the effects of monetary policy on interest rates is very robust when the aggregate NBR is used in the analysis. Regardless of whether we work with M- or R-rules, regardless of whether we work with monthly or quarterly data, and regardless of which postwar sample period we work with, the same result emerges. Unanticipated expansionary policy shocks drive down short-term interest rates for substantial periods of time. Measured in this way, expansionary monetary policy shocks also generate increases in real GNP. It is hard to imagine reconciling these findings with models that are empirically plausible and yet do not incorporate quantitatively important liquidity effects.[7] Building on earlier contributions by Grossman and Weiss (1983) and Rotemberg (1984), recent work by Lucas (1990), Fuerst (1990), Baxter et al. (1990), Christiano (1991), and Christiano and Eichenbaum (1991) has stressed the importance of liquidity effects for explaining the comovements between interest rates and monetary aggregates. We view our results as being very supportive of that work.

The chapter is organized as follows. In section 12.1 we present some basic facts about the dynamic (unconditional) correlations between different monetary aggregates and the federal funds rate. Three key facts emerge. First, the federal funds rate displays a sharp, robust, negative correlation with NBR. This negative correlation is masked by moving to higher-order monetary aggregates. Second, once we control for the behavior of borrowed reserves (BR), MO behaves much like NBR. Third, the federal funds rate displays sharp, persistent, negative comovements with real GNP. The dynamic correlations between these two time series are estimated very precisely and are very robust to sample period selection. While highly suggestive, the results cannot be taken as evidence of any specific causal mechanism. In particular, they cannot be used to formally infer that unanticipated expansionary monetary policy disturbances cause interest rates to fall and aggregate real output to rise. Such conclusions necessarily rely on theoretical restrictions that enable the analyst to identify the exogenous component of monetary policy disturbances. This issue is addressed in section 12.2, where we abandon the sharp distinction between theory and measurement and use vector autoregressions to interpret the relationship between money and interest rates. Finally, in section 12.3 we summarize our findings.

12.1 Some Basic Facts: The Dynamic Correlations Between Money, the Federal Funds Rate, and Real Output

In this section we report some basic facts about the dynamic correlations between different measures of money, the nominal federal funds rate, and aggregate output. Our primary findings are that the nominal federal funds rate displays strong negative comovements with different measures of the growth rate of money and of aggregate real output. The relationship between the federal funds rate and aggregate real output, as summarized by their dynamic correlations, is estimated very precisely and is very robust across different sampling periods as well as different stationary-inducing transformations of the data. The negative relationship between the federal funds rate and the growth rate of money is most pronounced and most stable when NBR is used as the measure of money.

In presenting these findings, we are mindful of the obvious caveat that correlations do not imply causality. Still, the results in this section serve at least three useful functions. First, these correlations represent important moments of the data that any business cycle model ought to be consistent with. Second, the correlations suggest that monetary business cycle models that display significant, persistent liquidity effects will be useful for interpreting the data. Finally, they provide a useful background for the vector autoregression analysis of section 12.2.

Choosing Measures of Short-Term Interest Rates and Money

Figure 12.1 displays the nominal federal funds rate (FF), the six-month nominal commercial paper rate, and the three-month nominal treasury bill rate over the sample period from the first quarter of 1959 to the first quarter of 1990 (1959:1–1990:1). Notice that these different short-term interest rates exhibit similar trends and move together quite closely. In what follows, we display results based on FF for two reasons. First, consistent with figure 12.1, our results are not very sensitive to which interest rate we work with. Second, numerous authors have stressed the important role that the federal funds rate plays in monetary policy. (See, for example, Bernanke 1990, Bernanke and Blinder 1990 and Kuttner and Friedman 1990.) Working with the federal funds rate facilitates comparisons with this literature.

Choosing which measure of money to work with is a much more difficult task. Existing monetary theories of the business cycle are simply too

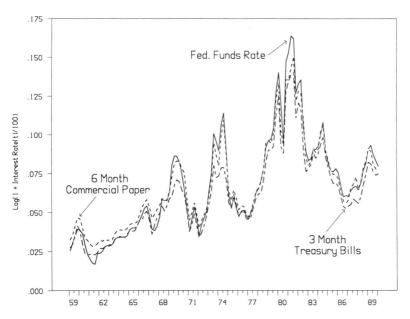

Figure 12.1
Three short-term interest rates, 1959:1–1990:1.

abstract to warrant focusing on any one measure of money. Adding to the difficulty is the fact that different components of any given measure of money often behave in very different ways. Consider, for example, high-powered money, M0, which is the sum of currency in the hands of the public, plus NBR, plus BR. As we shall show, the federal funds rate is negatively correlated with NBR but positively correlated with BR.

In part, the different behavior of NBR and BR simply reflects the institutional reality of how BR is determined. Of particular note is that discount window borrowing is administered under a set of guidelines that is independent of the deliberations of the FOMC. (See Goodfriend and Whelpley 1986 or Stigum 1990.)[8] In contrast, the FOMC directly controls, by open market operations, the level of NBR. From this perspective, NBR seems like a natural measure of money to use in identifying and estimating the effects of shocks to monetary policy. At the same time, we recognize that NBR is not necessarily the best measure of money for assessing the overall empirical plausibility of monetary business cycle models. Consequently, we also present results using M0 and M1. Finally, because of the importance of BR for some of the moments we discuss, we also display results using BR, M0 less BR, and M1 less BR.

Figures 12.2a and 12.2b display seasonally adjusted average quarterly NBR (adjusted to include extended credit) and FF over the sample period 1959:1 to 1990:1. As can be seen, both exhibit a strong positive trend. Other measures of the money supply, such as the level of M0 and M1, also display pronounced trends over this sample period. Consequently, some stationary-inducing transformation of the data must be adopted in order to calculate meaningful statistics. In this section, we work primarily with the filter developed by Hodrick and Prescott (1980). However, we also present results with linearly detrended data and growth rates. The bold lines in figures 12.2a and 12.2b display the Hodrick-Prescott (HP) trend component of NBR and FF, respectively. In figure 12.3a we display the HP-filtered versions of NBR and FF. Note the pronounced negative association between these variables. This basic fact is reflected in all of the formal statistics presented in this section. Figure 12.3b presents the HP-filtered versions of FF and real GNP. FF is positively correlated with the contemporaneous level of GNP but negatively correlated with future levels of GNP.

A Benchmark Scenario

Before discussing our empirical results, we digress to consider the question, What pattern of dynamic correlations would we expect to find in the

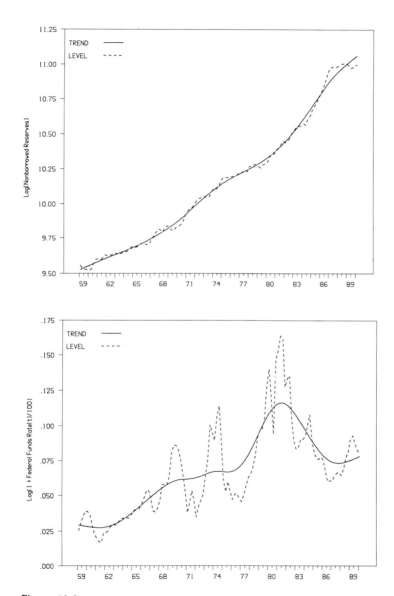

Figure 12.2
(a) Nonborrowed reserves with HP trend, 1959:1–1990:1; (b) federal funds rate with HP
trend, 1959:1–1990:1.

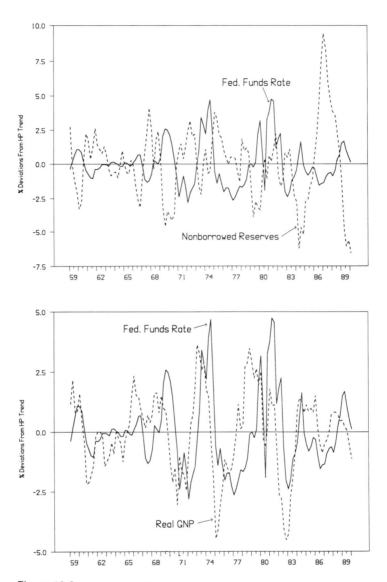

Figure 12.3
(a) HP-filtered federal funds rate and nonborrowed reserves, 1959:1–1990:1;
(b) HP-filtered federal funds rate and real GNP, 1959:1–1990:1.

presence of liquidity effects? A precise answer to this question obviously requires a formal model.[9] Still it seems worthwhile appealing to existing models in the literature to provide some perspective on our reduced-form results. In so doing we assume, as is the case for our measures of money, that money, M_t, is positively correlated over time. Also, for simplicity, we consider a benchmark scenario in which the only shocks are to the money supply.

Consider first the correlation between FF_t and future values of M_t. Suppose that, at time t, there was an unanticipated increase in the money supply. Given a liquidity effect, this would be associated with a decline in FF_t. With M_t positively correlated over time, high values of M_t would be associated with high values of $M_{t+\tau}$, for $\tau > 0$. Other things being equal, then, we would expect FF_t to be negatively correlated with future values of M_t, with the exact magnitude of the correlation depending on the size of the liquidity effect and the degree of serial correlation in M_t.

Next consider the correlation between FF_t and past values of M_t. Suppose that at time $t - \tau$, for $\tau > 0$, there was an unanticipated increase in the money supply. This would exert negative pressure on $FF_{t-\tau}$. Suppose that M_t is sufficiently autocorrelated that the initial increase in $M_{t-\tau}$ is associated with higher growth rates in $M_{t-\tau+j}$ for $j \geq 1$. This, we expect, would generate an increase in the anticipated rate of inflation from time $t - \tau + j$, for $j \geq 1$. If the liquidity effect lasted only one period, then the inflation effect would dominate after one period, so that $FF_{t-\tau+j}$, for $j \geq 1$, would rise. Consequently, $FF_{t-\tau+j}$, for $j \geq 1$, would be positively correlated with $M_{t-\tau}$, that is, $\rho(FF_t, M_{t-\tau}) > 0$ for $\tau \geq 1$, where $\rho(\cdot, \cdot)$ denotes the correlation operator. In fact, there is no reason to believe that the liquidity effect lasts for only one period. Suppose instead that it dominated the expected inflation effect for k periods. Then $\rho(FF_t, M_{t-\tau})$ would be negative for $\tau \leq k$, but positive for $\tau > k$. In this sense, k can be thought as measuring the persistence of the liquidity effect.

While useful for pedagogical purposes, the logic of the previous scenario holds only if the sole source of aggregate uncertainty is shocks to the money supply. With other shocks to the system, the dynamic correlation between FF and the stock of money depends, at least in part, on the way the FOMC reacts to the other shocks. For example, shocks that stimulate money demand tend to create a positive association between money and interest rates in an environment where the Fed seeks to smooth nominal interest rates. Still, were the pattern of correlations arising from our benchmark scenario completely absent from the data, we would have no obvious reason to seek evidence for liquidity effects in the context of more complicated, multiple-shock representations of the data. In fact, the actual pattern of correlations is consistent with our benchmark scenario. This provides additional motivation for the analysis of section 12.2, where we abandon the one-shock premise of the benchmark scenario and analyze the data using exactly identified vector autoregressive representations of the data.

The Dynamic Correlations between the Nominal Federal Funds Rate and Money

Figure 12.4 presents, graphically, our point estimates of $\rho(FF_t, M_{t-\tau})$ for $\tau = -8, \ldots, 8$, corresponding to three stationary-inducing transformations of the data: HP-filtered (the first column), linear detrending (the second column), and growth rates (the third column). The three rows contain results pertaining to NBR, M0, and M1 as the measure of money. All correlations

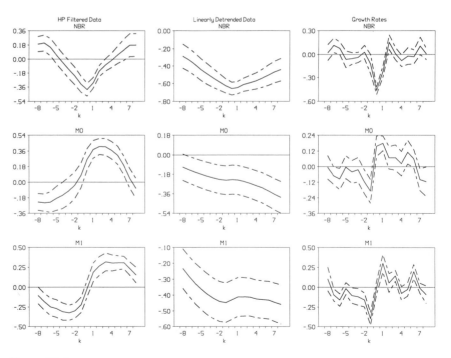

Figure 12.4
Correlation (federal funds rate(t), M(t − k)), k = −8, . . . , 8, M = NBR, M0, M1, 1959:1−1990:1.

are based on variables that have been logged prior to the stationary-inducing transformation. Figure 12.5 presents the analog results for BR, M0 less BR, and M1 less BR. The solid lines in figures 12.4 and 12.5 denote point estimates of the correlations in question, along with a two-standard-deviation band, given by the dashed lines. (Standard errors were computed using a generalized method of moments procedure.)

We begin by discussing results obtained with HP-filtered versions of the data. Consider first the estimated values for $\rho(FF_t, M_{t-\tau})$ for $\tau = -8, \ldots, 8$, when NBR is used as the measure of money. Three findings here are notable. First, there is a strong, statistically significant, negative contemporaneous correlation (equal to -0.39) between FF_t and M_t. This is consistent with the impression conveyed by figure 12.3. Second, FF_t is negatively correlated with leads and lags of M_t up to one year. Third, FF_t is positively correlated with $M_{t-\tau}$ for $\tau > 4$. These three findings are consistent with the benchmark scenario in which a liquidity effect of a monetary policy shock dominates the anticipated inflation effect for a period as long as a year.[10]

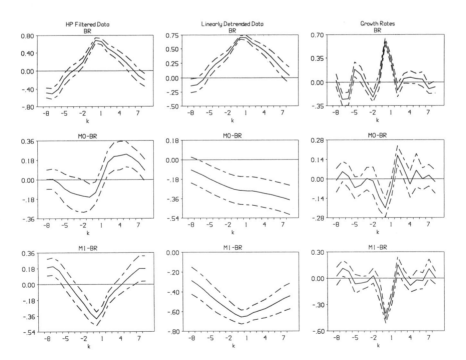

Figure 12.5
Correlation (federal funds rate(t), M($t - k$)), $k = -8, \ldots, 8$, M = BR, M0 $-$ BR, M1 $-$ BR, 1959:1–1990:1.

The point estimates obtained with the broader measures of money display a somewhat different pattern. As with NBR, our point estimate of $\rho(FF_t, M_t)$ is negative when M1 is used as the measure of money (-0.02). However, unlike with NBR, the maximal negative correlation occurs at $\tau = -3$ rather than $\tau = 0$ ($\rho(FF_t, M_{t+3}) = -0.33$). With M1, as with NBR, FF_t is negatively correlated with current and future values of money. But unlike the results obtained with NBR, with M1, FF_t is positively correlated with all past values of money. Interpreted from the perspective of the benchmark scenario, these results are consistent with the existence of a strong liquidity effect, but one which is less persistent than the effect observed with NBR.

The only measure of money with which FF_t displays a positive contemporaneous correlation is M0 ($\rho(FF_t, M_t) = 0.25$). Even here, though, FF_t is negatively correlated with $M0_{t+\tau}$, for $\tau \geqslant 1$. As it turns out, the negative contemporaneous correlation between M0 and FF is attributable entirely to the BR component of M0. As figure 12.5 reveals, HP-filtered BR displays a very strong positive contemporaneous correlation with HP-filtered FF_t. Presumably this reflects the incentive of banks to increase BR in response to an increase in FF and the practice of accommodating transient increases in bank demand for reserves through discount window lending. (See Thomas 1982, Goodfriend 1983, Goodfriend and Whelpley 1986, and Stigum 1990.) Notice that when BR is subtracted from M0, the resulting dynamic correlations are very similar to those between FF and NBR. As might be expected, subtracting BR from M1 strengthens the negative correlation between FF_t and current and future values of M_t but dampens the positive correlation between FF_t and past values of M_t.

Consider next the results of working with growth rates of the data. Three features of these results are worth noting. For every measure of money, there is a strong negative correlation between FF_t and M_t, regardless of whether or not we control for BR. In addition, the growth rate of FF_t is negatively correlated with future values of the growth rates in NBR, M0, and M1. Finally, FF_t is positively correlated with past values of growth rates in M0 and M1. This tendency is less pronounced with NBR.

Consider next our results with linearly detrended data. A number of comments are in order here. First, with this stationary-inducing transformation, FF is negatively correlated with current levels of the money supply and all its leads and lags ($\tau = -8, \ldots, 0, \ldots, +8$) regardless of whether NBR, or M0, or M1 is used. Second, with M0 and M1, the shape of the correlation functions using HP-filtered data and linearly detrended data are quite different. In our view, this reflects the dubious validity of the assump-

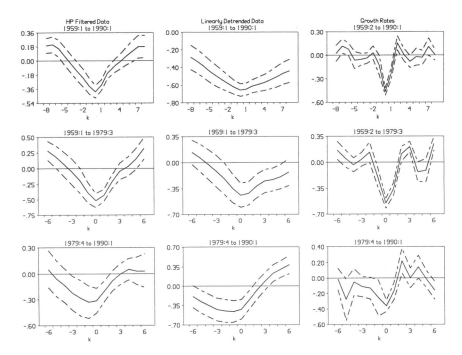

Figure 12.6
Correlation (federal funds rate(t), NBR$(t - k)$), $k = -8, \ldots, 8$.

tion that M0 and M1 are well represented as trend-stationary processes with a constant trend over the sample period as a whole. (See Stock and Watson 1989b, who argue that, over this period, the money growth rate has an upward trend.)

In order to assess the sensitivity of our results to sample period selection, we redid our analysis allowing for a break in the data at 1979:3. Figures 12.6, 12.7, and 12.8 present our results for NBR, M0, and M1, respectively, for the sampling intervals 1959:1–1990:1, 1959:1–1979:3, and 1979:4–1990:1. From figure 12.6 we see that, despite some differences, the results obtained with NBR are very stable across sample periods. However, figure 12.7 reveals considerable sample period sensitivity with M0. As a rule, the post-1979 and full sample correlation functions are similar, at least when we work with HP-filtered data or growth rates. However, the pre- and post-1979 periods results are quite different—so different, in fact, that inference regarding the plausibility of the benchmark scenario is substantially influenced by sample period selection. For the post-1979 period, the dynamic

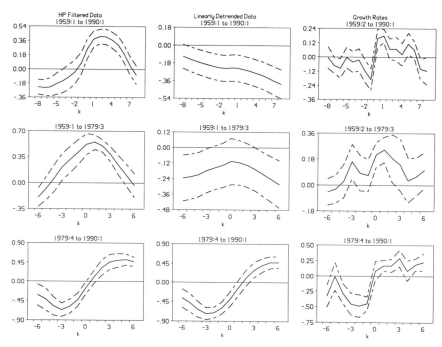

Figure 12.7
Correlation (federal funds rate(*t*), M0(*t* − *k*)), *k* = −8, ..., 8.

correlations appear to be entirely consistent with that scenario. For example, working with HP-filtered data, we find that $\rho(FF_t, M0_{t-\tau}) < 0$ for $\tau < 1$. In contrast, the pre-1979 results seem difficult to reconcile with the benchmark scenario. Finally, figure 12.8 reveals that sample period sensitivity with M1 is intermediate to the two polar cases of NBR and M0.

We summarize our findings for the correlations between money and interest rates as follows. First, when NBR is used, our results are consistent with what is to be expected from the benchmark scenario. This is true regardless of which stationary-inducing transformation or sample period is used. Second, the results with M0 and M1 seem to depend more sensitively on the sample period used. For the post-1979 period the dynamic correlations of these aggregates seem to accord well with the benchmark scenario. Third, we find that the time series properties of BR and NBR are very different. Simply adding the two when working with monetary aggregates like M0 obscures fundamental differences in the ways that these two types of reserves interact with interest rates.

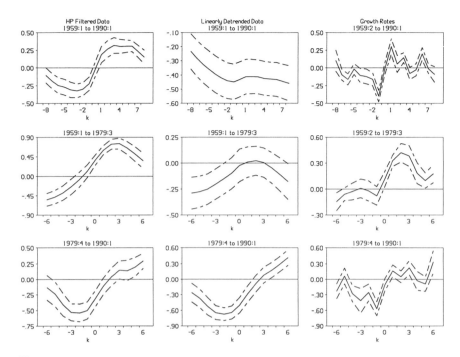

Figure 12.8
Correlation (federal funds rate(t), M1($t - k$)), $k = -8, \ldots, 8$.

We conclude this section by briefly discussing the dynamic correlations between FF and per capita real GNP (Y). These are summarized in figure 12.9, which displays our point estimates of the correlations for three stationary-inducing transformations of the data and three sample periods. Notice that, while the contemporaneous correlation between FF_t and Y_t is positive, FF_t displays a strong, sharp, negative correlation with future values of Y_t. This is true independent of which stationary-inducing transformation is used or which sample period is investigated. Interestingly, the correlation function of FF_t and Y_t seems to be estimated much more precisely than the correlation functions between money and interest rates. These results are consistent with findings by Kuttner and Friedman (1990), Bernanke (1990), Bernanke and Blinder (1990), and Stock and Watson (1989b). They show that the nominal federal funds rate is an excellent statistical predictor of real GNP, with positive movements in FF preceding declines in real GNP.

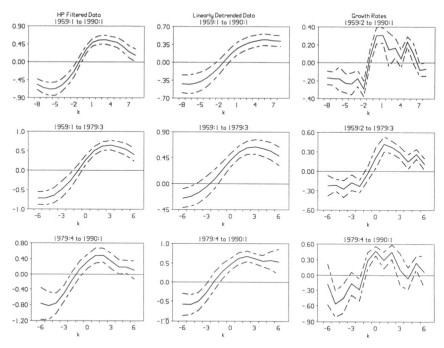

Figure 12.9
Correlation (federal funds rate(*t*), GNP(*t* − *k*)), *k* = −8, ..., 8.

12.2   Vector Autoregressions and the Liquidity Effect

We have documented the existence of a strong negative correlation between different measures of the growth rates of the money supply and GNP with the federal funds rate. However, while highly suggestive, these correlations cannot, in and of themselves, be taken as evidence that unanticipated expansionary monetary policy disturbances drive interest rates down and aggregate output up. At a minimum, providing such evidence requires identifying assumptions that are sufficiently strong to isolate a measure of monetary policy disturbances. As it turns out, inference regarding the effects of monetary policy on interest rates hinges critically on two factors: the identifying assumptions used to obtain measures of unanticipated shocks to monetary policy and the measure of money used in the analysis. As we shall show later in this section, these two factors are intimately connected. This connection is hardly surprising since the plausibility of any given set of identifying assumptions clearly depends on the measure of money used in the statistical analysis.

To clarify the nature of the identifying assumptions that have been used in the literature, suppose that the economy evolves according to

$$AZ_t = B(L)Z_{t-1} + \mu_t. \tag{1}$$

Here Z_t denotes the time t values of the variables summarizing the state of the economic system. For now we suppose that Z_t can be partitioned as $Z_t = [Z_{1t}, Z_{2t}]'$, where Z_{1t} denotes the time t values of the observable, endogenous nonpolicy variables in the system and Z_{2t} denotes the time t values of the policy instruments.

The fundamental sources of uncertainty in this economy are summarized by the i.i.d. random variable μ_t, which has the property that

$$E\mu_t\mu_t' = I, \tag{2}$$

where I denotes the identity matrix. The vector μ_t is partitioned as $\mu_t = [\mu_{1t}, \mu_{2t}]'$ where μ_{it} denotes the impulses to Z_{it} for $i = 1, 2$. With this notation, μ_{2t} represents the fundamental disturbances to policy. The constant matrix A summarizes the manner in which the contemporaneous values of Z_t are related to each other, while B(L) is a matrix polynomial in positive powers of the lag operator L. Notice that, absent restrictions on A or B(L), specification (1) embodies the notion that the reaction function of the policy maker, that is, the law of motion for Z_{2t}, depends on the current and past values of all the endogenous nonpolicy variables, Z_{1t}.

Now suppose we are interested in examining the historical effects of policy disturbances; that is, we want to characterize the dynamic effects of past variations in Z_{2t} arising from different values of μ_{2t}, on Z_{1t}. Given values for A and B(L), these responses can be calculated from the moving average representation of the system:

$$Z_t = C(L)\mu_t = \Sigma_0^\infty C_s\mu_{t-s}, \tag{3}$$

where

$$C(L) = A^{-1}[I - B(L)]^{-1}. \tag{4}$$

Under our assumptions, the (k, j) element of C_s gives the response of the kth element of Z_{t+s} to a unit disturbance in the jth element of μ_t.

In practice, the problem with this procedure is that we cannot directly observe or estimate the vector of policy disturbances, μ_{2t}. The vector autoregressive representation of Z_t implied by (1) is given by

$$Z_t = \bar{B}(L)Z_{t-1} + v_t, \tag{5}$$

where

$$\bar{B}(L) = A^{-1}B(L),$$ (6)

$$v_t = A^{-1}\mu_t,$$ (7)

and

$$Ev_t v_t' = A^{-1}(A^{-1})' = D.$$ (8)

Absent additional restrictions on the system, all that the econometrician can hope to estimate is the parameters of $\bar{B}(L)$ and D, while the parameters A and B(L) of the moving average representation (3) are not identified. One can calculate the moving average representation implied by (5),

$$Z_t = \bar{C}(L)v_t,$$ (9)

where

$$\bar{C}(L) = [I - \bar{B}(L)]^{-1}.$$ (10)

However, absent very special assumptions regarding the matrix A, the statistical innovations to Z_t, namely the v_t's, will not be the same as the fundamental disturbances to agents' environments as represented by the μ_t's. It follows that the dynamic response of nonpolicy variables in Z_t to shocks in μ_t will not coincide with the dynamic response of those variables to shocks in v_t.[11]

In order to resolve this problem, sufficiently strong restrictions must be imposed to identify the matrix A. While a variety of procedures have been adopted by empirical analysts, the type of restrictions most relevant for the existing liquidity literature is restrictions on the contemporaneous nature of feedback between the elements of Z_t, that is, restrictions on the matrix A. To this end, most researchers in the area have proceeded by adopting a particular Wold causal interpretation of the data.[12] The general idea here is to assume that the matrix A is triangular when the variables Z_t are ordered according to their causal priority. Under this assumption, there is a unique A which satisfies (8) for a given covariance matrix D. In the context of the liquidity literature, these types of identification schemes amount to a joint hypothesis about the nature of the contemporaneous portion of the monetary authority's feedback rule for its policy instruments and the sources of disturbances to the elements of Z_t. The set of M- and R-rules that we consider in this chapter fall within this class of identification schemes.

As an example, consider the sources of identification implicit in the work of Gordon and Leeper (1991), who analyze aggregate time-series data on the growth rate of the monetary base, $\Delta M0_t$; interest rates, R_t; consumer prices, P_t; and industrial production, Y_t; that is, $Z_t = [\Delta M0_t, R_t, P_t, Y_t]$. In looking for evidence of liquidity effects, Gordon and Leeper base the bulk of their inference on the moving average representation of Z_t corresponding to a lower triangular specification of the matrix A. In so doing, they identify a standardized version of the statistical innovation of $\Delta M0$ (that is, the first element in v_t) with monetary policy disturbances (that is, the first element in μ_t.) As a result, they assume monetary policy is an element of the class of M-rules, which we discussed in the introduction. The economic content of placing M0 first in the Wold causal chain is twofold: innovations to the monetary base are attributed solely to the actions of the FOMC, and in setting the growth rate of money, the FOMC does not consider the current period values of interest rates, real output, or the price level.[13] Although somewhat controversial when stated in this manner, this is perfectly consistent with the long tradition of identifying the innovation in some monetary aggregate with shocks to monetary policy. (See, for example, Mishkin 1982, Barro 1981, and R. King 1991.)[14]

In sharp contrast, Bernanke and Blinder (1990) and Sims (1986, 1991) adopt a very different set of identifying restrictions that associates innovations to the federal funds rate with unanticipated changes in monetary policy. (They analyze elements in the class of R-rules, which we referred to in the introduction.) Working with high-order monetary aggregates, these authors adopt Wold casual interpretations of the data in which some measure of short-term nominal interest rates is placed first in the ordering.[15] The economic content of this assumption is also twofold: innovations to the federal funds rate reflect solely the decisions of the FOMC, and the contemporaneous component of the FOMC's feedback rule for setting R_t does not include factors such as output, inflation, or the stock of money.

In what follows we present evidence on the liquidity effects of unanticipated changes in monetary policy using different identification schemes in conjunction with different measures of the monetary aggregate. Here, as in section 12.1, the three monetary aggregates considered are NBR, M0, and M1. All of the vector autoregressions we estimated included a measure of money, the federal funds rate, a measure of aggregate real output (Y), and the price level as measured by the GNP deflator.[16] Quarterly vector autoregressions including either NBR or M0 included five lags of all variables; those including M1 included nine lags of all variables.[17]

We begin by reporting results obtained using quarterly data over the period 1959:1–1990:1. The solid lines in figure 12.10 present the dynamic response of the federal funds rate to a shock in monetary policy, under five

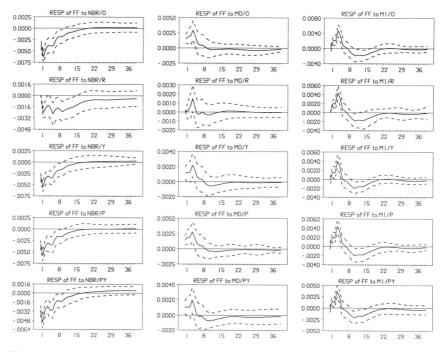

Figure 12.10
Response of federal funds rate to policy shock under M-rule (various measures of money, quarterly, 1959:1–1990:1).

different identification schemes. The dashed lines denote two standard deviation bands about point estimates of the dynamic response functions.[18] All of the identification schemes share the assumption that the unanticipated change in monetary policy is some orthogonalized component of the innovation to the monetary aggregate included in the vector autoregression. The three columns contain results pertaining to the case in which the measure of money is NBR, M0, and M1.

Each of the five rows displays the dynamic response of the federal funds rate to an unanticipated change in monetary policy generated under a different identification scheme, each of which is summarized by the label "RESP of FF to M/X," $M = \{NBR, M0, M1\}$ and $X = \{0, R, Y, P, (P, Y)\}$. The Wold ordering underlying the first row corresponds to $\{M, R, Y, P\}$. Placing M first in the ordering equates, after scaling by their standard deviation, innovations in M to unanticipated changes in monetary policy. This corresponds to the assumption that the contemporaneous portion of the monetary authority's feedback rule for setting M_t does not involve R_t, Y_t or P_t. The Wold ordering underlying the second row corresponds to $\{R, M, Y, P\}$, so that the unanticipated change in monetary policy is measured as the portion of the innovation in M_t that is orthogonal to the innovation in R_t. This corresponds to the assumption that the contemporaneous portion of the monetary authority's feedback rule involves R_t, but not P_t or Y_t. The Wold ordering underlying the third row is given by $\{Y, M, R, P\}$, so that the unanticipated change in monetary policy is measured as the portion of the innovation in M_t that is orthogonal to the innovation in Y_t, that is, the contemporaneous portion of the monetary authority's feedback rule for M_t involves Y_t, but not R_t or P_t. The Wold ordering underlying the fourth row is given by $\{P, M, R, Y\}$, so that the unanticipated change in monetary policy is measured as the portion of the innovation in M_t that is orthogonal to the innovation in P_t, that is, the contemporaneous portion of the monetary authority's feedback rule for M_t involves P_t, but not R_t or Y_t. Finally, the Wold ordering underlying the fifth row is $\{P, Y, M, R\}$, so that the unanticipated change in monetary policy is measured as the portion of the innovation in M_t that is orthogonal to innovations in P_t and Y_t; that is, in setting M_t the monetary authority looks at P_t and Y_t, but not R_t. In no case do we impose any restrictions on the lagged components of the vector autoregression (VAR).

Consider first our results with NBR. Notice that, regardless of which identification scheme is imposed, innovations to monetary policy are always followed by sharp, persistent, statistically significant declines in R_t. In all but one case, the dynamic response is the same: the immediate impact of the shock to monetary policy is to drive down R_t, which stays below its preshock level for approximately sixteen quarters. In the one exception, the second row, labeled "RESP of FF to NBR/R," the identification scheme rules out a priori a contemporaneous response of R_t. Even here, though, R_t falls in the period after the shock and stays below its preshock level for approximately twenty quarters.

The second and third columns of figure 12.10 reveal that changing the measure of money from NBR to either M0 or M1 has a drastic impact on inference. Measured this way, innovations to monetary policy are followed by increases in R_t. In the case of M0, the basic patterns are very similar across the different identification schemes; the immediate impact of the shock is to drive up R_t, which stays above its preshock level for approximately eight quarters but then falls and stabilizes at a level slightly below its preshock level.[19] Notice, though, that the standard errors associated with these impulse response functions are quite large. Indeed, one cannot

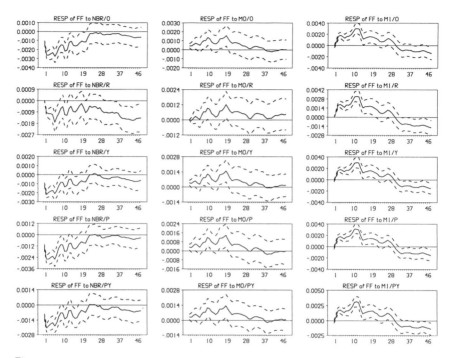

Figure 12.11
Response of federal funds rate to policy shock under M-rule (various measures of money, monthly, 1959:1–1990:1).

reject, at reasonable confidence levels, the null hypotheses that the federal funds rate rises, falls, or is unchanged following a shock in M0. Evidently, this monetary aggregate contains very little information for the federal funds rate. When M1 is used as the measure of money, the positive response of R_t to a policy shock is statistically more significant than is the case for M0.

In order to assess the sensitivity of results to the use of quarterly data, we redid our analysis using monthly data. These results are presented in figure 12.11. Since real GNP data are unavailable at the monthly level, we used industrial production as our measure of aggregate output and the consumer price index as our measure of the aggregate price level. As can be seen, these changes have very little impact on our results. Orthogonalized shocks to NBR continue to drive the federal funds rate down, M0 continues to contain very little information for the federal funds rate, and orthogonalized shocks to M1 drive the federal funds rate up.

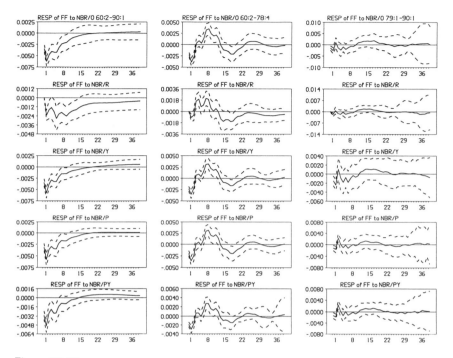

Figure 12.12
Response of federal funds rate to policy shock under M-rule (NBR, quarterly, various samples).

To address the issue of sample period sensitivity, we also redid our analysis using two distinct sample periods. Figures 12.12 and 12.13 report results for NBR using quarterly and monthly data respectively. Figures 12.14 and 12.15 report the analogous results for M0 and figures 12.16 and 12.17 display the analogous results for M1. The three columns of each figure display the response of R_t to unanticipated shocks to monetary policy for the periods 1959:1–1990:1, 1959:1–1978:4, and 1979:1–1990:1 respectively. The class of identification schemes considered is the same as that underlying figures 12.10 and 12.11.

Consider first our results for NBR. Figures 12.12 and 12.13 reveal that there is some sample period sensitivity. For both the monthly and quarterly data, the pre-1979 and post-1979 results appear quite different from the full sample results. Still, for the monthly data, it remains true that R_t always drops following an expansionary monetary disturbance. This is true regardless of which identification scheme or which sample period is adopted. At

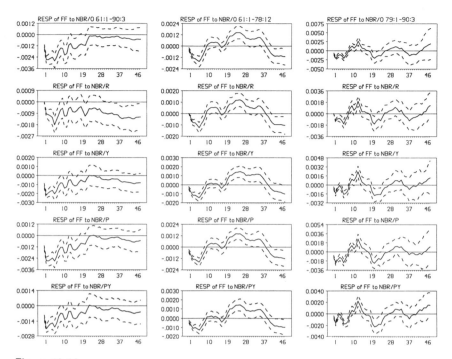

Figure 12.13
Response of federal funds rate to policy shock under M-rule (NBR, monthly, various samples).

the same time, the persistence of the drop in the federal funds rate seems much shorter in the post-1979 period. Figures 12.14 and 12.15 reveal that the response functions generated using M0 seem to be relatively stable across sample periods. Figures 12.16 and 12.17 reveal that the results obtained using M1 are the most sensitive to splitting the sample. Here, as with NBR, the pre-1979 period looks similar to the entire sample period, while the post-1979 period looks quite different.

To summarize this portion of our analysis, we find that when NBR is used as the measure of money, there is very strong evidence that, relative to the identification schemes considered, unanticipated expansionary changes in monetary policy drive the federal funds rate down. It is hard to imagine reconciling this finding with models that do not incorporate liquidity effects. In sharp contrast, when either M0 or M1 is used as the measure of money, unanticipated expansionary changes in monetary policy drive the federal funds rate up. Evidently, a given class of identification schemes

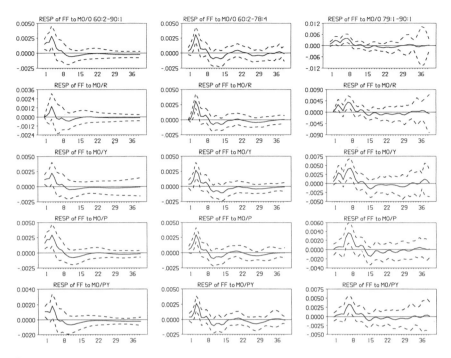

Figure 12.14
Response of federal funds rate to policy shock under M-rule (M0, quarterly, various samples).

generates very different results for different measures of money. This result is hardly surprising. As we stressed in the introduction, there is no reason to believe that a given set of identifying assumptions will be equally appropriate across high- and low-order measures of the monetary aggregate. Aggregates like NBR, M0, and M1 are influenced by very different sets of economics agents.

Given these apparently conflicting results, how can we realistically hope to proceed? One response is to investigate whether certain combinations of identification assumptions and monetary aggregates can be eliminated on the basis of their implications for variables other than interest rates. This seems to be the case for the class of identification schemes that equate unanticipated changes in monetary policy with some fraction of the innovations in M0 or M1. For example, figure 12.18 displays the dynamic response function of GNP to shocks in monetary policy for the M-rule class of identification schemes underlying figures 12.10 and 12.11. Notice that

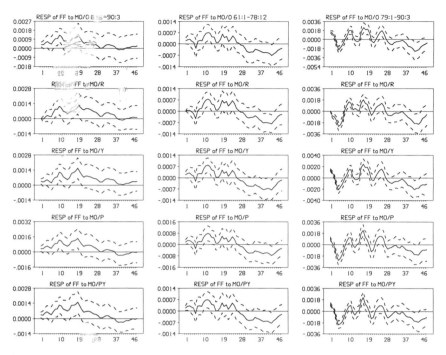

Figure 12.15
Response of federal funds rate to policy shock under M-rule (M0, monthly, various samples).

when M1 is used in the analysis, shocks to monetary policy are followed by sharp persistent declines in GNP that last over nine years. While less pronounced with M0, the salient effect of such shocks is also a large persistent decline in GNP.[20] Even taking sampling uncertainty into account, these declines last for roughly three years, with the exact horizon depending on the identification scheme used. In sharp contrast, when NBR is used in the analysis, these types of shocks generate increases in aggregate output.[21] We conclude that if one conditions on the class of M-rules considered here, then the results based on NBR are the most plausible. Those results provide strong support for the importance of the liquidity effect.

A different class of identifying restrictions not captured in figures 12.10–12.17 emerges from the analyses of McCallum (1983), Bernanke and Blinder (1990), and Sims (1986, 1991). These authors argue that, at least relative to high-order monetary aggregates like M1 or M2, the innovation in R_t is a

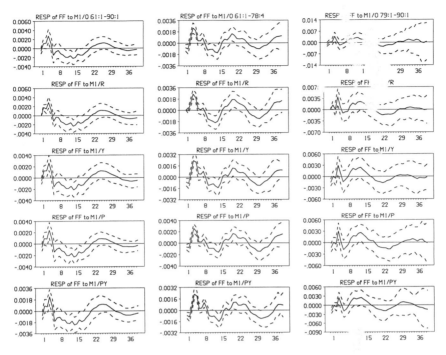

Figure 12.16
Response of federal funds rate to policy shock under M-rule (M1, quarte..y, various samples).

better measure of unanticipated changes in monetary policy than the innovation to the stock of money. In pursuing this idea, Bernanke and Blinder (1990) and Sims (1986, 1991) assume that innovations in R_t arise solely from the actions of the monetary authority and that the contemporaneous portion of the feedback rule for setting R_t does not include M_t, Y_t, or P_t. In short, they place R_t first in their Wold causal chain. More generally, their arguments suggest measuring monetary policy as some orthogonalized component of the innovation in the federal funds rate.

Figure 12.19 reports a subset of the implications of this class of identifying restrictions. In particular, each row displays the response function of R_t to a shock in monetary policy measured using a different identification scheme. The graphs labeled "RESP of M to FF/X," $M = \{NBR, M0, M1\}$ and $X = \{0, R, Y, P, (P, Y)\}$ denote the response of the monetary aggregate to a contractionary monetary policy disturbance, where the latter is identified as the component of the innovation in R_t that is orthogonal to X. The

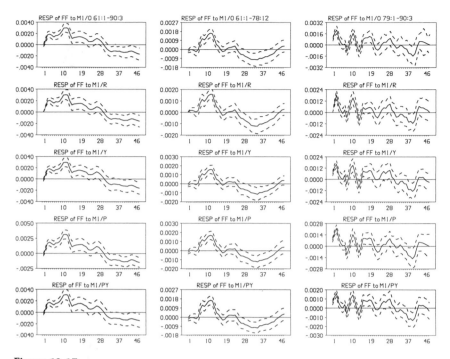

Figure 12.17
Response of federal funds rate to policy shock under M-rule (M1, monthly, various samples).

Wold ordering underlying the first row is $\{R, M, Y, P\}$. This corresponds to the identification scheme imposed by Bernanke and Blinder (1990) as well as Sims (1986, 1991). The Wold ordering underlying the second row is $\{M, R, Y, P\}$, so that the unanticipated change in monetary policy is measured as the portion of the innovation in R_t that is orthogonal to the innovation in M_t. This corresponds to the assumption that the contemporaneous portion of the monetary authority's feedback rule for setting R_t involves M_t, but not P_t or Y_t. The Wold ordering underlying the third row is $\{Y, R, M, P\}$, so that the unanticipated change in monetary policy is measured as the portion of the innovation in R_t that is orthogonal to the innovation in Y_t. This corresponds to the assumption that the only contemporaneous variable the FOMC looks at when setting R_t is Y_t. The Wold ordering underlying the fourth row is $\{P, R, M, Y\}$, so that the unanticipated change in monetary policy is measured as the portion of the innovation in R_t that is orthogonal to the innovation in P_t. This corresponds to the assumption that the only contemporaneous variable which the FOMC

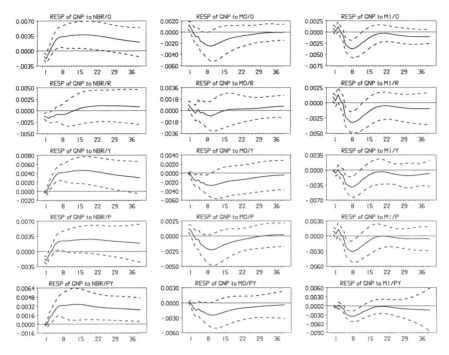

Figure 12.18
Response of GNP to policy shock under M-rule (various measures of money, quarterly, 1959:1–1990:1).

looks at when setting R_t is P_t. Finally, the Wold ordering underlying the entries of the fifth row is $\{P, Y, R, M\}$, so that the unanticipated change in monetary policy is measured as the portion of the innovation in R_t that is orthogonal to the innovations in both P_t and Y_t. This corresponds to the assumption that in setting R_t, the FOMC looks at P_t and Y_t, but not M_t.

Figure 12.19 reveals that, with one important exception, unanticipated changes in monetary policy, corresponding to an increase in R_t, are followed by long declines in the stock of money, regardless of whether the latter is measured as NBR, M0, or M1. The only exception to this pattern arises with NBR under the identification scheme generating the graph labeled "RESP of NBR to FF/NBR." Here NBR rises for approximately fifteen quarters before falling below its preshock level. One possible interpretation of this uses the fact that the monetary shock here is the component of the innovation to R_t that is orthogonal to NBR, that is, it is the movement in R_t that cannot be predicted on the basis of the current level of NBR. Viewed from this perspective, the increase in NBR after such a

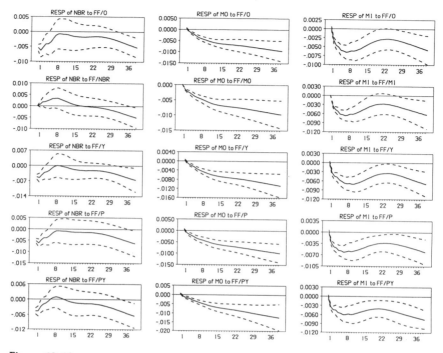

Figure 12.19
Response of money to policy shock under R-rule (various measures of money, quarterly, 1959:1–1990:1).

shock may be the consequence of a policy in which the monetary authority smooths fluctuations in the federal funds rate arising from what it perceives to be shocks to the demand for money. Goodfriend (1991) and others argue forcefully that this has been an important feature of postwar federal reserve policy. Finally, figure 12.20 presents the analog to figure 12.19 obtained with monthly data. As can be seen, our results are quite insensitive to this perturbation. Thus, abstracting from one identification scheme, conditioning on the R-rules leads to the inference that there is an important liquidity effect.

12.3 Summary

We conclude this paper by summarizing our two main findings.

First, we found that when nonborrowed reserves are used as the measure of money, inference regarding the effects of unanticipated changes in

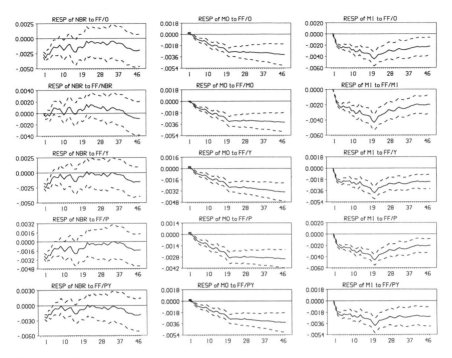

Figure 12.20
Response of money to policy shock under R-rule (various measures of money, monthly, 1959:1–1990:1).

monetary policy on interest rates is very robust. When the shock to monetary policy is measured as some orthogonalized component of the innovation to nonborrowed reserves, the federal funds rate displays a sharp, large, persistent decline in response to expansionary monetary policy. When the shock to monetary policy is measured as some orthogonalized component of the innovation to the federal funds rate, unanticipated contractionary monetary policy, corresponding to an increase in the federal funds rate, is accompanied by a sharp, large, persistent decline in NBR.

To us, these findings constitute strong evidence in favor of the view that unanticipated expansionary open market operations drive interest rates down, at least in the short run—that is, the federal reserve lowers interest rates by withdrawing nonborrowed reserves from the system. It seems unlikely that these findings can be reconciled with models that do not incorporate liquidity effects.

Second, we found that when either M0 or M1 is used as the measure of money, inference regarding the effects of unanticipated changes in monetary policy on interest rates is very sensitive to the identification scheme adopted. When the shock to monetary policy is measured as some orthogonalized component of the innovation to the federal funds rate, unanticipated contractionary monetary policy, corresponding to an increase in the federal funds rate, is accompanied by a sharp, large, persistent decline in M0 and M1. Thus, this class of monetary rules generates evidence in support of liquidity effects. In contrast, when the shock to monetary policy is measured as some orthogonalized component of the innovation to M0 or M1, the federal funds rate displays a large, persistent rise in response to expansionary monetary policy. However, these shocks generate implications for real output that seem to us implausible. We conclude that the balance of the evidence, including the dynamic correlations discussed in section 12.1, is consistent with the conventional view of the effects of monetary policy disturbances on interest rates.

Notes

We thank Steve Strongin and Mark Watson for many helpful discussions. Jonas Fisher provided excellent research assistance. Support from the National Science Foundation is gratefully acknowledged.

1. For example, Mishkin (1981, 1982), Cochrane (1989), and R. King (1991) use M1; Melvin (1983) uses M2; and Reichenstein (1987) uses both M1 and M2. Indeed, Reichenstein's (1987) review of this literature does not contain even one reference to a study that uses NBR or even M0 as the measure of money. Recently, Gordon and Leeper (1991) use M0 in their analysis and Terhan (1991) uses weekly data on NBR.

2. This assumption is implicit in studies that regress the interest rate on the unanticipated change in money, where the latter is the residual from an equation in which the time t value of a monetary aggregate is regressed against time $t - 1$ variables. Such a procedure is asymptotically equivalent to running a vector autoregression that contains, among other things, money and interest rates and then calculating the moving average representation implied by the assumption that the time t disturbance to money is orthogonal to innovations in the other variables in the system. In Sims' (1986) terminology, this identification scheme amounts to adopting a Wold causal chain in which money is placed first in the ordering.

3. NBR is total reserves, less total borrowings, of depository institutions from the Federal Reserve. (See U.S. Federal Reserve System, Board of Governors, 1991a, p A12, table 1.20.) NBR is the monetary aggregate most closely controllable by the FOMC. Broader aggregates like M1 and M2 are less closely controllable, because the non-NBR component in these aggregates is observed with a lag.

4. Sims (1986) looks at different identifying assumptions conditional on using a particular monetary aggregate, M1, in his analysis.

5. A simple way to understand the difference between M- and R-rules is to consider the extreme case in which each fails to feed back on the contemporaneous value of any other variable. This version of the M-rule corresponds to a perfectly interest-inelastic, short-run money supply rule, while this version of the R-rule corresponds to a perfectly elastic short-run money supply rule in which all shocks to money demand are completely accommodated.

6. Economic models do exist that can rationalize a fall in output following a money shock. (See Cooley and Hansen 1989, Christiano 1991, and Christiano and Eichenbaum 1991.) However, we suspect that plausibly parameterized versions of these models will have difficulty accounting for the magnitude and persistence of the fall in output.

7. For example, one could construct a model in which the fundamental shocks driving the business cycle are nonmonetary and have the effect that, in equilibrium, there is a positive association between output growth and the interest rate. If such a model incorporated a monetary policy of "leaning against the wind"—tightening money in a boom and easing in a recession—then it would imply a negative association between money and interest rates, even if the model had no liquidity effect. However, such a model would have the counterfactual implication that output growth and the interest rate are positively correlated.

8. The basis for lending at the discount window is laid out in the Fed's Regulation A, according to which, "Federal reserve credit is available on a short-term basis to a depository institution under such rules as may be prescribed to assist the institution, to the extent appropriate, in meeting temporary requirements for funds, or to cushion more persistent outflows of funds pending an orderly adjustment of the institution's assets and liabilities." (U.S. Federal Reserve Board, 1991, sec. 201.3, par. (a)).

9. Recent examples of such models are provided by Baxter et al. (1990); Lucas (1990); Fuerst (1990); Christiano (1991); and Christiano and Eichenbaum (1991).

10. In order to check the robustness of these results, we redid our calculations using the nominal three-month treasury bill as our measure of the interest rate. This change has virtually no impact on our conclusions.

11. For a further discussion of the problems of identifying a moving average representation like (3), see Hansen and Sargent (1991).

12. Some important exceptions are Gali (1991), King and Watson (1991), and Sims (1986, 1991) who impose exclusion restrictions on the contemporaneous component of determinants of money supply and demand to identify monetary policy shocks. The first two of these also impose restrictions on the long-run relationships between the variables in their vector autoregressions. Although we do not consider the kind of identification schemes considered by these authors, they reach the same conclusion we do: that the balance of the evidence favors the conventional view that short-term interest rates fall in response to an unanticipated monetary tightening.

13. Placing R second in the Wold causal chain amounts to the assumption that time *t* movements in interest rates are independent of contemporaneous movements in

both output and prices. Placing Y third in the Wold casual chain amounts to the assumption that time t movements in output are independent of contemporaneous movements in the price level.

14. As Gordon and Leeper (1991) point out, there are important differences in this literature regarding which variables are allowed to enter the law of motion for the monetary aggregate.

15. Sims (1986, 1991) works exclusively with M1; Bernanke and Blinder (1990) experiment with both M1 and M2.

16. We found that our results were not affected when we used either the consumer price index or the constant weighted GNP deflator instead of the GNP deflator as our measure of the price level.

17. Lag lengths were selected based on evidence regarding the serial correlation in the error term in the vector autoregression, as measured using the Q statistic discussed in Doan (1990).

18. These were computed using the method described in Doan (1990), example 10.1, using 100 draws from the estimated asymptotic distribution of the vector autoregressive coefficients.

19. The identification scheme labeled "RESP of FF to M0/R" precludes an immediate reaction of R_t to a shock in monetary policy.

20. This effect emerges most clearly under the assumption that the monetary authority sets M0, taking into account the contemporaneous values of the price level and/or GNP.

21. There is some sensitivity to when the rise in GNP begins.

References

Barro, R. J. 1981. "Unanticipated Money Growth and Economic Activity in the U.S.," in *Money, Expectations and Business Cycles*, Academic Press, New York.

Baxter, M., S. Fischer, R. G. King, and K. G. Rouwenhorst. 1990. "The Liquidity Effect in General Equilibrium," manuscript, Rochester University.

Bernanke, B. 1990. "On the Predictive Power of Interest Rates and Interest Rate Spreads," manuscript, Princeton University.

Bernanke, B., and A. Blinder. 1990. "The Federal Funds Rate and The Channels of Monetary Transmission," Working Paper 3487, National Bureau of Economic Research.

Christiano, L. J. 1991. "Modeling The Liquidity Effect of A Monetary Shock," *Federal Reserve Bank of Minneapolis Quarterly Review*, 15, Winter.

Christiano, L. J., and M. Eichenbaum. 1991. "Liquidity Effects, Monetary Policy, and the Business Cycle," manuscript, Northwestern University.

Cochrane, J. H. 1989. "The Return of the Liquidity Effect: A Study of the Short-Run Relation Between Money Growth and Interest Rates," *Journal of Business and Economic Statistics*, 17.

Cooley, T. F., and G. D. Hansen. 1989. "The Inflation Tax in a Real Business Cycle Model," *American Economic Review*, 79, September, 733–748.

Doan, T. 1990. "User's Manual, RATS Version 3.10," VAR Econometrics, Evanston, Ill.

Fuerst, T. 1990. "Liquidity, Loanable Funds and Real Activity," manuscript, Northwestern University.

Gali, J. 1991. "How Well Does the IS-LM Model Fit Postwar U.S. Data?", forthcoming, *Quarterly Journal of Economics*.

Goodfriend, M. 1991. "Interest Rates and the Conduct of Monetary Policy," in *Carnegie-Rochester Conference Series on Public Policy*, vol. 34, Spring, edited by C. I. Plosser and A. H. Meltzer.

Goodfriend, M. 1983. "Discount Window Borrowing, Monetary Policy, and the Post-October 1979 Federal Reserve Operating Procedures," *Journal of Monetary Economics*, 12:345–356.

Goodfriend, M. and Whelpley, M. 1986. "Federal Funds" In *Instruments of the Money Market* (6th edition), edited by T. Cook and T. Rowe. Richmond, VA: Federal Reserve Bank of Richmond.

Gordon, D. and E. Leeper. 1991. "In Search of the Liquidity Effect," manuscript, Federal Reserve Board of Governors.

Grossman, S. and L. Weiss. 1983. "A Transactions Based Model of the Monetary Transmission Mechanism," *American Economic Review*, 73 (December): 871–80.

Hansen, L. P., and T. J. Sargent, 1991, "Two Difficulties in Interpreting Vector Autoregressions," in *Rational Expectations Econometrics*, Westview Press.

Hodrick, R. J. and E. C. Prescott. 1980. "Post War Business Cycles: An Empirical Investigation," manuscript, Carnegie Mellon University.

King, S. R. 1983. "Real Interest Rates and the Interaction of Money, Output, and Prices," manuscript, Northwestern University.

King, R. 1991. "Money and Business Cycles," manuscript, University of Rochester.

King, R., and M. Watson. 1991. "Comparing the Fit of Dynamic Models," manuscript, University of Rochester.

Kuttner, K. and B. A. Friedman. 1990. "Money, Income, and Prices After the 1980's," Working Paper 2852, National Bureau of Economic Research, forthcoming, *American Economic Review*.

Lucas, R. E. Jr. 1990. "Liquidity and Interest Rates," *Journal of Economic Theory* 50:237–264.

McCallum, B. T. 1983. "A Reconsideration of Sims' Evidence Concerning Monetarism," *Economic Letters* 13 (2–3): 167–171.

Melvin, M. 1983. "The Vanishing Liquidity Effect of Money on Interest: Analysis and Implications for Policy," *Economic Inquiry* 21 (April): 188–202.

Mishkin, F. 1981. "Monetary Policy and Long Term Interest Rates: An Efficient Markets Approach," *Journal of Monetary Economics* 7: 29–55.

Mishkin, F. 1982. "Monetary Policy and Short Term Interest Rates: An Efficient Markets Rational Expectations Approach," *Journal of Finance* 37: 63–72.

Reichenstein. 1987. "The Impact of Money on Short-Term Interest Rates," *Economic Inquiry* 25 (1): 67–82.

Rotemberg, J. 1984. "A Monetary Equilibrium Model with Transaction Costs," *Journal of Political Economy* 92 (February): 40–58.

Sims, C. A. 1986. "Are Forecasting Models Usable for Policy Analysis?" *Federal Reserve Bank of Minneapolis Quarterly Review* 10 (Winter): 2–16.

Sims, C. A. 1991. "Interpreting the Macroeconomic Time Series Facts: The Effects of Monetary Policy," manuscript, Yale University, forthcoming, *European Economic Review.*

Stigum, M. L. 1990. *The Money Market,* 3rd ed. Homewood, Ill.: Dow Jones-Irwin.

Stock, J. H. and M. W. Watson. 1989a. "Interpreting The Evidence on Money Income Causality," *Journal of Econometrics* 40: 161–181.

Stock, J. H. and M. W. Watson. 1989b. "New Indexes of Coincident and Leading Economic Indicators, *NBER Macroeconomics Annual,* edited by O. J. Blanchard and S. Fischer, pp. 351–394.

Terhan, V. 1991. "Does the Federal Reserve Affect Asset Prices?," manuscript, Federal Reserve Bank of San Francisco.

Thomas, L. B., Jr. 1982. *Money, Banking and Economic Activity,* Third Edition, New York: Prentice-Hall.

U.S. Federal Reserve System. Board of Governors. 1991a. *Federal Reserve Bulletin,* October.

U.S. Federal Reserve System, Board of Governors. 1991b. "Regulation A: Extensions of Credit by Federal Reserve Banks." In *Monetary Policy and Reserve Requirements Handbook.* Washington, D.C.: Board of Governors of the Federal Reserve System.

V

**Labor Market
Regulations and
Industry Equilibrium**

13

A Framework for Assessing Aggregate Consequences of Labor Market Regulations

Hugo Hopenhayn and Richard Rogerson

Comparisons of labor market performance in Europe and the United States in the post-1970 period has led to considerable interest in the aggregate implications of regulations affecting the costs that individual firms must bear in making labor force adjustments. Two casual observations seem to motivate this interest. On the one hand, European economies are typically characterized as having a stricter regulatory environment with respect to these matters, and on the other hand, European economies have been much less proficient at .job creation during the last twenty years. Recent policy discussions that emphasize a need for a more "flexible" labor market indicate a tendency by some to attach a causal link between these two observations.

In light of this, it is perhaps surprising that there have been relatively few attempts by academic economists to assess the validity of arguments that stress labor market institutions as a prominent factor in explaining Europe's relatively poor record of job creation. (Some exceptions include Gavin 1986, Bertola 1990, Bentolila and Bertola 1990, and Lazear 1990.) One factor contributing to this situation may be that the theoretical structures commonly used by economists to address aggregate effects of policy are particularly ill suited to studying the impact of many labor market policies. This is because models that capture the important aspects of firm-level employment dynamics must stress heterogeneity and the process of firm entry and exit, while many commonly used models of aggregate economic activity (for example, the stochastic one-sector growth model) abstract from these considerations.

This chapter lays out a framework that we believe is a natural and useful structure in which to carry out the analysis of labor market regulations. The type of policy analysis we have in mind is a fairly standard one. Individual agents are posited to engage in optimizing behavior, leading to individual decision rules. Combined with an equilibrium concept, this yields a mapping from structural (policy invariant) and policy parameters into observable outcomes. Invoking a procedure to uncover the values of the structural parameters, one can then consider alternative values for the policy variables, re-solve the model, and determine how different settings of policy variables will influence the values of endogenous variables. This calls for a structure that can take into account the tremendous heterogeneity in firm-level employment dynamics yet maintain sufficient tractability to allow for analysis of aggregate behavior. The structure that we develop is a generalization of the industry equilibrium model of Hopenhayn (1989).

The focus of this chapter is the development of a framework in which one can assess the quantitative impact of various labor market regulations, not an analysis of why the regulations were adopted in the first place. One perspective explaining the existence of such regulations is that the political process operates in such a way that society adopts policies that effectively transfer resources from one group to another, possibly at the cost of generating some inefficiencies. In the case of legislated severance payments, for example, one might argue that labor is attempting to extract resources from capital through the political process. (The reader is referred to Alesina and Rodrik (1990) for an interesting analysis that focuses on the political economy of conflicts between labor and capital.) In such a context, it seems of particular interest to understand the costs associated with regulations that attempt to influence the distribution of income, since holding redistribution constant there is clearly a general desire to achieve it in the most cost-effective manner. The work described in this chapter can be interpreted as trying to assess the costs of some of these policies.

An outline of the chapter follows. The next section presents an example that illustrates some important aspects of the analysis. Section 13.2 presents the general framework, and section 13.3 develops the notion of a stationary equilibrium for the structure. As an illustration of the framework's usefulness for policy analysis, section 13.4 reports results from Hopenhayn and Rogerson (1990) on the effects of a tax on job destruction. Section 13.5 contains some closing remarks.

13.1   Preliminaries

A natural starting point for analyzing policies that affect the employment decisions of firms is the firm's decision problem. The analysis of this section takes place in a very simple framework and focuses on the particular policy that requires firms to make a fixed monetary payment for every job that is destroyed.

The firm uses labor to produce output, and revenues in period t are given by $R(n_t, s_t)$, where n_t is current employment and s_t is a stochastic shock. The shock may operate either through technology or demand, a distinction that is not important for the current discussion. The shock s is assumed to follow a first-order Markov process, and the revenue function is twice continuously differentiable, increasing in both arguments, with a positive cross partial. The firm faces a constant wage rate of w, a constant interest rate of r, and the dismissal cost is denoted by f. The firm's expected discounted profit maximization problem can then be written as the following dynamic program:

$$V(s, n) = \max_{n' \geqslant 0} \{R(s, n'\} - wn' - f \cdot \max(0, n - n') + 1/(1 + r)E_s V(s', n')\}$$

where n is last period's employment level, n' is this period's choice of employment, E_s is the expectations operator conditioned upon this period's value of s, and s' is next period's value of the shock.

Qualitative implications of firing costs on the optimal employment decision of the individual firm can be obtained, as Bentolila and Bertola (1990) illustrate in a similar setting. Note first that in the absence of firing costs, the above maximization problem is effectively static, and the period t employment level is given by the solution to

$$R_1(n_t, s_t) = w. \tag{1}$$

Denote the solution to this by $n^*(s)$, and note that by assumption this function is strictly increasing in s. How does the solution change when f assumes a positive value? The introduction of firing costs affects both hiring and firing decisions, as summarized by the next proposition, which is stated without proof.

Proposition: Let (s, n) be the state variable for a firm, and $N(s, n)$ be the decision rule for current employment. There exist functions $n_1(s)$, $n_2(s)$, which are continuous and increasing, with $n_1(s) \leqslant n_2(s)$ such that:

(1) if $n_1(s) \leqslant n \leqslant n_2(s)$ then $N(s, n) = n$,

(2) if $n \leqslant n_1(s)$ then $N(s, n) = n_1(s)$, and

(3) if $n \geqslant n_1(s)$ then $N(s, n) = n_2(s)$.

Moreover, $n_1(s) \leqslant n^*(s) \leqslant n_2(s)$.

This result is fairly intuitive. In the absence of firing costs, the firm always hires labor until the marginal increase in revenue with respect to employment (hereafter simply called marginal revenue) equals the wage rate.

Consider first the case where $f > 0$ and the combination of last period's employment level and this period's shock is such that maintaining last period's employment results in marginal revenue being lower than the wage rate. With f equal to zero the firm would decrease the size of its labor force, but with f positive the firm must factor into the calculation the (constant) marginal cost associated with decreasing employment. Because the marginal firing cost is constant, conditional upon doing some firing, the employment level that the firm chooses is independent of its initial employment level. Also, because of the firing cost, employment will be at least as great as it would have been in the absence of a firing cost, i.e., $n^*(s)$. Hence, the introduction of a firing cost has the anticipated affect of discouraging firms from firing workers, resulting in a level of employment greater than it would have been in the absence of such costs.

A similar situation arises if the combination of the current shock and last period's employment are such that the marginal revenue is greater than the wage rate when the firm maintains its labor force at last period's level, although the argument is slightly more subtle. From a static perspective the firm would like to hire more workers, and because there are no hiring costs, static considerations alone would suggest that the firm choose current employment equal to $n^*(s)$. From a dynamic perspective, however, the firm must take into account the probability that some of these workers may need to be fired in the future. Loosely speaking, this probability, suitably discounted, will be multiplied by the firing cost f. Effectively, it is as if the firm also faces a hiring cost, and thus in this case its decisions are affected in a manner similar to that discussed earlier. In particular, conditional upon hiring, the employment level chosen is independent of the starting position, and the level chosen will be less than or equal to the value that would be chosen in the absence of firing costs.[1] Hence, in this situation hiring is decreased by the presence of firing costs, resulting in a lower level of employment.

The above discussion indicates that both hiring and firing will be dampened by the introduction of firing costs. In fact, with a constant marginal firing cost it is possible that the firm chooses not to respond to a change in s. Essentially, if the firm is not "too far" from the optimal static employment $(n^*(s))$, then it may be in the firm's interest to not adjust its labor force at all. This is because the marginal revenue is close to w in a neighborhood of n^*, but the marginal firing cost is bounded away from zero when f is positive.

Because both hiring and firing decrease, it is not clear what the overall effect on employment will be. It follows that although one can obtain a fairly tight characterization of the qualitative effects of firing costs, this kind of exercise does little to ascertain the likelihood that such regulations lead to lower employment.

Even if one were able, in this context, to say something definitive about the direction in which firing costs affect employment, this still leaves unanswered the important question of how large the effects will be. Addressing this question requires being much more specific about the problem being solved by the firm. One point highlighted by the above discussion is that the impact of firing costs on the level of employment will depend very much on the stochastic environment in which the firm operates. To see this, consider the case of a firm that is faced with an improvement in its opportunities (i.e., a higher value of s). How will the presence of firing costs affect the manner in which the firm responds to this improvement? Clearly this will depend upon the firm's expectations of how long the improved situation is likely to last. If it is perceived to be temporary, then the firm may soon have to dismiss any newly hired workers and incur the firing cost. On the other hand, if it is expected to last a very long time, then even though the newly hired workers may eventually need to be dismissed, discounting will make the expected present value of the associated firing costs relatively small, diminishing their significance in the firm's current employment decision. An analogous argument applies to the situation where a firm is faced with a deterioration in its current prospects and is contemplating whether to decrease the size of its labor force. Obviously, determining the quantitative impact of firing costs will require some way to assess the stochastic environment in which individual firms operate, an issue to which we now direct our attention.

The firm decision problem formulated above defines a mapping from the (exogenous) stochastic process on s into the (endogenous) stochastic process on employment. Given time series on firm level employment, one can attempt to invert this mapping to uncover properties of the stochastic process describing the evolution of s. Although the topics of firm growth rates and the size distribution of firms have long attracted the attention of researchers, a number of recently completed studies have greatly expanded our knowledge about the process of firm-level employment dynamics, particularly in the context of the U.S. economy. Several data sets provide an opportunity to uncover the properties of this process, including Dun and Bradstreet, County Business Patterns, Longitudinal Research Data File, Wisconsin Unemployment Insurance Returns, and Compustat. Some of the many papers utilizing these sets are Birch (1981, 1986), Davis and Haltiwanger (1988, 1990), Dunne, Roberts, and Samuelson (1986, 1987,

1988, 1989), Ericson and Pakes (1989), Evans (1987a, 1987b), Hall (1987), Leonard (1987), Pakes and Erieson (1987) and Troske (1989). Each of these data sets has its particular strengths and weaknesses, relating to such issues as the extent of coverage, information included, frequency of data, and the ability to detect mergers, acquisitions, and transfers. The reader is referred to the above mentioned studies for details of these important measurement issues.

Despite differences in the various data sets and the studies that have utilized them, some robust findings have emerged. First, the rates of job creation and destruction at the level of the individual firm are very large, and in particular large relative to the net rate of job creation at the aggregate level. Second, the rates of entry and exit of firms are also very large. The exact magnitudes vary somewhat from study to study, but representative numbers are informative. Over the course of a year, roughly 10 percent of all jobs will be destroyed, with a corresponding number of new jobs created. Over a five-year interval, entry and exit rates are on the order of 40 percent. Furthermore, studies indicate that the majority of variance in firm-level employment growth cannot be explained by factors such as sector, geographic location, age, or aggregate factors.

The following picture of the economy emerges. Although aggregates tend to be quite stable, their relative constancy over time hides a great deal of turbulence that occurs "beneath the surface." There is an ongoing process whereby jobs are being reallocated across firms, with some growing, others shrinking, and some closing down completely, eventually to be replaced by new firms. Aggregates appear relatively stable over time only because most of these changes at the firm level tend to cancel out. An important message that we learn from these studies is that aggregate data provides very little information about the stochastic environment in which firms operate. For example, the variance of aggregate employment provides very little information about the variance of employment at the level of an individual firm. Hence, even if one's interest is the aggregate impact of firing costs, aggregate data do not contain the information that is relevant for the analysis. For this reason the recent empirical work listed above is of central importance in assessing the quantitative impact of regulations such as firing costs.

Although with appropriate data the above analysis can provide information about the quantitative impact of firing costs on the employment decisions of firms, it is still incomplete if one's ultimate objective is to assess the aggregate consequences of such costs. There are two issues here. First, one needs to aggregate over all firms in order to determine aggregate effects. In the example discussed above, the effect of firing costs upon the employment level at an individual firm depends upon the value of the firm's state variable (s, n); hence, the aggregate effect will depend upon the distribution of these state variables across existing firms. In carrying out this aggregation it is clearly important that the underlying distribution be close to that describing the actual economy. This consideration is closely related to appropriately matching the stochastic process on firm-level employment to that found in actual data.

The second issue concerns the fact that the above analysis has been decision theoretic in nature. It can be used to compute the change in labor demand assuming that all prices remain the same, but determining the aggregate impact of policies requires taking into account the possibility that these policies might affect the prices that firms take as given. This entails imbedding the analysis in a general equilibrium structure. In the present context, this involves explicitly bringing labor supply into the analysis. Moreover, in addition to simply closing the model, it is reasonable to expect that many policies affect not only labor demand but also labor supply. In the case of legislated severance payments one would also expect labor supply to be affected by the payments going from firms to workers. Obviously, it is necessary to include both labor supply and demand in order to determine the effect of a policy on total employment.

Combining the elements of the preceding discussion, the reader should be aware of several points that are relevant to a study of the aggregate consequences of labor market policies. First, the models must be able to account for the stochastic properties of firm-level employment dynamics found in actual data. This necessarily implies models in which heterogeneity plays a key role. Furthermore, entry and exit considerations must also be part of the analysis. Second, these issues must be handled in a general equilibrium framework. And finally, the structure must be amenable to quantitative analysis. The next section presents a framework that meets these requirements and hence is one we believe is useful for analyzing the macroeconomic effects of many labor market interventions.

13.2   Theoretical Framework

The framework to be described is designed for the purpose of studying a competitive economy that is in a stationary or long-run equilibrium. In this equilibrium, individual firms will be undergoing change over time, with some of them expanding, others contracting, some closing down, and others starting up. However, despite all of this change at the level of the individual firm, all aggregate variables, such as price, employment, output, and the number of firms, will be constant over time. Emphasis is placed on providing a general framework that can be used to analyze many different policies of interest. A later section reports results for the analysis of dismissal costs in a special case of this more general framework.

Each firm has a stochastic production function using labor and capital as inputs. If a firm employs n_t workers and has a capital stock of k_t in period t when the output price is p_t and the rental price of capital is r_t, it will receive period t profits equal to

$$p_t f(k_t, n_t, s_s) - n_t - r_t k_t - p_t c_f - p_t g_1(k_t, k_{t-1}) - p_t g_2(n_t, n_{t-1}).$$

Several elements require some elaboration. The wage rate has been normalized to one and hence does not appear explicitly. The variable s_t is a firm specific shock to this firm's production function in period t. This shock takes values in R_+ and follows a first-order Markov process described by a function $F(s, s')$, with the interpretation that for each current value of the shock, denoted by s, $F(s, \cdot)$ is the distribution function for next period's value of the shock, denoted by s'. Although the shocks are independent across firms, each firm's shock will evolve according to the same function F. The term c_f is a fixed operating cost (denominated in units of output) incurred by the firm in each period that it remains in operation. As will become clearer later, the role of this fixed cost is to make it meaningful to talk about a firm exiting, as opposed to temporarily producing zero output. The functions g_1 and g_2 capture the presence of (technological) adjustment costs that the firm faces in varying its capital stock or employment level from one period to the next. These costs are also denominated in units of output. The rental price of capital is denoted by r_t. It is assumed that capital depreciates at the rate δ each period.

We now consider the decisions made by each firm and in particular the timing of these decisions. The diagram in figure 13.1 shows the sequence of decisions made by both incumbent and new firms. We begin with the period t decisions made by a firm that was in operation in period $t-1$, at which time the firm had a shock equal to s_{t-1}, employment level of n_{t-1}, and a capital stock of k_{t-1}. At the beginning of period t, before receiving any new information, the firm must first make a decision about whether or not to remain in operation. If the firm exits, it implicitly chooses current employment and capital equal to zero and must pay the adjustment costs $g_1(0, k_{t-1})$ and $g_2(0, n_{t-1})$ associated with this choice, but it avoids paying the fixed operating cost c_f.[2] If a firm exits, it disappears from the model, receiving profits of zero in all future periods, with the value of zero simply

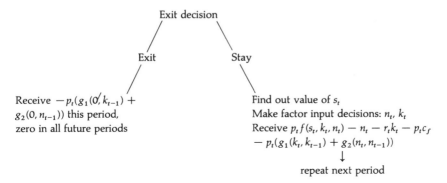

Figure 13.1
Timing of decisions

reflecting a normalization of outside opportunities.[3] If a firm chooses not to exit, it incurs the fixed cost c_f and finds out the current value of its shock, s_t. The firm then makes its choice for current employment and capital stock, produces output, sells it at the period t price, and repeats this process next period.

An important aspect of the exit decision is that firms whose prospects look sufficiently poor (because of their last period realization of s and the serial correlation in this process) will choose to exit to avoid the fixed cost. If there are no fixed costs, then the firm would not have to exit but could simply wait for the possibility of better times (higher realization of s), even if that implies output of zero in the immediate future.

Now consider the decisions made by potential entrants in period t. We assume that there is a large number (in fact a continuum) of ex ante identical potential entrants in each period. Entering requires that a firm incur a one-time cost of c_e, again denominated in units of output. Once this cost has been paid, the entrant is basically in the same position as an incumbent who has chosen to remain in the industry and had zero capital and employment in the previous period. The specification is completed by assuming that each new entrant receives its current value of s as a draw from the distribution v. These draws are i.i.d. across entering firms, but the distribution v is allowed to depend on the number of entering firms, which we will denote by M. This dependence allows for the possibility that when entry is high the marginal firms are in some sense worse. After the initial period, entering firms evolve in the same fashion as incumbent firms. Finally, we assume that all firms behave so as to maximize the expected discounted present value of profits, net of entry costs.

Having described the technology available to the economy, it remains to describe preferences and endowments. There is a continuum of identical agents, uniformly distributed over the unit interval, with preferences defined by

$$\sum_{t=1}^{\infty} \beta^t (u(c_t) - v(n_t))$$

where c_t and n_t are consumption and labor supply in period t. Consumption is restricted to be nonnegative. In many representative agent models it is assumed that hours of work are perfectly divisible, implying that in equilibrium all adjustment in total hours takes place at the intensive margin, i.e., employment is constant but hours per worker fluctuates. For fairly obvious reasons, this is not a very useful setting in which to analyze labor market regulations that in particular penalize firms for some adjustments made along the extensive (number of workers) margin. In fact, data indicate that the majority of adjustments take place at the extensive margin. Rather than introduce some element into either technology or preferences that would result in movements along both margins, we adopt the extreme but simplifying assumption that all adjustment must take place along the extensive margin. This is accomplished by restricting labor supply n_t for an individual to take on only the values of zero or one in any period, a restriction that has been studied by Hansen (1985) and Rogerson (1988). They show that optimal allocations involve individuals choosing lotteries over employment and providing insurance to cover the associated fluctuations in labor income. It can be shown that the economy behaves as if there were a representative agent with preferences defined by

$$\sum_{t=1}^{\infty} \beta^t (u(c_t) - AN_t)$$

where N_t is the fraction of individuals who are employed in period t. A final point concerning the specification of the environment is that ownership of the technology is assumed to be uniformly distributed across the population, and profits will also be shared equally in equilibrium.

The model just described attributes all idiosyncratic firm-level uncertainty to supply shocks. There is, however, an interpretation of this same structure in which the disturbances reflect shocks on the demand side. The spirit of this interpretation is that firms produce differentiated products and that the distribution of consumer tastes across differentiated products is stochastic over time. Hence, even though a firm's technological ability to produce output over time is constant, the value that consumers attach to this output is not. To capture this in the existing structure, one can interpret the production function as specifying output measured in some efficiency units that reflect the existing distribution of tastes in the market, rather than output in physical terms. The price will then reflect the price of an efficiency unit of output rather than the price of a physical unit of output. On the consumer side, c_t measures consumption in efficiency units. The shocks to preferences are not modeled explicitly, but in equilibrium it must be that each firm receives the same price per efficiency unit of consumption. This alternative interpretation is not pursued further here, however it is important to note that the framework does not require taking a stand on the source of idiosyncratic shocks.

In contrast, Jovanovic (1982) and Pakes and Ericson (1987) have studied models that are similar in spirit and are more explicit about the source of uncertainty. In Jovanovic, employment dynamics are the result of a learning process in which firms receive noisy observations on their true quality. Ericson and Pakes consider uncertainty to be the result of firms investing in new technologies with uncertain outcomes. Although both of these possibilities are of interest in their own right, evidence presented in Leonard (1987) and Davis and Haltiwanger (1990) demonstrates rather convincingly that whatever the source of idiosyncratic shocks, a relatively small amount of the variance can be accounted for by variables such as sector, geographic region, macroeconomic factors, or proxies for firm and industry life cycles. Although our understanding of the job creation and destruction process will be furthered by greater knowledge about the sources of shocks, it seems appropriate for our exercise to take somewhat of a black-box perspective with respect to modeling the idiosyncratic disturbances.

13.3   Equilibrium

Notation

Before formally defining a stationary equilibrium for the model just described, it is necessary to introduce some notation. In anticipation of a stationary equilibrium in which the prices of output and capital will be constant, we begin by considering the decision problem of the firm in more detail for the case where these prices assume the constant values of p and

r. More specifically, consider a firm that had capital stock and employment last period of k and n respectively, has decided to remain in the industry for the current period, and has received a new value for its shock equal to s. The Bellman's equation corresponding to the firm's decision problem at this point is

$$W(s, k, n) = \max_{k', n' \geq 0} \{pf(k', n', s) - n' - k'r - pc_f - pg_1(k', k) - pg_2(n', n)$$

$$+ \beta \max(E_s W(s', k', n'), - pg_1(0, k) - pg_2(0, n))\}$$

where E_s represents expectations conditional upon the current value of s, and s' represents next period's (random) value of s. This equation is entirely straightforward with the possible exception of one feature, that being the maximization operator that is nested on the right-hand side. This reflects the fact that the firm will make a decision about exiting the industry at the beginning of the next period. Moreover, there will be no additional information revealed between the current decision point and the time of the exit decision, hence the firm can determine now whether it will choose to exit at that time. Of course, the decision to exit at the beginning of next period is not independent of the decision of how many workers or how much capital to employ this period. Conditional upon this period's factor input choice, the firm must evaluate the expected value of remaining in operation, which will be given by $E_s W(s', k', n')$, and compare this with the present discounted value of profits associated with leaving the industry, which are given by $- pg_1(0, k) - pg_2(0, n)$. Note also that we have implicitly made use of the fact that in a stationary equilibrium the inverse of one plus the rate of interest must be equal to the rate of subjective time discounting of utility.

The firm's decision problem produces three decision rules: one each for the optimal choice of current employment and capital, and the other for the optimal stay/exit decision at the beginning of next period, which we write as $N(s, k, n)$, $K(s, k, n)$ and $X(s, k, n)$, respectively, with the convention that $X = 1$ corresponds to exit and $X = 0$ corresponds to stay.

Once the value function W is known, the value of entering gross of entry costs, W^e, can be computed for any given amount of entry M, by

$$W^e(M) = \int W(s, 0, 0) dv(s, M).$$

The state of an individual firm is fully described by a triplet (s, k, n). It is also of interest to describe the state of the industry, and this is accomplished by giving the distribution of the state variables for individual firms in the industry. The natural way to express this is by a measure over triplets (s, k, n), which will be denoted by $\mu(s, k, n)$.

The information introduced thus far is sufficient to trace the evolution of the industry over time, assuming that prices are constant. Beginning in period t at the point where incumbents have made their stay/exit decision and new realizations of s have been revealed, let the incumbents be summarized by a measure μ, and assume that a mass of firms equal to M enter the industry this period. All these firms will make optimal factor input decisions using the decision rules $N(s, k, n)$ and $K(s, k, n)$, and at the beginning of next period some of them will exit according the the decision rule $X(s, k, n)$. As a result of this, the aggregate state of period $t + 1$'s incumbents after the exit decision has been made and new information has been revealed will be given by some measure μ'. The transition from μ to μ' will be written as

$$\mu' = T(\mu, M).$$

The amount of output produced in a given period, denoted by Y, as a function of the variables μ, M, r, and p introduced above can be determined as

$$Y(\mu, M, r, p) = \int f(K(s, k, n), N(s, k, n), s)d\mu(s, k, n)$$
$$+ M\int f(K(s, 0, 0), N(s, 0, 0), s)dv(s; M)$$
$$- Mc_e - \text{adjustment costs}$$

In the first integrand, the output for a firm with state variable (s, k, n) that results from using the optimal factor input rules K and N is determined and then integrated over the distribution of incumbents. The second integrand does the same for new entrants, with the only difference being that all new entrants have a value of zero for last period's capital and employment, and their distribution of idiosyncratic shocks is given by the distribution v.

Demands for labor and capital are given by

$$L^d(\mu, M, r, p) = \int N(s, k, n)d\mu(s, k, n) + M\int N(s, 0, 0)dv(s; M),$$

$$K^d(\mu, M, r, p) = \int K(s, k, n)d\mu(s, k, n) + M\int K(s, 0, 0)dv(s; M).$$

Profits are given by

$$\Pi(\mu, M, r, p) = pY(\mu, M, r, p) - L^d(\mu, M, r, p) - rK^d(\mu, M, r, p).$$

Some notation is also necessary to describe the consumer problem. With constant prices the individual optimization problem can be written as

$$\text{Max} \sum_{t=1}^{\infty} \beta^t (u(c_t) - aN_t)$$

s.t. $p(c_t + i_t) \leqslant rk_t + \Pi_t + N_t$

$\quad\quad k_t = (1 - \delta)k_{t-1} + i_t$

$\quad\quad k_t \geqslant 0, \, i_t \geqslant 0, \, c_t \geqslant 0, \, 1 \geqslant N_t \geqslant 0$

This problem is quite standard. The first constraint is the one-period budget constraint, stating that current spending on consumption and new investment must be less than or equal to the sum of rental income on current capital, profits, and labor income. It is implicitly assumed that current output can be either consumed or used to augment the capital stock. First-order conditions for an interior solution to this problem are straightforward, and it is then easy to obtain values for the stationary solution as a function of the stationary values of p, r, and Π. These we write as

$$N = L^s(r, p, \Pi)$$

$$K = K^s(r, p, \Pi)$$

Definition of Equilibrium

It is now possible to define a stationary equilibrium for the model introduced in section 13.2.

Definition: A stationary equilibrium consists of prices r^*, $p^* \geqslant 0$, a mass of entrants $M^* \geqslant 0$, and a measure of incumbents μ^*, such that:

(i) $\quad L^d(\mu^*, M^*, r^*, p^*) = L^s(r^*, p^*, \Pi(\mu^*, M^*, r^*, p^*))$
(ii) $\quad K^d(\mu^*, M^*, r^*, p^*) = K^s(r^*, p^*, \Pi(\mu^*, M^*, r^*, p^*))$
(iii) $\quad T(\mu^*, M^*) = \mu^*$
(iv) $\quad W^e(M^*) \leqslant p^*c_e$, with equality if $M^* > 0$.

These conditions require little explanation. Conditions (i) and (ii) state that demand must equal supply in both the labor and capital markets. Condition (iii) requires that the state of the industry be such that the optimal actions of firms result in this state being reproduced each period. Condition (iv) states that entering firms must be willing to enter, and that if M^* is strictly positive then $W^e(p)$ must equal p^*c_e. Note that in equilibrium $W^e(p^*)$ cannot be strictly bigger than p^*c_e because of the assumption that there is an unlimited supply of potential entrants. It is possible, however, for an equilibrium to entail $W^e(p^*) < p^* c_e$, although in this case there is no entry and consequently, by condition (ii), there must also be no exit.

13.4 Policy Analysis

Thus far the framework has not included any specification of government policies. Before doing so it is useful to examine the structure that has been laid out to understand why it is a good structure for the analyses of policies affecting the costs of firm-level labor force adjustments. The main qualitative feature of a stationary equilibrium for this economy is a situation where aggregates are constant at the same time that there is (significant) change occurring at the level of individual firms: some firms are expanding, others are contracting, while others are exiting and new firms are being created. Hence it can confront the dominant fact that has emerged from the study of firm-level data sets: the rates of gross Job creation and destruction as well as entry and exit of firms are both very large relative to the net or aggregate rates of job creation and destruction and firm entry and exit. Moreover, by explicitly modeling heterogeneity across individual firms, the model will imply values for a number of observables that are used to describe the distribution of employment across firms. For example, the model will produce a size distribution of firms and a size distribution of employment. It also predicts how individual firms move within this distribution over time and hence also implies a size distribution for hiring and firing. These all are important characteristics describing the job creation and destruction process at the firm level. It seems that any study that wants to analyze how policy interventions may affect this process must as a first step provide a model that incorporates these characteristics and has some claim to being consistent with the facts. Simulations presented later in this section will be used to suggest that versions of the model outlined in this chapter do accomplish this task.

The framework laid out previously lends itself quite naturally to the analysis of many labor market policies. These include policies that make it costly for firms to dismiss workers, policies that create incentives for firms to hire workers, policies that subsidize start-ups of new firms, policies that require advance notice for either layoffs or plant closings, and alternative arrangements for financing unemployment insurance payments. At a general level, we have a model of the reallocation of resources across firms, and any policy that interacts with this reallocation process could potentially be analyzed. Here we report results from Hopenhayn and Rogerson (1990), analyzing dismissal costs in a framework that is a special case of the one introduced in section 13.2. In particular, in their framework there is no accumulation of capital, either at the aggregate or firm level, the distribution of entrants is assumed to be independent of the amount of entry, and government policy is assumed to be the only source of adjustment costs. These simplifications serve primarily to ease the computational burden associated with solving the model, although we note that solving a version of the framework as presented in section 13.2 is technologlcally feasible. The reader is referred to Hopenhayn and Rogerson for details of the analysis; here we only summarize the findings.

The specification used in the analysis is

$$f(n, s) = sn^\theta \qquad 0 \leqslant \theta \leqslant 1$$
$$g_2(n_t, n_{t-1}) = 0$$
$$\log(s_t) = a + \rho \log(s_{t-1}) + \varepsilon_t \qquad \varepsilon_t \sim N(0, \sigma_\varepsilon^2) \qquad a \geqslant 0, 0 \leqslant \rho < 1$$
$$u(c) = \ln(c), v(n) = An, A > 0$$
$$v \text{ is uniform on } [s_1, s_2]$$

The dismissal cost policy is introduced by assuming firms face an adjustment cost function,

$$f \cdot \max(n_{t-1} - n_t, 0),$$

where f is a measure of the firing cost. The revenue raised by this policy is assumed to be redistributed to all workers in a lump-sum payment. The analysis treats the length of a period as five years, since this corresponds to the frequency of data that is used to calibrate the model. Because wages are normalized to 1, the magnitude of f can be interpreted by comparing it with the wage rate, taking into account the time interval. For example, a value of f equal to .2 corresponds to a firing cost equivalent to one year's wages.

In order to solve the model it is necessary to resort to numerical methods. This requires assigning values to all of the parameters of the model, which is accomplished using a calibration procedure that matches moments from the model with those found in actual data. The moments that were matched are the average firm size, the exit rate, first-order auto-correlation and variance in employment growth rates for surviving firms, labor's share, the employment-to-population ratio, the interest rate, and the size distribution of new entrants. These moments are matched assuming that f is equal to zero, and then the model is solved assuming f takes on nonzero values in order to ascertain the impact of firing costs. Firm-level data from the LRD were used to calibrate the firm-level stochastic process.

Table 13.1
Summary statistics for benchmark model

	1–19	20–99	100–499	500+
Average firm size				61.2
Coworker mean				747
Variance of growth rates (survivors)				.55
Serial correlation in log n (survivors)				.92
Exit rate of firms				.39
Turnover rate of jobs				.30
Fraction of hiring by new firms				.15
Average size of a new firm				7.5
Average size of an exiting firm				4.9
Size dist. of firms	.52	.37	.10	.01
Size dist. of employment	.06	.24	.37	.33
Size dist. of hiring	.05	.35	.41	.19
Size dist. of firing	.12	.19	.34	.35
Size dist. by cohort:				
One period	.88	.12	.00	.00
Two periods	.54	.45	.01	.00
Five periods	.29	.58	.12	.01
Ten periods	.20	.54	.20	.05
Hazard rates by cohort:				
One period	.75			
Two periods	.32			
Five periods	.15			
Ten periods	.10			

There are a number of statistics that can be reported in characterizing the equilibrium for this model, and some of them are reported in table 13.1. Several properties cap be observed. The size distribution of firms indicates that most firms are quite small. Although the size distribution of employment indicates that most firms are small, it is nonetheless true that most employment is accounted for by larger firms. The mean firm size and the coworker mean reported ln the top part of the table support this claim. Although these statistics were not explicitly calibrated, they are ln fact quite close to those reported ln Davis and Haltiwanger (1988), Birch (1986), and Troske (1989). The size distribution of hiring and firing provides an expected pattern given that firm-level employment is following a mean reverting process: most of the firing is done by larger firms and most of the hiring is done by smaller firms. However, even though most of the hiring is done by small firms, and new firms tend to be small, it turns out that in any period, the fraction of total hiring done by new firms is relatively small as a fraction of total hiring. The top part of the table also shows that the average size of entering and exiting firms is quite small, which is also consistent with available evidence (see Troske 1989 or Dunne et al. 1986, 1987, 1988).

The statistics related to cohorts indicate two patterns. First, the probability of exit is decreasing in age, and second, the size distribution of firms is stochastically increasing in age, that is, the size distribution moves to the right as the age of the cohort increases. Both of these properties have been noted by empirical work in this area (see for example Evans 1987b).

It is perhaps important to indicate how the reader might interpret these statistics. The chosen model specification has relatively few parameters, and as such it is to be expected that this specification will not match the data equally well on all dimensions. Moreover, by calibrating the model using a small set of empirical statistics, there are conceivably other dimensions along which the model may not fit particularly well. The above statistics are shown to indicate that the relatively simple structure with the calibrated parameter values seems to do a reasonable job of matching several aspects of the relevant data, both qualitatively and quantitatively.

Table 13.2 shows the effect of introducing firing costs into the model.

Qualitatively, these results are quite intuitive, although, in light of the results obtained by Bentolilla and Bertola (1991), they may be viewed as unexpected. One line of intuition about the effects of such a tax on dismissals is that firms will be more cautious about job creation. As a result of this, there will also be less job destruction, and firms will end up making fewer adjustments to their labor forces. All of these effects show up in the new equilibria. In particular, the serial correlation in log employment increases as f increases, whereas the variance in growth rates decreases, as does the job turnover rate. Of particular significance is the fact that total employment is decreasing in f. These results indicate a fairly strong trade-

Table 13.2
Effect of changes in f, benchmark model

	$f = 0$	$f = .1$	$f = .2$
Price	1.00	1.026	1.048
Total employment	.600	.590	.585
Average firm size	61.2	61.8	65.1
Exit rate	.39	.39	.39
Job turnover rate	.30	.26	.22
Serial corr. in $\log(n)$	.92	.94	.94
Variance in growth rates	.55	.45	.39

off between the average duration of a job and the total number of jobs. Moving from $f = 0$ to $f = .2$, the job destruction rate decreases by 8 percent whereas total employment goes down by roughly 2.5 percent. The impact of f is not reported for all variables listed in table 13.2, however, we note that for the most part the change in the size distribution of firms and the other distributional statistics is relatively minor.

By viewing the dismissal cost as a tax payment that is redistributed in a lump-sum fashion to all individuals, the analysis has abstracted from contracting issues, and hence it might be best to view the numbers obtained as upper bounds for the effects of these sorts of policies. A related issue is the extent to which the given specification of firing costs captures the schedules that firms actually face. In some countries the rules are not even explicit about the exact payments that need to be made, but even when the required payments are known fairly precisely, the form is not as simple as has been examined here. Typically the payments depend upon the length of service, and hence the costs that a firm faces will depend upon the distribution of tenure in its current workforce. Explicit modeling of this feature would appear to be beyond current technological capabilities, slice it requires using a distribution to characterize the state of each firm.

Nonetheless, to the extent that the value of f equal to .2 is a reasonable description (to a first approximation) of the magnitude of legislated severance payments in several countries (see Emerson 1988 and Lazear 1990 for more country-specific details), we believe that the 2.5 percent impact on employment is very significant, making it worthwhile to attempt to refine the results reported here.

There are many sensitivity tests that can be performed. One of particular interest is the impact of changes in the parameters governing the stochastic process on the ldiosyncratic shock. There are two reasons for this. One is the usual reason of wanting to know how robust the quantitative results are. The second concerns using these results to analyze differences between American and European employment experiences from the mid-seventies through the eighties. In some discussions, when the possibility of labor market regulations are put forward as an explanation, a counterargument is offered based on the fact that in many countries the regulations did not change in the seventies and hence could not be part of the explanation. This, however, ignores the possibility that there were changes in the stochastic properties of the environment in which firms operate that might have interacted with the existing regulations in a manner that would produce different results in a cross section of countries. In particular, if the firm-level environment became more uncertain, countries with more regula-

Table 13.3
Effect of changes in f, $\rho = .80$

	$f = 0$	$f = .1$	$f = .2$
Price	1.00	1.028	1.045
Total employment	.60	.587	.583
Average firm size	69.7	99.8	102.7
Exit rate	.46	.19	.18
Job turnover rate	.32	.25	.20
Serial corr. in $\log(n)$	.80	.82	.84
Variance in growth rates	.59	.45	.37

tions may have experienced a decrease in their employment levels. Table 13.3 shows for one case how the effect of increases in f will be dependent upon the stochastic environment in which they are introduced. This table shows what results if one uses a benchmark model identical to the previous one except that the persistence in the shock process is decreased to .80. All other values used in calibrating the model are left unchanged.

Qualitatively the pattern is basically the same as in the previous case, however, it is worth noting that the loss in employment is now slightly greater, as would be expected. Since shocks are less persistent, Jobs will be expected to have a shorter duration, and firms will be more reluctant to hire in response to good shocks. This shorter job duration is seen as a higher job turnover rate in the $f = 0$ case.

13.5 Final Remarks

The objective of this chapter has been to set out a framework in which recent theoretical work on equilibrium models of firm-level dynamics and empirical findings from firm panel data sets can be brought to bear on the quantitative evaluation of policies that directly affect firm-level employment decisions. As mentioned, a number of policies can be analyzed in this framework. The results reported from Hopenhayn and Rogerson (1990) concerning a tax on job destruction are one example. In addition to many policy analysis exercises, there are some interesting extensions to be considered. For example, the model studied here did not allow for growth at the aggregate level. It may be that the types of policies discussed earlier have important interactions with the rate at which the economy grows, thereby making this an important area of study. Also, the framework laid out here considered only the effects on the stationary equilibrium and did not address the issue of the adjustment path resulting from a change in policies as the economy moves between two stationary equilib .

Notes

We would like to thank Ben Benthal and Yoram Weiss for comments and the NSF for financial support.

1. Because the probability of future dismissals is not independent of today's hiring, these "costs" are not linear in hiring. The result about the independence of initial employment still holds because the costs are effectively concave.

2. This outcome explicitly assumes that if a firm closes down it still has to make good on all of its obligations. It is of some interest to consider relaxing this feature.

3. If outside opportunities were normalized to be some positive value, then exit could result even if the fixed operating cost were equal to zero.

References

Alesina, A. and D. Rodrik. 1990. "Distributive Politics and Economic Growth", mimeo.

Bentolila, S., and G. Bertola. 1990. "Firing Costs and Labor Demand: How Bad is Euroscleurosls?", *Review of Economic Studies* 57:381–402.

Bertola, G. 1990. "Job Security, Employment and Wages," *European Economic Review* 34:851–886.

Birch, David. 1981. *The Job Generation Process.* (Combridge, MA: MIT Press).

Birch, David. 1986. *Job Creation in America,* (Cambridge, MA: MIT Press).

Davis, S. and J. Haltiwanger. 1988. "The Distribution of Employees and Establishments by Establishment Size: Patterns of Change and Comovement in the United States," manuscript.

Davis, S. and J. Haltiwanger. 1990. "Gross Job Creation and Destruction: Microeconomic Evidence and Macroeconomic Implications, manuscript.

Dunne, T., M. Roberts and L. Samuelson. 1986. "The Impact of Plant Failure on Employment Growth in the US Manufacturing Sector," manuscript.

Dunne, T., M. Roberts and L. Samuelson. 1987. "Patterns of Entry and Exit in US Manufacturing Industries," manuscript.

Dunne, T., M. Roberts and L. Samuelson. 1988. "Firm Entry and Post Entry Performance in the US Chemical Industries," manuscript.

Dunne, T., M. Roberts and L. Samuelson. 1989. "Plant Turnover and Gross Employment Flows in the US Manufacturing Sector" *Journal of Labor Economics* 7:48–71.

Emerson, M. 1988. "Regulation or Deregulation of the Labor Market" *European Economic Review* 32:775–817.

Ericson R. and A. Pakes. 1989. "An Alternative Theory of Firm and Industry Dynamics," manuscript.

Evans, D. 1987a. "The Relationship Between Firm Growth, Size and Age: Estimates for 100 Manufacturing Industries" *Journal of Industrial Economics*.

Evans, D. 1987b. "Tests of Alternative Theories of Firm Growth" *Journal of Political Economy* 95:657–674.

Gavin, M. 1986. "Labor Market Rigidities and Unemployment: The Case of Severance Costs," mimeo.

Hall, Bronwyn. 1987. "The Relationship Between Firm Size and Firm Growth in the U.S. Manufacturing Sector," *Journal of Industrial Economics* 35: 583–606.

Hansen, G. 1985. "Indivisible Labor and the Business Cycle," *Journal of Monetary Economics* 16:309–328.

Hopenhayn, H. 1989. "A Dynamic Stochastic Model of Entry and Exit to an Industry," manuscript.

Hopenhayn. H. and R. Rogerson. 1989. "Job Turnover and Policy Evaluation in a Model of Industry Equilibrium," mimeo.

Jovanovic, B. 1982. "Selection and the Evolution of Industry" *Econometrica* 50: 649–670.

Lazear, E. 1990. "Job Security Provisions and Employment," *Quarterly Journal of Economics.* CV:699–726.

Leonard J. 1987. "In the Wrong Place at the Wrong Time: the Extent of Frictional and Structural Unemployment" in *Unemployment and the Structure of Labor Markets*, edited by K. Lang and J. Leonard, (New York: Basil Blackwell).

Pakes, A. and R. Ericson. 1987. "Empirical Implications of Alternative Models of Firm Dynamics," manuscript.

Rogerson, R. 1988. "Indivisible Labor, Lotteries, and Equilibrium," *Journal of Monetary Economics* 21:3–16.

Troske, K. 1989. "The Life Cycle of Firms and the Expansion and Contraction of Industries," manuscript.

List of Contributors

Alberto Alesina
Harvard University

Robert J. Barro
Harvard University

Ricardo J. Caballero
MIT

V. V. Chari
Federal Reserve Bank of
Minneapolis

Lawrence J. Christiano
Federal Reserve Bank of
Minneapolis and Institute for
Empirical Macroeconomics

Gerald D. Cohen
Harvard University

Alex Cukierman
Tel Aviv University

Martin Eichenbaum
Northwestern University and
Federal Reserve Bank of Chicago

Jeremy Greenwood
Federal Reserve Bank of
Minneapolis and The University of
Western Ontario

Elhanan Helpman
Tel Aviv University

Zvi Hercowitz
Tel Aviv University

Hugo Hopenhayn
Stanford University

Patrick J. Kehoe
University of Minnesota and
Federal Reserve Bank of
Minneapolis

Leonardo Leiderman
Tel Aviv University

John Londregan
Princeton University

Richard K. Lyons
Columbia University

Stephen L. Parente
Northeastern University

Torsten Persson
Institute for International Economic
Studies

Keith Poole
Carnegie Mellon University

Edward C. Prescott
Federal Reserve Bank of
Mineapolis and University of
Minnesota

Dani Rodrik
Harvard University

Richard Rogerson
University of Minnesota

Nouriel Roubini
Yale University

Xavier Sala-i-Martin
Yale University

Guido Tabellini
Universita di Brescia and
University of California at Los
Angeles

Sweder van Wijnbergen
World Bank

Index